COVERED CALLS FOR BEGINNERS: THE COMPLETE STEP-BY-STEP GUIDE TO GENERATING MONTHLY INCOME FROM YOUR STOCK PORTFOLIO

First edition. December 23, 2025.

ISBN: 979-8233054624

Written by janice green.

Table of Contents

Covered Calls for Beginners:

The Complete Step-by-Step Guide to Generating Monthly Income from Your Stock Portfolio

By

Janice Green

Acknowledgments

This book represents the collective wisdom of thousands of covered call traders who've generously shared their experiences, mistakes, and successes over the years. While I cannot name them all, several deserve special recognition.

To the members of online trading communities who patiently answered my endless questions when I was learning—your willingness to help a beginner shaped my approach to education. Pay-it-forward mentality creates better traders and better markets.

To my early readers and beta testers who reviewed draft chapters and provided invaluable feedback—your honest critiques improved every section. Special thanks to the retirement-focused investors who helped me understand their unique needs and concerns.

To the professional options traders and market makers who've shared institutional-level insights—your perspective on what really works versus what sounds good in theory grounds this book in reality.

To my family, who endured countless evenings and weekends of "I just need to finish this chapter." Your patience, support, and understanding made this project possible.

To my students over the years whose questions revealed gaps in my knowledge and explanations—you taught me how to teach, which made me a better trader.

To the pioneers of options education whose books and teachings laid the foundation—we all stand on the shoulders of giants. Lawrence McMillan, Sheldon Natenberg, and countless others created the knowledge base we benefit from today.

And finally, to you, the reader, for investing your time and trust in this book. May your covered call journey be profitable, educational, and fulfilling.

With gratitude, Janice Green

DISCLAIMER

Important Investment Disclaimer

The information contained in this book is for educational and informational purposes only and should not be construed as financial, investment, legal, or tax advice. The strategies, techniques, and examples discussed are presented for educational purposes to help readers understand covered call options trading.

No Guarantee of Results

Past performance is not indicative of future results. The examples, case studies, and performance figures presented in this book are hypothetical or historical and are not guarantees of future performance. Options trading involves substantial risk and is not suitable for all investors. You can lose money trading options, including the entire amount of your investment.

Risk Disclosure

Options trading involves significant risk of loss. Before engaging in options trading, you should carefully consider your financial situation, investment objectives, risk tolerance, and level of experience. The strategies discussed in this book, including covered calls, can result in substantial losses if market conditions move unfavorably. Stock prices can decline significantly, and option premiums may not provide sufficient protection against such declines.

Not Professional Advice

The author is not a registered investment advisor, financial planner, or certified public accountant. This book does not provide personalized investment advice or recommendations specific to your individual circumstances. You should consult with qualified financial, legal, and tax professionals before making any investment decisions.

No Warranty

While the author has made every effort to ensure the accuracy and completeness of the information presented, no warranty is made regarding its accuracy, timeliness, or applicability to your specific situation. Financial markets, tax laws, and regulatory requirements change frequently, and information that was accurate at the time of publication may become outdated.

Your Responsibility

You are solely responsible for your investment decisions and their outcomes. The author and publisher shall not be liable for any losses, damages, or adverse consequences resulting from your use of the information in this book. By reading and using this book, you acknowledge and accept these terms.

Brokerage and Regulatory Compliance

Options trading requires approval from your brokerage firm. You must complete your broker's options application and be approved for the appropriate options trading level before implementing covered call strategies. Ensure you understand your broker's policies, fees, and margin requirements.

Tax Implications

The tax treatment of options trading can be complex. The information provided regarding taxes is general in nature and may not apply to your specific situation. Consult with a qualified tax professional to understand how covered call strategies will affect your individual tax situation.

Educational Purpose

This book is designed to educate readers about covered call strategies. It is not an offer to sell securities or a solicitation to buy securities. All investment decisions should be made after conducting thorough due diligence and consulting with appropriate professionals.

By purchasing and reading this book, you acknowledge that you have read and understood this disclaimer and agree to its terms.

Dedication

To every investor who has ever looked at their portfolio and wished it could do more—this book is for you.

To my family, whose unwavering support gave me the time and encouragement to pursue this project. Your patience during the countless evenings and weekends I spent writing, researching, and refining these strategies made this book possible.

To my mentors in the options trading community, who generously shared their knowledge, experiences, and hard-won lessons. Your willingness to teach and guide others elevated my understanding from theory to practice.

To the thousands of retail investors I've encountered in trading forums, investment clubs, and online communities over the years. Your questions, challenges, and success stories shaped this book's content and approach. You taught me what beginners truly need to know versus what textbooks think they should learn.

To the pioneers of options education who came before me, whose books, articles, and teachings laid the foundation for modern options strategies. We all stand on the shoulders of giants.

And finally, to you, the reader, who is taking control of your financial future by learning a new skill. Your commitment to education and self-improvement is admirable. May this book serve as a trusted guide on your journey to consistent income generation and financial independence.

The covered call strategy has transformed countless portfolios from passive holdings into active income producers. My sincere hope is that it will do the same for you.

With gratitude and best wishes for your trading success,

Janice Green

About the Author

Janice Green is an experienced options trader, educator, and financial writer specializing in income-generation strategies for individual investors. With over 15 years of active trading experience and a decade spent teaching retail investors how to implement covered call strategies, Janice has helped thousands of people transform their portfolios from passive holdings into consistent income producers.

Professional Background

Janice began her investment journey like many readers of this book—as a traditional buy-and-hold stock investor frustrated by portfolio volatility and inconsistent returns. After discovering covered calls in 2009 during the aftermath of the financial crisis, she immersed herself in options education, eventually developing systematic approaches that generated 15-25% annual returns with significantly reduced volatility compared to stock ownership alone.

What started as personal portfolio management evolved into a passion for teaching others. Janice began writing educational content for investment websites, contributing to leading financial publications, and conducting workshops at investment clubs and online forums. Her clear, jargon-free explanations and practical, real-world examples quickly gained a following among retail investors seeking actionable strategies rather than theoretical concepts.

Educational Philosophy

Janice's teaching philosophy centers on three core principles:

Accessibility: Options trading shouldn't require advanced mathematics, expensive software, or full-time attention. Her strategies are designed for part-time investors who have other careers, families, and responsibilities.

Practicality: Every concept must translate into concrete actions. Theoretical knowledge that cannot be implemented serves little purpose for retail investors seeking to generate income.

Risk Management: Consistent returns matter more than occasional home runs. Janice emphasizes strategies that preserve capital, manage downside risk, and generate reliable cash flow rather than speculative approaches chasing maximum profits.

Teaching and Community Involvement

Beyond this book, Janice maintains an active presence in the investment education community:

- **Speaking:** Regular presenter at investment conferences and local investment club meetings
- **Writing:** Contributing writer for major financial education websites and investment publications
- **Mentoring:** One-on-one coaching for investors implementing covered call strategies
- **Community:** Active participant in online trading communities, answering questions and sharing insights

Investment Approach

Janice's personal portfolio reflects the strategies taught in this book: a diversified collection of blue-chip stocks and dividend aristocrats with systematic covered call programs. Her approach emphasizes:

- Quality stock selection over chasing premiums
- Systematic execution rather than market timing
- Position sizing and risk management
- Long-term consistency over short-term optimization
- Continuous learning and strategy refinement

Personal Life

When not analyzing options chains or writing about covered calls, Janice enjoys hiking, photography, and spending time with her family. She lives in the Pacific Northwest with her husband and two children. An advocate for financial literacy, she volunteers with local organizations teaching basic investing and money management skills to young adults.

Why This Book

Covered Calls for Beginners represents the culmination of Janice's experience teaching thousands of investors. She wrote this book because she noticed a gap in existing options education: most books either over-simplified the strategy to the point of uselessness or overwhelmed beginners with complexity and jargon.

This book strikes the balance—comprehensive enough to serve as a complete reference yet accessible enough for true beginners. Every chapter reflects real questions from real students, common mistakes Janice has observed (and made herself), and practical solutions that work in actual trading environments.

Connect with Janice

Readers can connect with Janice and access additional resources at:

Website: www.JaniceGreenTrading.com **Email:** janice@janiceegreentrading.com **Twitter:** @JaniceGreenOpts **LinkedIn:** linkedin.com/in/janicegreentrading

Janice welcomes questions, feedback, and success stories from readers implementing the strategies in this book. She regularly updates her website with current market commentary, strategy adjustments for changing conditions, and answers to frequently asked reader questions.

A Note from Janice

"I wrote this book for the investor I was 15 years ago—someone who knew stocks but felt intimidated by options, someone seeking consistent income but unsure how to generate it reliably, someone willing to learn but needing clear, practical guidance.

If that describes you, welcome. You're in the right place. The strategies in this book work—I use them in my own portfolio every day. They won't make you rich overnight, but they will transform how your portfolio generates income and how you think about investing.

My commitment to you is simple: everything in this book is practical, tested, and actionable. No theoretical fluff, no get-rich-quick schemes, just systematic strategies that generate consistent returns when implemented with discipline and patience.

I look forward to hearing about your covered call success stories. May your journey be profitable and your portfolio generate the income you deserve."

—*Janice Green*

Endorsements

"Janice Green has written the definitive guide to covered calls for retail investors. This book strikes the perfect balance between comprehensive education and practical application. Whether you're completely new to options or looking to refine your strategy, this book belongs on your shelf." — [Financial Expert Name], Author of [Investment Book]

"Finally, an options book that speaks to real investors! Janice's clear explanations and practical examples make covered calls accessible to everyone. This is the book I wish existed when I started trading options." — [Trading Educator Name], Founder of [Trading Education Company]

"Mastering Covered Calls goes far beyond basic mechanics to address the real challenges of implementation: position sizing, market conditions, psychology, and systematic execution. Janice's teaching shines through every chapter." — [Investment Advisor Name], CFP®, [Advisory Firm]

Introduction:

Your Journey to Income Generation

Why Covered Calls Matter for Everyday Investors

If you've ever wished your stock portfolio could generate consistent monthly income—the kind of predictable cash flow that arrives whether markets go up, down, or sideways—then you've discovered the right book. Covered calls represent one of the most accessible, practical, and time-tested strategies for transforming ordinary stock holdings into income-producing assets.

Unlike many complex financial instruments that require specialized knowledge, expensive software, or full-time attention, covered calls work with stocks you may already own. They don't require predicting market direction, timing dramatic moves, or risking more than your initial investment. Instead, covered calls allow you to collect premium income by temporarily limiting your upside potential—a trade-off millions of investors gladly accept in exchange for consistent cash flow.

The Power of Consistent Income

Consider a typical investor holding $100,000 in blue-chip stocks. In a traditional buy-and-hold approach, this portfolio generates returns entirely from stock appreciation and dividends. Some years deliver excellent gains; other years bring disappointing losses. The unpredictability creates stress and makes financial planning difficult.

Now imagine that same $100,000 portfolio systematically generating $1,500 to $3,000 in monthly premium income through covered calls—$18,000 to $36,000 annually—regardless of whether the overall market rises or falls. This income arrives like clockwork, deposited into your account every month. Combined with dividends, your total annual income could reach $30,000 to $45,000, representing a 30-45% return on invested capital even if stock prices remain flat.

This transformation from passive stock ownership to active income generation is not hypothetical. Thousands of investors employ covered call strategies daily, creating reliable cash flows that fund retirements, supplement wages, or accelerate wealth accumulation. The strategy works because you're selling something valuable—optionality—to other market participants willing to pay for the possibility of outsized gains.

Who This Strategy Serves

Covered calls particularly benefit several investor categories:

Retirement-focused investors seeking to replace employment income with portfolio income find covered calls attractive because the strategy generates predictable monthly cash flow similar to a paycheck. Unlike dividend income alone, which typically yields 2-3% annually, covered call strategies can produce 15-30% annual returns in well-managed portfolios.

Conservative investors uncomfortable with market volatility appreciate that covered calls reduce portfolio risk. The premium income you collect provides a cushion against price declines, effectively lowering your cost basis and reducing losses during market corrections.

Long-term stock holders who believe in their companies but don't expect dramatic short-term appreciation can monetize the "waiting period" by collecting premiums. Rather than watching positions sit idle during consolidation phases, you transform that stability into income.

Accumulators building wealth benefit from the compounding effect of consistent returns. Reinvesting monthly premiums accelerates portfolio growth dramatically over time. A portfolio generating 20% annual returns doubles approximately every 3.6 years through compounding—a powerful wealth-building tool.

Why Covered Calls Work

The covered call strategy succeeds because of a persistent market phenomenon: implied volatility consistently exceeds realized volatility. In simpler terms, options buyers pay more for potential price movements than those movements typically deliver. This "volatility risk premium" creates a structural advantage for option sellers.

When you sell a covered call, you're essentially accepting payment from someone betting your stock will rise dramatically. Most of the time, stocks move less dramatically than options buyers expect. This allows you to collect premiums repeatedly as options expire worthless or lose value through time decay. Even when stocks do rise and you're assigned (forced to sell), you've typically collected premium at prices above your entry point, creating profitable outcomes.

The strategy also benefits from time decay—the mathematical certainty that options lose value as expiration approaches. Unlike stock investing where you must correctly predict direction, covered calls profit from the simple passage of time. Every day that passes without dramatic stock movement works in your favor as the options you sold lose value.

What You'll Learn in This Book

This comprehensive guide takes you from absolute beginner to confident practitioner through five carefully structured parts:

Part I: Foundations of Covered Call Trading establishes the essential knowledge base. You'll understand exactly what options are, how covered calls work mechanically, and why they differ fundamentally from risky strategies like naked option writing. We'll explore the risk-reward profile honestly, examining both the income potential and the limitations. You'll learn the terminology that seemed confusing—Greeks, strike prices, expirations—in plain language with practical applications. By the end of Part I, you'll understand not just the what of covered calls but the why.

Part II: Selecting Ideal Stocks for Covered Calls addresses perhaps the most critical success factor: choosing the right underlying stocks. Not all stocks make suitable covered call candidates. We'll explore the characteristics that distinguish excellent candidates from poor choices, including volatility metrics, liquidity requirements, dividend considerations, and sector stability. You'll learn systematic fundamental analysis to evaluate financial health, dividend sustainability, and competitive position. Technical analysis chapters teach you to identify optimal entry points using support and resistance, moving averages, RSI, and Bollinger Bands. Sector-specific chapters recognize that technology stocks, financials, utilities, and energy companies each require adapted approaches. We'll also examine blue-chip stocks and dividend aristocrats—the foundation of conservative covered call portfolios.

Part III: Strategy and Execution transforms knowledge into action. Here you'll master strike price selection, learning when to be aggressive (maximizing premium) versus conservative (preserving upside). The 30-delta rule provides a simple framework for consistent strike selection. You'll understand the trade-offs between weekly and monthly options, developing a systematic approach to expiration selection. Entry and exit strategies guide you through position initiation, management of winning trades, handling assignment gracefully, and the sophisticated technique of rolling positions to extend income. Position sizing and portfolio management ensure you allocate capital appropriately, diversify effectively, and track performance accurately.

Part IV: Advanced Concepts for Beginners addresses the real-world complexity beyond the basics. Markets don't remain static—they cycle through bull phases, bear phases, and sideways consolidation. Each environment requires adapted strategies. You'll learn how to adjust approaches based on market conditions, maximizing returns during favorable periods while protecting capital during challenging times. The common mistakes chapter draws from decades of collective experience to help you avoid costly errors: chasing high premiums on risky stocks, ignoring earnings announcements, poor strike selection, emotional decision-making, and overtrading. Tax considerations ensure you understand the implications of covered call income, qualified covered calls rules, and wash sale provisions. Tools and resources guide you to the best brokerage platforms, options calculators, and continuing education sources.

Part V: Putting It All Together provides the practical implementation roadmap. The step-by-step implementation guide walks you through building your first covered call portfolio with sample portfolios tailored to different goals: conservative income, growth with income, and retirement applications. Real-world case studies examine actual trades, analyzing what worked, what didn't, and lessons learned. The scaling chapter explains how to grow your strategy over time, when to add complexity, and explores advanced variations like poor man's covered calls and collar strategies.

Throughout the book, you'll find:

- **Practical examples** with real numbers showing exactly how trades work

- **Case studies** examining actual covered call positions from start to finish
- **Decision frameworks** providing systematic approaches to common choices
- **Checklists** ensuring you consider all relevant factors before trading
- **Visual aids** including charts, tables, and diagrams clarifying complex concepts
- **Pro tips** highlighting insights from experienced practitioners
- **Warning boxes** alerting you to common pitfalls and risks

How to Use This Guide Effectively

This book is designed for progressive learning, with each chapter building upon previous concepts. However, your specific situation may call for a customized approach:

For absolute beginners with limited options knowledge: Read the book sequentially from cover to cover. Don't skip ahead even if certain chapters seem basic. The foundational concepts in Part I are essential for understanding the more sophisticated strategies later. Plan to spend 2-3 weeks absorbing the material before placing your first trade. Reread chapters as needed—options concepts often require multiple exposures before becoming intuitive.

For investors with some options experience: You may be tempted to skip directly to Part III (Strategy and Execution). Resist this urge. Instead, quickly review Parts I and II to ensure your foundational knowledge is comprehensive, then focus detailed attention on Parts III, IV, and V. Pay particular attention to Chapter 14 (Common Mistakes)—experienced traders often have the hardest time identifying their own blind spots.

For active traders exploring covered calls: You likely understand options mechanics already. Focus your attention on Chapters 4-8 (stock selection) and Chapters 13-15 (managing market conditions, avoiding mistakes, and tax considerations). The stock selection criteria for covered calls differ significantly from stock selection for outright trading. What makes a great growth stock often makes a terrible covered call candidate.

For retirement-focused investors: Your primary concern is consistent income with limited risk. Prioritize Chapters 4-5 (stock characteristics and fundamental analysis), Chapter 8 (dividend stocks), Chapter 12 (position sizing), and Chapter 18 (real-world case studies, particularly the retirement account application). The conservative approaches outlined throughout the book align with retirement objectives.

Regardless of your background, follow this implementation timeline:

Weeks 1-2: Education Phase

- Read through the book without placing any trades
- Take notes on concepts that seem unclear
- Create a list of questions for further research
- Review the glossary (Appendix A) to ensure terminology fluency

Weeks 3-4: Preparation Phase

- Open or verify you have an options-enabled brokerage account
- Build your candidate stock watchlist using criteria from Chapters 4-8
- Paper trade (practice with virtual money) several positions to understand the mechanics
- Develop your record-keeping system using the template in Appendix C

Week 5: Implementation Phase

- Place your first covered call trade on a single position
- Start small—one or two contracts maximum
- Choose the most conservative approach (quality stock, OTM strike, 30-45 day expiration)

- Document everything: entry price, strike selected, premium received, reasoning

Weeks 6-12: Experience Building Phase

- Add one new covered call position every 2-3 weeks
- Focus on diverse stocks across different sectors
- Experiment with different strike selections and expirations
- Review what works and what doesn't in your trading journal

Month 4 and Beyond: Systematic Execution Phase

- Scale to your target portfolio size (typically 5-10 positions)
- Develop systematic processes for position management
- Refine your approach based on actual results
- Continuously educate yourself on market conditions and advanced strategies

Active Reading Techniques

To maximize retention and application:

Engage actively with the material: Don't just passively read. Highlight key passages, write margin notes, and create your own summary points at the end of each chapter. Studies show active engagement improves retention by 300-400% compared to passive reading.

Work through every example: When mathematical examples appear, grab a calculator and verify the calculations yourself. Understanding comes from doing, not just reading. Calculate premiums, breakeven points, returns on capital, and maximum profits for each example.

Create personal application notes: After each chapter, write 2-3 bullet points on how the concepts apply specifically to your situation. "Chapter 5 taught me that I need to check debt-to-equity ratios. My current holdings XYZ and ABC both exceed 1.5, which concerns me based on this chapter's guidance."

Build your reference system: As you progress, create a personal reference guide extracting the most relevant information for your strategy. This might include your customized stock selection checklist, strike selection decision tree, and position management rules. This reference guide becomes your operational manual for actual trading.

Return to challenging sections: Options concepts can be abstract and counterintuitive initially. If something doesn't click immediately, mark it and return after completing the chapter or section. Often, later material provides the context that makes earlier concepts clear.

Setting Realistic Expectations

Before embarking on your covered call journey, understand what this strategy can and cannot deliver. Realistic expectations prevent disappointment and help you maintain the discipline necessary for long-term success.

What Covered Calls Can Do:

Generate consistent income: Well-executed covered call strategies consistently produce 1-3% monthly returns (12-36% annually) on invested capital. These returns come primarily from option premiums supplemented by dividends. Conservative approaches targeting 1-1.5% monthly still dramatically outperform typical dividend yields. Aggressive approaches can achieve 2-3% monthly but with increased risk.

Reduce portfolio volatility: Collecting premium provides a cushion against price declines. If you collect $2.00 per share in premium monthly and the stock declines $1.50, you've still netted $0.50 positive. This cushion effect makes covered call portfolios less volatile than stock-only portfolios, reducing the emotional stress of market downturns.

Outperform buy-and-hold in sideways markets: During extended periods of market consolidation—which occur more frequently than dramatic moves—covered calls significantly outperform passive stock ownership. While buy-and-hold investors watch their portfolios tread water for months or years, covered call traders collect premium consistently regardless of price direction.

Provide downside protection: The premium income effectively lowers your cost basis. If you purchase stock at $50 and collect $6 in annual premiums, your effective cost basis drops to $44 over the first year. This provides meaningful protection during market corrections.

Create predictable cash flow: Unlike capital gains (which require selling assets) or dividends (which companies can cut), covered call premiums are yours to keep the moment you sell the option. This creates reliable cash flow for budgeting and planning purposes.

What Covered Calls Cannot Do:

Make you rich quickly: Covered calls are an income strategy, not a get-rich-quick scheme. Expecting 100% annual returns or doubling your money in months will lead to disappointment and excessive risk-taking. The strategy works through consistency and compounding over time, not dramatic gains.

Eliminate all risk: You still own stock, which can decline in value. While premium provides a cushion, significant stock declines will result in losses. Covered calls reduce risk compared to stock ownership alone but don't eliminate it. A stock falling 20% won't be offset by 2% monthly premiums.

Capture unlimited upside: By selling calls, you cap your gains at the strike price. If you sell a $55 call and the stock rallies to $70, you must sell at $55 (plus premium collected). This opportunity cost is the price you pay for consistent income. Accepting this trade-off is fundamental to the strategy.

Work on autopilot: Covered calls require active management. You must monitor positions, make decisions about rolling or assignment, track expirations, and adjust to changing market conditions. While not time-intensive (perhaps 30-60 minutes weekly for a 10-position portfolio), it's not completely passive like index fund investing.

Guarantee profits every month: Some months, stocks decline more than the premium collected. Some positions get assigned at inopportune times. Some trades simply don't work out. Success comes from overall portfolio results across months and years, not perfection in every position.

Replace professional income immediately: Building a covered call portfolio that generates substantial monthly income requires capital. A $50,000 portfolio generating 2% monthly produces $1,000 in income—helpful but unlikely to replace most salaries. Growing a portfolio to generate $5,000+ monthly income requires hundreds of thousands in capital or years of compounding smaller initial amounts.

Realistic Return Targets:

Set your expectations using these guidelines based on strategy aggressiveness:

Conservative approach (OTM strikes on stable blue-chips, emphasizing capital preservation):

- Monthly returns: 0.8-1.5%
- Annual returns: 10-18%
- Suitable for: Retirees, risk-averse investors, large portfolios

Moderate approach (blend of ATM and OTM strikes on quality stocks):

- Monthly returns: 1.5-2.5%
- Annual returns: 18-30%
- Suitable for: Most investors seeking balanced risk-reward

Aggressive approach (ATM strikes, higher volatility stocks, maximum premium):

- Monthly returns: 2.5-4%
- Annual returns: 30-48%
- Suitable for: Risk-tolerant investors, smaller portfolio allocations

Important reality check: Achieving even the conservative returns consistently places you in the top quartile of investment performance. The S&P 500 averages approximately 10% annually long-term. Generating 15-20% annually through covered calls represents exceptional performance. Don't let relative comparisons to aggressive targets obscure the absolute achievement of beating market benchmarks consistently.

Time Commitment Expectations:

Covered calls are not day trading but aren't completely passive either:

Initial setup (first month): 10-15 hours learning, researching stocks, establishing positions **Ongoing management** (per week): 30-60 minutes reviewing positions, checking for adjustments **Monthly activities** (per month): 2-4 hours researching new positions, rolling expiring options, rebalancing **Quarterly review** (per quarter): 3-5 hours comprehensive portfolio analysis, tax planning, strategy refinement

This totals approximately 5-8 hours monthly once established—manageable for busy professionals, retirees, or anyone willing to dedicate one Saturday morning monthly to portfolio management.

Capital Requirements:

While you can technically begin covered calls with a single 100-share position, practical considerations suggest minimum capital levels:

Absolute minimum: $5,000 (one position on a $50 stock) **Practical minimum**: $15,000-25,000 (3-5 positions providing basic diversification) **Comfortable minimum**: $50,000-100,000 (8-10 positions with good diversification) **Optimal range**: $100,000+ (10-15+ positions, full strategy implementation)

Smaller accounts can participate successfully but face limitations in diversification and stock selection (forced toward lower-priced stocks). Larger accounts enjoy greater flexibility, better diversification, and access to higher-quality blue-chip stocks.

Your Success Mindset:

Approach covered calls with these attitudes for optimal results:

Patience: Success accumulates over months and years, not days and weeks. Trust the process.

Discipline: Follow your rules even when tempted to chase high premiums or deviate from your plan.

Realism: Accept that some trades will disappoint. Focus on overall portfolio performance across all positions.

Consistency: Regular, systematic execution beats sporadic brilliance. Develop routines and stick to them.

Continuous learning: Markets evolve, and your knowledge should too. Commit to ongoing education.

Emotional control: Don't get euphoric after great months or despondent after difficult periods. Maintain equilibrium.

Beginning Your Journey

You now stand at the threshold of a powerful income-generation strategy used successfully by individual investors, financial advisors, and institutional money managers worldwide. The covered call approach you're about to master has generated consistent returns through bull markets, bear markets, and everything between for decades.

The journey from novice to proficient practitioner typically spans 6-12 months. You'll make mistakes—every trader does—but each mistake teaches valuable lessons if you approach them as learning opportunities rather than failures. Your first few trades may feel uncomfortable or confusing, but this discomfort is normal and temporary. Within months, the process becomes routine and comfortable.

Remember: every expert covered call trader started exactly where you are now. They read books, studied strategies, placed their first nervous trade, made mistakes, adjusted their approach, and ultimately developed the consistency that generates reliable income. You can do the same by combining the knowledge in this book with practical experience, patience, and discipline.

The following chapters provide everything you need to succeed. Read carefully, think critically, start conservatively, and scale gradually. Your future income awaits.

Let's begin.

PART I: FOUNDATIONS OF COVERED CALL TRADING

Chapter 1:

Understanding Options and Covered Calls

What Are Options? A Clear Foundation

Options are financial contracts that derive their value from underlying assets, such as stocks, commodities, or indices. Unlike traditional stock ownership, which represents a direct equity stake in a company, options provide traders with strategic flexibility and leverage. An option grants the holder specific rights without imposing obligations, creating a unique risk-reward dynamic that has made options trading increasingly popular among both individual and institutional investors.

At their core, options function as agreements between two parties: the buyer (holder) and the seller (writer). The buyer pays a premium to acquire rights that the seller must honor if exercised. This asymmetric relationship—where buyers have rights and sellers have obligations—forms the foundation of all options strategies, including the covered call approach that this book focuses on.

The Two Types of Options:

Call Options give the buyer the right, but not the obligation, to purchase an underlying asset at a predetermined price (the strike price) before or at expiration. Call buyers profit when the underlying asset's price rises above the strike price by more than the premium paid. They're essentially betting on upward price movement.

Put Options give the buyer the right, but not the obligation, to sell an underlying asset at the strike price before or at expiration. Put buyers profit when the underlying asset's price falls below the strike price by more than the premium paid. They're betting on downward price movement or hedging existing positions.

Critical Options Terminology:

Understanding these fundamental terms is essential before implementing any options strategy:

Strike Price (Exercise Price): The predetermined price at which the option holder can buy (for calls) or sell (for puts) the underlying asset. The strike price remains fixed throughout the option's life, regardless of the underlying asset's market price movements. Strike prices are set at regular intervals (typically $2.50 or $5.00 apart, depending on the stock's price level) and are determined by the options exchange.

Expiration Date: The specific date when the option contract becomes void and all rights cease to exist. In the United States, equity options traditionally expire on the third Friday of the expiration month, though weekly options and other variations now exist. After expiration, an option has no value and cannot be exercised, bought, or sold.

Premium: The price paid by the option buyer to the option seller for the rights conveyed by the contract. Premiums are quoted on a per-share basis but represent 100 shares per standard contract. For example, a premium quoted at $2.50 means the buyer pays $250 per contract ($2.50 × 100 shares). The premium compensates the seller for taking on the obligation and represents the maximum loss for the buyer.

Underlying Asset: The financial instrument (stock, ETF, index, commodity) upon which the option contract is based. The underlying asset's price movements directly affect the option's value. For covered calls, we focus primarily on individual stocks and stock-based ETFs as underlying assets.

In-the-Money (ITM): An option with intrinsic value. For call options, this means the current stock price exceeds the strike price. For put options, it means the stock price is below the strike price. ITM options have immediate exercise value.

At-the-Money (ATM): An option whose strike price equals (or very closely approximates) the current market price of the underlying asset. ATM options have no intrinsic value but typically have the highest time value.

Out-of-the-Money (OTM): An option with no intrinsic value. For calls, the strike price is above the current stock price. For puts, the strike price is below the current stock price. OTM options consist entirely of time value and will expire worthless if the underlying doesn't move favorably.

Intrinsic Value: The portion of an option's premium that represents real, tangible value if exercised immediately. For call options, intrinsic value equals the difference between the stock price and strike price (when positive). For example, if a stock trades at $55 and you own a $50 call, the intrinsic value is $5. Options cannot have negative intrinsic value—the minimum is zero.

Time Value (Extrinsic Value): The portion of an option's premium above its intrinsic value, representing the potential for the option to gain additional intrinsic value before expiration. Time value depends on several factors: time remaining until expiration, volatility expectations, interest rates, and dividend expectations. Time value always decreases as expiration approaches—a phenomenon called time decay or theta decay.

Example of Premium Components:

Let's say XYZ stock trades at $52 per share. A call option with a $50 strike price expiring in 30 days trades for $3.50.

- **Intrinsic Value:** $52 - $50 = $2.00
- **Time Value:** $3.50 - $2.00 = $1.50
- **Total Premium:** $3.50

The buyer pays $350 per contract ($3.50 × 100 shares). Of this, $200 represents intrinsic value (immediate exercise value), while $150 represents time value (the premium for 30 days of potential additional movement).

The Anatomy of a Call Option

To fully grasp covered calls, we must first understand call options in detail, as they form one half of the strategy (stock ownership being the other half).

The Call Option Contract Specifications:

Every standardized equity option contract in the United States represents control over 100 shares of the underlying stock. This standardization, established by the Options Clearing Corporation (OCC), ensures liquidity and uniform terms across all market participants. When you buy or sell one call option contract, you're dealing with rights or obligations concerning exactly 100 shares.

Key Elements of Every Call Option:

1. **The Underlying Security Identifier:** The specific stock ticker symbol (e.g., AAPL for Apple Inc., MSFT for Microsoft Corporation)
2. **The Option Type:** Call or Put (we focus on calls for covered call strategies)
3. **The Strike Price:** The price at which the call buyer can purchase the stock
4. **The Expiration Date:** When the option contract expires
5. **The Premium:** The current market price of the option
6. **The Option Symbol:** A standardized code that uniquely identifies each specific option contract

How Call Options Work in Practice:

When you purchase a call option, you pay a premium for the right to buy 100 shares of stock at the strike price any time before expiration (for American-style options, which most equity options are). You're not obligated to exercise this right—you can simply let the option expire or sell it to another trader.

Call Buyer's Perspective:

Imagine you're bullish on Tesla (TSLA), currently trading at $250 per share. You believe it will rise to $280 within the next month, but you don't have $25,000 to buy 100 shares. Instead, you purchase one call option:

- **Underlying:** TSLA
- **Strike Price:** $260
- **Expiration:** 30 days from now
- **Premium:** $8.00 per share ($800 total per contract)

Your investment: $800 (instead of $25,000 for 100 shares)

Potential Outcomes:

Scenario 1: Stock rises to $280

- Your call option is now worth at least $20 (the intrinsic value: $280 - $260)
- Your profit: $20 - $8 = $12 per share, or $1,200 per contract
- Your return: 150% on your $800 investment
- Compare this to buying stock: $3,000 profit on $25,000 = 12% return

Scenario 2: Stock stays at $250

- Your call option expires worthless (it's out-of-the-money)
- Your loss: The entire $800 premium paid
- Compare this to buying stock: $0 loss (you still own stock worth $25,000)

Scenario 3: Stock rises to $265

- Your call option is worth $5 at expiration ($265 - $260)
- Your net loss: $8 - $5 = -$3 per share, or -$300 total
- You lost money even though you were right about direction
- Compare this to buying stock: $1,500 profit on $25,000

Call Seller's Perspective (The Foundation of Covered Calls):

When you sell (write) a call option, you receive the premium immediately but take on an obligation. If the buyer exercises the option, you must sell 100 shares at the strike price, regardless of the current market price.

Using the same Tesla example, if you sell the $260 call for $8.00:

Your immediate income: $800 (premium received)

Your obligation: Sell 100 shares at $260 if exercised

Potential Outcomes:

Scenario 1: Stock rises to $280

- Your call will likely be exercised
- You must sell 100 shares at $260 (you miss the move from $260 to $280)

- You keep the $800 premium
- If you don't own the shares (naked call): You must buy at $280 and sell at $260 = $2,000 loss, partially offset by the $800 premium for a net loss of $1,200

Scenario 2: Stock stays at $250

- Your call expires worthless (good for you as the seller)
- You keep the entire $800 premium as profit
- You have no obligation to deliver shares

Scenario 3: Stock rises to $265

- Your call will likely be exercised
- You must sell shares at $260
- You keep the $800 premium
- Net outcome depends on whether you own the shares (covered) or must buy them (naked)

The Critical Distinction: Covered vs. Naked Calls:

A **naked call** (also called an uncovered call) is sold without owning the underlying stock. This is one of the riskiest options strategies because potential losses are theoretically unlimited. If the stock skyrockets, you must buy it at the market price (which could be very high) to deliver it at the lower strike price.

A **covered call** is sold against stock you already own. This is a conservative strategy with defined risk. If the stock rises and your call is exercised, you simply deliver the shares you own. Your maximum profit is capped (strike price + premium - your cost basis), but you eliminate the catastrophic risk of naked calls.

Why This Matters:

Understanding the mechanics of call options from both buyer and seller perspectives is crucial because:

1. **As a covered call writer, you are the seller** taking on

obligations in exchange for premium income
2. **Your profits and risks are the mirror image** of the call buyer's position
3. **Stock ownership transforms your risk profile** from unlimited (naked) to defined (covered)
4. **Time decay becomes your friend** as the seller, working to erode the option's value

This foundational knowledge sets the stage for understanding why covered calls work, when they work best, and how to implement them effectively to generate consistent income from your stock portfolio.

Why Covered Calls? The Income-Generation Strategy Explained

The covered call strategy has gained tremendous popularity among individual investors, professional money managers, and institutional traders because it addresses a common challenge: generating consistent income from stocks that may not appreciate rapidly or pay substantial dividends.

The Core Concept:

A covered call combines two positions:

1. **Long stock position:** You own 100 shares (or multiples of 100)
2. **Short call position:** You sell call options against those shares

This combination creates a new risk-reward profile that differs from simply holding the stock.

Why Investors Use Covered Calls:

1. Income Generation in Flat or Slow-Moving Markets

Traditional stock investing relies on two income sources: capital appreciation and dividends. But what happens when your stock moves sideways for months? Without price appreciation, you earn only the dividend yield (if any). Covered calls add a third income stream: option premiums.

Example:

- You own 500 shares of Johnson & Johnson (JNJ) at $160 per

share = $80,000 position

- JNJ pays a 2.8% annual dividend = $2,240 per year
- The stock trades in a range between $155-$165 for months (no capital appreciation)
- Traditional return: Just the 2.8% dividend yield

With covered calls:

- You sell 5 call contracts (500 shares ÷ 100) monthly at strikes slightly above current price
- Average premium: $2.00 per share = $1,000 per month ($200 per contract × 5 contracts)
- Annual premium income: $12,000
- Total income: $2,240 (dividends) + $12,000 (premiums) = $14,240
- Enhanced yield: 17.8% on your $80,000 position

This transforms a stagnant position into a meaningful income generator.

2. Reducing Cost Basis Over Time

Each premium collected effectively lowers your cost basis in the stock, creating a cushion against potential losses.

Example:

- You buy 100 shares of Microsoft (MSFT) at $380 per share = $38,000 investment
- Month 1: Sell $390 call for $5.00 premium = $500 income (new cost basis: $375)
- Month 2: Call expires, sell $395 call for $4.50 = $450 income (new cost basis: $370.50)
- Month 3: Call expires, sell $400 call for $5.50 = $550 income (new cost basis: $365)
- After 3 months: Your effective cost basis has dropped from $380 to $365 per share

If MSFT drops to $370, you're still showing a $500 profit instead of a $1,000 loss.

3. Enhanced Returns in Moderately Bullish Markets

Covered calls can actually outperform simple stock ownership when stocks rise moderately, because you capture both appreciation (up to the strike price) and premium income.

Example:

- Stock purchase price: $50 per share
- Sell $55 call for $2.00 premium
- Stock rises to $54 at expiration
- Return: $4 capital gain + $2 premium = $6 per share (12% return)
- Stock-only return: $4 per share (8% return)

You outperform by 50% due to the premium income.

4. Emotional Discipline and Structured Profit-Taking

Many investors struggle with knowing when to sell winners. Covered calls create a disciplined framework for taking profits at predetermined price levels.

Example: You own Apple (AAPL) at $175 and would be happy to sell at $185. Instead of trying to time the perfect exit:

- Sell the $185 call for $3.00 premium
- If AAPL reaches $185, your shares are automatically sold
- Your total gain: $10 (appreciation) + $3 (premium) = $13 per share
- If AAPL doesn't reach $185, you keep your shares and the $3 premium, then repeat

This removes emotional decision-making from profit-taking.

5. Leveraging Time Decay

One of the most powerful aspects of covered calls is that time decay (theta) works in your favor. Every day that passes, the option you sold loses value, even if the stock price doesn't move.

How Time Decay Benefits Covered Call Sellers:

Options have two value components: intrinsic value and time value. Time value decays exponentially as expiration approaches, with the most rapid decay occurring in the final 30 days.

Example:

- 60 days to expiration: $55 call on $50 stock = $3.00 premium (mostly time value)
- 30 days to expiration: Same call = $2.00 premium
- 10 days to expiration: Same call = $0.75 premium
- At expiration: $0 premium if stock remains at $50

As the seller, you collect $3.00 upfront. Each day, the option becomes less valuable, and you can potentially buy it back cheaper or let it expire worthless, keeping the full premium.

6. Portfolio Diversification of Income Streams

Covered calls add a new income dimension to your portfolio, creating returns that are partially uncorrelated with stock price movements.

Your portfolio income sources:

- Stock appreciation (correlated with market movements)
- Dividends (relatively stable, company-specific)
- Option premiums (dependent on volatility and time, partially independent of direction)

This diversification can smooth overall portfolio returns.

The Mathematics of Covered Call Income:

Let's examine a realistic portfolio example to see the cumulative power of covered calls:

Portfolio Details:

- Total value: $100,000
- 10 different stocks, $10,000 position each
- Average dividend yield: 2.5% = $2,500 annual dividend income

- Strategy: Sell monthly covered calls on all positions

Monthly Covered Call Activity:

- Each position: 100 shares
- Average premium per position: $150 per month
- Total monthly premium: $1,500
- Annual premium income: $18,000

Total Annual Income:

- Dividends: $2,500
- Option premiums: $18,000
- **Total: $20,500**
- **Effective yield: 20.5% on $100,000 portfolio**

This compares to 2.5% from dividends alone—more than an 8x improvement in income generation.

Important Considerations:

The math assumes:

- You successfully manage 12 monthly cycles per year
- You don't get assigned on all positions immediately
- You actively manage and roll positions when appropriate
- Transaction costs are factored into premium calculations

Real-World Performance Expectations:

While the example above shows impressive potential, realistic covered call returns typically fall into these ranges:

Conservative Approach (Out-of-the-Money Strikes):

- Additional annual yield: 4-8% above dividends
- Lower assignment probability
- More stock appreciation potential retained

Moderate Approach (At-the-Money Strikes):

- Additional annual yield: 8-15% above dividends
- Moderate assignment probability
- Balanced income and appreciation

Aggressive Approach (In-the-Money Strikes):

- Additional annual yield: 15-25% above dividends
- High assignment probability
- Limited appreciation potential

Who Benefits Most from Covered Calls?
Covered calls are particularly suitable for:

1. **Income-focused investors** seeking cash flow from their portfolios
2. **Retirees** needing to supplement fixed income without selling principal
3. **Conservative investors** wanting to enhance returns without taking excessive risk
4. **Tax-advantaged account holders** (IRAs, 401(k)s) where premium income compounds tax-free
5. **Patient investors** comfortable holding quality stocks long-term
6. **Investors with large unrealized gains** seeking to monetize positions without triggering capital gains taxes immediately

When Covered Calls May Not Be Optimal:
The strategy has limitations and isn't suitable for:

1. **Strongly bullish markets** where stocks may significantly exceed strike prices
2. **High-growth stocks** expected to make large, rapid moves upward
3. **Small positions** where transaction costs consume too much of the premium
4. **Very volatile stocks** where assignment risk is too high relative

to premiums

5. **Short-term traders** not planning to hold stocks long-term

The Covered Call Mindset:

Successful covered call investors embrace a specific mindset:

- **You're trading upside for income:** You accept capping your gains in exchange for immediate cash
- **You're a stock owner first:** The options strategy enhances your stock investment, not replaces it
- **You're patient and systematic:** Consistent execution over time matters more than perfect timing
- **You're willing to have stocks called away:** At profitable prices, letting go is part of the strategy
- **You focus on total return:** You measure success by combining appreciation, dividends, and premiums

---

How Covered Calls Differ from Naked Call Writing

Understanding the critical distinction between covered and naked call writing is essential for every options trader. While both strategies involve selling call options, their risk profiles differ dramatically—one is among the most conservative options strategies, while the other ranks among the most dangerous.

The Fundamental Difference: Stock Ownership

Covered Call Writing:

- You own 100 shares of the underlying stock (or multiples thereof)
- You sell call options against these owned shares
- Your shares serve as "coverage" for your obligation
- If assigned, you deliver the shares you already own
- Maximum loss is limited to your stock's decline, partially offset by premium

Naked (Uncovered) Call Writing:

- You sell call options without owning the underlying stock
- You have an obligation with no coverage
- If assigned, you must purchase shares at market price to deliver
- Maximum loss is theoretically unlimited as stock prices can rise indefinitely
- Requires substantial margin and broker approval

Risk Profile Comparison

Covered Call Risk:

Your risk is essentially identical to owning stock, with slight modification:

Maximum Loss: Your stock's decline to zero, minus the premium collected

Example:

- Buy 100 shares of XYZ at $50 = $5,000 investment
- Sell $55 call for $2 = $200 premium received
- Stock declines to $30 = $2,000 loss on stock
- Net loss: $2,000 - $200 = $1,800
- Stock-only loss would have been: $2,000

The premium provides a small cushion but doesn't fundamentally change the downside risk of stock ownership.

Maximum Gain: Limited to (Strike Price - Purchase Price) + Premium

Example:

- Buy stock at $50, sell $55 call for $2
- Maximum gain: ($55 - $50) + $2 = $7 per share = $700 total
- This occurs if stock reaches or exceeds $55 at expiration
- Gain percentage: 14% on your $5,000 investment

Breakeven: Purchase price minus premium received

Example:

- Purchase price: $50
- Premium received: $2
- Breakeven: $50 - $2 = $48
- Your position is profitable as long as stock stays above $48

Naked Call Risk:
The naked call exposes you to catastrophic risk:
Maximum Loss: Theoretically unlimited
Example:

- Sell $55 call on XYZ for $2 = $200 premium received
- You don't own the stock (currently at $50)
- Stock skyrockets to $150 due to acquisition announcement
- You must buy shares at $150 and deliver at $55 = $9,500 loss per contract
- Net loss: $9,500 - $200 = $9,300
- Your loss is nearly 50 times the premium received!

Maximum Gain: Limited to premium received
Example:

- Sell $55 call for $2 = $200 maximum profit
- This profit requires stock to stay below $55 at expiration
- Your best case is a $200 gain
- Your worst case is unlimited loss
- Risk-reward ratio is extremely unfavorable

Breakeven: Strike price plus premium received
Example:

- Strike price: $55
- Premium received: $2
- Breakeven: $55 + $2 = $57
- You begin losing money if stock exceeds $57

Capital Requirements

Covered Call:

- Must purchase 100 shares (or already own them)
- If stock costs $50/share: $5,000 capital required
- Premium received reduces net capital deployed
- No margin requirement if shares are paid for in cash
- Can be executed in retirement accounts (IRAs)

Example Investment:

- 100 shares at $50 = $5,000
- Sell call, receive $200 premium
- Net capital deployed: $4,800
- You own a real asset (the stock)

Naked Call:

- No stock purchase required initially
- Must meet substantial margin requirements (typically 20-40% of stock value)
- Broker requires Level 4 or 5 options approval (highest levels)
- Cannot be executed in standard retirement accounts
- Requires maintenance of margin throughout position

Example Margin Requirement:

- Stock price: $50
- Margin requirement: 20% of $5,000 = $1,000
- Plus: Premium received = $200
- Total margin: $1,200 minimum
- Margin increases as stock price rises
- Can receive margin call requiring immediate cash deposit

Critical Point: While naked calls require less initial capital, the margin requirement can increase dramatically if the trade moves against you, and brokers can force you to close the position at the worst possible time.

Broker Approval and Account Requirements

Covered Calls:

- Typically require Level 2 options approval
- Available to most investors after basic options education
- Can be executed in cash accounts (no margin needed)
- Permitted in IRAs and other retirement accounts
- Considered a conservative strategy by most brokers
- No special financial requirements beyond ability to buy stock

Naked Calls:

- Require Level 4 or 5 options approval (highest levels)
- Demand extensive options trading experience
- Require substantial liquid net worth (often $100,000+)
- Need significant margin account with substantial equity
- Prohibited in retirement accounts
- Require signed acknowledgment of unlimited risk
- Subject to pattern day trading rules if actively managed

Practical Implications:

Most individual investors can implement covered calls after minimal experience and education. Naked calls are restricted to sophisticated traders with substantial financial resources, and even experienced traders often avoid them due to risk.

Strategic Intent: Why Choose One Over the Other?

When Covered Calls Make Sense:

1. **You want to own the stock anyway**
   - You're bullish long-term on the company
   - You're comfortable holding through market

fluctuations
    - You want to enhance returns on an existing holding
2. **You seek income generation**
    - You need cash flow from your portfolio
    - You're willing to cap upside for immediate income
    - You want to reduce cost basis over time
3. **You expect modest appreciation or sideways movement**
    - Stock is in a trading range
    - Volatility is elevated (increasing premiums)
    - You don't expect dramatic moves in the near term
4. **You practice conservative risk management**
    - You want defined, quantifiable risk
    - You can't afford unlimited loss potential
    - You want to sleep well at night

When Naked Calls Might Be Considered (by professionals):

1. **You're extremely bearish on the stock**
    - You believe stock will decline or stay flat
    - You want to profit from that view without shorting stock
    - You're willing to accept unlimited risk for limited reward
2. **You're implementing advanced strategies**
    - Part of a complex spread strategy
    - Hedged with other positions
    - Using sophisticated risk management
3. **You're a professional with appropriate capital**
    - Substantial liquid net worth
    - Professional risk management systems
    - Ability to monitor positions constantly

Note: Even professional traders often prefer covered calls or defined-risk strategies over naked calls due to the catastrophic risk potential.

***

Real-World Scenarios Comparing Both Strategies

Scenario 1: Moderate Upside Move

Setup:

- Stock XYZ currently trading at $100
- Both traders sell the $110 call for $3 premium
- Stock rises to $108 at expiration

Covered Call Trader:

- Owns 100 shares purchased at $100 = $10,000 investment
- Stock gains: $8 per share = $800
- Premium kept: $3 per share = $300
- Total profit: $1,100 on $10,000 = 11% return

Naked Call Trader:

- No stock ownership
- Option expires worthless (out-of-the-money)
- Profit: $300 premium kept
- Return: $300 on ~$2,000 margin = 15% return
- But exposed to unlimited risk for this gain

Winner: Covered call trader has better absolute profit and no catastrophic risk exposure.

Scenario 2: Large Upside Move (The Nightmare for Naked Calls)

Setup:

- Stock XYZ trading at $100
- Both sell $110 call for $3 premium
- Unexpected buyout offer at $150 per share announced

Covered Call Trader:

- Owns stock bought at $100
- Stock assigned at $110 (call exercised)
- Gain: $10 per share + $3 premium = $13 per share = $1,300 profit
- Return: 13% on $10,000
- **Emotions:** Slight regret for missing the move from $110-$150, but still profitable

Naked Call Trader:

- Must buy stock at $150 to deliver at $110
- Loss: $40 per share loss - $3 premium = $37 per share = $3,700 loss
- Return: -185% loss on $2,000 margin
- Potential margin call requiring immediate capital
- **Emotions:** Panic, catastrophic loss, possible account termination

Winner: Covered call trader suffers opportunity cost but remains profitable. Naked call trader faces devastating loss.

Scenario 3: Downward Move

Setup:

- Stock XYZ trading at $100
- Both sell $110 call for $3 premium
- Stock declines to $85 at expiration

Covered Call Trader:

- Owns stock bought at $100
- Stock loss: $15 per share = $1,500 loss
- Premium offset: $3 per share = $300 gain
- Net loss: $1,200 on $10,000 = -12% return
- Still owns stock with potential to recover

Naked Call Trader:

- Option expires worthless
- Keeps entire $300 premium
- Return: 15% profit on $2,000 margin
- No stock ownership = no loss from decline

Winner: Naked call trader in this specific scenario, but only because no stock ownership means no participation in the decline.

Critical Analysis: While the naked call trader profits in this scenario, they took unlimited risk to earn $300. The covered call trader's loss is from stock ownership itself, not the options strategy. If bearish, simply don't own the stock—don't sell naked calls.

***

The Risk-Reward Mathematics

Covered Call Risk-Reward Profile:

Best Case: Strike price reached or exceeded

- Profit = (Strike - Purchase Price) + Premium
- Example: Buy at $100, sell $110 call for $3
- Maximum profit = $13 per share = 13%

Worst Case: Stock declines to zero

- Loss = Purchase Price - Premium
- Example: Buy at $100, collect $3 premium
- Maximum loss = $97 per share = -97%

Risk-Reward Ratio: Approximately 7.5:1 (risk $97 to make $13)

But remember: You own the stock for its long-term potential, not just this options cycle.

Naked Call Risk-Reward Profile:

Best Case: Stock stays below strike at expiration

- Profit = Premium received
- Example: Collect $3 premium
- Maximum profit = $3 per share

Worst Case: Stock rises dramatically

- Loss = (Stock Price - Strike Price) - Premium
- Example: Stock rises to $200, strike is $110, premium was $3
- Loss = ($200 - $110) - $3 = $87 per share

But it can be worse: Stock could rise to $300, $500, or higher

- At $300: Loss = $187 per share
- At $500: Loss = $387 per share
- Theoretically unlimited

Risk-Reward Ratio: Potentially 100:1 or worse (risk $300+ to make $3)

Professional Assessment: Financial professionals universally agree that naked call writing offers one of the worst risk-reward ratios in investing. You accept unlimited risk for limited reward—the exact opposite of what sound investing principles recommend.

***

Chapter 2: Essential Options Terminology and Concepts

Before implementing sophisticated covered call strategies, you must understand the language of options trading. This chapter demystifies the terminology and mathematical concepts that drive option pricing and behavior.

The Greeks: Delta, Theta, Vega, and Gamma Explained

The Greeks are mathematical measures that describe how option prices respond to various market factors. For covered call traders, these metrics provide crucial insights into risk management and profit optimization.

Delta: The Directional Sensitivity Measure

Delta measures how much an option's price changes for every one-dollar move in the underlying stock. Call options have positive delta values ranging from 0 to 1.00 (sometimes expressed as 0 to 100).

A covered call with a delta of 0.30 means the option premium will increase by approximately $0.30 for every $1.00 increase in the stock price. Conversely, if the stock drops $1.00, the option premium decreases by about $0.30, which benefits you as the option seller.

For covered call writers, understanding delta helps determine the probability of assignment. A delta of 0.30 suggests roughly a 30% chance the option will finish in-the-money at expiration. Out-of-the-money calls typically have lower deltas (0.15 to 0.35), while hover around 0.50, and in-the-money calls approach 1.00.

Strategic consideration: Lower delta options provide greater downside protection but generate less premium income. Higher delta options maximize premium but increase assignment likelihood.

Theta: Time Decay, Your Greatest Ally

Theta represents the rate at which an option loses value as time passes, measured as the dollar amount lost per day. For covered call sellers, theta decay is your friend because you profit as the option you sold loses value.

A call option with a theta of -0.05 loses approximately $5.00 in value per day (remember, one contract represents 100 shares). Time decay accelerates as expiration approaches, with the most rapid decay occurring in the final 30 days before expiration.

This phenomenon explains why many covered call traders prefer selling options with 30 to 45 days until expiration, maximizing the sweet spot where theta decay is most aggressive while still collecting meaningful premiums.

Practical example: You sell a covered call for $2.00 premium with 30 days to expiration and theta of -0.06. All else being equal, the option's value drops to approximately $1.40 after one week, allowing you to potentially buy it back for a profit or simply let theta continue working in your favor.

Vega: Volatility's Price Impact

Vega measures how much an option's price changes for every 1% change in implied volatility. Covered call writers benefit from understanding vega because selling options during high volatility periods generates higher premiums.

A vega of 0.15 means the option price increases by $0.15 for every 1% increase in implied volatility. When you sell a covered call, you want high vega and high implied volatility because you collect more premium. After you've sold the call, you benefit if volatility decreases because the option value declines faster.

Market conditions matter significantly. During earnings announcements, geopolitical events, or market uncertainty, implied volatility spikes, creating ideal covered call selling opportunities. After these events pass, volatility typically contracts, accelerating your profits.

Gamma: The Rate of Delta Change

Gamma measures how much delta changes when the stock price moves $1.00. While gamma is crucial for options traders who actively manage complex positions, covered call writers need only basic awareness.

Higher gamma values appear in at-the-money options near expiration, meaning delta becomes increasingly sensitive to stock price movements. For covered call traders, this translates to increased uncertainty about assignment as expiration approaches for at-the-money positions.

Long-term covered call positions generally have lower gamma, providing more predictable behavior and easier position management.

Intrinsic Value vs. Time Value

Every option's premium consists of two components: intrinsic value and time value. Understanding this distinction is fundamental to selecting optimal strike prices and managing positions effectively.

Intrinsic Value: Real, Tangible Worth

Intrinsic value is the amount by which an option is in-the-money. For call options, intrinsic value equals the stock price minus the strike price, but never less than zero.

Examples:

- Stock trading at $52, call strike at $50: Intrinsic value = $2.00
- Stock trading at $52, call strike at $55: Intrinsic value = $0 (out-of-the-money options have no intrinsic value)

When you sell an in-the-money covered call, you're selling intrinsic value plus time value. The intrinsic value component represents guaranteed profit for the option buyer if they exercise immediately, which is why in-the-money options command higher premiums.

Time Value: The Price of Possibility

Time value represents the additional premium beyond intrinsic value that buyers pay for the possibility the option will become more profitable before expiration. Time value depends on several factors: time until expiration, implied volatility, interest rates, and dividends.

Using our example of a $52 stock with a $50 strike call trading at $3.50:

- Intrinsic value: $2.00
- Time value: $1.50 ($3.50 premium - $2.00 intrinsic value)

The time value component is pure profit potential for covered call writers because it evaporates completely by expiration through theta decay. Even if the stock price remains perfectly flat, you capture the entire time value as profit.

Strategic Implications for Covered Call Selection

Out-of-the-money covered calls consist entirely of time value, offering maximum upside potential if the stock appreciates but lower immediate premium income. At-the-money and in-the-money calls include intrinsic value, providing larger premiums but capping gains at the strike price.

Conservative traders favor out-of-the-money strikes to preserve capital appreciation potential. Aggressive income seekers select at-the-money or slightly in-the-money strikes to maximize premium collection, accepting that significant stock appreciation would be capped.

In-the-Money, At-the-Money, and Out-of-the-Money Options

These three classifications describe the relationship between the stock price and the option's strike price. Each category offers distinct advantages and trade-offs for covered call strategies.

Out-of-the-Money (OTM) Covered Calls

Out-of-the-money calls have strike prices above the current stock price. These options contain only time value, no intrinsic value.

Example: Stock at $48, selling the $50 call for $0.75 premium.

Advantages:

- Preserves upside potential (stock can appreciate to $50 before assignment)
- Lower assignment probability
- Allows continued participation in stock appreciation
- Ideal for moderately bullish outlooks

Disadvantages:

- Lower premium income compared to ATM or ITM options
- Provides less downside protection
- May require stock appreciation to maximize profitability

OTM covered calls suit investors who believe their stock will appreciate modestly and want to capture that upside while generating supplemental income. The typical sweet spot is selecting strikes 2% to 5% above the current stock price.

At-the-Money (ATM) Covered Calls

At-the-money options have strike prices equal or very close to the current stock price, typically within $0.50 for most stocks.

Example: Stock at $50, selling the $50 call for $2.25 premium.

Advantages:

- Higher premium income than OTM options
- Balanced risk-reward profile
- Maximum time value (theta decay most beneficial)
- Reasonable assignment protection while stock is below strike

Disadvantages:

- Caps gains immediately at current price level
- Higher assignment probability than OTM calls
- No participation in stock appreciation beyond the strike

ATM covered calls represent the middle ground, popular among traders who expect neutral to slightly bullish price action and prioritize income over capital appreciation.

In-the-Money (ITM) Covered Calls

In-the-money calls have strike prices below the current stock price, containing both intrinsic and time value.

Example: Stock at $52, selling the $48 call for $4.75 premium (with $4.00 intrinsic value and $0.75 time value).

Advantages:

- Highest premium collection
- Excellent downside protection (premium cushions losses)
- More defensive strategy during uncertain markets
- Captures profit from stock positions above the strike price

Disadvantages:

- Very high assignment probability
- Eliminates upside potential (already in-the-money)
- Functions more like a stock exit strategy than income generation
- Intrinsic value is not "earned" income but rather foregone appreciation

ITM covered calls work best when you're willing to sell the stock at the strike price, essentially treating the covered call as an enhanced sell order. The strategy also suits bearish or neutral outlooks where downside protection outweighs upside potential.

Implied Volatility and Its Impact on Premiums

Implied volatility (IV) is the market's forecast of how much a stock will fluctuate in the future, expressed as an annualized percentage. Unlike historical volatility, which measures past price movements, implied volatility looks forward and profoundly impacts option premiums.

Understanding Implied Volatility

Implied volatility is derived from option prices using the Black-Scholes model, essentially backing out the volatility assumption that justifies current premium levels. An IV of 25% suggests the market expects the stock to move within a 25% range (up or down) over the next year, with about 68% probability.

For covered call traders, higher implied volatility creates opportunity. When IV increases, option premiums inflate, allowing you to collect more income for the same strike price and expiration. When IV decreases after you've sold calls, the option value declines faster, enhancing your profits.

Volatility's Premium Impact

Consider a $50 stock with different IV levels:

- IV at 15%: 30-day ATM call trades at $1.00
- IV at 30%: same call trades at $1.85
- IV at 45%: same call trades at $2.65

The premium nearly triples as volatility increases from 15% to 45%, even though the strike price, stock price, and expiration remain identical. This relationship makes volatility analysis crucial for maximizing covered call returns.

IV Rank and IV Percentile

Two metrics help assess whether current volatility is relatively high or low for a particular stock:

IV Rank compares current implied volatility to its 52-week high and low range. An IV rank of 75 means current volatility is at the 75th percentile of its annual range, suggesting elevated premiums and attractive selling opportunities.

IV Percentile measures what percentage of days over the past year had lower IV than today. An IV percentile of 80 indicates that 80% of recent days showed lower volatility, again signaling rich premiums.

Professional covered call traders prefer selling when IV rank or IV percentile exceeds 50, ensuring above-average premium collection.

Volatility Patterns and Events

Implied volatility follows predictable patterns:

Earnings announcements typically spike IV by 20% to 100%, creating exceptional covered call opportunities immediately before earnings. However, this strategy requires careful risk assessment because unexpected earnings surprises can trigger large stock movements.

Market-wide volatility, measured by the VIX index, affects all stocks during periods of economic uncertainty, geopolitical events, or market corrections. Covered call premiums across the board increase during these periods.

Post-event volatility crush occurs after earnings or significant announcements, causing IV and option premiums to collapse suddenly.

Selling calls before these events and buying them back immediately after can generate outsized returns.

Practical Application for Covered Call Selection

Compare IV across multiple stocks in your portfolio or watchlist before deciding where to write calls. A stock with 35% IV might generate $2.50 premium while an equivalent stock with 18% IV produces only $1.20, making the high-IV choice far more attractive.

Additionally, avoid selling covered calls during unusually low volatility periods. Instead, wait for IV to revert toward its historical average, which typically generates 30% to 50% higher premiums for identical positions.

The 100-Share Contract Standard

Options contracts in U.S. markets follow a standardized structure: one contract represents 100 shares of the underlying stock. This convention affects position sizing, premium calculations, and risk management for covered call traders.

Contract Specifications

When you sell one covered call contract, you're obligating yourself to sell 100 shares at the strike price if the buyer exercises the option. Therefore, covered call positions require owning at least 100 shares per contract sold.

Premium quotes appear on a per-share basis but represent the per-contract value when multiplied by 100. A call option quoted at $2.35 actually costs $235.00 per contract ($2.35 × 100 shares).

Position Sizing Implications

The 100-share standard creates natural position sizing increments:

- 100 shares: One covered call contract
- 250 shares: Two contracts (with 50 shares uncovered)
- 500 shares: Five covered calls
- 1,000 shares: Ten contracts

Fractional positions create complications. If you own 250 shares and sell three covered calls, you're exposed to naked call risk on 50 shares, fundamentally changing your risk profile and margin requirements.

Always ensure your stock holdings equal or exceed 100 times the number of calls sold.

Mathematical Examples

Position 1: Conservative covered call

- Own 500 shares of XYZ at $48.00 per share: $24,000 investment
- Sell 5 covered calls, $50 strike, $1.40 premium: $700 income ($1.40 × 100 × 5)
- Total premium yield: 2.92% ($700 ÷ $24,000)

Position 2: Partial position coverage

- Own 300 shares of ABC at $65.00 per share: $19,500 investment
- Sell 2 covered calls (covering 200 shares), $67.50 strike, $2.10 premium: $420 income
- Keep 100 shares uncovered for unlimited upside potential
- Blended strategy balancing income and appreciation

Contract Standard and Account Size

The 100-share requirement creates minimum position sizes that may challenge smaller accounts. At a $50 stock price, one covered call position requires $5,000 in capital. This consideration influences stock selection for traders with limited capital, often pushing them toward lower-priced stocks or ETFs.

Some brokers offer "mini options" on select securities, representing 10 shares instead of 100, though these are uncommon and typically limited to specific stocks.

Options Chains: How to Read and Interpret Them

An options chain displays all available call and put options for a specific stock, organized by expiration date and strike price. Mastering options chain analysis is essential for efficient covered call trading.

Basic Options Chain Structure

Options chains contain several critical data columns:

Strike Price: The price at which the option can be exercised, displayed in ascending order.

Bid: The highest price buyers are currently offering for the option. When you sell to open a covered call, you receive approximately the bid price.

Ask: The lowest price sellers are currently requesting. When you buy to close a covered call, you pay approximately the ask price.

Last: The most recent trade price, which may not reflect current market conditions if trading volume is low.

Volume: The number of contracts traded during the current session, indicating liquidity and market interest.

Open Interest: The total number of outstanding contracts not yet closed or exercised. Higher open interest suggests better liquidity and tighter bid-ask spreads.

Implied Volatility: The market's volatility forecast reflected in option prices, typically shown as a percentage.

The Greeks: Delta, theta, vega, and gamma values for each strike and expiration.

Analyzing Strike Prices

Options chains typically display strikes in standardized increments:

- Stocks under $25: $0.50 or $1.00 intervals
- Stocks $25 to $200: $2.50 or $5.00 intervals
- Stocks above $200: $5.00 or $10.00 intervals

Higher-priced stocks may also offer $1.00-increment strikes near the current stock price for precision.

When selecting covered call strikes, compare premiums across multiple strikes within your strategy parameters. A $50 strike might offer $2.20 while the $52.50 strike provides $1.35, allowing you to calculate whether the additional $2.50 of upside potential justifies the $85 premium reduction.

Evaluating Bid-Ask Spreads

The bid-ask spread represents trading costs and liquidity quality. Narrow spreads (under $0.10 for liquid stocks) indicate efficient markets where you receive fair pricing. Wide spreads (over $0.30) suggest low liquidity, potentially costing you significant premium.

Example comparison:

- Liquid option: Bid $2.30, Ask $2.35 (spread: $0.05 or 2.2%)
- Illiquid option: Bid $1.80, Ask $2.25 (spread: $0.45 or 22.5%)

For a one-contract trade, the wide spread costs you $45 in reduced premium compared to the theoretical mid-point. This emphasizes the importance of selecting liquid underlyings with active options markets.

Comparing Multiple Expirations

Most options chains allow toggling between expiration dates. Comparing premiums across different expirations reveals the term structure of option pricing:

30-day $50 call: $1.45 premium 60-day $50 call: $2.15 premium

90-day $50 call: $2.70 premium

Notice the premium doesn't increase linearly with time. The 60-day option costs 48% more than the 30-day option but provides twice the time, illustrating that shorter-term options offer better time decay efficiency.

Many covered call traders calculate monthly premium yield by dividing premium by days until expiration and comparing results:

- 30-day option: $1.45 ÷ 30 = $0.048 per day
- 60-day option: $2.15 ÷ 60 = $0.036 per day
- 90-day option: $2.70 ÷ 90 = $0.030 per day

The 30-day option generates 60% more daily premium than the 90-day option, supporting the common practice of selling monthly covered calls.

Practical Chain Navigation Strategy

Follow this systematic approach when analyzing options chains:

1. Filter for your preferred expiration timeframe (typically 30-45 days)

2. Identify strikes within your strategic range (typically 2-7% out-of-the-money)
3. Verify adequate open interest (minimum 100 contracts) and volume
4. Check bid-ask spreads (should be under 5% of premium)
5. Review delta to assess assignment probability
6. Compare premiums across strikes to optimize risk-reward
7. Note implied volatility to ensure favorable selling conditions

This methodical analysis takes mere minutes with practice and dramatically improves position selection quality.

***

Position Greeks Comparison

Understanding how option Greeks differ between covered and naked calls helps illustrate their different risk characteristics.

Covered Call Greeks (Long Stock + Short Call):

Delta: Approximately +0.50 to +0.70

- Positive delta from stock ownership (+1.00)
- Negative delta from short call (typically -0.30 to -0.50)
- Net effect: You still profit from upward moves, but less than stock-only
- You still lose from downward moves, but same as stock-only

Theta: Positive (time decay helps you)

- You benefit as option loses time value
- Every day that passes increases your probability of keeping premium
- Maximum theta benefit in final 30 days

Vega: Negative (volatility decrease helps you)

- You benefit from declining volatility
- Options become less expensive when volatility drops
- You can potentially buy back calls cheaper

Gamma: Negative (acceleration risk is limited)

- Your delta changes as stock moves
- Limited impact because you own the stock
- Risk is manageable and defined

Naked Call Greeks (Short Call Only):

Delta: Negative (-0.30 to -0.50 typically)

- You lose money as stock rises
- Loss accelerates as stock moves above strike
- No positive delta from stock ownership to offset

Theta: Positive (time decay helps you)

- Same benefit as covered call
- But benefit is small relative to potential loss
- $3 daily time decay doesn't help if stock rises $20

Vega: Negative (volatility decrease helps you)

- Same as covered call
- But volatility spike can be devastating
- Volatility tends to increase with sharp upward moves

Gamma: Highly negative (acceleration risk is severe)

- Your delta becomes more negative as stock rises
- Losses accelerate exponentially above strike
- This is where "unlimited risk" becomes reality
- At-the-money options have highest gamma risk

Example of Gamma Risk:
Stock at $100, you're short the $105 call:

- Delta = -0.40 (you lose $40 for every $1 stock rise)
- Stock rises to $105: Delta now -0.50
- Stock rises to $110: Delta now -0.85
- Stock rises to $115: Delta now -0.95
- Each subsequent $1 move costs you nearly $1 per share

With covered calls, this gamma risk is neutralized by stock ownership. With naked calls, it creates a feedback loop of accelerating losses.

***

Margin and Maintenance Requirements

Covered Call Margin:

- **If stock owned outright:** No margin requirement
- **If on margin:** Standard stock margin (typically 50% of stock value)
- **Premium received:** Credited to account immediately
- **Maintenance:** No ongoing margin calls related to option
- **Risk to broker:** Minimal—they can liquidate stock if needed

Example:

- Own 100 shares at $100 = $10,000 value
- Sell $110 call, receive $300
- No additional margin requirement
- No risk of margin call from option position

Naked Call Margin:
Much more complex and dynamic:
Initial Margin Requirement: The greater of:

1. 20% of stock value + premium - out-of-money amount
2. 10% of stock value + premium

Example Calculation (Stock at $100, short $110 call for $3):

- Method 1: (20% × $10,000) + $300 - $1,000 = $1,300
- Method 2: (10% × $10,000) + $300 = $1,300
- Required margin: $1,300

But here's the danger:
As stock rises, margin requirement increases:
Stock rises to $110:

- Method 1: (20% × $11,000) + premium - $0 = $2,500
- Your margin requirement nearly doubles!

Stock rises to $120:

- Method 1: (20% × $12,000) + premium + $1,000 = $4,400
- Now you need $4,400 in margin (up from $1,300)

Stock rises to $150:

- Method 1: (20% × $15,000) + premium + $4,000 = $7,300
- Margin requirement has increased 5.6x

Margin Call Risk:
If your account doesn't have sufficient equity to meet increasing margin requirements:

1. Broker issues margin call
2. You must deposit cash immediately (often within 24-48 hours)
3. If you can't meet call, broker liquidates positions
4. Broker closes your position at the worst possible time
5. You're locked into the loss with no chance of recovery

Real-World Horror Story:
A trader with $10,000 account equity sells 5 naked calls on a $50 stock ($55 strike, $2 premium).

- Initial margin required: ~$6,500
- Remaining buying power: $3,500
- Feels comfortable

Stock gaps up 30% overnight on earnings to $65:

- New margin requirement: ~$18,000
- Account equity: $10,000 - $5,000 loss = $5,000
- Margin call: $13,000 needed immediately

Trader can't meet call:

- Broker closes all positions at market open
- Loss locked in at $5,000 (50% of account)
- Had trader been able to hold, stock later declined to $58
- But broker forced liquidation for protection

With covered calls, this nightmare scenario cannot happen. Your shares satisfy the obligation.

***

Tax Treatment Differences

Covered Call Taxation:

Premium received:

- Generally treated as short-term capital gain when position closes
- If option expires: Premium is short-term gain
- If option is bought back: Net premium (sold - bought back) is gain/loss
- If assigned: Premium added to sale price of stock

Stock holding period:

- Can maintain long-term capital gains treatment
- If held 12+ months before writing call
- And call is "qualified" (not too deep in-the-money)

Example:

- Bought stock 2 years ago at $50
- Now worth $100, sell $110 call for $3
- Assigned at expiration
- Sale price for tax purposes: $110 + $3 = $113
- Purchase price: $50

- Long-term capital gain: $63 per share
- Tax rate: 15-20% (depending on income)

Naked Call Taxation:
Premium received:

- Always short-term capital gain
- No long-term treatment available
- Taxed as ordinary income (up to 37% federal rate)

If assigned:

- You buy stock at market price
- Immediately sell at strike price
- Creates short-term capital gain/loss
- Higher tax rate than long-term gains

Example:

- Sell $110 call for $3 premium
- Stock rises to $150, you're assigned
- You buy at $150, sell at $110 = $40 loss
- Net after premium: $37 loss
- Loss offsets other gains, but at short-term rates

Tax Efficiency Verdict:
Covered calls offer potential for:

- Long-term capital gains treatment (lower rates)
- Tax-loss harvesting opportunities
- Strategic timing of income recognition

Naked calls result in:

- Short-term gains only (highest rates)
- Less tax-planning flexibility

- Potential for large short-term losses

Psychological and Emotional Factors
Covered Call Psychology:
Peace of Mind:

- Sleep well knowing maximum loss is defined
- No 3 AM panic checking stock prices
- Can go on vacation without constant monitoring
- Stress level similar to owning stock

Emotional Discipline:

- Strategy enforces profit-taking discipline
- Less emotional attachment to positions
- Acceptance of trading upside for income
- Logical exit points predetermined

Regret Management:

- Minor regret if stock soars past strike
- But still profitable = easier to accept
- Can immediately write new covered call
- Learning opportunity, not devastating loss

Naked Call Psychology:
Constant Anxiety:

- Every market open is stressful
- After-hours and pre-market moves cause panic
- Vacation is impossible without constant monitoring
- Sleep disruption common

Emotional Breakdown:

- When position moves against you, emotions intensify

- Paralysis from fear of realizing loss
- Hope that stock will reverse (often doesn't)
- Catastrophic losses create psychological trauma

Account Destruction:

- Single bad trade can wipe out months/years of gains
- Some traders quit after naked call disasters
- Relationships strained from financial stress
- Long-term psychological impact

Professional Traders' Perspective:

Even experienced traders who occasionally use naked calls universally agree:

- The risk doesn't justify the reward
- The stress isn't worth the premium
- Better strategies exist for bearish views
- Covered calls offer superior risk-adjusted returns

***

Why Covered Calls Are Called "Conservative"

Despite being an options strategy, covered calls are considered conservative because:

1. **Risk is defined and acceptable:** Maximum loss is the same as stock ownership (which you were willing to accept)
2. **Premium provides downside cushion:** Every dollar collected reduces your breakeven point
3. **You own the underlying asset:** Unlike many derivative strategies, you hold real equity value
4. **Suitable for retirement accounts:** IRAs and 401(k)s permit covered calls, indicating regulatory approval of their conservative nature
5. **Income without leverage:** You're not borrowing or using

margin to amplify returns

6. **Institutional adoption:** Conservative institutions (pension funds, endowments) use covered calls for income enhancement
7. **Mathematical risk-reward:** Studies show covered call portfolios have lower volatility than stock-only portfolios

Industry Classification:

- **CBOE:** Rates covered calls as Level 2 (basic)
- **FINRA:** Considers them suitable for conservative investors
- **Academic Research:** Multiple studies show reduced portfolio volatility
- **Financial Planners:** Often recommend for retirees needing income

When Covered Calls Beat Naked Calls

Covered calls outperform naked calls in:

1. **Risk-adjusted returns:** Better Sharpe ratios and risk metrics
2. **Downside protection:** Stock ownership provides asset value
3. **Psychological sustainability:** Strategy you can maintain long-term
4. **Tax efficiency:** Potential for long-term gains treatment
5. **Regulatory approval:** Access for all investors, not just sophisticated
6. **Capital preservation:** No catastrophic loss potential
7. **Sleep quality:** Literally better rest (stress affects health)
8. **Long-term wealth building:** Compound returns without account destruction

The Only Scenario Where Naked Calls "Win":

Naked calls only outperform when:

- Stock declines or stays flat
- You correctly predict this movement

- You don't need the capital for other opportunities
- Volatility doesn't spike
- No unexpected news occurs

Even then, the profit is small relative to risk taken. Other bearish strategies (put spreads, short stock, inverse ETFs) offer better risk-reward profiles.

Conclusion: The Clear Choice

For individual investors, the choice is unambiguous: **covered calls** provide a conservative, sustainable approach to income generation with defined risk. Naked calls belong only in the hands of the most sophisticated traders with substantial capital reserves and professional risk management systems—and even they often choose other strategies.

Throughout this book, we focus exclusively on covered calls because they:

- Preserve capital
- Generate consistent income
- Require no special account status
- Work in retirement accounts
- Provide tax efficiency
- Enable long-term wealth building
- Let you sleep at night

The slight reduction in potential upside is a small price to pay for eliminating catastrophic risk.

The Risk-Reward Profile of Covered Calls

Understanding the risk-reward profile of covered calls is essential for setting realistic expectations and making informed decisions about when and how to implement this strategy. Unlike simple stock ownership or more complex options strategies, covered calls create a unique asymmetric profile that offers defined risks and capped rewards.

The Three-Dimensional Risk-Reward Framework

Traditional stock ownership has a straightforward risk-reward profile:

- **Unlimited upside potential** (stock can rise indefinitely)
- **Limited downside risk** (stock can only fall to zero)
- **1:1 participation** in price movements (stock up $1 = you gain $1)

Covered calls modify this profile across three dimensions:

1. Return Enhancement Through Premium Income 2. Upside Cap at Strike Price 3. Downside Cushion from Premium

Let's explore each dimension in detail.

***

Dimension 1: Return Enhancement Through Premium Income

The primary benefit of covered calls is the immediate income generated from selling call options. This premium income enhances your total return regardless of the stock's price movement (within certain ranges).

Premium Income Characteristics:

Immediate and Certain:

- Premium is credited to your account the moment the trade executes
- You keep this money regardless of what happens next (unless you buy back the option)

- It's real cash that can be withdrawn, reinvested, or used for other purposes

Repeatable:

- After expiration or assignment, you can write new calls
- Monthly cycles create 12 income opportunities per year
- Even weekly options allow 52+ income cycles annually
- Compounds over time as you repeat the strategy

Market-Condition Independent (Partially):

- You collect premium even if stock stays flat
- You collect premium even if stock declines slightly
- Premium compensates for lack of appreciation
- Creates positive returns in sideways markets

Quantifying Premium Income Potential:
Realistic premium ranges for different stock types and strike selections:
Conservative Stocks (Low Volatility: β < 0.8):

- **Examples:** Utilities, Consumer Staples, REITs
- **Out-of-the-Money strikes (5% above current price):**
    - Monthly premium: 0.5-1.0% of stock price
    - Annual potential: 6-12% additional yield
    - Example: $100 stock, collect $0.50-$1.00 per month
- **At-the-Money strikes (current price):**
    - Monthly premium: 1.0-2.0% of stock price
    - Annual potential: 12-24% additional yield
    - Example: $100 stock, collect $1.00-$2.00 per month

Moderate Volatility Stocks (β = 0.8-1.2):

- **Examples:** Large-cap technology, Financials, Industrials

- **Out-of-the-Money strikes (5% above):**
    - Monthly premium: 1.0-2.0% of stock price
    - Annual potential: 12-24% additional yield
    - Example: $100 stock, collect $1.00-$2.00 per month
- **At-the-Money strikes:**
    - Monthly premium: 2.0-3.5% of stock price
    - Annual potential: 24-42% additional yield
    - Example: $100 stock, collect $2.00-$3.50 per month

High Volatility Stocks (β > 1.2):

- **Examples:** Small-cap growth, Biotechnology, Emerging tech
- **Out-of-the-Money strikes (5% above):**
    - Monthly premium: 2.0-4.0% of stock price
    - Annual potential: 24-48% additional yield
    - Example: $100 stock, collect $2.00-$4.00 per month
- **At-the-Money strikes:**
    - Monthly premium: 4.0-7.0% of stock price
    - Annual potential: 48-84% additional yield
    - Example: $100 stock, collect $4.00-$7.00 per month

Important Reality Check:
While high-volatility stocks offer tempting premiums, they also carry significantly higher risks:

- Greater likelihood of large price swings
- Higher probability of assignment (calls finishing in-the-money)
- Increased downside risk if stock declines sharply
- More stressful to manage

Most successful covered call investors focus on **moderate volatility stocks** that balance attractive premiums with manageable risk.

***

Real-World Example: Annual Income Calculation

Conservative Portfolio Approach:

Let's build a realistic covered call portfolio and calculate expected annual income:

Portfolio Composition:

- $100,000 total portfolio value
- 10 positions of $10,000 each (100 shares at $100/share)
- Mix of dividend-paying, moderate-volatility stocks
- Average beta: 1.0
- Average dividend yield: 2.5%

Covered Call Strategy:

- Sell monthly calls 3-5% out-of-the-money
- Average premium: 1.5% of stock price per month
- Target 10-11 successful cycles per year (accounting for occasional assignments)

Annual Income Calculation:

Dividend Income:

- Portfolio value: $100,000
- Dividend yield: 2.5%
- Annual dividends: $2,500

Option Premium Income:

- Monthly premium per position: $150 (1.5% of $10,000)
- 10 positions: $1,500 per month
- Successful months per year: 10.5 (accounting for assignments/rollovers)
- Annual premium income: $1,500 × 10.5 = $15,750

Total Annual Income:

- Dividends: $2,500

- Premiums: $15,750
- **Total: $18,250**
- **Effective yield: 18.25%**

Breakdown by Source:

- Traditional stock appreciation: Variable (market-dependent)
- Dividend yield: 2.5% (relatively stable)
- Option premium yield: 15.75% (strategy-generated)
- **Income enhancement: 7.3x over dividends alone**

Risk-Adjusted Comparison:
Compare this to alternative income strategies:
High-Dividend Stock Portfolio (No Covered Calls):

- Average yield: 4-5%
- Annual income on $100,000: $4,000-$5,000
- Full upside potential retained
- No option management required

Bond Portfolio:

- Investment-grade corporate bonds: 4-5%
- Annual income on $100,000: $4,000-$5,000
- Limited price appreciation potential
- Interest rate risk

Dividend Growth + Covered Calls:

- Dividend yield: 2.5%
- Premium income: 15.75%
- Total income: 18.25%
- Some upside retained (up to strike prices)
- **Best income-to-risk ratio for most investors**

***

Dimension 2: Upside Cap at Strike Price

The trade-off for premium income is that you cap your upside potential at the strike price. This is the most significant limitation of covered calls and requires careful consideration.

Understanding the Upside Cap:

When you sell a call option, you grant the buyer the right to purchase your shares at the strike price. If the stock rises above the strike, you must sell at that predetermined price, missing any additional gains.

Mathematical Impact:

Basic Scenario:

- Stock purchased at: $100
- Sell $110 call for: $3 premium
- Maximum gain: ($110 - $100) + $3 = $13 per share
- Maximum return: 13%

If stock rises to $120:

- Your actual gain: $13 per share (10% appreciation + 3% premium)
- Missed opportunity: $7 per share (the move from $110 to $120)
- Stock-only gain would have been: $20 per share (20% return)
- Covered call return: 13%
- **Opportunity cost: 7% (35% of potential gain)**

If stock rises to $150:

- Your actual gain: Still $13 per share (capped at strike)
- Missed opportunity: $37 per share
- Stock-only gain would have been: $50 per share (50% return)
- Covered call return: 13%
- **Opportunity cost: 37% (74% of potential gain)**

The Opportunity Cost Equation:

Opportunity Cost = (Actual Stock Price - Strike Price) - Premium Collected

When opportunity cost = $0: Stock finishes at or below strike **When opportunity cost > $0:** Stock finishes above strike **When opportunity cost > Premium:** You would have been better off with stock only

Frequency of Assignment (Upside Cap Triggered):

Statistical probabilities based on strike selection:

5% Out-of-the-Money Strikes:

- Historical assignment rate: 30-40% of the time
- You keep full premium without assignment: 60-70% of the time
- When assigned, you capture: 5% appreciation + 1-2% premium = 6-7% total
- Annualized (if monthly): 72-84% potential return

At-the-Money Strikes:

- Historical assignment rate: 50-60% of the time
- You keep full premium without assignment: 40-50% of the time
- When assigned, you capture: 0% appreciation + 2-3% premium = 2-3% total
- Annualized (if monthly): 24-36% potential return

5% In-the-Money Strikes:

- Historical assignment rate: 70-85% of the time
- You keep full premium without assignment: 15-30% of the time
- When assigned, you capture: -5% loss + 6-7% premium = 1-2% net
- Annualized (if monthly): 12-24% potential return

Key Insight: Out-of-the-money strikes provide the best balance of:

- Lower assignment probability (you keep the stock more often)
- Meaningful appreciation potential (5%+ before cap)

- Attractive premiums (1-2% monthly)
- Repeatable strategy (can rewrite calls after expiration)

Managing the Upside Cap:

Successful covered call investors employ several tactics to mitigate upside limitation:

1. Strike Selection Strategy:

Choose strikes that represent satisfactory profit targets.

Example:

- You bought stock at $100
- You'd be happy to sell at $115 (15% gain)
- Current stock price: $108
- Sell the $115 call instead of $110 call
- Premium might be smaller ($2 instead of $3)
- But you capture more appreciation (15% instead of 10%)

The question to ask: "If someone offered to buy my shares at [strike price] today, would I happily sell?"

If yes, that strike price is appropriate for covered calls. If no, choose a higher strike or don't write calls at all.

2. Rolling Up Strategy:

When stock approaches or exceeds your strike price before expiration, you can "roll up" to a higher strike.

Example:

- Initial position: Own stock at $100, sold $110 call for $3
- Stock rallies to $112 with 2 weeks until expiration
- Current $110 call now worth $4 (intrinsic value + time value)
- Action: Buy back $110 call for $4, sell $115 call for $3.50
- Net cost: $0.50 ($4 paid - $3.50 collected)
- New position: Committed to sell at $115 instead of $110
- Benefit: Capture additional $5 of appreciation for just $0.50 cost

When rolling up makes sense:

- You want to hold the stock longer
- Strong bullish momentum continues
- Time until expiration is sufficient to collect meaningful premium at higher strikes
- Your cost to roll is less than the additional appreciation captured

3. Selective Writing Strategy:

Don't feel obligated to write covered calls every month. In strongly bullish markets or on your highest-conviction stocks, consider holding without calls to capture full upside.

Decision Framework:

- **Write calls when:** Market is sideways, stock is range-bound, volatility is elevated, you need income
- **Hold without calls when:** Strong bull market, stock has major catalyst ahead, you have high conviction on significant upside

4. Partial Position Coverage:

If you own 500 shares, consider writing calls on only 300 shares (3 contracts), leaving 200 shares with unlimited upside potential.

Benefits:

- Generate premium income on portion of position
- Retain full upside on remaining shares
- Flexibility to adjust coverage based on market conditions
- Psychological comfort from having "free" upside exposure

Example:

- Own 500 shares at $100 = $50,000 position
- Write calls on 300 shares, leave 200 uncovered
- If stock rises to $150:

    - 300 shares assigned at $110 = gain of $10/share = $3,000
    - Plus premium collected on 3 contracts = ~$900
    - 200 uncovered shares = gain of $50/share = $10,000
    - Total gain: $13,900
- Compare to all 500 shares covered: $5,000 + $1,500 = $6,500
- **Extra gain from partial coverage: $7,400**

***

The Psychological Reality of Upside Caps:

Common Investor Emotions:

When stock finishes just below strike:

- **Feeling:** Satisfaction and success
- **Thought:** "Perfect execution! Kept my shares and the premium."
- **Reality:** This is indeed the optimal outcome

When stock rises 5-10% above strike:

- **Feeling:** Mild regret, but acceptance
- **Thought:** "Missed some upside, but I made 13% in a month. That's great."
- **Reality:** Still a highly successful outcome

When stock rises 30-50% above strike:

- **Feeling:** Significant regret and frustration
- **Thought:** "I gave away massive gains for a tiny premium!"
- **Reality:** This is the emotional cost of the strategy

Managing the Emotional Impact:

1. Reframe the Narrative:

Instead of: "I lost $37 per share in potential gains" Think: "I made $13 per share (13% return) in 30 days, which annualizes to 156%"

Instead of: "I should have just held the stock" Think: "I executed my plan perfectly and achieved my target return"

2. Focus on Total Portfolio Returns:

Don't judge success by individual positions. Across a diversified covered call portfolio:

- Some stocks will exceed their strikes (frustrating)
- Some stocks will decline (premiums cushion losses)
- Most stocks will trade in ranges (optimal for the strategy)
- **Overall portfolio returns will be enhanced with lower volatility**

3. Remember the Alternative Scenario:

For every stock that soars past your strike, there are others that:

- Declined, but your premium cushioned the fall
- Went sideways, but you earned premium income
- Rose modestly, and you captured both appreciation and premium

The grass isn't always greener. Studies consistently show that covered call portfolios outperform stock-only portfolios on a risk-adjusted basis over long time periods.

4. Celebrate Successes:

When you achieve your target return and get assigned:

- You executed the strategy perfectly
- You made the return you targeted
- You can now redeploy capital into new opportunities
- **This is success, not failure**

Assignment is not a bad outcome—it's often the best outcome.

Statistical Reality Check:

Research by the CBOE (Chicago Board Options Exchange) shows:
BXM Index (Covered Call Performance):

- Tracks S&P 500 with monthly at-the-money covered calls
- Period analyzed: 1986-2023 (37 years)

Results:

- **Total return:** Within 1-2% of S&P 500 total return
- **Volatility:** 25% lower than S&P 500
- **Maximum drawdown:** 30% less severe than S&P 500
- **Risk-adjusted return (Sharpe Ratio):** Superior to S&P 500
- **Income generated:** Significantly higher than dividends alone

Key Finding: You give up some upside in massive bull markets, but gain significantly better risk-adjusted returns and income generation.

Downside: In prolonged strong bull markets (like 2013-2021), covered call strategies underperform stock-only approaches.

Upside: In normal, volatile, or declining markets (the majority of market conditions), covered calls outperform significantly.

***

Dimension 3: Downside Cushion from Premium

While covered calls don't eliminate downside risk, the premium collected provides a meaningful cushion against losses.

How the Cushion Works:

Every dollar of premium collected effectively lowers your breakeven point on the stock.

Example:

- Buy stock at $100
- Sell call for $3 premium
- New breakeven: $100 - $3 = $97
- You don't start losing money until stock falls below $97
- You have a 3% buffer against declines

Quantifying Downside Protection:

The protection equals the premium as a percentage of stock price:

Conservative Strategy (1% monthly premium):

- 12-month protection: ~12% cushion
- Stock can decline 12% before you have losses
- Beyond 12% decline, you lose dollar-for-dollar with stock-only investor

Moderate Strategy (2% monthly premium):

- 12-month protection: ~24% cushion
- Stock can decline 24% before you have losses
- Significant protection against moderate bear markets

Aggressive Strategy (3% monthly premium):

- 12-month protection: ~36% cushion
- Stock can decline 36% before you have losses
- Substantial protection, but higher assignment risk

Real-World Downside Scenarios:

Scenario 1: Minor Decline (5-10%)

Setup:

- Stock purchased at $100
- Sell $105 call for $2.50
- Stock declines to $92 over the month

Covered Call Result:

- Stock loss: -$8 per share
- Premium collected: +$2.50
- Net loss: -$5.50 per share (-5.5%)
- Breakeven at expiration: $97.50

Stock-Only Result:

- Loss: -$8 per share (-8%)

Benefit: Premium cushioned 31% of the loss ($2.50 of $8.00 decline)

Scenario 2: Moderate Decline (15-20%)

Setup:

- Stock purchased at $100
- Monthly covered calls written for 6 months, averaging $2.50 premium
- Stock gradually declines from $100 to $82 over 6 months

Covered Call Result:

- Stock loss: -$18 per share
- Total premiums collected: +$15 (6 months × $2.50)
- Net loss: -$3 per share (-3%)
- Cumulative breakeven: $85

Stock-Only Result:

- Loss: -$18 per share (-18%)

Benefit: Premiums cushioned 83% of the loss ($15 of $18 decline)

Scenario 3: Severe Decline (30%+)

Setup:

- Stock purchased at $100
- Monthly covered calls for 12 months, averaging $2.50 premium
- Stock declines from $100 to $70 over 12 months (bear market)

Covered Call Result:

- Stock loss: -$30 per share

- Total premiums collected: +$30 (12 months × $2.50)
- Net loss: $0 per share (breakeven)
- Cumulative breakeven: $70

Stock-Only Result:

- Loss: -$30 per share (-30%)

Benefit: Premiums completely offset the stock decline!

Critical Understanding: The premium cushion is most powerful in moderate, gradual declines. In severe, rapid crashes, the cushion helps but doesn't eliminate losses entirely.

The Math of Downside Protection Over Time:

Single Month:

- Premium: 2.5% of stock price
- Protection: 2.5% decline buffer
- Modest protection

Six Months:

- Cumulative premium: 15% of original stock price
- Protection: 15% decline buffer
- Meaningful protection

Twelve Months:

- Cumulative premium: 30% of original stock price
- Protection: 30% decline buffer
- Substantial protection against all but severe bear markets

Key Insight: Time is your friend with covered calls. The longer you consistently implement the strategy, the more downside cushion you build.

***

Comparison to Other Downside Protection Strategies:

Covered Calls vs. Protective Puts:

Protective Put:

- Buy put option as insurance
- Costs money (premium paid)
- Provides hard downside protection (guaranteed sell price)
- Expensive over time (negative carry)
- Unlimited upside retained

Covered Call:

- Sell call option for income
- Generates money (premium received)
- Provides soft downside cushion (premium offset)
- Positive carry over time
- Upside capped at strike

Example Comparison:

- Stock at $100
- 6-month protective put at $95 strike costs $4 (hard protection, lose only $1 if stock crashes to $50)
- 6-month covered calls generate $15 in premiums (soft protection, lose $35 if stock crashes to $50, but made $15 income along the way)

Verdict: Protective puts are better for crash protection; covered calls are better for income generation with moderate downside cushion.

Covered Calls vs. Stop-Loss Orders:

Stop-Loss Order:

- Automatic sale at specified price

- No cost, no income
- Hard protection (guaranteed sale)
- Risk of being stopped out on temporary dip
- Full upside retained if not stopped out

Covered Call:

- Income generating
- Soft protection through premium cushion
- No forced sale on temporary dips
- Upside capped at strike

Example:

- Stock at $100
- Stop-loss at $90 triggers if stock hits $90, locking in $10 loss
- Covered call with $3 premium doesn't force sale, reduces loss to $7 at $90 stock price

Verdict: Stop losses are better for limiting large losses; covered calls are better for weathering volatility while generating income.

The Downside Protection Reality:

What covered call premiums DO:

- Reduce cost basis immediately
- Provide cushion against 5-15% declines
- Turn small losers into breakevens or small winners
- Generate income during sideways markets
- Compound protection over time through repeated cycles

What covered call premiums DON'T DO:

- Protect against crashes (still lose significantly if stock drops 40%+)
- Eliminate risk (you still own a volatile asset)
- Guarantee profits (bear markets can still cause losses)

- Replace proper diversification (still need portfolio-wide risk management)

Realistic Expectations:
Think of covered call premiums as:

- **Shock absorbers, not airbags** (cushion bumps, don't prevent crashes)
- **Income enhancement, not insurance** (generate returns, not guaranteed protection)
- **Margin of safety, not bullet-proof vest** (reduce risk, don't eliminate it)

***

The Complete Risk-Reward Profile: Putting It All Together

Now let's synthesize all three dimensions into a comprehensive understanding of covered call risk-reward characteristics.

The Covered Call Return Matrix:
Different market conditions produce different outcomes:
Strong Bull Market (Stock +25% annually):
Stock-Only:

- Return: +25%
- Volatility: High
- Income: Dividends only

Covered Calls (5% OTM strikes):

- Return: +18-22% (some assignments limit upside)
- Volatility: Moderate-High
- Income: Dividends + Substantial premiums
- **Verdict:** Underperforms stock-only, but still excellent returns

Moderate Bull Market (Stock +10-15% annually):

Stock-Only:

- Return: +10-15%
- Volatility: Moderate
- Income: Dividends only

Covered Calls:

- Return: +15-20% (appreciation + premiums)
- Volatility: Moderate
- Income: Dividends + Premiums
- **Verdict:** Outperforms stock-only significantly

Sideways Market (Stock ±5% annually):
Stock-Only:

- Return: 0-5% (mostly dividends)
- Volatility: Moderate
- Income: Dividends only

Covered Calls:

- Return: +12-18% (premiums dominate)
- Volatility: Low-Moderate
- Income: Dividends + Substantial premiums
- **Verdict:** Vastly outperforms stock-only

Bear Market (Stock -15-25% annually):
Stock-Only:

- Return: -15-25%
- Volatility: High
- Income: Dividends only

Covered Calls:

- Return: -5-15% (premiums cushion losses)
- Volatility: Moderate-High
- Income: Dividends + Premiums offset losses
- **Verdict:** Outperforms stock-only substantially

Severe Bear Market (Stock -35-50% annually):
Stock-Only:

- Return: -35-50%
- Volatility: Extreme
- Income: Dividends (possibly cut)

Covered Calls:

- Return: -20-35% (premiums help but don't prevent major losses)
- Volatility: High
- Income: Dividends + Premiums provide some cushion
- **Verdict:** Outperforms stock-only, but both suffer significantly

Historical Performance Summary:
Over market cycles (combining all conditions):

- **Covered calls outperform stock-only 60-70% of the time**
- **Especially outperform in:** Sideways markets, moderate bear markets, volatile markets
- **Underperform in:** Sustained strong bull markets (2013-2021 type periods)
- **Risk-adjusted returns (Sharpe Ratio):** Consistently superior to stock-only

The Probability Distribution of Returns:
Stock-Only Annual Returns:

- Best years: +30-40%

- Worst years: -30-40%
- Median years: +10-12%
- Standard deviation: ~15-18%

Covered Call Annual Returns:

- Best years: +20-30% (capped upside)
- Worst years: -20-30% (cushioned downside)
- Median years: +12-15% (enhanced median)
- Standard deviation: ~10-13% (reduced volatility)

Translation: You give up some of the best years to avoid some of the worst years, while improving average returns.

Risk-Reward Visualization:

Imagine a bell curve of possible returns:

Stock-Only:

- Wide distribution (high volatility)
- Fat tails on both ends (extreme outcomes possible)
- Center at ~10% annual return

Covered Calls:

- Narrower distribution (lower volatility)
- Right tail cut off (limited extreme gains)
- Left tail elevated (cushioned extreme losses)
- Center at ~12-13% annual return
- **Result:** Higher average returns with lower volatility = superior risk-adjusted performance

Maximum Loss, Maximum Gain, and Breakeven Analysis

Maximum Loss Formula:

Max Loss = (Stock Purchase Price - $0) - Total Premiums Collected

In theory: You could lose everything if stock goes to zero **In practice:** Premiums cushion losses, and most stocks don't go to zero

Example:

- Purchase price: $100
- First-year premiums: $30 (monthly calls)
- If stock goes to $0: Loss = $100 - $30 = $70 per share
- Stock-only loss: $100 per share
- **Premium cushion: $30 (30% of loss prevented)**

Maximum Gain Formula:
Max Gain = (Strike Price - Purchase Price) + Premium Received
Example:

- Purchase price: $100
- Strike price: $110
- Premium received: $3
- Maximum gain: ($110 - $100) + $3 = $13 per share = 13%

If you wrote monthly calls for a year:

- Assuming average assignment every 3 months
- 4 cycles per year × $3 average premium = $12 annual premium
- Plus appreciation on re-bought shares
- Total potential annual return: 15-25% (depending on management)

Breakeven Formula:
Breakeven = Purchase Price - Total Premiums Collected
Example:

- Purchase price: $100
- Monthly premium: $2.50
- After 6 months: Total premiums = $15
- Breakeven: $100 - $15 = $85
- Stock can decline 15% before you have any loss

Dynamic Breakeven Over Time:

The breakeven point improves with each premium collected:
Month 1:

- Breakeven: $97.50 (one $2.50 premium)
- Protection: 2.5%

Month 6:

- Breakeven: $85 (six $2.50 premiums)
- Protection: 15%

Month 12:

- Breakeven: $70 (twelve $2.50 premiums)
- Protection: 30%

Key Insight: The longer you hold and consistently write calls, the better your risk profile becomes.

***

Risk-Reward Comparison: Covered Calls vs. Alternative Strategies

Let's compare covered calls to other common investment approaches:

1. Covered Calls vs. Buy-and-Hold Stocks:

Buy-and-Hold:

- **Pros:** Unlimited upside, simple, tax-efficient (long-term gains), no management required
- **Cons:** High volatility, no income unless dividends, fully exposed to declines
- **Best for:** Strong bull markets, high-conviction long-term holds

Covered Calls:

- **Pros:** Enhanced income, reduced volatility, downside cushion, consistent cash flow

- **Cons:** Capped upside, requires active management, more complex taxes
- **Best for:** Sideways/volatile markets, income seekers, risk-averse investors

Verdict: Covered calls offer superior risk-adjusted returns in most market conditions, but underperform in sustained bull markets.

2. Covered Calls vs. Dividend Stocks Only:

High-Dividend Stocks:

- **Pros:** Reliable income, simple, often stable companies, tax-qualified dividends
- **Cons:** Limited to 3-6% yields typically, stock appreciation often limited, dividend cuts possible
- **Best for:** Conservative income investors, retirees, passive investors

Covered Calls on Dividend Stocks:

- **Pros:** Double income (dividends + premiums), 15-25% total yields possible, flexibility to adjust
- **Cons:** More management required, options learning curve, some upside traded away
- **Best for:** Income investors willing to actively manage, those wanting higher yields

Verdict: Covered calls on dividend stocks offer dramatically higher income potential for those willing to manage positions actively.

3. Covered Calls vs. Bonds:

Bonds:

- **Pros:** Predictable income, capital preservation (if held to maturity), lower volatility than stocks
- **Cons:** Low yields (2-5%), interest rate risk, no growth

potential, inflation risk

- **Best for:** Very conservative investors, capital preservation focus, income with no volatility tolerance

Covered Calls:

- **Pros:** Higher income (12-20%+ potential), stock appreciation potential, inflation hedge through equity ownership
- **Cons:** Higher volatility, principal at risk, requires stock market knowledge
- **Best for:** Income investors comfortable with moderate risk, those wanting growth potential

Verdict: Covered calls offer significantly higher income potential with moderate additional risk compared to bonds.

4. Covered Calls vs. REITs:

REITs (Real Estate Investment Trusts):

- **Pros:** High yields (4-8%), real estate diversification, professional management, liquidity
- **Cons:** Interest rate sensitive, sector-specific risk, high taxes on distributions
- **Best for:** Income investors, real estate exposure seekers, diversification

Covered Calls on Diversified Stocks:

- **Pros:** Comparable or higher yields, sector flexibility, more control, potential tax advantages
- **Cons:** Requires options knowledge, more active management, individual stock risk
- **Best for:** Investors wanting high income with flexibility, those willing to manage actively

Verdict: Similar income potential; choice depends on real estate exposure desire and management preferences.

***

The Risk-Reward Sweet Spot: Finding Your Ideal Strike Selection

The strike price you choose dramatically affects your risk-reward profile. Let's analyze the optimal approach for different investor profiles:

Conservative Investor Profile:

Goal: Capital preservation with moderate income enhancement **Risk Tolerance:** Low **Time Horizon:** Long-term

Optimal Strategy:

- **Strike Selection:** 7-10% out-of-the-money
- **Expected Premium:** 0.75-1.5% monthly
- **Assignment Probability:** 20-30%
- **Upside Retained:** Significant (can capture 7-10%+ appreciation)

Example:

- Stock at $100, sell $108 or $110 call
- Premium: ~$1.00-$1.50
- If assigned: Capture 8-10% appreciation + 1-1.5% premium = 9-11.5% total
- If not assigned: Keep stock + 1-1.5% premium, repeat next month

Risk-Reward Result:

- Lower income than aggressive approach
- Higher probability of keeping stock long-term
- Significant appreciation potential retained
- Best balance for risk-averse investors

Moderate Investor Profile:

Goal: Balance of income and appreciation **Risk Tolerance:** Moderate **Time Horizon:** Medium-term

Optimal Strategy:

- **Strike Selection:** 3-5% out-of-the-money
- **Expected Premium:** 1.5-2.5% monthly
- **Assignment Probability:** 40-50%
- **Upside Retained:** Moderate (can capture 3-5% appreciation)

Example:

- Stock at $100, sell $103 or $105 call
- Premium: ~$2.00-$2.50
- If assigned: Capture 3-5% appreciation + 2-2.5% premium = 5-7.5% total
- If not assigned: Keep stock + 2-2.5% premium, repeat

Risk-Reward Result:

- Good income generation
- Reasonable probability of keeping stock
- Meaningful appreciation potential
- **Optimal for most covered call investors**

Aggressive Investor Profile:

Goal: Maximum income generation **Risk Tolerance:** Moderate-High **Time Horizon:** Short-term

Optimal Strategy:

- **Strike Selection:** At-the-money or 1-2% out
- **Expected Premium:** 2.5-4% monthly
- **Assignment Probability:** 60-70%
- **Upside Retained:** Minimal (capped at current price or slightly above)

Example:

- Stock at $100, sell $100 or $102 call
- Premium: ~$3.00-$4.00
- If assigned: Capture 0-2% appreciation + 3-4% premium = 3-6% total
- If not assigned: Keep stock + 3-4% premium, repeat

Risk-Reward Result:

- Highest income generation
- High probability of assignment
- Limited appreciation participation
- Best for pure income focus

Very Aggressive Investor Profile:
Goal: Maximize short-term income, willing to sell stock **Risk Tolerance:** High **Time Horizon:** Very short-term
Optimal Strategy:

- **Strike Selection:** 1-3% in-the-money
- **Expected Premium:** 4-7% monthly
- **Assignment Probability:** 80-90%
- **Upside Retained:** None (already in-the-money)

Example:

- Stock at $100, sell $97 or $98 call
- Premium: ~$5.00-$7.00
- Almost certainly assigned
- Net result: Small loss on stock (-$2-3) + large premium (+$5-7) = +$2-5 net

Risk-Reward Result:

- Maximum income in short term

- Virtually certain assignment
- No appreciation potential
- Only for investors ready to sell stock

Recommendation for Most Investors:

The **moderate investor profile** (3-5% OTM strikes) provides the optimal balance:

- Meaningful premium income (18-30% annualized)
- Reasonable chance of keeping stock (50-60%)
- Significant upside participation (3-5%+ before cap)
- Manageable assignment rates
- Sustainable long-term strategy

Chapter 3:

The Mechanics of Covered Call Execution

Step-by-Step: Setting Up Your First Covered Call

Understanding the theory of covered calls is one thing; executing your first trade is where knowledge becomes practical skill. This section provides a comprehensive, step-by-step guide to implementing your first covered call, from pre-trade preparation through execution and post-trade management.

Pre-Trade Preparation Checklist

Before placing your first covered call trade, ensure you have the following foundation in place:

1. Account Requirements

Brokerage Account Setup:

- Standard brokerage account (taxable or IRA)
- Options trading enabled (requires application and approval)
- Level 1 or Level 2 options approval (covered calls are basic level)
- Sufficient funds to purchase 100 shares of chosen stock

Options Approval Process:

Most brokers require you to complete an options application that assesses:

- Investment experience and knowledge
- Financial situation (income, net worth, liquid assets)
- Risk tolerance
- Investment objectives
- Understanding of options risks

For covered calls specifically:

- Lowest level of options approval (Level 1 or 2)
- Process typically takes 1-3 business days
- Some brokers offer instant approval for basic strategies

- Educational requirements may include reading disclosure documents

Account Type Considerations:
Taxable Brokerage Account:

- Pros: No restrictions on withdrawals, can use losses to offset gains
- Cons: Annual tax reporting on all option income and stock gains
- Best for: Investors with maxed-out retirement accounts or needing access to funds

Traditional IRA:

- Pros: Tax-deferred growth on all premium income and gains
- Cons: RMDs after age 73, taxes on withdrawals
- Best for: Long-term retirement savers

Roth IRA:

- Pros: Tax-free growth on all income and gains, no RMDs
- Cons: Contribution limits, income restrictions
- Best for: Long-term savers who qualify, optimal for covered calls

2. Capital Requirements
Minimum Investment:

For your first covered call, you need enough capital to purchase 100 shares of your chosen stock (one standard options contract = 100 shares).

Examples by stock price:

- \$25 stock: \$2,500 required (100 shares × \$25)
- \$50 stock: \$5,000 required (100 shares × \$50)
- \$100 stock: \$10,000 required (100 shares × \$100)

- $200 stock: $20,000 required (100 shares × $200)

Practical Starting Point:
For beginners, ideal first positions:

- **$3,000 - $7,000 per position:** Manageable risk, meaningful learning experience
- **Start with 1-3 positions:** Gain experience before scaling up
- **Total initial commitment:** $10,000-$20,000 allows proper diversification

Important: Never invest money you can't afford to lose or will need within 12-24 months. Stocks can decline significantly, and while covered calls provide downside cushion, they don't eliminate risk.

3. Stock Selection for Your First Trade

Your first covered call should be on a stock that meets these beginner-friendly criteria:

Stability and Quality:

- Established company (10+ years operating history)
- Market cap $20 billion+ (large-cap)
- Consistent profitability (positive earnings past 5 years)
- Dividend-paying (indicates financial stability)
- Low-to-moderate volatility (beta 0.7-1.3)

Liquidity Requirements:

- Average daily volume: 1 million+ shares
- Tight bid-ask spread on options: $0.05-$0.15
- Multiple strike prices available
- Open interest on options: 500+ contracts

Favorable Options Characteristics:

- Active options market (many buyers and sellers)

- Reasonable premiums (1-3% monthly at ATM or slightly OTM)
- Weekly and monthly options available
- Liquid enough to exit easily if needed

Beginner-Friendly Examples:
Tier 1 - Most Conservative (Ideal for first trade):

1. **Johnson & Johnson (JNJ)** - Healthcare, stable dividend aristocrat
2. **Procter & Gamble (PG)** - Consumer staples, consistent performer
3. **Coca-Cola (KO)** - Beverages, global brand, reliable
4. **Verizon (VZ)** - Telecom, high dividend, low volatility
5. **Duke Energy (DUK)** - Utilities, stable, defensive

Tier 2 - Moderate (After gaining experience):

1. **Microsoft (MSFT)** - Technology, but very stable large-cap
2. **Apple (AAPL)** - Technology, massive market cap, liquid options
3. **JPMorgan Chase (JPM)** - Financials, dividend-paying, established
4. **Walmart (WMT)** - Retail, defensive, stable
5. **Costco (COST)** - Retail, quality business, consistent

Stocks to AVOID for first trades:

- High-volatility growth stocks (TSLA, NVDA in volatile periods)
- Small-cap stocks (unpredictable movements)
- Penny stocks or stocks under $10
- Companies with upcoming earnings in next 2 weeks
- Stocks in bankruptcy or financial distress
- Meme stocks or heavily shorted names

- Biotech with binary FDA events
- Stocks with low options volume (wide bid-ask spreads)

4. Educational Preparation

Before executing your first trade:

Required Knowledge:

- Understanding of call options (right to buy at strike price)
- Knowledge of covered call mechanics (sell call on owned stock)
- Familiarity with options terminology (strike, premium, expiration)
- Awareness of assignment risk (stock can be called away)
- Understanding of breakeven calculations
- Knowledge of tax implications (consult tax advisor)

Recommended Pre-Trade Activities:

- Watch broker's covered call tutorial videos (most offer free education)
- Paper trade for 1-2 months (practice without real money)
- Read your broker's options disclosure document
- Join online community (Reddit r/options, Bogleheads forum, etc.)
- Review 5-10 real examples of covered call trades
- Understand your broker's platform mechanics

5. Tools and Resources Needed

Essential Tools:

Options Chain Access:

- Real-time options quotes from your broker
- Ability to view multiple strikes and expirations
- Bid-ask spread visibility
- Volume and open interest data

Stock Analysis Tools:

- Real-time stock quotes
- Basic charts (identify support/resistance)
- Dividend calendar (know ex-dividend dates)
- Earnings calendar (avoid earnings surprises)

Position Tracking:

- Portfolio management within broker platform
- Spreadsheet for tracking cost basis, premiums, realized gains
- Calendar reminders for expiration dates

Educational Resources:

- Broker's education center
- Options Clearing Corporation (OCC) educational materials
- CBOE (Chicago Board Options Exchange) learning resources
- Books on covered calls and options basics

Helpful but Not Required:

- Options profit/loss calculators (many free online)
- Implied volatility charts
- Greeks calculators (delta, theta, etc.)
- Third-party research platforms

Step 1: Purchase the Underlying Stock

Your first action in creating a covered call is purchasing 100 shares of your selected stock. This is a straightforward stock purchase, but timing and execution matter.

Decision Point: Market Order vs. Limit Order

Market Order:

- Executes immediately at current market price
- Guarantees execution (you will get filled)

- Price paid may be slightly higher than last quote (slippage)
- Use when: Stock is highly liquid, market is calm, price moving favorably

Limit Order:

- You specify maximum price willing to pay
- Only executes if stock reaches your price
- May not fill if stock moves away from your limit
- Use when: Stock is volatile, you have target entry price, patient approach

Example:
You want to buy 100 shares of Johnson & Johnson (JNJ):

- Current bid: $156.25
- Current ask: $156.30
- Last trade: $156.27

Market Order: You'll likely pay $156.30 (ask price) = $15,630 total
Limit Order at $156.25:

- Might fill immediately if someone sells at bid
- Might wait minutes/hours if stock moves up
- Saves $5 if filled at bid instead of ask
- Risk: Stock rises to $157, you miss entry, have to chase

Recommendation for Beginners: Use limit orders midway between bid-ask to ensure reasonable price while maintaining high fill probability.

Example Limit Order: $156.27 (the last trade price)

- Likely fills quickly
- Pays fair price
- Avoids worst-case ask price

Execution Example:
Let's walk through buying JNJ for your first covered call:
Step-by-Step Stock Purchase:

1. **Log into your broker platform**
2. **Navigate to stock trading section**
3. **Enter stock symbol:** JNJ
4. **Select "Buy" order**
5. **Enter quantity:** 100 shares
6. **Select order type:** Limit Order
7. **Enter limit price:** $156.27 (current mid-price)
8. **Select duration:** Day Order (good for today only)
9. **Review order:**
    - Symbol: JNJ
    - Quantity: 100 shares
    - Order type: Limit Buy
    - Limit price: $156.27
    - Total cost: $15,627 + commission (if any)
    - Commission: $0 (most brokers offer free stock trades)
10. **Submit order**
11. **Wait for confirmation** (usually seconds for liquid stocks)
12. **Verify fill:** Check that 100 shares now appear in your portfolio

Order Confirmation Details:
Your confirmation should show:

- Symbol: JNJ
- Quantity: 100 shares
- Fill price: $156.27 (or very close)
- Total cost: $15,627.00
- Commission: $0.00
- Net cost: $15,627.00
- Settlement date: T+1 (next business day)

Important Note on Settlement:

Stocks settle T+1 (trade date plus one business day). Your shares will be officially "yours" the next business day, but most brokers allow you to trade options against them immediately. This is called "trading on good faith settlement."

Common Beginner Mistakes to Avoid:

Mistake 1: Buying odd lots

- ◈ Buying 50 shares or 150 shares
- ✓ Buy exactly 100 shares (or multiples: 200, 300, etc.)
- Why: One options contract = 100 shares

Mistake 2: Market orders in volatile stocks

- ◈ Using market order on gapping stock at market open
- ✓ Using limit orders or waiting for market to stabilize
- Why: Can pay significantly more than expected

Mistake 3: Ignoring ex-dividend dates

- ◈ Buying 1 day before ex-dividend, writing calls immediately
- ✓ Checking dividend calendar, planning call strike accordingly
- Why: Stock typically drops by dividend amount on ex-date

Mistake 4: Buying without checking options liquidity

- ◈ Buying stock with illiquid options (wide bid-ask spreads)
- ✓ Verifying active options market before buying stock
- Why: Difficult to execute calls profitably with wide spreads

Mistake 5: Buying at 52-week highs without analysis

- ◈ Chasing stock that's extended 30% above moving averages
- ✓ Buying at reasonable valuations or after minor pullbacks
- Why: Higher risk of decline, difficult to write profitable calls above current price

Your Stock Purchase Checklist:

Before submitting your stock buy order, verify:

- ☐ Account has sufficient funds (+ cushion for options commission)
- ☐ Purchasing exactly 100 shares (or 200, 300, etc.)
- ☐ Stock meets beginner-friendly criteria
- ☐ Options on this stock have good liquidity
- ☐ No earnings announcement in next 2 weeks
- ☐ No ex-dividend date in next 3 days
- ☐ Using appropriate order type (limit preferred)
- ☐ Limit price is reasonable vs. current bid-ask
- ☐ Ready to write covered call immediately after fill

Step 2: Understanding the Options Chain

Once you own 100 shares, it's time to select and sell a call option. The options chain is where you'll find all available options for your stock.

What is an Options Chain?

An options chain is a comprehensive listing of all available options contracts for a stock, organized by:

- **Expiration dates** (weekly, monthly, quarterly)
- **Strike prices** (ascending from low to high)
- **Option type** (calls vs. puts)
- **Bid and ask prices** (what buyers pay, sellers receive)
- **Volume and open interest** (trading activity)
- **Greeks** (delta, theta, gamma, vega)

Anatomy of an Options Chain:

Let's examine a real example for JNJ (Johnson & Johnson) trading at $156.27:

Sample Options Chain (Calls, 30-day expiration):

Strike	Bid	Ask	Volume	Open Int	Delta	Theta
150	$7.80	$7.95	245	3,842	0.78	-0.03

152 | $6.15 | $6.30 | 189 | 2,567 | 0.71 | -0.04
154 | $4.65 | $4.80 | 312 | 4,123 | 0.63 | -0.04
156 | $3.35 | $3.50 | 876 | 8,945 | 0.54 | -0.05
158 | $2.30 | $2.45 | 534 | 6,234 | 0.44 | -0.05
160 | $1.50 | $1.65 | 423 | 5,678 | 0.33 | -0.04
162 | $0.95 | $1.05 | 198 | 3,456 | 0.24 | -0.03
165 | $0.45 | $0.55 | 156 | 2,134 | 0.14 | -0.02

Understanding Each Column:

Strike Price:

- The price at which call buyer can purchase your stock
- **Lower strikes** = More likely to be assigned (in-the-money or near it)
- **Higher strikes** = Less likely to be assigned (out-of-the-money)
- Stock currently at $156.27 in this example

Bid Price:

- What buyers are willing to pay for the option
- **This is what YOU receive** when selling a covered call
- Always lower than ask price
- Example: $160 strike has $1.50 bid = you'd collect $150 per contract

Ask Price:

- What sellers are asking for the option
- Not relevant when you're selling (you use bid price)
- Useful to see spread: Ask - Bid = market maker's profit
- Narrow spreads (< $0.15) indicate good liquidity

Volume:

- Number of contracts traded today
- Higher volume = more active interest

- Confirms liquidity (easier to exit if needed)
- Look for 100+ daily volume on strikes you consider

Open Interest:

- Total number of outstanding contracts at this strike
- Higher open interest = more liquid, established market
- Look for 1,000+ open interest for best liquidity
- Updates once daily (after market close)

Delta:

- Probability option finishes in-the-money (approximate)
- Also: How much option price changes per $1 stock move
- Range: 0.00 to 1.00 for calls
- Examples:
    - Delta 0.54 ($156 strike): ~54% chance of assignment
    - Delta 0.33 ($160 strike): ~33% chance of assignment
    - Delta 0.14 ($165 strike): ~14% chance of assignment

Theta:

- Time decay per day (in dollars)
- How much option loses in value each day
- Always negative (time works against option buyers)
- Theta of -0.05 = option loses $5/day in time value
- This is YOUR profit as seller (time decay helps you)

Interpreting the Sample Chain:
Looking at our JNJ example (stock at $156.27):
$150 Strike (In-the-Money):

- **Bid:** $7.80 premium
- **Analysis:** Stock already $6.27 above strike
- **Intrinsic value:** $6.27

- **Time value:** $1.53 ($7.80 - $6.27)
- **Delta:** 0.78 (78% probability of assignment)
- **Use case:** Very aggressive income, almost certain assignment
- **Annualized premium:** ~60% (but stock likely called away)

$156 Strike (At-the-Money):

- **Bid:** $3.35 premium
- **Analysis:** Strike equals current stock price
- **Intrinsic value:** $0.27
- **Time value:** $3.08
- **Delta:** 0.54 (54% probability of assignment)
- **Use case:** High income, moderate assignment risk
- **Annualized premium:** ~26% (solid income generation)

$160 Strike (Out-of-the-Money):

- **Bid:** $1.50 premium
- **Analysis:** Stock must rise $3.73 (2.4%) to reach strike
- **Intrinsic value:** $0 (out-of-the-money)
- **Time value:** $1.50 (all premium is time value)
- **Delta:** 0.33 (33% probability of assignment)
- **Use case:** Moderate income, lower assignment risk
- **Annualized premium:** ~12% (balanced approach)

$165 Strike (Far Out-of-the-Money):

- **Bid:** $0.45 premium
- **Analysis:** Stock must rise $8.73 (5.6%) to reach strike
- **Intrinsic value:** $0
- **Time value:** $0.45
- **Delta:** 0.14 (14% probability of assignment)
- **Use case:** Conservative, retain most upside
- **Annualized premium:** ~3.5% (minimal income)

Selecting Expiration Date:
Options are available in multiple expiration cycles:
Weekly Options (Fridays):

- Expire every Friday
- Short-term (7 days or less)
- Higher annualized returns but more management
- Best for: Active traders, volatile markets
- Example: Sell Friday expiration on Monday = 4-day hold

Monthly Options (Third Friday):

- Standard expiration cycle
- 30-45 days typical timeframe
- Balance of premium income and management burden
- Best for: Most covered call investors (recommended for beginners)
- Example: Sell 35-day option, manage once monthly

Quarterly Options (LEAPS):

- Expire in 3, 6, 9, or 12+ months
- Lower monthly income but less frequent management
- More time value at risk
- Best for: Very long-term, hands-off investors
- Example: Sell 6-month option, check quarterly

Recommendation for First Trade:
Choose monthly options (30-45 days to expiration):

- Optimal balance of time decay acceleration and premium
- Industry standard for covered calls
- Manageable timeline for beginners
- Theta decay strongest in final 30-45 days
- Enough time to adjust if needed
- Not so long that you're locked in uncomfortably

Visual Guide to Options Chain Navigation:
Step 1: Open options chain in your broker platform

- Find "Trade Options" or "Options Chain" button
- Select your stock (JNJ in our example)

Step 2: Filter to Calls only

- Toggle off Puts (you're only selling calls)
- Display only Call options

Step 3: Select expiration date

- Choose monthly expiration ~30 days out
- Example: If today is May 15, choose June 16 expiration (32 days)

Step 4: Review strike prices

- Identify current stock price
- Look 2-3 strikes above (out-of-the-money)
- Look at at-the-money strike
- Compare premiums and probabilities

Step 5: Check liquidity metrics

- Volume: 100+ contracts today
- Open interest: 1,000+ contracts
- Bid-ask spread: < $0.15
- If metrics are poor, choose different strike/expiration

Step 6: Calculate annualized return

- Premium ÷ Stock Price ÷ Days to Expiration × 365
- Example: $1.50 premium on $156 stock, 32 days
- Calculation: ($1.50 ÷ $156) × (365 ÷ 32) = 10.9% annualized

Common Mistakes When Reading Options Chains:
Mistake 1: Confusing bid and ask

- ⟐ Thinking you'll receive ask price ($1.65)
- ✓ Understanding you receive bid price ($1.50)
- Impact: Overestimating income by 10-20%

Mistake 2: Ignoring liquidity

- ⟐ Selecting strike with wide $0.40 bid-ask spread
- ✓ Choosing liquid strikes with $0.05-0.15 spreads
- Impact: Losing 20-30% of premium to spread

Mistake 3: Only looking at premium amount

- ⟐ "This $5 premium looks better than $2 premium"
- ✓ Comparing premium as % of stock price and annualized return
- Impact: Missing better risk-adjusted opportunities

Mistake 4: Misunderstanding delta

- ⟐ Delta 0.60 = "60% profit probability"
- ✓ Delta 0.60 = "60% probability option finishes in-the-money"
- Impact: Wrong expectations about outcomes

Mistake 5: Selecting wrong expiration

- ⟐ Accidentally choosing June 2025 instead of June 2024
- ✓ Verifying expiration date before order
- Impact: Locked into year-long position unintentionally

Options Chain Best Practices:

1. **Always verify you're viewing CALLS not PUTS**
2. **Double-check expiration date** (look for year: 2024 vs 2025)

3. **Use mid-price as reference** ((Bid + Ask) ÷ 2) for fair value
4. **Compare multiple strikes** before deciding
5. **Check volume and open interest** for every strike considered
6. **Calculate annualized return** for apples-to-apples comparison
7. **Review delta for assignment probability** before committing
8. **Consider upcoming events** (earnings, dividends) before selecting expiration

---

Step 3: Selecting Your Strike Price

Choosing the right strike price is the most critical decision in covered call execution. It determines your income, risk of assignment, and upside potential. This decision should align with your investment goals and risk tolerance.

The Strike Price Spectrum:

Strike prices exist on a spectrum from aggressive (more income, higher assignment risk) to conservative (less income, lower assignment risk).

Aggressive ← → Conservative

ITM ATM 1% OTM 3% OTM 5% OTM 7% OTM 10% OTM

Let's analyze each approach using our JNJ example (stock at $156.27):

1. In-the-Money (ITM) Strikes: $150-$154

Characteristics:

- Strike price below current stock price
- Option has intrinsic value already
- Highest premium income
- Highest probability of assignment (70-90%)
- Limited upside potential (already above strike)

Example: $154 Strike

- Stock price: $156.27
- Strike: $154.00
- Difference: Stock is $2.27 above strike (already in-the-money)

- Premium (bid): $4.65
- Intrinsic value: $2.27
- Time value: $2.38
- Delta: 0.63 (63% assignment probability)

Outcome Scenarios:
If assigned (likely):

- Sell stock at $154 = ($2.27) loss vs. current price
- Keep premium = +$4.65
- Net per share: $2.38 profit
- Return: 1.5% in 30 days = 18.7% annualized
- But you lose the stock

If not assigned (stock drops):

- Keep stock + $4.65 premium
- Breakeven: $156.27 - $4.65 = $151.62
- Downside cushion: 3% before losses begin

Best for:

- Investors ready to sell stock
- Maximum income priority
- Don't care about keeping shares
- Want highest probability profit trade

2. At-the-Money (ATM) Strikes: $156
Characteristics:

- Strike price equals (or very close to) current stock price
- Balanced intrinsic and time value
- High premium income
- Moderate assignment probability (50-60%)
- Some upside potential if stock rises modestly

Example: $156 Strike

- Stock price: $156.27
- Strike: $156.00
- Difference: Essentially at current price
- Premium (bid): $3.35
- Intrinsic value: $0.27
- Time value: $3.08
- Delta: 0.54 (54% assignment probability)

Outcome Scenarios:
If assigned:

- Sell stock at $156 = ($0.27) tiny loss vs. entry
- Keep premium = +$3.35
- Net per share: $3.08 profit
- Return: 2.0% in 30 days = 24.7% annualized

If not assigned:

- Keep stock + $3.35 premium
- Breakeven: $156.27 - $3.35 = $152.92
- Downside cushion: 2.1% before losses

Best for:

- High income with reasonable assignment risk
- Willing to sell at current price
- Market neutral outlook
- Balanced approach

3. Slightly Out-of-the-Money (OTM) Strikes: $158-$160 (2-3% above)
Characteristics:

- Strike price 2-3% above current stock price

- Mostly time value (little/no intrinsic value)
- Good premium income
- Moderate assignment probability (35-45%)
- Meaningful upside potential

Example: $160 Strike

- Stock price: $156.27
- Strike: $160.00
- Difference: $3.73 above current (2.4% upside needed)
- Premium (bid): $1.50
- Intrinsic value: $0
- Time value: $1.50 (all time value)
- Delta: 0.33 (33% assignment probability)

Outcome Scenarios:
If assigned:

- Sell stock at $160 = +$3.73 appreciation
- Keep premium = +$1.50
- Net per share: $5.23 total profit
- Return: 3.3% in 30 days = 42.1% annualized
- **Excellent outcome if achieved**

If not assigned:

- Keep stock + $1.50 premium
- Can write another call next month
- Breakeven: $156.27 - $1.50 = $154.77
- Downside cushion: 1% before losses

Best for:

- Balanced income and appreciation
- Want to keep stock if possible
- Slightly bullish outlook

- **Optimal for most investors (RECOMMENDED)**

4. Moderately Out-of-the-Money Strikes: $162-$165 (4-6% above)

Characteristics:

- Strike price 4-6% above current stock price
- All time value (no intrinsic value)
- Moderate premium income
- Lower assignment probability (20-30%)
- Significant upside potential retained

Example: $162 Strike

- Stock price: $156.27
- Strike: $162.00
- Difference: $5.73 above current (3.7% upside needed)
- Premium (bid): $0.95
- Intrinsic value: $0
- Time value: $0.95
- Delta: 0.24 (24% assignment probability)

Outcome Scenarios:

If assigned:

- Sell stock at $162 = +$5.73 appreciation
- Keep premium = +$0.95
- Net per share: $6.68 total profit
- Return: 4.3% in 30 days = 53.8% annualized
- **Outstanding outcome, but less likely**

If not assigned (more likely):

- Keep stock + $0.95 premium
- Can write another call
- Breakeven: $156.27 - $0.95 = $155.32

- Downside cushion: 0.6% before losses

Best for:

- Conservative income enhancement
- Definitely want to keep stock
- Bullish outlook
- Long-term holders supplementing with income

5. Far Out-of-the-Money Strikes: $165+ (6%+ above)
Characteristics:

- Strike price significantly above current stock price
- All time value, very small premium
- Low assignment probability (< 20%)
- Maximum upside potential
- Minimal income generation

Example: $165 Strike

- Stock price: $156.27
- Strike: $165.00
- Difference: $8.73 above current (5.6% upside needed)
- Premium (bid): $0.45
- Intrinsic value: $0
- Time value: $0.45
- Delta: 0.14 (14% assignment probability)

Outcome Scenarios:
If assigned (unlikely):

- Sell stock at $165 = +$8.73 appreciation
- Keep premium = +$0.45
- Net per share: $9.18 total profit
- Return: 5.9% in 30 days = 73.3% annualized
- **Fantastic if it happens, but don't count on it**

If not assigned (very likely):

- Keep stock + $0.45 premium
- Breakeven: $156.27 - $0.45 = $155.82
- Downside cushion: 0.3% only

Best for:

- Very conservative approach
- Strongly bullish outlook
- Want maximum upside
- Income is secondary goal
- **Generally NOT recommended** (insufficient income for effort)

Strike Selection Decision Matrix:

To help choose the right strike for YOUR situation, use this decision framework:

Question 1: Are you ready to sell the stock?

- **Yes, I want to sell:** Consider ITM or ATM strikes ($150-$156)
- **Maybe, at the right price:** Consider 2-5% OTM strikes ($158-$162)
- **No, I want to keep it:** Consider 5-7% OTM strikes ($162-$165)

Question 2: What's your primary goal?

- **Maximum income:** ATM or 1-2% OTM ($156-$158)
- **Balance income and appreciation:** 3-5% OTM ($160-$162)
- **Mostly appreciation, some income:** 6-8% OTM ($165+)

Question 3: What's your market outlook for next 30 days?

- **Bearish (stock may decline):** ATM or ITM ($150-$156) for max cushion
- **Neutral (sideways trading):** 2-4% OTM ($158-$160) for optimal balance
- **Bullish (stock will rise):** 5-7% OTM ($162-$165) to capture more upside

Question 4: How much do you need the income?

- **Critical income needs:** ATM for ~$3.35 premium ($335)
- **Nice supplemental income:** 3% OTM for ~$1.50 premium ($150)
- **Just experimenting:** 5-7% OTM for ~$0.50-$1.00 premium

Question 5: How will you feel if assigned?

- **Happy to take profit:** Any strike at profit above your cost basis
- **Neutral:** Strikes giving satisfactory return
- **Regretful:** Choose higher strikes, consider not writing calls

Recommended Strike Selection for Beginners:
For your first 3-5 covered call trades, use this approach:
Strike: 3-5% Out-of-the-Money

- Provides meaningful premium ($1.00-$2.00 range)
- Reasonable assignment risk (30-40%)
- Captures most strong upward moves
- Good learning balance

Using JNJ Example ($156.27 stock):

- **First choice:** $160 strike (2.4% OTM, $1.50 premium)
- **Alternative:** $162 strike (3.7% OTM, $0.95 premium)

Why this is optimal for beginners:

1. Premium is large enough to be meaningful (~1-2% monthly)
2. Assignment risk is moderate (won't happen every month)
3. If assigned, you capture appreciation + premium (great outcome)
4. If not assigned, keep stock and repeat (learning continues)
5. Strikes are liquid (easy to exit if needed)
6. Less stressful than ATM (not assigned constantly)
7. More income than far OTM (worth the effort)

Advanced Consideration: Adjusting Based on Volatility:

When options premiums are elevated due to market volatility, you can select strikes further OTM while still collecting attractive premiums.

Normal volatility environment:

- $160 strike (2.4% OTM): $1.50 premium (normal)

High volatility environment:

- $160 strike (2.4% OTM): $2.50 premium (elevated)
- Could move to $162 strike (3.7% OTM): $1.80 premium
- Collect good premium while retaining more upside

Low volatility environment:

- $160 strike (2.4% OTM): $0.90 premium (depressed)
- Might need to use $158 strike (closer) to collect $1.50
- Trade-off: More income but less upside/higher assignment risk

---

Continuing with **Step 4: Executing the Covered Call Trade.**

Step 4: Executing the Covered Call Trade

Now that you own 100 shares and have selected your strike price, it's time to execute the actual covered call trade. This involves selling (writing) a call option through your broker's platform.

The Sell-to-Open Order:

When you sell a covered call, you're placing what's called a "Sell to Open" order. This terminology is important because it distinguishes your action from other option transactions:

Types of Options Orders:

- **Buy to Open:** Opening a new long position (buying calls/ puts)
- **Sell to Open:** Opening a new short position (selling calls/ puts) ← **This is what you're doing**
- **Buy to Close:** Closing an existing short position
- **Sell to Close:** Closing an existing long position

Why "Sell to Open" matters:

Your broker needs to know you're:

1. **Selling** (not buying) the option
2. **Opening** a new position (not closing an existing one)
3. Creating an obligation that requires stock ownership as collateral

Pre-Trade Verification Checklist:

Before submitting your sell-to-open order, verify:

☐ **You own exactly 100 shares** (or multiples) of the underlying stock ☐ **Shares are settled** (or broker allows trading on unsettled shares)

☐ **Options trading is enabled** on your account

☐ **You have Level 1 or 2 approval** (covered calls)

☐ **Strike price is confirmed** (double-check you didn't click wrong strike)

☐ **Expiration date is correct** (not accidentally selecting wrong month/year)

☐ **You're selling CALLS not PUTS** (easy mistake for beginners)

☐ **Quantity is 1 contract** (not 10 contracts accidentally)

☐ **No earnings announcement** before expiration

☐ **No ex-dividend date** that will affect your strategy

Step-by-Step Trade Execution:

Let's execute our JNJ covered call using the $160 strike, 30-day expiration:

Trade Parameters:

- Stock: JNJ, currently at $156.27
- You own: 100 shares (purchased at $156.27)
- Strike: $160
- Expiration: June 16, 2024 (32 days away)
- Premium (bid): $1.50
- Premium (ask): $1.65
- Mid-price: $1.575
- Target premium: $1.50-$1.55 (bid to mid)

Platform Execution (General Steps for Most Brokers):

1. Navigate to Options Trading Section

- Log into your broker platform
- Find your JNJ position in your portfolio
- Click "Trade Options" or "Options Chain" button
- Or navigate to Trade → Options → Select JNJ

2. Locate Your Strike in the Options Chain

- Filter to: Calls Only
- Select expiration: June 16, 2024
- Find strike: $160
- Verify bid: $1.50, ask: $1.65

3. Initiate Sell-to-Open Order

- Click on the $160 strike row (usually clickable)
- Select "Sell" or "Sell to Open"
- Or click "Sell" button in the bid column

4. Configure Order Parameters

Action: Sell to Open (should auto-populate) **Symbol:** JNJ 06/16/24 $160 Call (verify this carefully) **Quantity:** 1 (one contract = 100 shares) **Order Type:** (choose one)

Order Type Options:

A. Market Order

- Executes immediately at current bid price
- Guaranteed fill
- Likely receive: ~$1.50 (current bid)
- Use when: Need immediate execution, liquid option, tight spread

Pros:

- Instant execution
- No risk of missing trade
- Simple

Cons:

- May get filled at bid price (not better)
- During fast markets, could get poor fill
- Less control over premium received

B. Limit Order (RECOMMENDED)

- You specify minimum acceptable premium
- Only executes if buyer pays your price or better
- May not fill if market moves away
- Use when: Want specific premium, patient, normal market conditions

Pros:

- Control exact premium received
- Can set limit between bid-ask for better fill

- Protects against poor execution in volatile conditions

Cons:

- May not fill if too aggressive
- Could miss trade if market moves
- Requires monitoring

C. Stop-Limit Order

- Advanced order type, not typically used for opening covered calls
- More relevant for closing positions
- Skip this for your first trades

Recommendation for First Trade: Limit Order at Mid-Price
Set limit at $1.55 (between bid $1.50 and ask $1.65):

- Higher than bid = more income
- Lower than ask = realistic fill probability
- Fair market price
- Likely fills within minutes in normal markets

5. Complete Order Details
Order Entry Form Example:

COVERED CALL - SELL TO OPEN

Action: SELL TO OPEN
Symbol: JNJ 160616C00160000
(JNJ $160 Call Exp 06/16/24)
Quantity: 1 contract (100 shares)
Order Type: LIMIT
Limit Price: $1.55
Duration: DAY (Good for Today Only)

ORDER SUMMARY

Credit: $155.00 (Premium received)
Commission: $0.00 (Most brokers free)
Net Credit: $155.00
Covered Stock: 100 shares JNJ @ $156.27
Obligation: Sell at $160 if assigned
Max Profit: $528.00 [(160-156.27+1.55)×100]
Breakeven: $154.72 (156.27-1.55)
Profit if Flat: $155.00 (Premium)

---

6. Review and Verify
Critical Verification Points:
Symbol Check:

- Correct underlying: JNH? No! JNJ? YES! ✓
- Correct strike: $160? YES! ✓
- Correct expiration: June 16, 2024? YES! ✓
- Correct type: CALL? YES! ✓

Quantity Check:

- 1 contract for 100 shares owned? YES! ✓
- Not 10 contracts? Correct! ✓

Action Check:

- SELL to Open? YES! ✓
- Not BUY to Open? Correct! ✓

Price Check:

- Limit price $1.55? YES! ✓
- Within bid-ask range? YES! ($1.50-$1.65) ✓
- Credit to account? YES! (selling = credit) ✓

Order Summary Check:

- Net credit $155? YES! ($1.55 × 100) ✓
- Commission reasonable? YES! ($0 or < $1) ✓
- Duration Day Order? YES! ✓

7. Submit Order
Once all verifications pass:

- Click "Submit Order" or "Review and Submit"
- Some brokers require additional confirmation screen
- Re-verify details one final time
- Click "Confirm" or "Place Order"
- Order is now live in the market

8. Monitor Order Status
After submission, your order goes through stages:
Status: PENDING

- Order received by broker
- Being routed to exchange
- Usually lasts seconds
- No action needed

Status: WORKING

- Order is live in the market
- Available for execution
- Waiting for buyer at your limit price
- Monitor if concerned about fill

Status: FILLED (Success!)

- Your order executed
- Premium credited to account
- Position now shows in portfolio

- Time to celebrate first covered call! ◈

Status: PARTIALLY FILLED

- Part of order filled (if you sold multiple contracts)
- Not common with single-contract orders
- Can choose to cancel remaining

Status: CANCELLED

- Order not filled before day end
- Your limit price wasn't reached
- Can resubmit tomorrow with adjusted price
- No harm done, try again

Typical Fill Times:
Highly liquid stock (JNJ, AAPL, MSFT):

- Limit order at mid-price: Usually seconds to minutes
- Limit order at bid+$0.05: Nearly instant
- Limit order at ask-$0.05: Usually fills within an hour

Moderately liquid stock:

- Limit order at mid-price: Minutes to hours
- May need to adjust price if not filling
- Monitor first 30 minutes, adjust if needed

Pro tip: If your order doesn't fill within 30 minutes in a normal market, consider:

1. Adjusting limit price down $0.05
2. Checking if market moved significantly
3. Verifying your limit is within bid-ask spread
4. Calling broker if spread seems wrong

9. Confirmation and Record Keeping

Once filled, you'll receive trade confirmation:

Sample Trade Confirmation:

TRADE CONFIRMATION

Trade Date: May 15, 2024
Settlement Date: May 16, 2024
Account: XXX-XXXXX
Action: SELL TO OPEN
Symbol: JNJ 06/16/24 $160 Call
Quantity: 1 contract
Fill Price: $1.55 per share
Total Credit: $155.00
Commission: $0.00
Net Credit: $155.00

POSITION DETAILS

Long Stock: 100 shares JNJ @ $156.27
Short Call: 1 contract $160 strike
Expiration: June 16, 2024 (32 days)
Obligation: Sell at $160 if assigned
Max Profit: $528.00 (if assigned at $160)
Max Loss: $15,472.00 (if stock to $0)
Breakeven: $154.72
Profit if Flat: $155.00 (1.0% return)

Important Information to Record:

Create a spreadsheet or notebook entry:

Position Entry Log:

- **Date opened:** 5/15/2024
- **Stock:** JNJ
- **Shares:** 100

- **Stock cost basis:** $156.27
- **Call strike:** $160
- **Expiration:** 6/16/2024
- **Premium received:** $155.00
- **Days to expiration:** 32
- **Effective cost basis:** $154.72 ($156.27 - $1.55)
- **Max profit potential:** $528.00
- **Annualized return if assigned:** 42.1%
- **Notes:** First covered call trade, conservative 2.4% OTM strike

Why Record Keeping Matters:

1. **Tax purposes:** You'll need this for Schedule D
2. **Performance tracking:** Measure success over time
3. **Strategy refinement:** Learn what works
4. **Assignment preparation:** Know your obligations
5. **Position management:** Track multiple positions easily

10. Post-Execution Verification
Immediately after your order fills, verify in your account:
Check Your Portfolio:
Positions Should Show:
STOCK POSITION:
JNJ - Johnson & Johnson
Quantity: 100 shares
Cost Basis: $156.27
Current Price: $156.45
Market Value: $15,645.00
Unrealized Gain: $18.00
OPTIONS POSITION:
JNJ Jun 16 2024 160.00 Call (SHORT)
Quantity: -1 contract (negative = short/sold)
Entry Price: $1.55 credit
Current Price: $1.52 bid / $1.67 ask
Market Value: -$152.00

Unrealized Gain: $3.00
Days to Expiration: 32
Account Balance:
Before Trade: $5,000.00 (example)
Premium Credit: +$155.00
After Trade: $5,155.00
Buying Power:
Your buying power may be affected:

- Some brokers: No change (covered by stock)
- Some brokers: Slight reduction (maintenance requirement)
- Generally: Covered calls don't require additional margin

Position Greeks (Advanced, but good to understand):
Delta: +0.67 (Long stock +1.00, Short call -0.33)
Theta: +0.05 (Time decay helping you)
Vega: -0.15 (Volatility decrease helps you)
Translation:

- Stock moves $1 up, position gains $0.67
- Each day passing, you gain ~$5 from time decay
- If volatility drops, your option becomes cheaper (good for you)

Common Execution Errors and How to Avoid Them:
Error 1: Selling Puts Instead of Calls
What happened:

- Clicked wrong column in options chain
- Sold put instead of call
- Now obligated to BUY stock at strike, not sell

How to avoid:

- Double-check "CALL" appears in order summary
- Verify symbol ends with "C" (calls) not "P" (puts)

- Example: JNJ 160616C00160000 (C = call)

If you make this mistake:

- Close the position immediately (Buy to Close)
- Accept small loss on bid-ask spread
- Re-enter correct trade

Error 2: Wrong Expiration Date
What happened:

- Clicked June 2025 instead of June 2024
- Sold 1-year option instead of 1-month
- Locked in for way too long

How to avoid:

- Always verify YEAR in confirmation screen
- Check "Days to Expiration" in order summary
- 32 days? Right. 397 days? WRONG!

If you make this mistake:

- Close position immediately (Buy to Close)
- Loss will be small if caught quickly
- Re-enter with correct expiration

Error 3: Wrong Strike Price
What happened:

- Meant to click $160 strike
- Accidentally clicked $150 strike
- Sold call already in-the-money

How to avoid:

- Verify strike price in confirmation
- Check delta: Should be 0.30-0.40 for OTM, not 0.70+
- If delta looks too high, check strike again

If you make this mistake:

- Might be okay if you're willing to sell there
- Or close immediately and re-enter correct strike
- Evaluate: Is this outcome acceptable?

Error 4: Wrong Quantity
What happened:

- Meant to enter "1" contract
- Accidentally entered "10" contracts
- Sold options on 1,000 shares (you only own 100)

How to avoid:

- Verify quantity matches shares owned ÷ 100
- Look for warning: "Not enough shares to cover"
- Check total premium: $1,550 (10 contracts) vs $155 (1 contract)

If you make this mistake:

- Close 9 contracts immediately (Buy to Close on 9)
- Could be expensive if caught late
- Most brokers prevent this with warnings

Error 5: Buying Instead of Selling
What happened:

- Selected "Buy to Open" instead of "Sell to Open"
- Bought call option (spent money) instead of selling
- Now you own a call, not created covered call

How to avoid:

- Verify "SELL" in order action
- Check that premium is CREDIT (+$155) not DEBIT (-$155)
- Order summary should say "Credit" not "Debit"

If you make this mistake:

- Sell the call you just bought (Sell to Close)
- Loss: Bid-ask spread (~$10-20)
- Then properly sell to open the covered call

Error 6: Using Market Order in Volatile Conditions
What happened:

- Used market order during high volatility
- Got filled at bid price ($1.50) instead of better price
- Gave up $5-10 in premium

How to avoid:

- Use limit orders, especially when learning
- Only use market orders in calm, liquid conditions
- Accept that limit orders might not fill immediately

If you make this mistake:

- Learn for next time
- Not a major error, just suboptimal
- Loss is small ($5-10 typically)

Error 7: Not Checking for Earnings
What happened:

- Sold 30-day call

- Earnings announcement in 2 weeks (didn't check)
- Stock gaps up 8% on earnings, assigned immediately

How to avoid:

- Check earnings calendar BEFORE selling call
- Don't sell calls expiring after earnings (unless intentional)
- Or sell strike well above current price if earnings approaching

If you make this mistake:

- If caught before earnings: Close position (Buy to Close)
- If after earnings: Accept assignment or manage position
- Learn to always check earnings calendar

The First Trade Emotional Experience:
What you might feel immediately after executing:
Relief: "I did it! Order filled successfully!"
Nervousness: "Did I do this right? Is everything correct?"
Excitement: "I just made $155 in seconds!"
Confusion: "Why does my account show different values now?"
Concern: "What if the stock drops? What if it rises too much?"
All of these are completely normal!
What to expect in first 24-48 hours:
Hour 1-2:

- Obsessively check stock price
- Watch option value fluctuate
- Feel every $0.10 move intensely
- Question your strike selection
- → **Normal! Resist urge to close immediately**

Day 1:

- Stock might move $1-2 in either direction

- Option value changes accordingly
- Temptation to "take profits" or "cut losses"
- → **Normal! Stick with your 32-day plan**

Day 2-3:

- Nervousness starts to fade
- Getting comfortable with position
- Understanding daily fluctuations
- → **Good! This is the learning phase**

Week 1:

- Position feels "normal" now
- Checking less obsessively
- Starting to understand time decay
- → **Excellent! You're becoming a covered call investor**

Beginner Mindset Mantras:

1. **"I have a 32-day plan. I will not react to daily moves."**
2. **"If assigned, I make $528. That's success, not failure."**
3. **"The premium is already mine. Time is working for me."**
4. **"I'm learning with one position. No need to rush."**
5. **"Profitable assignment is the GOAL, not something to avoid."**

Post-Execution Action Items:

Immediately After Fill:

☐ Screenshot confirmation for records
☐ Update position tracking spreadsheet
☐ Verify position appears correctly in portfolio
☐ Check that premium credit is in account
☐ Set calendar reminder for expiration date
☐ Note any upcoming events (earnings, dividends)

Within 24 Hours:

☐ Re-read your plan for this position
☐ Identify what you'll do at expiration
☐ Calculate returns under different scenarios
☐ Join covered call community for support
☐ Review position once, then stop obsessing

Within First Week:

☐ Observe how time decay affects option value
☐ Watch how stock price moves affect option
☐ Get comfortable with the position
☐ Learn your broker's position management tools
☐ Plan your second covered call trade

Common First-Week Questions:

Q: "The stock is up $2 and my option is worth more. Did I lose money?"

A: No! Your stock gain offsets option value increase. Your net position value is higher. Remember: you're still collecting that premium, and if assigned, you make maximum profit.

Q: "The stock is down $1. Should I close the call and cut losses?"

A: Probably not. The premium you collected cushions this loss. Give the position time to work. Stocks fluctuate—this is normal. Your breakeven is $154.72, not $156.27.

Q: "The option is now worth $1.30 (I sold at $1.55). Should I buy it back for $0.25 profit?"

A: You could, but there's still 29 days of time decay left. Many investors hold for larger gains or full expiration. Closing at 80% profit ($0.25 ÷ $0.30 decay = 83%) is reasonable if you want to redeploy capital.

Q: "I'm scared the stock will drop a lot. Should I sell my shares?"

A: If you're genuinely concerned about a major drop, you can close both positions (sell stock + buy back call). But remember: you chose this stock thinking it was solid. Short-term volatility is normal. The premium cushions minor drops.

Q: "The stock rallied to $159. Will I be assigned early?"

A: Extremely unlikely. Early assignment typically only happens right before ex-dividend dates. With 30 days left, no one will exercise because the option has significant time value remaining.

Execution Success Confirmation:

You've successfully executed your first covered call if you can answer YES to all:

☐ I own 100 shares of a quality stock
☐ I sold 1 call option against those shares (Sell to Open)
☐ I received premium credit to my account (~$100-200+)
☐ The call strike is at or above my stock purchase price
☐ I understand I might be assigned (required to sell at strike)
☐ I'm comfortable holding this position for 30+ days
☐ I've recorded all position details for tracking
☐ I have a plan for what to do at expiration
☐ I'm not panicking over daily price fluctuations
☐ I understand this is a learning experience

If you checked all boxes: CONGRATULATIONS! ◈

You are now officially a covered call investor. You've taken the most important step: actual execution. The learning accelerates from here as you manage this position to expiration.

Shall I continue with **Understanding Premiums and Their Components**?

years

Step 2: Screen for Candidates

Using free screeners (Yahoo Finance, Finviz):

Filter inputs:

- Market cap: Mega ($200B+) or Large ($10-200B)
- Dividend yield: 2-5%
- Beta: 0.5-1.3
- Average volume: > 1M
- Price: $30-$200 (affordable for 100 shares)

Results example:

1. Johnson & Johnson (JNJ)
2. Procter & Gamble (PG)
3. Coca-Cola (KO)
4. Verizon (VZ)
5. Microsoft (MSFT)
6. JPMorgan Chase (JPM)
7. Home Depot (HD)
8. Walmart (WMT)
9. Costco (COST)
10. Duke Energy (DUK)

Step 3: Verify Options Liquidity
Check each stock's options:
JNJ example:

- ATM call bid-ask: $3.35-$3.50 ($0.15 spread) ✓
- Daily volume: 2,400 contracts ✓
- Open interest: 12,500 ✓
- **Liquid - Good candidate**

Small-cap example:

- ATM call bid-ask: $1.20-$1.65 ($0.45 spread) ✗
- Daily volume: 45 contracts ✗
- Open interest: 230 ✗
- **Illiquid - Avoid**

Step 4: Assess Fundamentals
Review for each candidate:

- Recent earnings: Positive? Stable?
- Dividend history: Any cuts?
- Debt levels: Manageable?
- Business outlook: Favorable?

Red flags to avoid:

- Recent dividend cut
- Negative earnings trend
- High debt (> 2.0 debt-to-equity)
- Major litigation or regulatory issues
- Declining market share

Step 5: Check Technical Levels
Simple technical review:

- Current price vs. 52-week range
- Near 52-week high: May wait for pullback
- Near 52-week low: Investigate why (problem or opportunity?)
- Uptrend, downtrend, or range: Range-bound ideal

Support/resistance:

- Identify key price levels
- Use these to inform strike selection
- Sell calls near resistance levels

Step 6: Review Earnings Calendar
Avoid stocks with earnings in next 30 days (for first trades)
Check:

- Next earnings date
- Historical earnings volatility
- Analyst expectations

Once experienced, can trade through earnings strategically.

Diversification Strategy
Position Sizing
General rules:
Single position: 5-10% of portfolio maximum

- $50,000 portfolio: $2,500-$5,000 per stock
- Limits single-stock risk

- Allows for 10-20 different positions

Beginner approach:

- Start with 3-5 positions
- Equal weight each position
- Gradually expand to 8-12 positions

Example $50,000 portfolio:

- 5 positions of $10,000 each
- Each position: 100 shares of $100 stock
- Write 1 call contract per position
- Monthly premium: ~$150 per position = $750 total

Sector Diversification
Don't concentrate in single sector:
Poor diversification:

- 80% Technology stocks
- 20% Communication stocks
- High correlation = high risk

Good diversification:

- 20% Healthcare (JNJ, ABBV)
- 20% Consumer Staples (PG, KO)
- 20% Financials (JPM, V)
- 20% Technology (MSFT, AAPL)
- 20% Utilities/Other (DUK, WMT)

Benefits:

- Sector rotation: One sector down, another up
- Lower portfolio volatility
- Consistent income across cycles

- Better risk management

Staggered Expirations
Don't expire all positions same day:
Poor timing:

- All 10 positions expire 3rd Friday of month
- All decisions at once
- Bulk assignment risk
- Time-intensive single day

Better timing:

- 5 positions: 3rd Friday
- 5 positions: 4th Friday (or next week)
- Or use weekly options on some
- Spreads management throughout month

Building Your Watchlist
Top 20 Beginner-Friendly Covered Call Stocks
Tier 1: Ultra-Conservative (Start Here)

1. **Johnson & Johnson (JNJ)** - Healthcare, dividend aristocrat
2. **Procter & Gamble (PG)** - Consumer staples, 67 years dividends
3. **Coca-Cola (KO)** - Beverages, Warren Buffett holding
4. **Walmart (WMT)** - Retail, defensive
5. **Duke Energy (DUK)** - Utilities, stable income

Tier 2: Conservative (Next Step)

1. **Verizon (VZ)** - Telecom, high yield
2. **AT&T (T)** - Telecom, high yield
3. **Costco (COST)** - Retail, quality business
4. **Home Depot (HD)** - Home improvement, solid
5. **AbbVie (ABBV)** - Pharma, strong pipeline

**Tier 3: Moderate (After Experience

***

Chapter 3: The Mechanics of Covered Call Execution (Continued)

Understanding Premiums and Their Components

The option premium is the price you receive when selling a covered call. It's the immediate cash credited to your account, and understanding what drives premium values is essential for making informed trading decisions. The premium represents compensation for taking on the obligation to potentially sell your shares at the strike price.

Premium Breakdown: Intrinsic Value vs. Time Value

Every option premium consists of two distinct components, and understanding this breakdown is crucial for evaluating whether you're getting fair value when selling calls.

Premium = Intrinsic Value + Time Value

This simple formula governs all option pricing, but each component behaves differently and responds to different market forces.

Intrinsic Value: The "Real" Money

Intrinsic value represents the tangible, immediate profit that would result from exercising the option right now. It's the amount by which an option is "in-the-money."

For Call Options:

- **Intrinsic Value = Stock Price - Strike Price** (when positive)
- **Intrinsic Value = Zero** (when stock price is at or below strike)

Intrinsic value can never be negative—the minimum is always zero.

Detailed Examples:

Example 1: In-the-Money Call

- Stock trading at: $100
- Strike price: $95
- Intrinsic value: $100 - $95 = **$5.00**
- Meaning: If exercised immediately, buyer could buy at $95 and sell at $100 for $5 profit

If the call is trading at $7.50:

- Intrinsic value: $5.00
- Time value: $2.50 ($7.50 total - $5.00 intrinsic)

Example 2: At-the-Money Call

- Stock trading at: $100
- Strike price: $100
- Intrinsic value: $100 - $100 = **$0.00**
- Meaning: No immediate profit from exercise

If the call is trading at $3.00:

- Intrinsic value: $0.00
- Time value: $3.00 (entire premium is time value)

Example 3: Out-of-the-Money Call

- Stock trading at: $100
- Strike price: $105
- Intrinsic value: Cannot be negative, so = **$0.00**
- Meaning: Worthless if exercised now (why buy at $105 when stock trades at $100?)

If the call is trading at $1.50:

- Intrinsic value: $0.00
- Time value: $1.50 (entire premium is time value)

Key Principle: When you sell out-of-the-money calls (recommended for most covered call strategies), you're selling pure time value with no intrinsic value. This is advantageous because time value decays predictably as expiration approaches.

Time Value: The "Hope" Premium

Time value represents the additional amount option buyers are willing to pay beyond intrinsic value, based on the possibility that the option will become more valuable before expiration. It's essentially a bet on future price movement.

Time Value = Total Premium - Intrinsic Value

Why Time Value Exists:

1. **Potential for favorable movement:** The stock might move above the strike price (for OTM calls) or move further above it (for ITM calls)
2. **Time creates opportunity:** More time = more chance for significant price changes
3. **Volatility expectation:** Higher expected volatility = higher time value
4. **Optionality has value:** The right without obligation has inherent worth

Real-World Example: Understanding Both Components

Let's examine Johnson & Johnson (JNJ) trading at $156.27 with various strike prices for a 30-day expiration:

$150 Strike (Deep In-the-Money):

- Stock price: $156.27
- Strike price: $150.00
- Intrinsic value: $156.27 - $150.00 = **$6.27**
- Option premium (bid): $7.80
- Time value: $7.80 - $6.27 = **$1.53**
- Analysis: 80% intrinsic value, 20% time value

$154 Strike (In-the-Money):

- Intrinsic value: $156.27 - $154.00 = **$2.27**
- Option premium (bid): $4.65
- Time value: $4.65 - $2.27 = **$2.38**
- Analysis: 49% intrinsic value, 51% time value

$156 Strike (At-the-Money):

- Intrinsic value: $156.27 - $156.00 = **$0.27**
- Option premium (bid): $3.35
- Time value: $3.35 - $0.27 = **$3.08**
- Analysis: 8% intrinsic value, 92% time value

$160 Strike (Out-of-the-Money):

- Intrinsic value: **$0.00** (stock below strike)
- Option premium (bid): $1.50
- Time value: **$1.50** (100% of premium)
- Analysis: 0% intrinsic value, 100% time value

$165 Strike (Far Out-of-the-Money):

- Intrinsic value: **$0.00**
- Option premium (bid): $0.45
- Time value: **$0.45** (100% of premium)
- Analysis: 0% intrinsic value, 100% time value

What This Means for Covered Call Sellers:

When you sell the $160 strike call (3-5% OTM strategy), you're collecting $1.50 per share ($150 total) in pure time value. This is ideal because:

1. **Time decay is your friend:** The $1.50 will decay to $0 by expiration if stock stays below $160
2. **No intrinsic value risk:** You're not giving away existing equity value
3. **Probabilistic edge:** The stock must rise 2.4% just to reach your strike
4. **Optimal premium-to-risk ratio:** Good income without excessive assignment risk

Compare this to selling the $150 ITM call:

- You collect $7.80 total premium (looks attractive)
- But $6.27 is intrinsic value you're already giving up
- Only $1.53 is actual time value you're earning
- Assignment probability is 78% (very high)
- You're essentially agreeing to sell stock $6.27 below current price
- Not ideal for most covered call strategies

The Time Value Advantage:

Professional covered call investors focus on maximizing time value capture while minimizing intrinsic value giveaway. This is why the 3-5% OTM strike range is optimal—it offers substantial time value ($1.50-$2.50 typically) with zero intrinsic value sacrifice.

What Influences Premium Amounts: The Five Key Factors

Understanding what drives option premiums helps you time your trades better and select optimal strikes. Premiums are determined by a combination of factors that interact in complex ways.

Factor 1: Time Until Expiration (Theta)

Time is the most predictable component of option pricing. The longer until expiration, the higher the premium, but the relationship is not linear—it's exponential.

Time Decay Curve:

Premium Value Over Time (Hypothetical $105 Strike on $100 Stock)

90 days out: $3.50 premium | Daily decay: ~$0.01
60 days out: $2.80 premium | Daily decay: ~$0.02
45 days out: $2.30 premium | Daily decay: ~$0.03
30 days out: $1.80 premium | Daily decay: ~$0.05
15 days out: $0.90 premium | Daily decay: ~$0.08
7 days out: $0.40 premium | Daily decay: ~$0.10
1 day out: $0.05 premium | Daily decay: ~$0.05
Expiration: $0.00 premium | (worthless if OTM)

Key Insights:

The 30-45 Day Sweet Spot:

- Time decay accelerates significantly in the final 45 days
- 30-45 days captures the "acceleration zone" of decay
- You collect substantial premium while benefiting from rapid decay
- This is why monthly options (30-45 days) are standard for covered calls

Weekly Options (7 Days):

- Extremely rapid decay (good for seller)
- But smaller absolute premium amounts
- Requires more frequent management
- Higher annualized returns but more work

Longer-Term Options (90+ Days):

- Larger upfront premium (looks attractive)
- But slow decay in early weeks
- Locks you in for extended period
- Lower annualized returns
- Less flexibility to adjust

Practical Example:
Stock at $100, $105 strike:
Weekly Option (7 days):

- Premium: $0.50
- Weekly return: 0.5%
- Annualized: 26% (if repeated 52 times successfully)
- Management: 52 decisions per year
- Risk: Easier to make mistakes with frequency

Monthly Option (30 days):

- Premium: $1.80
- Monthly return: 1.8%
- Annualized: 21.6% (if repeated 12 times successfully)
- Management: 12 decisions per year
- **Optimal balance** for most investors

Quarterly Option (90 days):

- Premium: $3.50
- Quarterly return: 3.5%
- Annualized: 14% (if repeated 4 times successfully)
- Management: 4 decisions per year
- Less optimal return-to-time ratio

The monthly approach captures 84% of the quarterly premium in just 33% of the time. This is the mathematical advantage of the 30-45 day window.

Factor 2: Stock Price Volatility (Vega)

Volatility measures how much a stock's price moves up and down. Higher volatility creates higher option premiums because there's greater uncertainty—and therefore more risk for option buyers and more potential profit for them.

Two Types of Volatility:

Historical Volatility (HV):

- Measures actual past price movements
- Backward-looking metric
- Calculated using standard deviation of returns
- Expressed as annualized percentage

Example:

- Low volatility stock: HV = 15% (utility company)
- Moderate volatility stock: HV = 25% (large-cap tech)
- High volatility stock: HV = 50% (small-cap growth)

Implied Volatility (IV):

- Measures market's expectation of future volatility
- Forward-looking metric
- Derived from current option prices
- More important for option sellers

How IV Affects Your Premiums:
Low Volatility Stock Example (Utility Company):

- Stock: $50 per share
- Historical volatility: 12%
- Implied volatility: 15%
- $52 strike call (4% OTM), 30 days:
- Premium: **$0.60** (1.2% of stock price)
- Annualized yield: ~14%

Moderate Volatility Stock Example (Large-Cap Blue Chip):

- Stock: $50 per share
- Historical volatility: 22%
- Implied volatility: 25%
- $52 strike call (4% OTM), 30 days:
- Premium: **$1.50** (3.0% of stock price)
- Annualized yield: ~36%

High Volatility Stock Example (Tech Growth):

- Stock: $50 per share
- Historical volatility: 45%
- Implied volatility: 50%
- $52 strike call (4% OTM), 30 days:
- Premium: **$3.00** (6.0% of stock price)
- Annualized yield: ~72%

The Volatility Trade-Off:

Higher premiums are tempting, but they come with increased risks:
Low Volatility (Utility):

- ✓ Stable, predictable price movement
- ✓ Lower assignment risk
- ✓ Sleep well at night
- ✗ Lower premium income ($0.60 or 14% annually)
- **Best for:** Conservative investors, retirees, risk-averse traders

Moderate Volatility (Blue Chip):

- ✓ Good premium income ($1.50 or 36% annually)
- ✓ Manageable price swings
- ✓ Quality underlying stocks
- ✓ Balance of income and stability
- **Best for:** Most covered call investors** ← RECOMMENDED

High Volatility (Growth):

- ✓ Excellent premium income ($3.00 or 72% annually)
- ✗ Large, unpredictable price swings
- ✗ Higher assignment risk
- ✗ Higher stress and monitoring required
- ✗ Greater risk of significant stock declines
- **Best for:** Aggressive traders comfortable with volatility

Practical Strategy: Volatility-Based Strike Selection
When IV is LOW (stock quiet, market calm):

- Premiums are compressed
- Consider waiting for IV spike
- Or select strikes closer to current price for better premium
- Example: Use 2% OTM instead of 5% OTM

When IV is ELEVATED (market uncertainty, volatility spike):

- Premiums are inflated (good for sellers!)
- Can select strikes further OTM while still collecting good premiums
- Example: Use 5-7% OTM strikes, still collect 1.5-2% premiums
- Lower assignment risk + good income = optimal

IV Percentile Tool:

Many platforms show IV percentile—comparing current IV to past year:

- **IV percentile 80%:** Current IV in top 20% of past year (GOOD time to sell calls)
- **IV percentile 50%:** Current IV at median (NORMAL time to sell)
- **IV percentile 20%:** Current IV in bottom 20% (WAIT if possible)

Real-World Example: Same Stock, Different Volatility Environments

Microsoft (MSFT) at $380 per share:

Normal Market Conditions (IV = 22%):

- $390 strike call (2.6% OTM), 30 days
- Premium: $7.00 (1.8% of stock price)
- Assignment probability: 38%

Elevated Volatility Period (IV = 35%, market uncertainty):

- $390 strike call (2.6% OTM), 30 days
- Premium: $11.00 (2.9% of stock price)
- Assignment probability: 42% (slightly higher)

Same strike, 57% higher premium during volatility spike!

Strategic Implication: Patient covered call sellers wait for IV spikes to optimize income. During calm markets, either wait or adjust strikes closer for better premium.

Factor 3: Proximity to Strike Price (Moneyness)

The closer the strike price to the current stock price, the higher the premium. This reflects the increased probability that the option will finish in-the-money.

Premium Progression Example (Stock at $100):

Deep In-the-Money Strikes:

- $90 strike: $12.00 premium (10% ITM)
    - Intrinsic: $10.00
    - Time: $2.00
    - Delta: 0.85 (85% assignment probability)
- $95 strike: $7.50 premium (5% ITM)
    - Intrinsic: $5.00
    - Time: $2.50
    - Delta: 0.75 (75% assignment probability)

At-the-Money Strike:

- $100 strike: $3.50 premium (ATM)
    - Intrinsic: $0.00
    - Time: $3.50
    - Delta: 0.50 (50% assignment probability)

Out-of-the-Money Strikes:

- $102 strike: $2.40 premium (2% OTM)
    - Intrinsic: $0.00
    - Time: $2.40
    - Delta: 0.42 (42% assignment probability)
- $105 strike: $1.50 premium (5% OTM)
    - Intrinsic: $0.00
    - Time: $1.50

    - Delta: 0.30 (30% assignment probability)
- $108 strike: $0.85 premium (8% OTM)
    - Intrinsic: $0.00
    - Time: $0.85
    - Delta: 0.20 (20% assignment probability)
- $110 strike: $0.50 premium (10% OTM)
    - Intrinsic: $0.00
    - Time: $0.50
    - Delta: 0.14 (14% assignment probability)

The Premium Decay Pattern:

Notice how premiums don't decline linearly—they decay exponentially as you move further OTM:

- ATM to 2% OTM: Lose 31% of premium ($3.50 → $2.40)
- 2% to 5% OTM: Lose 38% of premium ($2.40 → $1.50)
- 5% to 8% OTM: Lose 43% of premium ($1.50 → $0.85)
- 8% to 10% OTM: Lose 41% of premium ($0.85 → $0.50)

Strategic Sweet Spot: 3-5% OTM

The 3-5% OTM range offers the best balance:

- Premium: Still substantial ($1.50-$2.00 range)
- Assignment risk: Moderate (30-40%)
- Upside retained: Meaningful (3-5% appreciation possible)
- Time value: 100% of premium is time value
- Delta: 0.25-0.40 (comfortable probability)

Example Comparison:

Too Aggressive (ATM $100 strike):

- Premium: $3.50 ✓
- Assignment risk: 50% ✗
- Upside: $0 ✗
- Gets assigned frequently, miss appreciation

Too Conservative (10% OTM $110 strike):

- Premium: $0.50 ✗
- Assignment risk: 14% ✓
- Upside: $10 ✓
- Premium too small, not worth the effort

Optimal (5% OTM $105 strike):

- Premium: $1.50 ✓
- Assignment risk: 30% ✓
- Upside: $5 ✓
- Best balance of all factors

Factor 4: Dividends

Dividend-paying stocks have an interesting effect on option premiums, particularly as ex-dividend dates approach.

How Dividends Affect Calls:

Call premiums are LOWER for dividend-paying stocks because:

1. Stock price typically drops by dividend amount on ex-dividend date
2. Call holders don't receive the dividend (stock owners do)
3. This anticipated drop is priced into the call premium

Example Without Dividend:

- Stock at $100 (no dividend)
- $105 strike call, 30 days: $1.50 premium

Example With Dividend:

- Stock at $100 (pays $1.00 dividend in 15 days)
- $105 strike call, 30 days: $1.20 premium
- Premium is $0.30 lower due to dividend

Why this matters for covered calls:
Advantage: You collect both premium AND dividend

- Premium income: $1.20 per share
- Dividend income: $1.00 per share
- Total income: $2.20 per share
- Better than $1.50 from non-dividend stock!

Strategic Timing Around Ex-Dividend Dates:
Scenario 1: Call Expiring BEFORE Ex-Dividend

- You keep the stock through ex-dividend
- You collect the dividend ✓
- Lower assignment risk (buyers have no dividend incentive)
- **Optimal for dividend capture**

Scenario 2: Call Expiring AFTER Ex-Dividend

- Risk of early assignment right before ex-dividend
- Call holder might exercise to capture dividend
- You'd lose both stock and dividend
- **Use higher strikes if this structure**

Example: Dividend Capture Strategy
Setup:

- Stock: Johnson & Johnson (JNJ) at $156
- Quarterly dividend: $1.19 per share
- Ex-dividend date: May 25
- Current date: May 1

Strategy:

- Sell May 19 calls (expire before ex-dividend)
- Strike: $160 (2.6% OTM)
- Premium: $2.30

- Calls expire May 19, ex-dividend May 25
- You keep stock through ex-dividend

Income potential:

- Call premium: $2.30
- Dividend: $1.19
- Total income: $3.49 per share ($349 per contract)
- If not assigned: 2.2% return in one month (26.4% annualized)

Repeating Quarterly:

- 4 cycles per year capturing dividends
- Annual dividend income: $4.76
- Annual premium income: ~$9.20 (4 cycles × $2.30)
- Total annual income: ~$13.96 (8.9% yield on $156 stock)

This is why dividend stocks are particularly attractive for covered call strategies—you're generating income from TWO sources simultaneously.

Factor 5: Interest Rates (Rho)

Interest rates have a minor but measurable effect on option premiums. This is the least important factor for most covered call traders but worth understanding.

How Rising Interest Rates Affect Calls:

- Call premiums increase slightly
- Reflects opportunity cost of capital
- Effect is small compared to other factors

Example:

- Stock at $100, $105 strike call
- 2% interest rate environment: $1.50 premium
- 5% interest rate environment: $1.58 premium
- Difference: $0.08 (5% increase in premium)

Practical Impact:

For covered call sellers, rising interest rates are mildly beneficial (slightly higher premiums), but the effect is small enough to largely ignore in decision-making. Focus on time, volatility, and strike selection instead.

Combined Factor Example: Real-World Premium Analysis

Let's see how all factors work together:

Stock: Apple (AAPL) at $175

Scenario A: Normal Market Conditions

- Time: 30 days to expiration
- IV: 25% (moderate)
- Strike: $180 (2.9% OTM)
- Dividend: $0.24 next month
- Interest rates: 5%
- **Premium: $4.50**

Scenario B: High Volatility Event

- Time: 30 days to expiration
- IV: 40% (elevated due to earnings)
- Strike: $180 (2.9% OTM)
- Dividend: $0.24 next month
- Interest rates: 5%
- **Premium: $7.00** (56% higher!)

Scenario C: Low Time Remaining

- Time: 7 days to expiration
- IV: 25% (moderate)
- Strike: $180 (2.9% OTM)
- Dividend: $0.24 next month
- Interest rates: 5%
- **Premium: $1.20** (73% lower than Scenario A)

Key Takeaway: Volatility and time are the dominant factors affecting premiums. Master timing your trades around these two factors for optimal results.

Premium Collection Strategies

Strategy 1: The Steady Eddie (Monthly Moderate OTM)

- Strike: 3-5% OTM
- Expiration: 30-45 days
- Expected monthly premium: 1.5-2.5%
- Frequency: 12 cycles per year
- **Annualized yield: 18-30%**
- Best for: Most covered call investors

Strategy 2: The Income Maximizer (Monthly ATM)

- Strike: At-the-money
- Expiration: 30-45 days
- Expected monthly premium: 2.5-4%
- Frequency: 12 cycles (with frequent assignments)
- **Annualized yield: 30-48%**
- Best for: Maximum income priority, willing to replace stock often

Strategy 3: The Conservative Holder (Monthly Far OTM)

- Strike: 6-8% OTM
- Expiration: 30-45 days
- Expected monthly premium: 0.8-1.5%
- Frequency: 12 cycles per year
- **Annualized yield: 9-18%**
- Best for: Long-term holders wanting modest enhancement

Strategy 4: The Active Trader (Weekly Options)

- Strike: 2-3% OTM
- Expiration: 7 days

- Expected weekly premium: 0.5-1%
- Frequency: 52 cycles per year
- **Annualized yield: 26-52%**
- Best for: Active traders with time for management

Strategy 5: The Hands-Off Approach (Quarterly Options)

- Strike: 4-6% OTM
- Expiration: 90 days
- Expected quarterly premium: 3-5%
- Frequency: 4 cycles per year
- **Annualized yield: 12-20%**
- Best for: Minimal management desired

Recommended Starting Strategy:
For your first 6-12 months of covered call trading:

- Use **Strategy 1: The Steady Eddie**
- Sell calls 30-45 days to expiration
- Select strikes 3-5% OTM
- Target 1.5-2.5% monthly premium
- This provides optimal learning experience with good returns

Once comfortable, you can adjust based on your preferences and results.

Time Decay: Your Edge as a Covered Call Seller

Time decay, measured by the Greek letter **Theta**, is arguably the most important concept for covered call sellers to understand. Unlike option buyers who fight against time decay, sellers benefit from it every single day.

Understanding Theta (Time Decay)

Theta Definition: The amount an option's price decreases each day, assuming all other factors remain constant.

Theta is always negative for option buyers (they lose value daily)
Theta is always positive for option sellers (they gain value daily)

Example:

- Option premium: $2.00
- Theta: -0.05
- Tomorrow (all else equal): Option worth $1.95
- Day after: Option worth $1.90
- You profit $0.05 per day per share = $5 per day per contract

The Time Decay Curve

Time decay does NOT happen linearly—it accelerates as expiration approaches.

Visual Representation:

$3.00 premium (90 days out)
|
| Slow decay phase
$2.80 |—-—(60 days)
|
$2.50 | Moderate decay phase
|_____ (45 days)
$2.00 |
| Acceleration phase
$1.50 |_____ (30 days)
|
| Rapid decay phase
$0.80 |_______ (15 days)
|
$0.30 | Extreme decay
|___________ (5 days)
$0.00 EXPIRATION

Actual Theta Values by Time Period:

90 to 60 Days Out:

- Daily theta: -$0.01 to -$0.02
- Decay rate: Slow, linear
- Seller advantage: Minimal

60 to 45 Days Out:

- Daily theta: -$0.02 to -$0.03
- Decay rate: Steady
- Seller advantage: Building

45 to 30 Days Out:

- Daily theta: -$0.03 to -$0.05
- Decay rate: Accelerating
- Seller advantage: Good

30 to 15 Days Out:

- Daily theta: -$0.05 to -$0.08
- Decay rate: Rapid
- Seller advantage: **Excellent** ← OPTIMAL ENTRY POINT

15 to 0 Days Out:

- Daily theta: -$0.08 to -$0.15+
- Decay rate: Extreme
- Seller advantage: Maximum but risky (gamma risk increases)

The 30-45 Day Sweet Spot

Professional covered call sellers target options with 30-45 days to expiration because this window captures the acceleration zone of time decay while avoiding the risks of the final week.

Why 30-45 Days is Optimal:

1. Maximum Theta Efficiency

Example comparison (all $105 strike on $100 stock):

90-Day Option:

- Premium collected: $3.50
- Average daily decay: $0.02
- Days held: 30 days (then roll or close)

- Decay captured: $0.60 (17% of premium)
- **Efficiency: Low**

45-Day Option:

- Premium collected: $2.30
- Average daily decay: $0.04
- Days held: 30 days
- Decay captured: $1.20 (52% of premium)
- **Efficiency: Good**

30-Day Option:

- Premium collected: $1.80
- Average daily decay: $0.06
- Days held: 30 days (to expiration)
- Decay captured: $1.80 (100% of premium)
- **Efficiency: Excellent** ← OPTIMAL

15-Day Option:

- Premium collected: $0.90
- Average daily decay: $0.09
- Days held: 15 days
- Decay captured: $0.90 (100% of premium)
- **Efficiency: Excellent BUT smaller absolute dollars**

Takeaway: 30-day options give you substantial absolute premium ($1.80) with maximum theta efficiency. 15-day options are efficient but collect less total premium per cycle.

2. Better Premium-to-Risk Ratio

30-45 day options balance:

- Enough premium to be worthwhile ($1.50-$2.50 typical)
- Not so much time that market conditions might drastically change

- Flexibility to adjust or roll if needed
- Less stress than weekly management

3. Optimal Theta-to-Gamma Trade-off

Gamma measures how quickly delta changes. It creates risk for sellers in the final week:

- **30-45 days out:** Low gamma (stable, predictable)
- **15 days out:** Moderate gamma (increasing risk)
- **5 days out:** High gamma (rapid delta changes, unpredictable)

Example of Gamma Risk:
Stock at $100, you're short the $105 call:
With 30 days to expiration:

- Delta: 0.30
- Gamma: 0.02
- Stock moves to $103: Delta becomes 0.34
- Predictable, manageable change

With 5 days to expiration:

- Delta: 0.30
- Gamma: 0.12
- Stock moves to $103: Delta becomes 0.54
- Dramatic change, higher assignment risk, stressful

The final week is when options become most unpredictable. By targeting 30-45 day options, you capture most of the decay without the final week's stress.

Practical Theta Application
Monthly Covered Call Cycle Example:
Day 1 (Sell call 35 days out):

- Stock: $100
- Sell $105 call

- Premium: $2.00
- Theta: -0.04

Day 7:

- Stock: $101
- Option value: $1.75 (gained $0.25 from theta)
- Still 28 days to expiration

Day 14:

- Stock: $100 (back where started)
- Option value: $1.50 (gained $0.50 total)
- Still 21 days to expiration
- **You're profitable even though stock unchanged**

Day 21:

- Stock: $99 (down $1)
- Option value: $1.15 (gained $0.85 total)
- Still 14 days to expiration
- **You're profitable even though stock down $1**

Day 28:

- Stock: $98 (down $2)
- Option value: $0.70 (gained $1.30 total)
- Still 7 days to expiration
- **You're still profitable even though stock down $2**

Day 35 (Expiration):

- Stock: $101 (up $1 overall)
- Option expires worthless (OTM)
- **You keep entire $2.00 premium + $1 stock gain = $3 profit**

Key Insight: Time decay worked in your favor every single day, creating profit even during periods when the stock was flat or down. This is the power of theta for covered call sellers.

Maximizing Time Decay Benefits

Best Practice 1: Enter at 30-45 Days

Don't sell options that are 60-90 days out thinking "more premium is better":

- You collect more premium upfront (true)
- But theta decay is much slower (also true)
- You'd be better off selling two 30-day cycles instead of one 60-day
- Two

***

30-day cycles typically generate 30-40% more total premium

Example:

- One 60-day option: $2.80 premium
- Two 30-day options: $1.80 + $1.80 = $3.60 total premium
- **28% more income with the monthly approach**

Best Practice 2: Close or Roll at 50-70% Profit

Many professional traders don't hold covered calls until expiration. Instead:

Traditional approach:

- Sell call for $2.00
- Hold 30 days
- Expires worthless
- Profit: $2.00 (100%)
- Return: 2% in 30 days

Professional approach:

- Sell call for $2.00
- After 15 days, option worth $0.60
- Buy back for $0.60 (close position)
- Profit: $1.40 (70%)
- Immediately sell new call for $1.90
- Total potential: $1.40 + $1.90 = $3.30 over 30 days
- **65% more income than holding to expiration**

Why this works:

- You captured most of the theta (70% in half the time)
- Reinvesting in new option captures more theta
- Reduces risk of adverse movements in final days
- More frequent trading = more compounding opportunities

Best Practice 3: Avoid Holding Through Final Week
The final 5-7 days of an option's life are when gamma risk is highest:
Recommendation:

- Target entry: 30-45 days
- Target exit: 7-10 days remaining OR when 60-70% profit achieved
- This captures optimal theta while avoiding final week stress

Exception: If option is very far OTM (worth < $0.20) and you're confident in direction, letting it expire worthless is fine—not worth transaction cost to close.

Time Decay Scenarios
Scenario 1: Optimal Decay (Stock Stays Stable)
Setup:

- Day 0: Stock $100, sell $105 call for $2.00
- Day 30: Stock $101, option expires worthless
- Result: Keep $2.00 + $1 stock gain = $3 total ✓

What happened: Perfect execution. Stock stayed below strike, theta worked every day, total profit maximized.

Scenario 2: Profitable Even in Decline

Setup:

- Day 0: Stock $100, sell $105 call for $2.00
- Day 30: Stock $99, option expires worthless
- Result: Keep $2.00 premium, offset $1 stock loss = $1 net profit ✓

What happened: Premium cushioned the loss. Still profitable despite stock declining 1%.

Scenario 3: Assignment (Stock Rallies)

Setup:

- Day 0: Stock $100, sell $105 call for $2.00
- Day 20: Stock rallies to $108
- Day 30: Stock at $107, assigned at $105
- Result: $5 stock gain + $2 premium = $7 total ✓

What happened: Assigned but still excellent outcome. Made 7% in one month. Theta worked for 30 days before assignment.

Scenario 4: Early Exit Strategy

Setup:

- Day 0: Stock $100, sell $105 call for $2.00
- Day 15: Stock $101, option now worth $0.65
- Action: Buy back for $0.65
- Profit: $1.35 (67.5% of max profit in 50% of time)
- Immediately sell new $106 call (15 days out) for $1.80
- Potential total: $1.35 + $1.80 = $3.15 over 30 days

What happened: Professional management captured most theta early, reinvested in new option, potentially increased total return by 57.5%.

Expiration Dates: Monthly vs. Weekly vs. Quarterly Options

Choosing the right expiration timeline is a crucial decision that affects your premium income, management requirements, and stress levels.

Monthly Options: The Industry Standard

Expiration Schedule:

- Third Friday of every month
- Standard expiration cycle
- Examples: Jan 20, Feb 17, Mar 17, Apr 21, May 19, etc.

Characteristics:

Time Frame:

- Typically sell with 30-45 days remaining
- Hold through one monthly cycle
- 12 decision points per year

Premium Amounts:

- Moderate per-contract premium
- Example: $150-$250 per contract typical for $100-$150 stocks

Management Requirements:

- Review positions weekly
- Make adjustments as needed
- Monthly expiration management
- Time commitment: 2-3 hours per month

Theta Decay:

- Optimal decay curve (30-45 day sweet spot)
- Balanced approach
- Not too slow, not too fast

Advantages:
✓ **Optimal return-per-effort ratio**
✓ **Industry standard with highest liquidity**
✓ **Balanced premium income**
✓ **Manageable time commitment**
✓ **Less stressful than weekly options**
✓ **More income than quarterly options**
✓ **Captures prime theta decay period**
Disadvantages:
✗ Monthly commitment (can't adjust as quickly as weekly)
✗ 12 decisions per year (some prefer fewer)
✗ Transaction costs if broker charges (12 cycles)
Best For:

- 95% of covered call investors ← **HIGHLY RECOMMENDED**
- Beginners learning the strategy
- Investors with moderate time availability
- Those wanting good returns without excessive management

Monthly Options Strategy:
Implementation:

1. First Monday of each month: Review portfolio
2. Select stocks for covered calls
3. Sell calls 30-35 days to expiration (targeting 3rd Friday)
4. Monitor weekly but don't over-manage
5. Week before expiration: Decide on roll, close, or let expire
6. Expiration Friday: Positions close or assigned
7. Following Monday: Start new cycle

Example Monthly Calendar:
May 2024
Week 1 (May 1-5): Sell June 16 calls
Week 2 (May 8-12): Monitor, no action needed

Week 3 (May 15-19): Monitor, no action needed
Week 4 (May 22-26): Monitor, no action needed
Week 5 (May 29-Jun 2): Monitor, no action needed
June 2024
Week 1 (Jun 3-7): Monitor, no action needed
Week 2 (Jun 10-14): Review positions, decide on management
Week 3 (Jun 17-21): Expiration June 16 - positions close
Monday June 17: Sell July 21 calls

Time Commitment: Approximately 2-3 hours monthly (30 minutes weekly + 60 minutes expiration week)

Weekly Options: For Active Traders

Expiration Schedule:

- Every Friday
- 52 expirations per year
- Short-term commitments

Characteristics:

Time Frame:

- Typically sell Monday-Tuesday for Friday expiration
- 3-5 day holding periods
- 52 decision points per year

Premium Amounts:

- Smaller per-contract premium
- Example: $40-$80 per contract typical
- But 52 opportunities vs. 12 monthly

Management Requirements:

- Daily monitoring recommended
- Weekly decision-making
- More frequent adjustments
- Time commitment: 1-2 hours per week

Theta Decay:

- Extremely rapid (final week decay)
- Maximum theta per day
- High stress due to gamma

Advantages:
✓ **Highest annualized returns possible** (if executed well)
✓ **Quick adjustments** to market changes
✓ **Rapid compounding** of premiums
✓ **Flexibility** to be in or out weekly
✓ **Lower absolute risk** per trade (shorter exposure)
Disadvantages:
✗ **Time-intensive** (52 decisions per year)
✗ **Higher stress** (daily monitoring needed)
✗ **More transaction costs** (52 cycles)
✗ **Easier to make mistakes** with frequency
✗ **Higher gamma risk** (unpredictable final days)
✗ **Fatigue** from constant management
Best For:

- Active traders with significant time
- Experienced options traders (not beginners)
- Those comfortable with daily monitoring
- Traders wanting maximum control and flexibility
- People who enjoy active management

Weekly Options Strategy:
Implementation:

1. Monday morning: Review positions from previous week
2. Analyze market conditions
3. Select strikes for Friday expiration
4. Sell calls Monday or Tuesday
5. Monitor daily (especially Thursday/Friday)

6. Let expire Friday or roll if needed
7. Repeat next Monday

Example Weekly Pattern:
Week 1: May 3 expiration
Mon Apr 29: Sell May 3 calls
Tue-Thu: Monitor
Fri May 3: Expiration, collect premium or assigned
Week 2: May 10 expiration
Mon May 6: Sell May 10 calls
Tue-Thu: Monitor
Fri May 10: Expiration
[Continues weekly...]
Time Commitment: 1-2 hours every week (52 weeks)
Annualized Return Example:
Stock at $100:

- Weekly premium: 0.6% ($0.60 per share)
- If repeated 52 weeks successfully: 31.2% annual return
- Monthly premium: 1.8% ($1.80 per share)
- If repeated 12 months successfully: 21.6% annual return

Weekly advantage: 44% higher annualized return

BUT: Requires 4.3x more decisions (52 vs 12) and significantly more time/stress

Is the extra 9.6% annual return worth 4.3x the work? For most investors: No. For active traders who enjoy it: Possibly.

Beginner Recommendation: Start with monthly options. After 6-12 months of success, consider testing weekly options on 1-2 positions while maintaining monthly on others. Don't switch entirely to weekly until proven you can manage the workload.

Quarterly Options (LEAPS): For Hands-Off Investors
Expiration Schedule:

- March, June, September, December

- Long-term commitments
- Often called LEAPS (Long-term Equity AnticiPation Securities) when 9+ months out

Characteristics:
Time Frame:

- Typically sell 90-180 days to expiration
- Hold through one or more quarters
- 4 decision points per year (if 90-day cycles)

Premium Amounts:

- Large per-contract premium
- Example: $400-$700 per contract for $100-$150 stocks (90 days)
- $800-$1,200 for 180-day options

Management Requirements:

- Quarterly review
- Minimal management needed
- Set-and-forget approach
- Time commitment: 1 hour per quarter

Theta Decay:

- Very slow initially
- Accelerates only in final 45 days
- Inefficient theta capture

Advantages:
✓ **Minimal time commitment** (4 decisions/year)
✓ **Large upfront premium** (satisfying psychologically)
✓ **Less stressful** (not checking weekly)
✓ **Fewer transaction costs**

✓ **Good for busy professionals**
✓ **Works well in tax-advantaged accounts**
Disadvantages:
✗ **Lowest annualized returns** (13-18% typical vs 20-30% monthly)
✗ **Slow theta decay** (inefficient premium capture)
✗ **Locked in long-term** (less flexibility)
✗ **Difficult to adjust** to market changes
✗ **More time value at risk** (if market moves against you)
✗ **Opportunity cost** (could generate more with shorter cycles)
Best For:

- Very busy professionals with minimal time
- Extremely long-term holders (10+ year horizon)
- Very conservative investors wanting minimal management
- Those uncomfortable with frequent trading
- Tax-advantaged retirement accounts (fewer taxable events)

Quarterly Options Strategy:
Implementation:

1. Beginning of quarter: Sell 90-day calls
2. Monthly monitoring (optional)
3. Minimal adjustment
4. Near expiration: Decide to roll or let expire
5. New quarter: Repeat

Example Quarterly Cycle:
Q2 2024
April 1: Sell July 19 calls (110 days out)
Premium: $6.00 per share
April-May: Minimal monitoring
June: Review position
July 19: Expiration
Total return: 6% in one quarter (24% annualized if repeated)
Q3 2024

July 22: Sell October 18 calls

[Continue cycle]

Time Commitment: Approximately 1 hour per quarter = 4 hours annually

Annualized Return Comparison:

90-Day Option on $100 Stock:

- Quarterly premium: 4% ($4.00)
- Annualized (4 quarters): 16%

30-Day Option on Same $100 Stock:

- Monthly premium: 1.8% ($1.80)
- Annualized (12 months): 21.6%

Monthly advantage: 35% higher annualized returns

The Math:

- Quarterly: 4 trades = $16 annual income
- Monthly: 12 trades = $21.60 annual income
- **$5.60 more with monthly approach (35% increase)**

Why Quarterly Underperforms:

The math is clear: selling three 30-day options generates more total premium than one 90-day option because:

1. Theta decay is concentrated in the final 45 days
2. You're collecting the "good part" of decay three times
3. More frequent cycles = more compounding
4. Greater flexibility to adjust strikes based on conditions

When Quarterly Makes Sense:

Despite lower returns, quarterly options are appropriate for:

1. **Retirement accounts** where you want minimal activity
2. **Very busy professionals** (doctors, lawyers, executives) with

zero time

3. **Extremely conservative investors** uncomfortable with monthly decisions
4. **Large portfolios** (1M+) where 16% on large capital is satisfactory
5. **Complementary strategy**: Keep 70% in monthly, 30% in quarterly for balance

Comparison Summary Table

Factor	Weekly	Monthly	Quarterly
Frequency	52/year	12/year	4/year
Time needed	1-2 hrs/week	2-3 hrs/mo	1 hr/quarter
Annualized	26-52%	18-30%	12-20%
Stress	High	Moderate	Low
Flexibility	Maximum	Good	Limited
Learning	Steep	Gradual	Minimal
Best for	Active traders	Most investors	Hands-off investors

Hybrid Approaches

Many sophisticated covered call investors use combination approaches:

Strategy 1: Core-Satellite

- Core 70%: Monthly options (reliable income, moderate management)
- Satellite 30%: Weekly options (higher returns, active management)
- Result: Balanced returns with manageable workload

Strategy 2: The Lazy 80/20

- 80%: Quarterly options (minimal effort)
- 20%: Monthly options (some activity, learning)
- Result: Mostly passive with some engagement

Strategy 3: The Time-Based Rotation

- Busy months (work/travel): Use quarterly or skip
- Normal months: Use monthly
- Light months (vacation/break): Try weekly
- Result: Adapt to life circumstances

Strategy 4: The Conviction-Based

- High conviction stocks: Quarterly (want to hold long-term)
- Moderate conviction: Monthly (balanced approach)
- Lower conviction: Weekly (willing to churn)
- Result: Strategy matches conviction level

Recommended Progression for New Traders

Months 1-3: Learn with Monthly

- Start with 1-2 positions
- Use monthly 30-45 day options
- Focus on understanding mechanics
- Goal: Comfortable with process

Months 4-6: Scale with Monthly

- Expand to 5-8 positions
- Continue monthly approach
- Develop routine and system
- Goal: Consistent execution

Months 7-12: Experiment (Optional)

- Keep 70-80% monthly
- Try 1-2 weekly positions if desired
- Or try 1 quarterly position
- Compare results
- Goal: Find your optimal mix

After Year 1: Your Personal System

- By now you know:
    - How much time you want to spend
    - What returns you're achieving
    - What stress level is comfortable
    - Which approach fits your life

Most traders end up 80-90% monthly with occasional weekly or quarterly positions based on circumstances.

Shall I continue with **Strike Price Selection: The Critical Decision?**

Strike Price Selection: The Critical Decision

Strike price selection is arguably the most important decision in covered call trading. It determines your maximum profit, assignment probability, and how you'll feel about the trade outcome. This decision should align with your investment goals, market outlook, and risk tolerance.

Understanding the Strike Price Spectrum

Strike prices exist on a continuum from aggressive (maximum income, high assignment risk) to conservative (lower income, minimal assignment risk). Understanding where each approach falls on this spectrum helps you make informed decisions.

The Complete Spectrum:

AGGRESSIVE

←————————————————————————————————————→

CONSERVATIVE

Deep ITM | ITM | ATM | 1-2% OTM | 3-5% OTM | 6-8% OTM | 9%+ OTM

$95 $98 $100 $102 $105 $108 $112

↓ ↓ ↓ ↓ ↓ ↓ ↓

Max Very High Good OPTIMAL Lower Minimal

Income High Income Income ZONE Income Income

Income

Assumes stock trading at $100

Each position on this spectrum represents a different trade-off between income, assignment risk, and upside potential.

Strike-by-Strike Analysis

Let's analyze each major strike selection approach in detail using a $100 stock as our example:

AGGRESSIVE STRATEGY: Deep In-the-Money (ITM) Strikes

Strike Selection: $95 (5% ITM)

Current Situation:

- Stock price: $100
- Strike: $95
- Already in-the-money by: $5

Premium Breakdown:

- Total premium: $7.50
- Intrinsic value: $5.00
- Time value: $2.50
- Delta: 0.78 (78% assignment probability)

What This Means:

You're essentially agreeing to sell your stock for $5 less than current price, but collecting $7.50 for doing so. The net effect is selling for $2.50 above your purchase price (assuming you bought at $100).

Outcome Scenarios:

If assigned (very likely - 78% probability):

- Sell stock at: $95 (appears to be a $5 loss)
- Keep premium: $7.50
- Net gain: $2.50 per share ($250 per contract)
- Return: 2.5% in 30 days = 30% annualized
- **Stock is called away**

If not assigned (unlikely - 22% probability):

- Means stock fell below $95 (at least -5% decline)
- Stock loss: At least -$5
- Premium cushion: +$7.50
- Net result: +$2.50 or worse depending on final price
- Still own stock but it's down significantly

Risk Analysis:

Maximum profit: $2.50 (achieved if stock stays above $95) **Breakeven:** $92.50 ($100 - $7.50) **Protection:** 7.5% downside cushion before losses

Pros:

✓ Highest probability of profit (78%)
✓ Excellent downside protection (7.5%)
✓ Significant premium income
✓ Works well in declining or flat markets
✓ Good for stocks you're ready to sell

Cons:

✗ No appreciation potential (capped at current price)
✗ Very high assignment probability (give up stock)
✗ Most of premium is intrinsic value (already giving away $5)
✗ Only earning $2.50 time value
✗ Miss any rallies above $100

Best Used When:

- You want to exit the stock but not immediately
- Market outlook is bearish or neutral
- You want maximum probability of profit
- Downside protection is highest priority
- You're comfortable with near-certain assignment

Example Scenario:

You bought stock at $95, it's now $100, and you're ready to take profits:

- Current price: $100

- Your cost: $95
- Sell $95 call for $7.50
- If assigned: Sell at $95 + $7.50 premium = $102.50 effective
- Total gain: $7.50 per share (7.9% profit)
- **This strategy locked in profits while collecting premium**

Not Recommended For:

- Long-term holders who want to keep stock
- Bullish market outlooks
- Stocks with strong upside potential
- Most covered call strategies (too aggressive)

AGGRESSIVE STRATEGY: In-the-Money (ITM) Strikes
Strike Selection: $98 (2% ITM)
Current Situation:

- Stock price: $100
- Strike: $98
- Already in-the-money by: $2

Premium Breakdown:

- Total premium: $4.50
- Intrinsic value: $2.00
- Time value: $2.50
- Delta: 0.68 (68% assignment probability)

What This Means:
You're selling slightly below current price but collecting attractive premium that more than compensates.
Outcome Scenarios:
If assigned (likely - 68% probability):

- Sell stock at: $98 (appears to be $2 loss)
- Keep premium: $4.50

- Net gain: $2.50 per share
- Return: 2.5% in 30 days = 30% annualized
- **Stock is called away**

If not assigned (32% probability):

- Stock stayed below $98 (declined 2%+)
- Stock loss: At least -$2
- Premium cushion: +$4.50
- Net result: +$2.50 or less depending on price
- Still own stock but it's down

Risk Analysis:

Maximum profit: $2.50 **Breakeven:** $95.50 ($100 - $4.50) **Protection:** 4.5% downside cushion

Pros:

✓ High probability of profit (68%)
✓ Good downside protection (4.5%)
✓ Substantial premium income
✓ Balanced intrinsic/time value mix
✓ Slightly less certain assignment than deep ITM

Cons:

✗ Limited appreciation potential ($0 if assigned)
✗ High assignment probability
✗ Half of premium is intrinsic value (giving away $2)
✗ Miss rallies above $100

Best Used When:

- Slightly bearish to neutral outlook
- Want high probability income
- Ready to sell at current price levels
- Seeking strong downside cushion

Example Use Case:

Stock has rallied from your purchase price and you want to lock in gains while collecting premium, but you'd prefer not to be assigned immediately:

- Purchase price: $95
- Current price: $100
- Sell $98 call for $4.50
- If assigned: $98 + $4.50 = $102.50 effective sale price
- Gain: $7.50 from $95 entry (7.9%)
- Lower assignment probability than $95 strike gives stock a chance to dip

---

MODERATE AGGRESSIVE: At-the-Money (ATM) Strikes
Strike Selection: $100 (ATM)
Current Situation:

- Stock price: $100
- Strike: $100
- Exactly at current market price

Premium Breakdown:

- Total premium: $3.50
- Intrinsic value: $0 (technically $0.00, practically negligible)
- Time value: $3.50 (virtually all time value)
- Delta: 0.50 (50% assignment probability)

What This Means:

You're agreeing to sell at exactly the current price, collecting significant premium for taking that obligation.

Outcome Scenarios:

If assigned (50% probability):

- Sell stock at: $100 (no gain from current)
- Keep premium: $3.50

- Net gain: $3.50 per share
- Return: 3.5% in 30 days = 42% annualized
- **Maximum profit achieved**

If not assigned (50% probability):

- Stock stayed below $100
- Potential stock loss: Variable
- Premium cushion: +$3.50
- Can write new call next month
- Still own the stock

Specific Scenarios:
Stock finishes at $98 (down 2%):

- Stock loss: -$2.00
- Premium kept: +$3.50
- Net gain: +$1.50 (1.5%)
- Can write new call at $100-$102

Stock finishes at $95 (down 5%):

- Stock loss: -$5.00
- Premium kept: +$3.50
- Net loss: -$1.50 (-1.5%)
- Can write new call to recover

Stock finishes at $103 (up 3%):

- Assigned at $100
- Missed $3 rally above strike
- Keep $3.50 premium
- Net gain: $3.50 (3.5%)
- **Opportunity cost of $3 per share**

Risk Analysis:

Maximum profit: $3.50 (3.5%) **Breakeven:** $96.50 ($100 - $3.50)
Protection: 3.5% downside cushion **Probability of max profit:** 50%

Pros:

✓ High premium income ($3.50 = 3.5% monthly)
✓ 100% time value (no intrinsic value given away)
✓ Balanced assignment probability (50/50)
✓ Good income in sideways markets
✓ Reasonable downside protection
✓ If not assigned, can repeat indefinitely

Cons:

✗ No upside participation (capped at entry price)
✗ High assignment risk in any rally
✗ Opportunity cost if stock surges
✗ Stressful when stock hovering near strike at expiration

Best Used When:

- Market outlook is neutral (sideways expected)
- Maximum income is priority
- You're neutral on keeping the stock
- Comfortable with frequent assignments
- Comfortable with zero appreciation capture

Who Uses This Strategy:

- Income-focused traders
- Market neutral strategies
- Traders willing to churn stocks frequently
- Those targeting 35-45% annualized returns
- Active portfolio managers

Example Monthly Cycle:
Month 1:

- Buy stock: $100
- Sell $100 call: +$3.50

- Stock finishes: $99
- Keep stock + premium
- Result: +$2.50 (stock -$1, premium +$3.50)

Month 2:

- Stock opens: $99
- Sell $100 call: +$3.20
- Stock finishes: $98
- Keep stock + premium
- Result: +$2.20 (stock -$1, premium +$3.20)

Month 3:

- Stock opens: $98
- Sell $100 call: +$2.80
- Stock rallies to $102
- Assigned at $100
- Result: +$4.80 (stock +$2, premium +$2.80)

Total 3-month result:

- Premiums: $9.50
- Stock movements: +$0 (bought $100, sold $100)
- **Total gain: $9.50 (9.5% in 3 months = 38% annualized)**

ATM Strategy Verdict:

Excellent for maximum income generation in neutral to slightly bearish markets. Not ideal for strong bull markets or stocks you want to hold long-term. Best suited for active traders comfortable with frequent assignments and re-establishing positions.

BALANCED APPROACH: 1-2% Out-of-the-Money (OTM)
Strike Selection: $102 (2% OTM)
Current Situation:

- Stock price: $100

- Strike: $102
- Stock needs to rise 2% to reach strike

Premium Breakdown:

- Total premium: $2.40
- Intrinsic value: $0
- Time value: $2.40 (100% time value)
- Delta: 0.42 (42% assignment probability)

What This Means:

You're collecting good premium while retaining $2 of appreciation potential. Balanced trade-off between income and upside.

Outcome Scenarios:

If assigned (42% probability):

- Sell stock at: $102
- Stock gain: $2.00
- Premium kept: $2.40
- Net gain: $4.40 per share
- Return: 4.4% in 30 days = 53% annualized
- **Excellent outcome**

If not assigned (58% probability):

- Stock stayed below $102
- Keep stock + premium
- Can write new call
- Multiple sub-scenarios:

Stock finishes at $101:

- Stock gain: +$1.00
- Premium kept: +$2.40
- Net gain: +$3.40 (3.4%)
- Can write $102-$104 call next month

- **Excellent outcome, not assigned**

Stock finishes at $100 (unchanged):

- Stock gain: $0
- Premium kept: +$2.40
- Net gain: +$2.40 (2.4%)
- Can write new $102 call
- **Good outcome**

Stock finishes at $97 (down 3%):

- Stock loss: -$3.00
- Premium kept: +$2.40
- Net loss: -$0.60 (-0.6%)
- Can write new call to recover
- **Small loss, recoverable**

Risk Analysis:

Maximum profit: $4.40 (4.4%) **Breakeven:** $97.60 ($100 - $2.40) **Protection:** 2.4% downside cushion **Probability of profit:** ~60% (includes partial profits)

Pros:

✓ Good premium income ($2.40 = 2.4% monthly)
✓ Captures $2 appreciation (2% upside retained)
✓ Moderate assignment probability (42%)
✓ 100% time value collected
✓ Good balance of income and growth
✓ Comfortable assignment rate (not too frequent)

Cons:

✗ Miss gains above $102
✗ Moderate downside protection only (2.4%)
✗ Not maximum income (ATM pays more)
✗ Not maximum upside retention (higher strikes retain more)

Best Used When:

- Slightly bullish outlook (expect 0-3% move up)
- Want good income with some appreciation
- Comfortable with moderate assignment risk
- Seeking balanced approach
- Active income generation but not max-aggressive

12-Month Performance Model:
Assuming this strategy on $100 stock, repeated monthly:
Scenario A: Choppy market (stock range $98-$103)

- 5 months: Not assigned, collect $2.40 avg = $12.00
- 3 months: Assigned, collect $4.40 avg = $13.20
- 4 months: Small losses, net $0.80 avg = $3.20
- **Annual return: $28.40 = 28.4%**

Scenario B: Steady bull market (+12% year)

- 8 months: Assigned, collect $4.40 = $35.20
- 4 months: Not assigned, collect $3.20 = $12.80
- **Annual return: $48.00 but miss some rally = effective 35%**
- Stock-only would return: 12%
- **Covered calls outperform by 23 percentage points**

Scenario C: Bear market (-15% year)

- 0 months: Assigned
- 12 months: Not assigned, collect $2.40 = $28.80
- Stock losses: -$15.00
- **Net return: +$13.80 = +13.8% despite 15% market decline**
- Stock-only would return: -15%
- **Covered calls outperform by 28.8 percentage points**

Verdict: This 1-2% OTM approach delivers strong results across most market conditions. Slight underperformance in extreme bull markets (+20%+) but outperforms in all other scenarios.

OPTIMAL ZONE: 3-5% Out-of-the-Money
Strike Selection: $105 (5% OTM)
Current Situation:

- Stock price: $100
- Strike: $105
- Stock needs to rise 5% to reach strike

Premium Breakdown:

- Total premium: $1.50
- Intrinsic value: $0
- Time value: $1.50 (100% time value)
- Delta: 0.30 (30% assignment probability)

What This Means:

You're collecting meaningful premium while retaining substantial upside potential. This is the "Goldilocks zone" for most covered call investors—not too aggressive, not too conservative.

Outcome Scenarios:
If assigned (30% probability):

- Sell stock at: $105
- Stock gain: $5.00
- Premium kept: $1.50
- Net gain: $6.50 per share
- Return: 6.5% in 30 days = 78% annualized
- **Fantastic outcome—if it happens**

If not assigned (70% probability):

- Stock stayed below $105
- Keep stock + premium
- Multiple scenarios:

Stock finishes at $104 (up 4%):

- Stock gain: +$4.00
- Premium kept: +$1.50
- Net gain: +$5.50 (5.5%)
- **Excellent outcome, nearly maximum**
- Can write $105-$108 call next month

Stock finishes at $102 (up 2%):

- Stock gain: +$2.00
- Premium kept: +$1.50
- Net gain: +$3.50 (3.5%)
- **Very good outcome**
- Can write $105-$107 call

Stock finishes at $100 (unchanged):

- Stock gain: $0
- Premium kept: +$1.50
- Net gain: +$1.50 (1.5%)
- **Acceptable outcome**
- Can write new $105 call

Stock finishes at $97 (down 3%):

- Stock loss: -$3.00
- Premium kept: +$1.50
- Net loss: -$1.50 (-1.5%)
- **Small loss**
- Can write new call to recover

Stock finishes at $93 (down 7%):

- Stock loss: -$7.00
- Premium kept: +$1.50
- Net loss: -$5.50 (-5.5%)
- **Meaningful loss but cushioned**

- Premium offset 21% of decline

Risk Analysis:

Maximum profit: \$6.50 (6.5%) **Breakeven:** \$98.50 (\$100 - \$1.50) **Protection:** 1.5% downside cushion **Probability of assignment:** 30% **Probability of keeping stock:** 70%

Pros:

✓ Balanced premium income (\$1.50 = 1.5% monthly)
✓ Captures significant appreciation (\$5 = 5% upside)
✓ Low assignment probability (30% = keep stock 7/10 months)
✓ 100% time value (optimal theta capture)
✓ Comfortable mentally (rarely assigned)
✓ **Perfect balance for most investors**
✓ Excellent risk-adjusted returns
✓ Sustainable long-term strategy

Cons:

✗ Lower absolute premium than closer strikes
✗ Modest downside protection (1.5% only)
✗ Requires stock appreciation for maximum profit
✗ May feel "too conservative" for income-focused traders

Why This Is the Optimal Zone:

Mathematical Efficiency:

- Annualized return if not assigned: 18% (from premiums alone)
- Annualized return if assigned: 78% (premiums + appreciation)
- Weighted expected return: ~30% annualized
- **Superior risk-adjusted returns**

Psychological Comfort:

- Not assigned 70% of time (keep your stocks)
- When assigned, it's at significant profit
- Never feels like "loss" or "mistake"
- Sustainable approach doesn't cause burnout

Portfolio Stability:

- Lower turnover (fewer assignments)
- Build long-term positions
- Compound dividends over time
- Reduced transaction costs
- More tax-efficient (fewer taxable events)

Flexibility:

- Can adjust strikes based on market conditions
- Not locked into aggressive strategy
- Room to become more/less aggressive as needed

12-Month Performance Model:
Scenario A: Normal market (+8% year):

- 3 months: Assigned at $105, collect $6.50 = $19.50
- 9 months: Not assigned, collect $1.50, capture partial gains = $22.50
- **Annual return: $42.00 = 42%**

Scenario B: Strong bull (+18% year):

- 7 months: Assigned, collect $6.50 = $45.50
- 5 months: Not assigned, collect $4.00 avg = $20.00
- **Annual return: $65.50 = 65.5%**
- Stock-only: 18%
- **Outperform by 47.5 percentage points**

Scenario C: Bear market (-12% year):

- 0 months: Assigned
- 12 months: Collect $1.50, stocks decline = $18.00 - $12.00
- **Net return: +$6.00 = +6%**
- Stock-only: -12%

- **Outperform by 18 percentage points**

Real-World Example: Johnson & Johnson
Position:

- Purchase: 100 shares at $156
- Current price: $156
- Dividend: 2.8% annually ($0.75 quarterly)

Strategy: Sell $162 call (3.8% OTM) monthly
Month 1:

- Sell $162 call for $1.80
- Stock finishes: $159
- Result: +$3 stock + $1.80 premium = +$4.80 (3.1%)
- Not assigned, keep stock

Month 2:

- Sell $165 call (stock now $159) for $1.70
- Stock finishes: $161
- Result: +$2 stock + $1.70 premium = +$3.70 (2.3%)
- Not assigned, keep stock

Month 3 (ex-dividend month):

- Sell $165 call for $1.60
- Collect $0.75 dividend
- Stock finishes: $163
- Result: +$2 stock + $1.60 premium + $0.75 dividend = +$4.35 (2.7%)
- Not assigned, keep stock

Quarter 1 Total:

- Stock appreciation: $7 ($156 → $163)

- Premiums: $5.10
- Dividend: $0.75
- **Total gain: $12.85 (8.2% in one quarter)**
- **Annualized: 32.8%**
- **Still own the stock**

This 3-5% OTM strategy delivered:

- Triple income streams (premiums + dividends + appreciation)
- Stock retained for long-term compound growth
- Minimal stress (never close to assignment)
- Sustainable approach repeatable indefinitely

CONSERVATIVE: 6-8% Out-of-the-Money
Strike Selection: $108 (8% OTM)
Current Situation:

- Stock price: $100
- Strike: $108
- Stock needs to rise 8% to reach strike

Premium Breakdown:

- Total premium: $0.85
- Intrinsic value: $0
- Time value: $0.85 (100% time value)
- Delta: 0.20 (20% assignment probability)

What This Means:

You're prioritizing stock ownership and upside retention over premium income. Very low probability of assignment.

Outcome Scenarios:
If assigned (20% probability - rare):

- Sell stock at: $108
- Stock gain: $8.00

- Premium kept: $0.85
- Net gain: $8.85 per share
- Return: 8.85% in 30 days = 106% annualized
- **Exceptional outcome, but unlikely**

If not assigned (80% probability - typical):

- Stock stayed below $108
- Keep stock + premium

Stock finishes at $107 (up 7%):

- Stock gain: +$7.00
- Premium kept: +$0.85
- Net gain: +$7.85 (7.85%)
- **Excellent, nearly maximum profit**

Stock finishes at $104 (up 4%):

- Stock gain: +$4.00
- Premium kept: +$0.85
- Net gain: +$4.85 (4.85%)
- **Good outcome**

Stock finishes at $100 (unchanged):

- Stock gain: $0
- Premium kept: +$0.85
- Net gain: +$0.85 (0.85%)
- **Modest outcome**

Stock finishes at $95 (down 5%):

- Stock loss: -$5.00
- Premium kept: +$0.85
- Net loss: -$4.15 (-4.15%)

- **Loss, minimal premium cushion**

Risk Analysis:

Maximum profit: \$8.85 (8.85%) **Breakeven:** \$99.15 (\$100 - \$0.85) **Protection:** 0.85% downside cushion (minimal) **Probability of assignment:** 20% **Probability of keeping stock:** 80%

Pros:

✓ Keep stock 80% of time (very low assignment)
✓ Capture significant upside (\$8 = 8% appreciation potential)
✓ Massive returns IF assigned (106% annualized)
✓ Comfortable for long-term holders
✓ Good for high-conviction stocks
✓ Good for strongly bullish outlook

Cons:

✗ Low premium income (\$0.85 = 0.85% monthly)
✗ Minimal downside protection
✗ May not be worth the effort/transaction costs
✗ Low annualized return if never assigned (~10%)
✗ Opportunity cost (could earn more with closer strikes)

Best Used When:

- Very bullish on the stock
- Want to hold long-term but earn small income
- High-conviction position
- Stock with strong upside potential
- Comfortable with minimal premium

12-Month Performance Model:

Scenario A: Normal market (+8% year):

- 1 month: Assigned, collect \$8.85 = \$8.85
- 11 months: Not assigned, collect \$0.85 = \$9.35
- **Annual return: \$18.20 = 18.2%**

Scenario B: Strong bull (+20% year):

- 4 months: Assigned, collect $8.85 = $35.40
- 8 months: Not assigned, collect $4.00 avg = $32.00
- **Annual return: $67.40 = 67.4%**

Scenario C: Bear market (-12%):

- 0 months: Assigned
- 12 months: Collect $0.85 = $10.20
- Stock losses: -$12.00
- **Net return: -$1.80 = -1.8%**
- Stock-only: -12%
- **Outperform by 10.2 percentage points**

Verdict:
This conservative approach works best for:

- Stocks you absolutely want to keep
- High-conviction long-term positions
- Strongly bullish markets
- Supplemental income (not primary strategy)

Not recommended as primary strategy due to low premium collection relative to risk taken and transaction costs involved.

ULTRA-CONSERVATIVE: 10%+ Out-of-the-Money
Strike Selection: $112 (12% OTM)
Current Situation:

- Stock price: $100
- Strike: $112
- Stock needs to rise 12% to reach strike

Premium Breakdown:

- Total premium: $0.35
- Intrinsic value: $0
- Time value: $0.35

- Delta: 0.10 (10% assignment probability)

What This Means:

You're basically holding the stock with minimal covered call overlay. Very unlikely to ever be assigned.

Outcome Scenarios:

If assigned (10% probability - very rare):

- Sell stock at: $112
- Stock gain: $12.00
- Premium kept: $0.35
- Net gain: $12.35 per share
- Return: 12.35% in 30 days = 148% annualized
- **Extraordinary outcome, extremely unlikely**

If not assigned (90% probability - typical):

- Stock stayed below $112
- Keep stock + tiny premium

Risk Analysis:

Maximum profit: $12.35 (12.35%) **Breakeven:** $99.65 ($100 - $0.35) **Protection:** 0.35% downside cushion (negligible) **Probability of assignment:** 10%

Pros:

✓ Virtually never assigned (keep stock indefinitely)
✓ Capture almost all upside
✓ No cap on gains for practical purposes

Cons:

✗ Tiny premium ($35 per contract)
✗ Barely worth transaction costs
✗ Negligible downside protection
✗ Extremely low income generation (4% annualized)
✗ Opportunity cost is enormous

Verdict:

Not recommended for covered calls.

If you want this much upside retention, just hold the stock without writing calls. The $0.35 premium isn't worth the effort, transaction costs, or tax complications.

Better alternatives:

- Hold stock outright
- Use 6-8% OTM strikes for better premium
- Write calls only occasionally when you choose

Strike Selection Decision Framework

Now that we've analyzed each strike approach, here's a practical decision framework to choose the right strike for YOUR situation:

Step 1: Define Your Primary Goal

Question: What matters most to you?

A. Maximum income generation → Use ATM or 1-2% OTM strikes → Accept frequent assignments → Focus: Cash flow, not stock ownership

B. Balance of income and growth → Use 3-5% OTM strikes ← **RECOMMENDED FOR MOST** → Moderate assignment rates → Focus: Total return optimization

C. Minimal assignments, keep stocks → Use 6-8% OTM strikes → Rare assignments → Focus: Long-term ownership with income supplement

Step 2: Assess Your Market Outlook

Question: What do you expect the stock to do in the next 30 days?

A. Strongly bullish (expect 8%+ gain) → Use 6-8% OTM or skip covered calls → Don't cap your upside in strong rally

B. Moderately bullish (expect 3-6% gain) → Use 4-6% OTM strikes → Capture most upside plus premium

C. Neutral/sideways (expect -2% to +3%) → Use 2-4% OTM strikes → Optimize income in range-bound market

D. Slightly bearish (expect 0-3% decline) → Use ATM to 2% OTM strikes → Generate income to offset expected decline

E. Very bearish (expect 5%+ decline) → Use ITM strikes or don't own the stock → Maximum downside protection

Step 3: Evaluate Your Emotional Comfort

Question: How will you feel in different scenarios?

Scenario Test:

"If the stock rises 10% above my strike price and gets called away, I will feel:"

A. Happy I made a profit → Any strike where you profit is fine → Use ATM to 5% OTM

B. Satisfied but slight regret → Use 5-7% OTM strikes → Captures most of rally before assignment

C. Very regretful → Use 7-10% OTM strikes or don't write calls → Your comfort > additional income

Step 4: Consider Your Time Commitment

Question: How actively do you want to manage?

A. Very active (check daily, willing to adjust frequently) → Can use ATM strikes with active rolling → Weekly options possible

B. Moderately active (check weekly, manage monthly) → Use 3-5% OTM strikes → Monthly options optimal

C. Minimal activity (check monthly or less) → Use 6-8% OTM strikes → Quarterly options possible → Let positions run with minimal intervention

Step 5: Factor In Stock-Specific Characteristics

Question: What type of stock is this?

High-quality dividend aristocrat (JNJ, PG, KO): → Use 4-6% OTM → Focus on long-term ownership → Coordinate with dividend dates

Large-cap tech with growth potential (MSFT, AAPL): → Use 3-5

Premium Calculation Examples and Expected Returns

Understanding how to calculate expected returns from covered calls helps you make informed decisions and set realistic expectations. Let's work through detailed examples across different strategies.

Basic Premium Math

Formula Components:

Monthly Return = Premium ÷ Stock Price Annualized Return = Monthly Return × 12 (if repeated monthly) **Total Return if Assigned = (Strike - Purchase Price + Premium) ÷ Purchase Price**

Example 1: Conservative Strategy (5% OTM)

Position Details:

- Stock: Procter & Gamble (PG)
- Purchase price: $150
- Current price: $150
- Strike selected: $158 (5.3% OTM)
- Premium received: $1.80
- Time: 30 days

Calculations:

Premium return:

- $1.80 ÷ $150 = 1.2% monthly
- 1.2% × 12 = 14.4% annualized

If assigned:

- Stock gain: $158 - $150 = $8
- Total gain: $8 + $1.80 = $9.80
- Return: $9.80 ÷ $150 = 6.5% in 30 days
- Annualized: 6.5% × 12 = 78%

If not assigned (stock flat at $150):

- Premium only: $1.80
- Return: 1.2% monthly
- Can repeat next month

Expected outcome over 12 months:

- Probability of assignment per month: ~25%
- Expected assignments per year: 3
- Expected months collecting premium: 9

Year calculation:

- 9 months premium: 9 × $1.80 = $16.20
- 3 assignments: 3 × $9.80 = $29.40
- Total: $45.60
- **Annual return: 30.4%**

Example 2: Moderate Strategy (3% OTM)
Position Details:

- Stock: Microsoft (MSFT)
- Purchase price: $380
- Current price: $380
- Strike selected: $390 (2.6% OTM)
- Premium received: $8.50
- Time: 30 days

Calculations:
Premium return:

- $8.50 ÷ $380 = 2.24% monthly
- 2.24% × 12 = 26.9% annualized

If assigned:

- Stock gain: $390 - $380 = $10

- Total gain: $10 + $8.50 = $18.50
- Return: $18.50 ÷ $380 = 4.87% in 30 days
- Annualized: 58.4%

Expected outcome over 12 months:

- Probability of assignment per month: ~40%
- Expected assignments: 5
- Expected premium-only months: 7

Year calculation:

- 7 months premium: 7 × $8.50 = $59.50
- 5 assignments: 5 × $18.50 = $92.50
- Total: $152.00
- **Annual return: 40%**

Example 3: Aggressive Strategy (ATM)
Position Details:

- Stock: JPMorgan Chase (JPM)
- Purchase price: $145
- Current price: $145
- Strike selected: $145 (ATM)
- Premium received: $4.50
- Time: 30 days

Calculations:
Premium return:

- $4.50 ÷ $145 = 3.1% monthly
- 3.1% × 12 = 37.2% annualized

If assigned:

- Stock gain: $145 - $145 = $0

- Total gain: $0 + $4.50 = $4.50
- Return: $4.50 ÷ $145 = 3.1% in 30 days
- Annualized: 37.2%

Expected outcome over 12 months:

- Probability of assignment per month: ~50%
- Expected assignments: 6
- Expected premium-only months: 6

Year calculation:

- 6 months premium only: 6 × $4.50 = $27.00
- 6 assignments: 6 × $4.50 = $27.00
- Total: $54.00
- **Annual return: 37.2%**

Reality: High turnover costs, frequent re-establishing positions

Comparison Summary Table

Strategy	Conservative	Moderate	Aggressive
Strike	5% OTM	3% OTM	ATM
Premium	1.2%/mo	2.2%/mo	3.1%/mo
Assignment	25%	40%	50%
Expected Annual	30.4%	40%	37.2%
Stress	Low	Moderate	High
Turnover	Low	Moderate	High
Best For	Long-term holders	Most investors	Income focused

Key Insight: Moderate strategy (3-5% OTM) delivers best risk-adjusted returns with manageable stress and turnover.

Chapter 4:

Stock Selection for Covered Calls

The foundation of successful covered call trading is selecting the right underlying stocks. Even the perfect strike selection and timing won't save you if the underlying stock is fundamentally flawed. This chapter provides a comprehensive framework for identifying and evaluating stocks suitable for covered call strategies.

The Covered Call Stock Selection Framework

Not all stocks are suitable for covered calls. The ideal candidates share specific characteristics that make them reliable income generators while minimizing risk.

The Five Pillars of Covered Call Stock Selection

Pillar 1: Financial Stability

You need stocks that won't suddenly collapse, as covered calls provide limited downside protection.

Required characteristics:

- Profitable for past 5+ years
- Positive free cash flow
- Manageable debt levels (debt-to-equity < 1.0)
- Strong balance sheet
- Investment-grade credit rating (BBB+ or higher)

Why this matters:

Covered calls give you 1-3% downside cushion monthly. If your stock drops 30% due to financial distress, your premiums won't save you.

Example of good financial stability: Johnson & Johnson (JNJ)

- Consecutive profitable years: 50+
- Free cash flow: $18B+ annually
- Debt-to-equity: 0.42
- Credit rating: AAA
- Dividend history: 61 years of increases

Example of poor financial stability: Struggling retailer

- Inconsistent profitability
- Negative free cash flow
- Debt-to-equity: 3.5
- Credit rating: BB (junk)
- Dividend cut 2 years ago

Pillar 2: Reasonable Volatility

You need volatility high enough for decent premiums, but not so high that stocks gap unpredictably.

Target range:

- Beta: 0.7 to 1.3
- Historical volatility: 15-35%
- Implied volatility: 20-40%

Sweet spot: Beta 0.9-1.1

Why this matters:

Too low volatility (Beta 0.3, HV 10%):

- Premium example: $0.40 on $100 stock (0.4% monthly)
- Annualized: 4.8%
- Not worth the effort

Optimal volatility (Beta 1.0, HV 22%):

- Premium example: $1.80 on $100 stock (1.8% monthly)
- Annualized: 21.6%
- Excellent risk-reward

Too high volatility (Beta 1.8, HV 55%):

- Premium example: $4.50 on $100 stock (4.5% monthly)
- Annualized: 54%
- But stock can gap 10-15% overnight

- High stress, frequent large losses

Volatility Assessment Tools:

1. Beta Calculation: Available on any financial website (Yahoo Finance, Bloomberg, etc.)

- Look for beta between 0.7-1.3
- Avoid anything above 1.5

2. Historical Volatility: Check past 52-week range:

- Calculate: (High - Low) ÷ Average Price
- Example: $150 high, $110 low, $130 avg
- Range: $40 ÷ $130 = 30.7% (acceptable)

3. Implied Volatility: Check options chain IV percentile

- IV Percentile > 50%: Above average (good time to sell)
- IV Percentile < 30%: Below average (consider waiting)

Pillar 3: Strong Liquidity

Both stock and options must trade actively for efficient execution.

Stock liquidity requirements:

- Average daily volume: 1 million+ shares
- Bid-ask spread: $0.03 or less
- Market cap: $10 billion minimum

Options liquidity requirements:

- Daily options volume: 500+ contracts
- Open interest (ATM strikes): 5,000+ contracts
- Bid-ask spread: $0.10 or less for ATM options

Why this matters:

Liquid stock (Apple - AAPL):

- Daily volume: 50M+ shares
- Bid: $175.23, Ask: $175.25 (2¢ spread)
- Options: 500K+ daily volume
- Bid-ask on ATM calls: $0.05
- **Easy to execute at fair prices**

Illiquid stock (Small-cap company):

- Daily volume: 50K shares
- Bid: $24.85, Ask: $25.25 (40¢ spread)
- Options: 12 daily contracts
- Bid-ask on ATM calls: $0.60
- **Lose 2-3% to spreads on every trade**

How to check liquidity:

1. **Stock volume:** Must average 1M+ daily
2. **Options volume:** Check any major strike, should see 100+ contracts traded
3. **Open interest:** View options chain, should see 1,000+ for popular strikes
4. **Bid-ask spread:** Calculate Ask - Bid, should be under $0.15

Pillar 4: Dividend Payments

Dividends provide a second income stream alongside premiums.

Optimal dividend characteristics:

- Yield: 2-5%
- Payout ratio: 30-60%
- History: 10+ years of payments
- Growth: Increasing or stable dividends

Why dividends matter for covered calls:

Example: Dividend stock (Coca-Cola - KO)

- Stock price: $60

- Dividend yield: 3.2% ($1.92 annual)
- Quarterly dividend: $0.48
- Monthly covered call premium: $0.90
- **Combined monthly income: $0.48 ÷ 3 + $0.90 = $1.06**
- Total annual income: $1.92 (dividend) + $10.80 (premiums) = $12.72
- **Total yield: 21.2%**

Example: Non-dividend stock

- Stock price: $60
- Dividend: $0
- Monthly covered call premium: $1.20 (higher premium due to no dividend)
- Total annual income: $14.40 (premiums only)
- **Total yield: 24%**

Verdict: Dividend stocks provide more stable total returns and psychological comfort. Non-dividend stocks may offer slightly higher option premiums but no dividend cushion.

Best practice: Prefer dividend-paying stocks with 2-4% yields for covered calls.

Dividend timing considerations:

Ex-dividend dates:

- Stock price drops by dividend amount on ex-date
- Call options account for this (lower premiums)
- Coordinate call expirations around ex-dates
- Strategy: Sell calls expiring BEFORE ex-date to capture dividend

Example:

- Stock: $100
- Ex-dividend date: June 15

- Dividend: $0.75
- Strategy: Sell June 9 calls (expire before ex-date)
- Result: Collect premium + keep stock through ex-date + receive dividend

Pillar 5: Sector Stability

Some sectors are inherently better for covered calls than others.

Best sectors for covered calls:

1. Consumer Staples

- Companies: PG, KO, PEP, CL, KMB
- Characteristics: Stable demand, predictable earnings
- Volatility: Low-moderate
- Why good: Consistent income, rarely collapse
- Premium range: 12-20% annualized

2. Healthcare (Large Cap)

- Companies: JNJ, ABBV, UNH, CVS
- Characteristics: Aging demographics, steady demand
- Volatility: Moderate
- Why good: Defensive, growth potential
- Premium range: 15-25% annualized

3. Utilities

- Companies: DUK, NEE, SO, D
- Characteristics: Regulated, high dividends
- Volatility: Very low
- Why good: Maximum stability
- Premium range: 8-15% annualized

4. Financials (Large Cap)

- Companies: JPM, BAC, WFC, GS
- Characteristics: Economic sensitivity, stable large banks

- Volatility: Moderate
- Why good: Decent premiums, dividends
- Premium range: 18-28% annualized

5. Telecommunications

- Companies: VZ, T
- Characteristics: Essential services, high dividends
- Volatility: Low-moderate
- Why good: Income focus, stability
- Premium range: 15-25% annualized

Sectors to approach carefully:
Technology (case by case):

- Mega-caps (MSFT, AAPL, GOOGL): Good for covered calls
- Mid-growth tech: Moderate (higher volatility)
- Small-cap tech: Avoid (too volatile)

Avoid these sectors:

- Biotechnology (binary FDA events)
- Small-cap anything (unpredictable)
- Meme stocks (manipulation risk)
- Penny stocks (illiquid, unstable)
- Highly shorted stocks (squeeze risk)

The Covered Call Stock Screening Process

Step 1: Set Your Screening Criteria

Use a stock screener (Yahoo Finance, Finviz, TradingView) with these filters:

Basic filters:

Market Cap: $20B minimum
Price: $30 - $250 (affordable for 100 shares)
Average Volume: 1M+ shares

Dividend Yield: 2-5%
Beta: 0.7 - 1.3
Sector: Consumer Staples, Healthcare, Utilities, Financials, Telecom
Results: Typically 50-150 stocks
Step 2: Verify Options Liquidity
Manually check each candidate:

1. Open stock page on your broker platform
2. View options chain
3. Check ATM strike (closest to current price)
4. Verify:
    - Daily volume: 100+ contracts minimum
    - Open interest: 1,000+ contracts
    - Bid-ask spread: Under $0.15

Eliminate stocks failing liquidity test
Results: Typically 30-60 stocks remain
Step 3: Fundamental Analysis
For remaining stocks, check:
Financial Health:

- Revenue trend: Growing or stable?
- Profit margins: Positive past 5 years?
- Debt-to-equity: Under 1.0?
- Free cash flow: Positive?

Dividend Quality:

- Payment history: 10+ years?
- Recent cuts: None in 5 years?
- Payout ratio: 30-70%?
- Growth rate: Stable or increasing?

Business Quality:

- Competitive position: Strong moat?

- Market share: Stable or growing?
- Management: Competent track record?
- Industry outlook: Favorable?

Eliminate stocks with red flags:

- Declining revenues
- Negative cash flow
- Recent dividend cuts
- Debt spiraling
- Major legal issues

Results: Typically 15-25 stocks remain
Step 4: Technical Analysis
Check current price vs historical ranges:
Price position:

- Near 52-week high (be cautious, may pull back)
- Near 52-week low (investigate why—opportunity or problem?)
- Middle of range (ideal—room to move either way)

Trend assessment:

- Uptrend: Good for covered calls
- Downtrend: Premiums help but stock falling
- Sideways: Ideal for covered calls

Support/Resistance:

- Identify key levels
- Use for strike selection

Results: Narrow to 10-15 highest quality stocks
Step 5: Check Earnings Calendar
Verify earnings dates:

- Avoid stocks with earnings in next 30 days (for first trades)
- Note upcoming earnings for future planning

Step 6: Final Portfolio Selection

From your final list, select 5-10 stocks for your covered call portfolio:

Diversification rules:

- Maximum 2 stocks from same sector
- Vary volatility levels (mix low and moderate beta)
- Include mix of dividend yields
- Different expiration calendars (stagger purchases)

The Top 25 Covered Call Stocks (Beginner-Friendly)

Here's a curated list of stocks that consistently meet covered call criteria:

Tier 1: Ultra-Conservative (Start Here)

1. Johnson & Johnson (JNJ) - Healthcare

- Market cap: $380B
- Dividend yield: 2.9%
- Beta: 0.54
- Why: 61 years dividend increases, AAA rated, stable
- Expected premium: 12-18% annually

2. Procter & Gamble (PG) - Consumer Staples

- Market cap: $360B
- Dividend yield: 2.5%
- Beta: 0.42
- Why: 67 years dividend increases, essential products
- Expected premium: 10-16% annually

3. Coca-Cola (KO) - Beverages

- Market cap: $260B
- Dividend yield: 3.1%

- Beta: 0.58
- Why: 61 years dividend increases, global brand
- Expected premium: 11-17% annually

4. Duke Energy (DUK) - Utilities

- Market cap: $75B
- Dividend yield: 4.2%
- Beta: 0.32
- Why: Regulated utility, consistent, high yield
- Expected premium: 8-14% annually

5. Walmart (WMT) - Retail

- Market cap: $400B
- Dividend yield: 1.5%
- Beta: 0.51
- Why: Defensive retail, strong business model
- Expected premium: 12-18% annually

Tier 2: Conservative (After Initial Experience)
6. Verizon (VZ) - Telecom

- Market cap: $170B
- Dividend yield: 6.5%
- Beta: 0.41
- Why: Essential service, very high yield
- Expected premium: 15-22% annually

7. AT&T (T) - Telecom

- Market cap: $125B
- Dividend yield: 6.8%
- Beta: 0.52
- Why: High yield, stabilized post-spin
- Expected premium: 16-24% annually

8. Home Depot (HD) - Retail

- Market cap: $320B
- Dividend yield: 2.4%
- Beta: 0.98
- Why: Strong business, housing market exposure
- Expected premium: 16-24% annually

9. Costco (COST) - Retail

- Market cap: $260B
- Dividend yield: 0.7%
- Beta: 0.68
- Why: Exceptional business quality, member loyalty
- Expected premium: 15-23% annually

10. AbbVie (ABBV) - Pharmaceuticals

- Market cap: $280B
- Dividend yield: 3.8%
- Beta: 0.62
- Why: Strong drug pipeline, good dividend
- Expected premium: 17-25% annually

Tier 3: Moderate (After 6+ Months Experience)
11. Microsoft (MSFT) - Technology

- Market cap: $2.8T
- Dividend yield: 0.8%
- Beta: 0.88
- Why: Mega-cap tech, stable, growing
- Expected premium: 18-28% annually

12. Apple (AAPL) - Technology

- Market cap: $2.7T

- Dividend yield: 0.5%
- Beta: 1.24
- Why: Most liquid stock, strong business
- Expected premium: 20-30% annually

13. JPMorgan Chase (JPM) - Financials

- Market cap: $450B
- Dividend yield: 2.5%
- Beta: 1.14
- Why: Leading bank, well-managed
- Expected premium: 20-30% annually

14. Visa (V) - Financials

- Market cap: $520B
- Dividend yield: 0.7%
- Beta: 0.96
- Why: Payment network, high margins
- Expected premium: 18-26% annually

15. UnitedHealth Group (UNH) - Healthcare

- Market cap: $480B
- Dividend yield: 1.3%
- Beta: 0.74
- Why: Healthcare leader, growth + stability
- Expected premium: 17-25% annually

Tier 4: Moderate-Aggressive (Experienced Traders)
16. Alphabet (GOOGL) - Technology

- Market cap: $1.7T
- Dividend yield: 0%
- Beta: 1.06
- Why: Search dominance, multiple revenue streams

- Expected premium: 20-32% annually

17. Meta Platforms (META) - Technology

- Market cap: $850B
- Dividend yield: 0%
- Beta: 1.19
- Why: Social media leader, recovered from 2022 lows
- Expected premium: 25-38% annually

18. Bank of America (BAC) - Financials

- Market cap: $280B
- Dividend yield: 2.8%
- Beta: 1.27
- Why: Large bank, economic sensitivity
- Expected premium: 22-32% annually

19. Wells Fargo (WFC) - Financials

- Market cap: $180B
- Dividend yield: 2.6%
- Beta: 1.19
- Why: Turnaround story, improving
- Expected premium: 23-33% annually

20. Chevron (CVX) - Energy

- Market cap: $290B
- Dividend yield: 3.5%
- Beta: 1.06
- Why: Integrated oil, good dividend
- Expected premium: 20-30% annually

Tier 5: Sector Diversification

21. NextEra Energy (NEE) - Utilities

- Market cap: $140B
- Dividend yield: 2.8%
- Beta: 0.47
- Why: Renewable energy leader
- Expected premium: 12-20% annually

22. Realty Income (O) - REIT

- Market cap: $43B
- Dividend yield: 5.2%
- Beta: 0.76
- Why: Monthly dividends, "The Monthly Dividend Company"
- Expected premium: 14-22% annually

23. McDonald's (MCD) - Consumer Discretionary

- Market cap: $210B
- Dividend yield: 2.2%
- Beta: 0.64
- Why: Global brand, consistent
- Expected premium: 13-20% annually

24. Lockheed Martin (LMT) - Industrials/Defense

- Market cap: $115B
- Dividend yield: 2.7%
- Beta: 0.71
- Why: Defense contractor, government contracts
- Expected premium: 14-22% annually

25. 3M Company (MMM) - Industrials

- Market cap: $60B
- Dividend yield: 5.8%
- Beta: 0.93
- Why: Diversified industrial, high yield

- Expected premium: 18-26% annually

Building Your Personal Covered Call Watchlist
Step 1: Select Your Starting 5
From the Tier 1-2 lists above, choose 5 stocks:
Recommended beginner portfolio:

1. Johnson & Johnson (JNJ) - Healthcare
2. Procter & Gamble (PG) - Consumer Staples
3. Verizon (VZ) - Telecom
4. Home Depot (HD) - Retail
5. Microsoft (MSFT) - Technology

Why this mix:

- Sector diversification (5 different sectors)
- Mix of volatility (beta 0.42 to 0.98)
- Mix of dividend yields (0.8% to 6.5%)
- All mega-caps ($170B to $2.8T)
- All highly liquid
- All beginner-friendly

Step 2: Calculate Your Capital Requirements
Example with $50,000 portfolio:

Stock	Price	Shares	Cost	Weight
JNJ	$156	100	$15,600	31.2%
PG	$150	100	$15,000	30.0%
VZ	$40	100	$4,000	8.0%
HD	$310	100	$31,000	Not affordable

Adjustment needed: HD too expensive at $310/share
Revised portfolio:

1. JNJ - $15,600 (31%)
2. PG - $15,000 (30%)
3. VZ - $4,000 (8%)

4. JPM - $150/share × 100 = $15,000 (30%)
5. Cash reserve - $400 (1%)

Total: $50,000

Step 3: Set Acquisition Targets

Don't buy all at once. Use dollar-cost averaging:

Month 1: Buy JNJ (100 shares) **Month 2:** Buy PG (100 shares) **Month 3:** Buy JPM (100 shares) **Month 4:** Buy VZ (100 shares)

Why stagger:

- Avoid buying everything at market top
- Learn gradually
- Test strategy before full deployment
- Better average entry prices

Step 4: Establish Your Strike Selection Rules

Document your strategy for each stock:

Stock: JNJ (Healthcare, stable)
Strike approach: 4-5% OTM
Expected premium: 1.2-1.5% monthly
Assignment acceptance: YES (quality stock, happy to hold or sell)
Stock: PG (Consumer staples, very stable)
Strike approach: 3-4% OTM
Expected premium: 1.0-1.3% monthly
Assignment acceptance: YES
Stock: JPM (Financial, moderate volatility)
Strike approach: 3-4% OTM
Expected premium: 1.8-2.2% monthly
Assignment acceptance: YES
Stock: VZ (Telecom, low price, high dividend)
Strike approach: 5-7% OTM
Expected premium: 1.5-2.0% monthly
Assignment acceptance: YES

Step 5: Create Your Monitoring System

Spreadsheet columns:

- Stock ticker
- Purchase date
- Purchase price
- Current price
- Shares owned
- Call strike sold
- Call expiration date
- Premium received
- Days to expiration
- Current call value
- Unrealized P/L (stock)
- Unrealized P/L (option)
- Total position P/L
- Next action date
- Notes

Step 6: Set Review Schedule
Weekly (15 minutes):

- Check stock prices
- Note significant moves (>3%)
- Verify no major news

Monthly (1-2 hours):

- Review all positions
- Decide: Roll, close, let expire, adjust
- Execute new covered calls
- Update tracking spreadsheet

Quarterly (2-3 hours):

- Comprehensive portfolio review
- Evaluate each stock fundamentals
- Consider adding/removing positions

- Assess strategy effectiveness
- Adjust approach if needed

Chapter 5: Managing Covered Call Positions

Successfully managing covered call positions separates profitable traders from those who struggle. This chapter covers the complete lifecycle of position management, from the day after opening through expiration and beyond.

The Covered Call Position Lifecycle

Every covered call position moves through distinct phases, each requiring different management approaches.

Phase 1: The First Week (Days 1-7)

What's Happening:

- Time decay is moderate (theta ~\$0.03-0.04 daily)
- Position has maximum time value
- Stock price movements have moderate impact
- Psychological adjustment period for new traders

Normal Price Behavior:

If stock unchanged:

- Option loses \$0.20-0.30 in value (10-15%)
- Your unrealized gain: \$20-30
- This is theta working in your favor

If stock up 2%:

- Option gains \$0.40-0.60 in value
- Your unrealized loss on option: \$40-60
- But stock gained 2% = offsetting gain
- Net position: Still slightly positive

If stock down 2%:

- Option loses \$0.60-0.80 in value

- Your unrealized gain on option: $60-80
- But stock lost 2%
- Net position: Premium cushions loss

Your Action Items:

☐ **Resist the urge to check constantly** (once daily maximum) ☐ **Don't close position early** (you have 30+ days for theta to work) ☐ **Document your emotions** (helps build discipline) ☐ **Trust your plan** (you set strikes for a reason)

Common First Week Mistakes:

Mistake 1: Panic Closing

- Stock down $1, you close call for $0.20 loss to "protect" stock
- Reality: Premium was $2.00, you gave up $1.80 of potential profit
- Stock recovers next week, you missed the theta decay
- **Solution:** Give positions time to work

Mistake 2: Greed Rolling

- Stock up $2, your call gained value
- You think "I should roll to higher strike to capture more upside"
- You pay $50 to roll, stock reverses next week
- **Solution:** Let the position work unless in Phase 3

Mistake 3: Over-monitoring

- Checking prices 10 times per day
- Causing stress over normal fluctuations
- Making impulsive decisions
- **Solution:** Check once daily or every other day maximum

Week 1 Checkpoint:

Healthy positions:

- Stock within 5% of entry price

- Option value decreased 10-20% from sale price
- You're feeling comfortable (or getting there)
- No major news or earnings surprises

Warning signs:

- Stock down 8%+ (consider adjustment in Week 3-4)
- Stock up 7%+ toward strike (monitor for potential early success)
- Major news (earnings surprise, acquisition rumors, etc.)

Phase 2: The Middle Period (Days 8-21)
What's Happening:

- Time decay accelerating (theta ~$0.04-0.06 daily)
- Option losing value steadily
- Stock price movements have moderate impact
- The "boring" phase where theta works

This is where covered calls make money. Most profitable outcomes occur because you patiently let theta work during this period.

Typical Scenarios:
Scenario A: Stock Drifting Sideways
Position:

- Entry: Stock $100, sold $105 call for $2.00
- Day 15: Stock at $101, call now worth $1.10

Analysis:

- Stock gain: $1.00
- Option decay: $0.90 (45% of premium captured)
- Net P&L: $1.90 unrealized gain
- **Status: Excellent—let it continue**

Your action: Nothing. Let theta work.

Scenario B: Stock Drifting Higher Toward Strike
Position:

- Entry: Stock $100, sold $105 call for $2.00
- Day 15: Stock at $104, call now worth $1.80

Analysis:

- Stock gain: $4.00
- Option against you: $0.20
- Net P&L: $3.80 unrealized gain
- **Status: Great—approaching maximum profit**

Your action: Nothing. Let position ride toward assignment.
If assigned: $5 stock gain + $2 premium = $7 profit (7% in 30 days)
Scenario C: Stock Declining Moderately
Position:

- Entry: Stock $100, sold $105 call for $2.00
- Day 15: Stock at $97, call now worth $0.50

Analysis:

- Stock loss: -$3.00
- Option decay: $1.50 (75% of premium captured)
- Net P&L: -$1.50 unrealized loss
- **Status: Premium cushioning loss, near breakeven**

Your action: Monitor. Consider closing option if reaches $0.20-0.30 and rewriting new call.
Scenario D: Stock Declining Significantly
Position:

- Entry: Stock $100, sold $105 call for $2.00
- Day 15: Stock at $93, call now worth $0.15

Analysis:

- Stock loss: -$7.00
- Option decay: $1.85
- Net P&L: -$5.15
- **Status: Premium helped but significant loss**

Your decision point:

- **Option 1:** Close call for $0.15, write new $95 call for $1.50
    - Improves cost basis by additional $1.35
    - New strike appropriate to current price
- **Option 2:** Let current call expire worthless, reassess at expiration
    - Simpler approach
    - Wait to see if stock recovers
- **Option 3:** Close entire position (sell stock + buy back call)
    - Only if fundamentally bearish on stock
    - Accept loss and redeploy capital

Management Decision Framework:

When to actively manage (adjust position):

✓ Stock moved 8%+ in either direction ✓ Major news changed outlook (earnings surprise, downgrade, acquisition) ✓ Option worth less than $0.20 (can close and rewrite) ✓ Better opportunity identified elsewhere ✓ Fundamental thesis broken (sell stock entirely)

When to do nothing (most common):

✓ Stock within 5% of entry (normal movement) ✓ Option behaving as expected (decaying with time) ✓ No major news ✓ Thesis intact ✓ **Default action for 80% of positions**

Phase 3: The Final Week (Days 22-30)

What's Happening:

- Time decay maximized (theta ~$0.06-0.12 daily)
- Gamma risk increasing (delta changes rapidly)

- Decision time approaching
- Most volatile phase for emotions

The final week is when options become unpredictable. Stock movements near your strike create stress.

Final Week Scenarios:

Scenario A: Deep Out-of-the-Money (OTM)

Position:

- Stock at $102, your strike is $105
- Call worth $0.30
- 5 days to expiration

Probability: Stock stays below $105 = 85%

Your options:

Option 1: Let it expire (most common)

- Wait 5 days
- Collect final $0.30 of decay
- 99% certain it expires worthless
- Simple, clean

Option 2: Close now for $0.30

- Buy back call
- Profit: $1.70 if sold for $2.00
- Redeploy capital immediately
- Good if you want to write new call

Recommendation: If option worth < $0.30 and deep OTM, close it and write new call for following month. If worth $0.30-0.50 and only 3-5 days left, let it expire.

Scenario B: Slightly Out-of-the-Money

Position:

- Stock at $104, your strike is $105

- Call worth $0.80
- 5 days to expiration

Probability: Could go either way
Analysis:

- If stock closes at $104.99 or below: Expires worthless, you keep full $2.00
- If stock closes at $105.01 or above: Assigned, you make maximum profit

Your options:
Option 1: Let it ride

- Gamble on expiring worthless
- Risk: Assignment if stock rises $1
- Reward: Keep extra $0.80 if stays below $105

Option 2: Close at $0.80, take $1.20 profit

- Lock in 60% of maximum profit
- Avoid weekend stress
- Immediately write new call for next month

Recommendation: Depends on conviction. If neutral, close at 60-70% profit. If bearish on stock, let it ride. If bullish, close and take profit.

Scenario C: At-the-Money (Stressful!)
Position:

- Stock at $105.00, your strike is $105
- Call worth $1.50
- 5 days to expiration

This is the stressful zone. Stock could finish $0.50 either side.
Your options:

Option 1: Let it play out

- Natural outcome
- If assigned: Make $2.00 premium (maximum)
- If not assigned: Make $2.00 premium (maximum)
- Either way, good outcome

Option 2: Close at $1.50, take $0.50 profit

- Lock in 25% profit (not great)
- Avoid stress
- Keep stock

Option 3: Roll up and out

- Buy back $105 call for $1.50
- Sell $108 call next month for $2.00
- Net credit: $0.50
- New position: Can capture $3 more appreciation + $0.50 premium

Recommendation: If you want to keep the stock (bullish), roll up and out. If neutral, let it play out naturally. The stress isn't worth $0.50 to close early.

Scenario D: In-the-Money (ITM)

Position:

- Stock at $108, your strike is $105
- Call worth $3.50 (intrinsic $3, time $0.50)
- 5 days to expiration

Reality: You're getting assigned. Accept it.

Your analysis:

- Stock gain: $8 if you bought at $100
- Premium kept: $2.00

- Total profit: $10.00 (10% in 30 days)
- **This is success, not failure**

Your options:
Option 1: Let assignment happen (recommended)

- Simple, clean exit
- Take your profit
- Redeploy capital into new stock

Option 2: Roll up and out

- Buy back $105 call for $3.50
- Sell $110 call next month for $3.00
- Net cost: $0.50 to capture $5 more upside
- **Only if very bullish on continued rally**

Option 3: Close everything (stock + call)

- Sell stock at $108
- Buy back call at $3.50
- Same profit as letting assignment happen
- More control over timing

Recommendation: Let assignment happen. This is the planned, successful outcome. Moving to Option 2 (rolling) is greed and often backfires when stock reverses.

Final Week Stress Management:

Mental Framework:

"I sold this call agreeing to sell at $105. If assigned at $105, I achieved my goal. The fact that the stock is now at $108 doesn't change that I'm profitable. Assignment is success."

Mantra: *"I made X% in 30 days. That's the goal. I cannot capture every dollar of every move."*

Final Week Action Items:

☐ Review each position 3 days before expiration

☐ Decide: Let expire, close early, or roll
☐ Set calendar reminder for expiration date (Friday 4pm EST)
☐ Prepare for next cycle (identify new strikes)
☐ Calculate returns achieved this cycle
☐ Celebrate wins (even assignments are wins!)

Expiration Day: Managing the Close

Expiration occurs:

- Third Friday of the month (for monthly options)
- Market close: 4:00 PM Eastern Time
- Assignment processing: Friday evening/Saturday morning

Expiration Day Timeline:

Morning (9:30 AM - 12:00 PM):

- Review all expiring positions
- Identify which are ITM (will be assigned)
- Identify which are OTM (will expire worthless)
- Make final adjustment decisions

Afternoon (12:00 PM - 3:45 PM):

- Execute any closing trades
- Roll positions if decided
- Let ITM positions ride to assignment
- Let OTM positions expire

Final Hour (3:00 PM - 4:00 PM):

- Stock prices fluctuating near strikes can be stressful
- Accept that some will be close calls
- Assignment is determined by 4:00 PM closing price
- Don't panic trade in final minutes

After Market Close (4:00 PM+):

- Positions are now settled
- ITM options will be assigned (processing overnight)
- OTM options expire worthless
- Your account will reflect changes Saturday morning

Understanding Assignment Processing:
What happens when assigned:

1. **Friday after close:** Assignment notices sent
2. **Saturday morning:** Stock automatically sold from your account
3. **Settlement:** Cash credited to account
4. **Notification:** Broker emails assignment notice

Example:

- Position: 100 shares JNJ, short $160 call
- Friday 4 PM: Stock closes at $162
- Call is $2 in-the-money → Assignment
- Saturday morning: Your account shows:
    - 100 shares JNJ removed
    - $16,000 cash added (100 × $160)
    - Short call position closed
    - Premium ($250) already in account from 30 days ago

Your realized gain:

- Stock bought at: $156 = $15,600 cost
- Sold via assignment: $160 = $16,000 received
- Premium collected: $2.50 = $250
- **Total gain: $650 (4.2% in 30 days = 50% annualized)**

What happens with expired worthless options:
Example:

- Position: 100 shares PG, short $155 call

- Friday 4 PM: Stock closes at $153
- Call is $2 out-of-the-money → Expires worthless
- Saturday morning: Your account shows:
    - 100 shares PG still owned
    - Short call position removed
    - Premium ($220) retained from 30 days ago

Your result:

- Still own 100 shares
- Kept entire $2.20 premium = $220 profit
- Can immediately write new call for next month

Edge Cases:
Stock closes exactly at strike:
Example: Stock closes at exactly $105.00, your strike is $105
What happens:

- Technically in-the-money by $0.00
- Assignment is at the option holder's discretion
- Most brokers auto-exercise options ITM by $0.01+
- You might or might not be assigned

Your action:

- If you want to keep stock: Call broker Friday afternoon, request to buy back call for $0.01-0.05 (prevents assignment)
- If neutral: Let it play out, accept either outcome
- Check account Saturday to see result

Pin risk: When stock closes very near your strike ($104.90 - $105.10), assignment is uncertain. This is annoying but rare. Simply accept the outcome.

Position Management Strategies

Beyond basic lifecycle management, specific strategies can improve your results.

Strategy 1: The 50-70% Profit Close

Concept: Don't hold until expiration. Close when you've captured 50-70% of maximum profit.

Example:

- Sold call for $2.00
- 15 days later, call worth $0.70
- Your profit: $1.30 (65% of max)
- Buy back for $0.70
- Immediately sell new call for $1.90
- Potential total: $1.30 + $1.90 = $3.20 over 30 days
- **60% more than holding to expiration**

When to use:

- Option has decayed to $0.50-0.80
- 15-20 days into 30-day cycle
- Stock is stable (not near strike)
- You want to compound faster

When NOT to use:

- Option still worth $1.50+ (not enough decay)
- Only 5 days left (let it expire)
- Stock near strike (outcome uncertain)
- Transaction costs eat into profit

Mathematical Justification:
Traditional approach (hold 30 days):

- Collect $2.00 once = $2.00/month

- Annual: $24.00

50-70% close approach:

- Collect $1.30 in 15 days
- Rewrite new call: $1.90
- But only hold 15 days of new cycle: $0.95 decay
- Total in 30 days: $1.30 + $0.95 = $2.25
- Annual: $27.00
- **12.5% improvement**

Professional traders use this approach to compound returns faster.

Strategy 2: Rolling Adjustments

Rolling means closing your current call and simultaneously opening a new call with different terms.

Three types of rolls:

Roll Up: New strike is higher **Roll Out:** New expiration is later

Roll Down: New strike is lower

Can combine: Roll up and out, Roll down and out, etc.

When and Why to Roll:

Roll Up (Stock Rallied):

Situation:

- Stock at $100, sold $105 call for $2.00
- Stock rallies to $108
- Call now worth $4.50 (you're losing $2.50)
- You want to capture more upside

Action:

- Buy back $105 call for $4.50 (debit $4.50)
- Sell $110 call for $3.50 (credit $3.50)
- Net cost: $1.00
- New position: Can capture $10 appreciation (up from $5)

Analysis:

- Original max profit: $7 ($5 stock + $2 premium)
- Spent $1 to roll
- New max profit: $12 ($10 stock + $2 original premium)
- Net: $11 ($12 - $1 roll cost)
- **Gained $4 potential profit for $1 cost** (if stock continues up)

When this works:

- Strong bullish momentum continuing
- Stock breaking out
- You have high conviction

When this fails:

- Stock reverses after you roll
- You spent $1 and stock comes back to $105
- You'd have been better off accepting assignment

Recommendation: Only roll up if you'd buy the stock at current price. If stock at $108 feels expensive, take your assignment profit.

Roll Out (Extend Time):

Situation:

- Stock at $100, sold $105 call expiring in 5 days for $2.00
- Call now worth $0.40
- Stock at $104, might finish above $105
- You want to keep stock

Action:

- Buy back $105 call this month for $0.40 (debit $0.40)
- Sell $105 call next month for $2.30 (credit $2.30)
- Net credit: $1.90
- New position: Same strike, 30 more days

Analysis:

- Collected $1.60 so far ($2.00 - $0.40)
- Can collect $2.30 more
- Total: $3.90 over 60 days
- **But gave up potential assignment at $105 this week**

When this works:

- You definitely want to keep the stock
- Stock near strike but might dip
- Can collect more total premium

When this fails:

- Stock rallies hard next month
- Gets assigned at $105 anyway
- You delayed the inevitable

Roll Down (Stock Declined):
Situation:

- Stock at $100, sold $105 call for $2.00
- Stock dropped to $95
- Call worth $0.20
- You want to collect more premium

Action:

- Buy back $105 call for $0.20 (debit $0.20)
- Sell $97 call for $1.80 (credit $1.80)
- Net credit: $1.60
- New position: Strike at $97 (near current price)

Analysis:

- Collected $1.80 from first call ($2.00 - $0.20)
- Can collect $1.80 more from new call
- Total: $3.60
- But new strike is at $97 (below your $100 cost)

Important: If assigned at $97, you'll sell at $97 when you paid $100. Your loss: -$3 + $3.60 premiums = $0.60 profit overall.

When this works:

- Stock stabilizes at lower level
- You collect additional premium
- Reduces cost basis further

When this fails:

- Stock continues dropping
- Get assigned at $97 (loss on stock)
- Though premiums helped

Roll Down and Out (Most Common Combination):

Situation:

- Stock declined from $100 to $95
- Want more time and premium

Action:

- Close current $105 call for $0.20
- Sell $97 call next month for $2.10
- Net credit: $1.90

Benefit: More time for stock to recover + more premium collected

Risk: If assigned at $97, you lock in stock loss (though premiums helped)

Strategy 3: Legging Out of Positions

Legging out means closing one part of a position (stock or option) while keeping the other.

Close Option, Keep Stock:

When:

- Option decayed to $0.10-0.20
- Stock stable or rising
- Want to immediately rewrite new call

Action:

- Buy back call for $0.15
- Profit: $1.85 if sold for $2.00
- Immediately sell new call for $2.00
- Total: $3.85 if both work

Close Stock, Keep Short Call:

DANGEROUS - Not recommended for beginners

This creates a "naked call" which has unlimited risk. Your broker may not allow it, and you'll need higher margin requirements.

Only mentioned for awareness: Don't do this unless you're an experienced trader with specific strategies.

Strategy 4: Defensive Adjustments

When stock moves against you significantly:

Scenario: Stock Down 10%

Position:

- Bought stock: $100
- Sold call: $105 for $2.00
- Stock now: $90
- Call now: $0.05

Your loss: -$10 stock + $1.95 option profit = -$8.05 (8% loss)

Options:

1. Do nothing (often best)

- Keep stock
- Let call expire worthless
- Write new call at $93-95 strike
- Collect more premiums while waiting for recovery

2. Close everything and take the loss

- Sell stock at $90: -$10 loss
- Buy back call for $0.05: +$1.95 profit
- Net: -$8.05 loss
- **Only if fundamentally bearish on stock**

3. Roll down to reduce cost basis

- Close $105 call for $0.05
- Sell $92 call for $1.50
- Additional premium: $1.45
- New cost basis: $100 - $2 - $1.45 = $96.55

4. Average down (add more shares)

- Buy 100 more shares at $90
- Average cost: ($100 + $90) ÷ 2 = $95
- Write 2 calls at $97 strike
- **Only if you have capital and conviction**

Recommendation: Usually #1 (do nothing, wait for recovery) is best. #2 (close everything) only if thesis is broken. #3 (roll down) is moderate approach. #4 (average down) only for high-conviction positions.

Strategy 5: Taking Assignment Gracefully

Assignment is not failure—it's often your best outcome.

Mental Framework for Assignment:

When you sell a $105 call for $2.00 on stock bought at $100, you're saying:

"I'm willing to sell this stock at $105. If assigned, I'll make $5 stock gain + $2 premium = $7 profit (7% in 30 days). This is my target profit. I accept this outcome."

If assigned at $105 while stock is $108:

Yes, you "missed" $3 of additional gains. But:

- You made your 7% target profit
- 7% in 30 days = 84% annualized
- This is excellent performance
- Chasing every dollar leads to worse outcomes

Professional Mindset:

"I don't need to capture every dollar of every move. I set a profit target, hit it, and moved on. Success."

After Assignment:

Immediate actions:

1. **Celebrate the win:** You profited! (Seriously, acknowledge the success)
2. **Review the trade:** What worked? What could improve?
3. **Plan next trade:** Find new stock or repurchase same stock
4. **Update tracking:** Record the completed cycle

Repurchasing the Same Stock:

Common scenario: You owned JNJ at $156, got assigned at $160, now want to repurchase.

Decision tree:

If stock at $161-165 (slightly higher):

- **Repurchase:** If you still like the stock fundamentally
- **Write call immediately:** $165 strike for $2.50
- **Continue the cycle:** Similar strategy, new cost basis

If stock at $170+ (significantly higher):

- **Wait for pullback:** Stock may be extended
- **Find different opportunity:** Many stocks in market
- **Don't chase:** Buying significantly higher adds risk

If stock at $158-160 (same range):

- **Good repurchase opportunity:** Similar to your previous cost
- **Write call:** Resume strategy
- **Lesson:** Market is giving you another chance at similar entry

After Assignment Checklist:
☐ Record final profit in tracking spreadsheet
☐ Calculate annualized return achieved
☐ Note lessons learned (what worked/didn't)
☐ Research replacement stock or repurchase decision
☐ If repurchasing, find good entry point
☐ Write new covered call within 1-2 days of repurchase
☐ Continue the cycle

The Monthly Covered Call Calendar

A systematic approach to managing multiple positions across the month:

Week 1 (Day 1-7): Opening Week

- **Monday/Tuesday:** New monthly options listed
- **Your action:** Review portfolio, select new strikes
- **Execute:** Sell new covered calls on all eligible positions
- **Focus:** Setting up positions correctly
- **Time required:** 1-2 hours

Week 2 (Day 8-14): Monitoring Week

- **Your action:** Check positions once
- **Look for:** Any major moves (±5%+)
- **Generally:** Let theta work, don't interfere
- **Focus:** Patience

- **Time required:** 15 minutes

Week 3 (Day 15-21): Assessment Week

- **Your action:** Review each position carefully
- **Evaluate:** Are positions on track?
- **Consider:** Early closes on deep profit (70%+ decay)
- **Focus:** Identifying adjustment opportunities
- **Time required:** 30-45 minutes

Week 4 (Day 22-28): Decision Week

- **Your action:** Plan for expiration
- **Decisions:** Roll, close, or let expire?
- **Execute:** Any adjustments needed
- **Focus:** Preparation for expiration
- **Time required:** 1 hour

Week 5 (Expiration Week):

- **Monday-Wednesday:** Final monitoring
- **Thursday:** Review likely outcomes
- **Friday:** Expiration day—let positions settle
- **Weekend:** Assignment processing
- **Focus:** Accepting outcomes gracefully
- **Time required:** 30 minutes

Following Monday: Start Week 1 again with new cycle

Common Management Mistakes and Solutions

Mistake 1: Over-Management (Over-Trading)

Symptom:

- Closing and reopening positions 2-3 times per month
- Constantly rolling
- Never letting positions work

- High transaction costs

Cost:

- 10-15 trades per position per year
- $5-10 per trade in slippage/costs = $50-150 lost annually per position
- Emotional exhaustion
- Often underperforms simple approach

Solution:

- Set it and forget it (mostly)
- Only adjust when position moves 8%+ or other clear trigger
- Let theta work without interference
- Review weekly, act monthly

Mistake 2: Under-Management (Neglect)
Symptom:

- Not reviewing positions for weeks
- Missing expirations
- Holding worthless options instead of rewriting
- Losing track of portfolio

Cost:

- Missed opportunities to redeploy capital
- Let profits stagnate
- Forget about positions until problems emerge

Solution:

- Set calendar reminders
- Weekly 15-minute review
- Use portfolio tracking spreadsheet

- Automate where possible (alerts at 70% profit)

Mistake 3: Emotional Rolling (Fighting Losses)
Symptom:

- Stock down 10%, you keep rolling down to "recover"
- Never accepting losses
- Adding good money to bad positions
- Hoping instead of analyzing

Example:

- Month 1: Stock \$100 → \$92, roll to \$93 strike
- Month 2: Stock \$92 → \$87, roll to \$88 strike
- Month 3: Stock \$87 → \$82, roll to \$83 strike
- After 3 months: Stock at \$82, you have \$9 premiums
- Net loss: Still -\$9 (-9%)
- **Should have cut losses at -8% after Month 1**

Solution:

- Set stop-loss rules: Exit if stock down 15% and thesis broken
- Don't roll down more than twice
- Accept some losses—not every trade wins
- Redeploy capital to better opportunities

Mistake 4: Greedy Rolling (Chasing Rallies)
Symptom:

- Stock hits your strike, you roll up for more gains
- This works once, so you keep doing it
- Eventually stock reverses and you miss the assignment
- End up with lower total return

Example:

- Month 1: Stock \$100 → \$105, roll to \$108 for \$1 cost
- Month 2: Stock \$108 → \$111, roll to \$113 for \$1 cost
- Month 3: Stock \$111 → \$106, expires below \$113
- Still assigned at \$113 but paid \$2 in rolling costs
- **Better to have taken first assignment at \$105**

Solution:

- Accept assignments as success
- Only roll up if strongly bullish and fundamentally justified
- Remember: "Bulls make money, bears make money, pigs get slaughtered"
- Take your profits and find next opportunity

Mistake 5: Calendar Confusion
Symptom:

- Forgetting ex-dividend dates
- Missing earnings announcements
- Not tracking expiration dates
- Surprised by events

Cost:

- Early assignment surprises
- Earnings volatility ruins positions
- Missed dividend income

Solution:

- Mark all ex-dividend dates on calendar
- Note earnings dates before selling calls
- Set expiration reminders
- Use broker's calendar tools

Advanced Management: The Professional Approach

Professional covered call managers use systematic rules:

Rule Set Example

Position Opening:

- Only sell calls with 30-45 days to expiration
- Only use 3-5% OTM strikes
- Never sell calls expiring before ex-dividend date
- Maximum 10 positions simultaneously

Ongoing Management:

- Check all positions every Monday morning
- Close any position showing 70% profit (buy back call)
- Roll down any position where stock dropped 8%+
- Exit any position where stock dropped 15% and thesis broken

Expiration Week:

- Thursday: Review all expiring positions
- Close any worth $0.10 or less (not worth holding)
- Accept all assignments gracefully
- Plan next week's new positions

Performance Tracking:

- Calculate return on each completed cycle
- Track annualized returns
- Compare to stock-only performance
- Adjust strategy quarterly based on results

This systematic approach removes emotion and creates consistency.

Position Management Tools

Excel/Google Sheets Template:

Create a tracking spreadsheet with these columns:

Date Ticker Shares Cost Strike Exp Premium Current Stock Current Option Days Left Status Action Needed

Broker Platform Tools:

- Options P/L calculator
- Expiration calendar
- Assignment risk indicator
- Position Greeks display

Third-Party Tools:

- OptionStrat (position visualization)
- ThinkorSwim (if using TD Ameritrade)
- Interactive Brokers (advanced tools)
- TastyWorks (designed for options)

Mobile Apps:

- Set price alerts on your phone
- Get expiration reminders

Chapter 6:

Characteristics of Covered Call Candidates

Not all stocks make suitable covered call candidates. This chapter identifies the key characteristics that distinguish excellent covered call stocks from poor choices, enabling you to build a portfolio optimized for consistent option income.

Stock Price Stability and Predictability

The ideal covered call stock exhibits moderate volatility with predictable trading ranges. Excessive volatility creates assignment risk and potential capital losses, while insufficient volatility generates inadequate premiums to justify the strategy.

The Goldilocks Zone of Volatility

Stocks with historical volatility between 20% and 40% annually typically provide the best covered call opportunities. This range generates attractive premiums without excessive risk of dramatic price swings.

Consider three scenarios:

Low volatility (10-15%): Utility stocks, stable consumer staples, and established dividend aristocrats often exhibit minimal price movement. While safe, their options generate minimal premium. A stable $50 utility stock might produce only $0.40 to $0.60 in monthly premium, yielding less than 1% monthly income.

Moderate volatility (20-40%): Established technology companies, financial stocks, healthcare firms, and diversified industrials occupy this sweet spot. These stocks move enough to generate meaningful premiums ($1.00 to $2.50 per month on a $50 stock) without excessive risk. Price movements remain largely predictable within established ranges.

High volatility (50%+): Speculative growth stocks, biotechnology companies, and momentum plays produce exceptional premiums but carry substantial risk. A volatile stock might generate $4.00 monthly premium but could easily gap down 15% overnight on disappointing news, overwhelming your premium income with capital losses.

Identifying Predictable Price Patterns

Review six-month to one-year price charts to identify stocks trading in established ranges or following predictable trends:

Range-bound stocks oscillate between clear support and resistance levels, ideal for covered calls when prices approach resistance. For example, a stock consistently bouncing between $45 and $55 over several months allows selling $55 calls when the price nears $52-$53.

Steady uptrends with moderate slopes (10-20% annually) combine capital appreciation with premium income. These stocks provide call premium while maintaining long-term appreciation, the optimal covered call scenario.

Stocks exhibiting unpredictable gaps, frequent reversals, or chaotic patterns make poor candidates. The uncertainty increases assignment risk and creates scenarios where you may be forced to sell appreciated shares or hold depreciated positions.

Standard Deviation and Price Confidence

Calculate or reference a stock's standard deviation to quantify price predictability. One standard deviation represents the range containing approximately 68% of price movements.

A stock trading at $50 with a 25% annual standard deviation should remain between $37.50 and $62.50 (one standard deviation) during 68% of the year. This allows confidence when selling $55 or $57.50 calls, as statistical probability suggests the stock will remain below these strikes most of the time.

Conversely, a stock with 60% standard deviation might trade anywhere from $20 to $80 during the year, making strike selection largely guesswork.

Liquidity Requirements for Efficient Trading

Liquidity determines your ability to enter and exit covered call positions at fair prices without excessive slippage or bid-ask spread costs. Always prioritize liquid stocks and options for covered call trading.

Stock Liquidity Metrics

Evaluate stock liquidity using these criteria:

Average daily volume should exceed 500,000 shares, preferably exceeding 1 million shares. High volume ensures you can buy or sell stock positions without materially impacting the price.

Tight bid-ask spreads, typically $0.01 to $0.03 for stocks under $100, indicate efficient pricing. Wide spreads increase your trading costs both when establishing positions and when potentially rolling or closing them.

Multiple market makers actively quoting prices throughout the trading session ensure continuous liquidity rather than sporadic availability.

Options Liquidity Standards

Options liquidity often matters more than stock liquidity for covered call traders:

Open interest for at-the-money and near-the-money strikes should exceed 100 contracts minimum, preferably exceeding 500 contracts. Higher open interest correlates with better pricing and easier execution.

Daily options volume provides additional confirmation. Options trading volume equivalent to at least 1% of stock volume suggests adequate liquidity.

Bid-ask spreads should remain under 5% of the option premium, preferably under 3%. A $2.00 call option should have a spread no wider than $0.10, and ideally $0.05 or less.

Liquidity Impact on Returns

Consider two equivalent covered call opportunities:

Stock A (highly liquid):

- Stock bid-ask: $50.00 - $50.02
- Option bid-ask: $2.30 - $2.35
- Effective premium received: $2.30 (or $2.32 with limit order)
- Round-trip trading costs: Minimal

Stock B (illiquid):

- Stock bid-ask: $49.85 - $50.20
- Option bid-ask: $2.00 - $2.50
- Effective premium received: $2.00 (or $2.25 if lucky)
- Round-trip trading costs: Significant

The illiquid stock costs you $0.30 per share in reduced premium plus $0.35 in wider stock spreads, totaling $65 per contract in unnecessary costs. Over multiple trades, illiquidity erodes 10-20% of your potential returns.

Identifying Liquid Covered Call Stocks

Several stock categories consistently offer excellent liquidity:

Large-cap stocks ($10 billion+ market capitalization) with S&P 500 inclusion typically provide superior liquidity. Companies like Microsoft, Johnson & Johnson, JPMorgan Chase, and Procter & Gamble trade enormous volumes with tight spreads.

Major ETFs such as SPY, QQQ, IWM, and sector-specific funds offer exceptional liquidity with very active options markets. ETFs often provide better liquidity than individual stocks while offering instant diversification.

High-profile growth stocks like Tesla, AMD, and Netflix, despite higher volatility, maintain tremendous liquidity due to significant retail and institutional interest.

Dividend-Paying Stocks: The Double Income Strategy

Combining covered calls with dividend-paying stocks creates dual income streams, enhancing total returns and providing downside cushions during market weakness. This strategy particularly appeals to income-focused investors.

The Dividend-Enhanced Covered Call Model

Dividend stocks provide quarterly cash payments independent of option premium income. This combination creates consistent cash flow:

Quarter 1: Sell three monthly covered calls at $1.50 premium each = $450 income Quarter 1: Receive quarterly dividend of $0.50 per share on 100 shares = $50 income

Quarterly total: $500 income ($450 premium + $50 dividend)

Annualized, this strategy on a $50 stock position produces $2,000 income, representing a 40% return on invested capital even if the stock price remains flat.

Dividend Capture and Ex-Dividend Dates

Understanding dividend mechanics prevents unwanted assignment and optimizes income:

The ex-dividend date determines dividend eligibility. Shareholders of record as of the ex-dividend date receive the dividend. If your stock gets called away before the ex-dividend date, you forfeit the dividend.

In-the-money covered calls face elevated assignment risk immediately before ex-dividend dates. Option holders may exercise early to capture the dividend, particularly when the dividend exceeds the remaining time value.

Strategic timing: Avoid selling in-the-money calls in the week preceding ex-dividend dates. Alternatively, sell out-of-the-money calls that are unlikely to be exercised early, preserving both dividend and premium income.

Selecting High-Quality Dividend Stocks

Prioritize dividend aristocrats and dividend achievers with 10+ years of consecutive dividend increases. These companies demonstrate financial stability and commitment to shareholders:

Dividend aristocrats (25+ years of increases): Companies like Coca-Cola, 3M, Johnson & Johnson, and Walmart combine reliable dividends with stable price action, ideal for covered calls.

Dividend yield considerations: Target yields between 2% and 5%. Exceptionally high yields (6%+) often signal distressed companies where dividend cuts loom, creating capital loss risk that overwhelms premium income.

Payout ratios under 70% ensure dividends are sustainable from earnings, reducing dividend cut risk. Calculate payout ratio by dividing annual dividend by earnings per share.

Case Study: Dividend Stock Covered Call Returns

Real-world example using Johnson & Johnson (JNJ):

- Stock price: $150.00 per share
- Annual dividend: $4.80 (3.2% yield)
- Quarterly dividend: $1.20

Monthly covered call strategy:

- Sell $155 call, 30 days to expiration: $2.25 premium

- Repeat monthly, assuming no assignment: $2.25 × 12 = $27.00 annual premium
- Annual dividend: $4.80
- Total annual income: $31.80 per share (21.2% return)

Even accounting for occasional assignment and position reestablishment costs, this strategy dramatically outperforms simple stock ownership or dividend collection alone.

Volatility Metrics: Finding the Sweet Spot

Volatility drives option premium values. Understanding and measuring volatility allows you to identify stocks offering optimal premium relative to risk.

Historical vs. Implied Volatility

Historical volatility (HV) measures actual past price fluctuations, calculated as the standard deviation of price changes over a specific period (typically 30, 60, or 90 days).

Implied volatility (IV), as discussed in Chapter 3, represents the market's forward-looking expectation embedded in option prices.

The relationship between HV and IV reveals trading opportunities:

IV > HV by 20%+: Options are expensive relative to historical movement, creating ideal covered call selling opportunities. The market is pricing in more volatility than the stock typically exhibits.

IV < HV by 20%+: Options are cheap relative to historical movement. Avoid selling covered calls in these conditions as premiums are inadequate.

IV ≈ HV: Fairly valued options. Covered calls remain viable but offer no special advantage.

Beta: Market Correlation and Systematic Risk

Beta measures how much a stock moves relative to the overall market (typically the S&P 500):

Beta = 1.0: Stock moves in line with the market Beta > 1.0: Stock is more volatile than the market

Beta < 1.0: Stock is less volatile than the market

For covered call purposes, stocks with beta between 0.8 and 1.3 provide good balance. Lower beta stocks are too stable to generate meaningful premiums. Higher beta stocks carry excessive risk of sharp moves against your position.

Technology stocks often carry beta of 1.2 to 1.5, generating attractive premiums but requiring careful position management. Defensive sectors like utilities and consumer staples typically show beta of 0.5 to 0.9, producing lower premiums but greater safety.

The Volatility Risk Premium

A persistent phenomenon in options markets: implied volatility consistently exceeds realized volatility over time. This "volatility risk premium" creates structural advantages for option sellers.

Research shows that implied volatility exceeds realized volatility by 3-5 percentage points on average for major stocks. This means option sellers (like covered call writers) systematically collect more premium than statistical risk justifies, creating a built-in edge.

This premium exists because option buyers pay for insurance and potential outsized gains, accepting negative expected value for the possibility of extraordinary returns. As a covered call seller, you're the insurance company collecting premiums that exceed actuarial risk.

Practical Volatility Analysis

Before selling covered calls on a stock, complete this volatility assessment:

1. Check current implied volatility (IV) on at-the-money options
2. Compare to the stock's 6-month average IV (IV percentile)
3. Confirm IV exceeds 20% (below 20%, premiums are typically inadequate)
4. Verify IV rank or IV percentile above 30 (preferably above 50)
5. Compare to beta to ensure volatility doesn't indicate excessive systematic risk

This analysis takes less than two minutes using standard options platforms and dramatically improves position selection quality.

Market Capitalization Considerations

Market capitalization (total value of all outstanding shares) correlates strongly with liquidity, stability, and options availability. Different cap ranges suit different covered call strategies.

Large-Cap Stocks ($10 Billion+)

Large-cap stocks represent established, mature companies with stable operations and substantial market presence.

Advantages for covered calls:

- Exceptional liquidity in stocks and options
- Predictable price behavior with less gap risk
- Extensive research coverage and information availability
- Lower bankruptcy and severe drawdown risk
- Tight bid-ask spreads minimizing transaction costs

Disadvantages:

- Lower volatility may produce modest premiums
- Less explosive upside potential compared to smaller companies
- Already efficient pricing may limit special opportunities

Best practices: Large-caps suit conservative covered call strategies emphasizing consistency over maximum yield. Target monthly returns of 1-2% through systematic premium collection.

Mid-Cap Stocks ($2 Billion to $10 Billion)

Mid-cap stocks balance growth potential with relative stability, often representing the sweet spot for covered call income.

Advantages:

- Higher volatility than large-caps, producing better premiums
- Adequate liquidity for efficient trading
- Growth potential while maintaining reasonable risk
- Often underfollowed by institutions, creating opportunities

Disadvantages:

- More susceptible to market volatility than large-caps

- Potentially wider bid-ask spreads
- Greater gap risk on earnings or news events
- Less analyst coverage may make research more challenging

Best practices: Mid-caps support aggressive income generation with target monthly returns of 2-3%. Emphasize quality names with strong fundamentals and established market positions.

Small-Cap Stocks (Under $2 Billion)

Small-cap stocks offer higher volatility and premium potential but carry substantially greater risk.

Advantages:

- Highest option premiums relative to stock price
- Potential for significant stock appreciation alongside premium income
- Less institutional competition may create mispricings

Disadvantages:

- Liquidity challenges in stocks and especially options
- Wide bid-ask spreads erode returns
- Greater business risk and potential for severe price declines
- More susceptible to manipulation and technical factors
- Gap risk on news is severe

Best practices: Limit small-cap positions to a minor portfolio allocation (under 20%). Verify exceptional liquidity before engaging. Accept that occasional losses will be larger but offset by higher premiums during profitable periods.

Mega-Cap Stocks ($200 Billion+)

Mega-caps including Apple, Microsoft, Amazon, and Alphabet warrant special mention.

These stocks offer unparalleled liquidity and options volume, making them ideal for covered call trading despite lower volatility. Their sheer size creates options markets so active that pricing is extremely efficient and spreads are minimal.

Many traders build core portfolios around 4-6 mega-cap positions, systematically selling covered calls against large positions (500+ shares) to generate meaningful absolute income even at lower percentage yields.

Sector Stability and Economic Sensitivity

Different economic sectors exhibit varying levels of stability, cyclicality, and sensitivity to economic conditions. Understanding these sector-specific characteristics allows you to construct a covered call portfolio that performs consistently across different market environments.

Defensive Sectors: Stability Over Growth

Defensive sectors provide essential goods and services that consumers need regardless of economic conditions. These sectors exhibit lower volatility but also generate lower premiums.

Consumer Staples (food, beverages, household products): Companies like Procter & Gamble, Coca-Cola, and Walmart demonstrate remarkable stability. Demand for toothpaste, groceries, and cleaning products remains constant during recessions and expansions alike.

For covered call purposes, consumer staples offer:

- Predictable, range-bound price action ideal for systematic call selling
- Consistent dividends supplementing premium income
- Lower premiums (typically 1-1.5% monthly) due to reduced volatility
- Minimal gap risk and assignment surprises
- Reliable performance during market downturns

Strategy recommendation: Consumer staples form the conservative foundation of covered call portfolios, suitable for 30-40% of holdings for risk-averse investors.

Utilities (electricity, gas, water): Regulated utility companies like Duke Energy, NextEra Energy, and Southern Company provide essential services with government-approved pricing.

Utilities characteristics:

- Extremely stable cash flows and dividends (often yielding 3-5%)
- Very low volatility, resulting in minimal option premiums
- Interest rate sensitivity (prices decline when rates rise)
- Limited capital appreciation potential
- Ideal for investors prioritizing dividend income over option premium

Strategy recommendation: Utilities work best for retirees and conservative investors comfortable with lower total returns (8-12% annually) in exchange for high predictability.

Healthcare (pharmaceuticals, medical devices, healthcare services): The healthcare sector bridges defensive and growth characteristics. Companies like Johnson & Johnson, UnitedHealth Group, and Pfizer benefit from aging demographics and consistent demand.

Healthcare advantages for covered calls:

- Moderate volatility generating reasonable premiums (1.5-2.5% monthly)
- Stable underlying demand with some growth potential
- Many companies pay reliable dividends
- Diversification across pharmaceuticals, biotechnology, insurance, and services
- Regulatory approval events create predictable volatility spikes

Healthcare considerations:

- FDA approval decisions can cause significant price movements
- Patent cliffs threaten pharmaceutical companies as blockbuster drugs lose exclusivity
- Political and regulatory risks surrounding drug pricing and

healthcare reform

- Biotechnology subsector exhibits high volatility unsuitable for covered calls

Strategy recommendation: Focus on diversified healthcare companies and established pharmaceutical firms rather than single-product biotechnology companies. Healthcare can represent 15-25% of a covered call portfolio.

Cyclical Sectors: Higher Returns, Greater Risk

Cyclical sectors fluctuate with economic conditions, producing higher volatility and premiums but requiring more active management.

Financials (banks, insurance, asset managers): The financial sector's performance correlates strongly with interest rates, economic growth, and credit conditions. Companies like JPMorgan Chase, Bank of America, and Citigroup dominate this space.

Financial sector characteristics:

- Moderate to high volatility, particularly during economic uncertainty
- Strong premium generation (2-3% monthly during favorable conditions)
- Dividend yields typically between 2-4%
- Highly sensitive to Federal Reserve policy and interest rate changes
- Quarterly earnings reports often trigger significant price movement

Optimal covered call timing for financials:

- Rising interest rate environments generally favor banks (higher net interest margins)
- Sell calls during periods of market optimism about economic growth
- Exercise caution during credit cycle downturns or regulatory changes

- Earnings season offers elevated premiums but increased assignment risk

Strategy recommendation: Financials suit moderately aggressive covered call traders comfortable with quarterly position management. Allocate 15-20% of portfolio during favorable economic conditions.

Technology (software, semiconductors, hardware): Technology represents perhaps the most complex sector for covered calls, ranging from stable mega-caps to volatile growth stocks.

Technology subcategories:

- Established mega-caps (Microsoft, Apple, Google): Lower volatility, enormous liquidity, moderate premiums (1.5-2.5% monthly)
- Semiconductor companies (Intel, AMD, NVIDIA): Cyclical volatility, strong premiums (2-4% monthly), subject to industry cycles
- Cloud and software (Salesforce, Adobe, Oracle): Growth-oriented with moderate volatility
- Emerging technology: High volatility unsuitable for most covered call strategies

Technology sector challenges:

- Rapid innovation creates obsolescence risk
- Earnings reports frequently trigger 5-15% single-day movements
- Competitive dynamics shift quickly
- Valuation multiples contract sharply during market selloffs

Technology sector advantages:

- Highest premium potential in stable subsegments
- Strong secular growth trends support long-term stock appreciation

- Mega-caps offer unparalleled liquidity
- Many companies now pay dividends (Apple, Microsoft, Cisco)

Strategy recommendation: Focus technology exposure on mega-cap, established companies with proven business models. Avoid emerging technology and unprofitable growth stocks. Technology can represent 20-30% of aggressive covered call portfolios.

Industrials (manufacturing, transportation, aerospace): Industrial companies like Caterpillar, Boeing, Union Pacific, and 3M serve businesses and government infrastructure projects.

Industrials exhibit:

- Strong correlation with GDP growth and capital expenditure cycles
- Moderate volatility producing reasonable premiums (1.5-2.5% monthly)
- Many pay consistent dividends with long increase histories
- Sensitivity to commodity prices, particularly steel and oil
- Government spending and infrastructure investment impacts demand

Covered call considerations:

- Economic expansion phases offer optimal conditions
- Trade policy and tariffs can create sudden volatility
- Aerospace companies face regulatory and certification risks
- Transportation companies are sensitive to fuel costs

Strategy recommendation: Industrials provide portfolio diversification with moderate risk-reward characteristics, suitable for 10-15% allocation.

Consumer Discretionary (retail, automotive, entertainment): This sector includes companies selling non-essential goods and services: Amazon, Tesla, Home Depot, McDonald's, and Disney.

Consumer discretionary traits:

- High economic sensitivity (consumers cut discretionary spending during recessions)
- Wide volatility range depending on subsector
- E-commerce and omnichannel retail dominate traditional retail
- Automotive cyclicality creates boom-bust patterns
- Entertainment and travel rebound strongly during economic expansions

Premium opportunities:

- Strong premiums during economic expansions (2-3.5% monthly)
- Significant volatility around earnings and economic data releases
- Consumer confidence and employment data drive sector sentiment

Strategy recommendation: Emphasize dominant market leaders with omnichannel capabilities or unique competitive advantages. Limit to 10-15% of portfolio and reduce exposure during economic uncertainty.

Commodity-Dependent Sectors: Volatility and Opportunity

Energy (oil & gas, renewables): Energy represents one of the most volatile sectors, creating substantial premium opportunities alongside considerable risk.

Energy sector dynamics:

- Extreme sensitivity to crude oil and natural gas prices
- Geopolitical events create sudden, sharp price movements
- OPEC decisions and global demand shifts drive volatility
- Transition to renewable energy creates long-term uncertainty for fossil fuel companies
- Quarterly earnings volatility based on commodity price fluctuations

Covered call approaches for energy:

- Highest premiums available (3-5% monthly during volatile periods)
- Integrated majors (ExxonMobil, Chevron) offer more stability than exploration and production companies
- Strong dividend yields (4-6%) supplement premium income
- Consider selling calls after significant price run-ups
- Avoid small-cap energy stocks due to bankruptcy risk during price collapses

Energy sector risks:

- Commodity price crashes can trigger 30-50% stock declines
- Political and regulatory risks surrounding climate policy
- Long-term secular decline concerns for fossil fuels
- Geopolitical conflicts create unpredictable volatility

Strategy recommendation: Energy suits experienced traders comfortable with volatility and active position management. Limit to 5-10% of portfolio. Consider energy exposure as tactical opportunities rather than core holdings.

Materials (mining, chemicals, construction materials): Basic materials companies like Freeport-McMoRan, Newmont Mining, and Dow Chemical extract and process raw materials.

Materials sector characteristics:

- Strong correlation with global economic growth, particularly Chinese demand
- Cyclical volatility based on commodity price cycles
- Moderate to high option premiums (2-3.5% monthly)
- Some companies pay dividends, though less consistently than other sectors
- Environmental regulations increasingly impact operations

Covered call timing:

- Best opportunities during commodity bull markets and economic expansions
- Sell calls when commodity prices approach cyclical highs
- Exercise caution during global economic slowdowns
- Chinese economic policy significantly impacts demand

Strategy recommendation: Materials work as tactical positions during favorable commodity cycles. Limit to 5-10% of core portfolio.

Real Estate Investment Trusts (REITs): Special Considerations

REITs own and operate income-producing real estate: office buildings, apartments, shopping centers, warehouses, and specialized properties like data centers and cell towers.

REIT characteristics for covered calls:

- Required to distribute 90% of taxable income as dividends (yields typically 3-6%)
- Interest rate sensitivity (prices decline when rates rise as alternative investments become more attractive)
- Moderate volatility suitable for covered calls (1.5-2.5% monthly premiums)
- Different REIT types exhibit different stability levels
- Tax treatment differs from regular stocks (dividends taxed as ordinary income)

REIT subcategories:

- Industrial/logistics REITs (warehouse, distribution): Benefit from e-commerce growth, relatively stable
- Residential REITs (apartments): Stable demand, moderate growth
- Retail REITs (shopping centers, malls): Declining due to e-commerce, higher risk
- Office REITs: Post-pandemic uncertainty about office space

demand
- Specialized REITs (data centers, cell towers, healthcare facilities): Higher growth, more stable

Covered call strategy for REITs:

- Combine high dividend yields with modest option premiums for total returns of 12-18%
- Focus on specialized and industrial REITs with favorable secular trends
- Avoid retail and potentially office REITs facing structural challenges
- Monitor Federal Reserve policy closely as rate changes significantly impact REIT prices
- Sell calls during periods of low interest rates and economic optimism

Strategy recommendation: REITs provide excellent income characteristics for covered calls, suitable for 10-20% allocation in income-focused portfolios.

Sector Diversification Strategy

Construct a balanced covered call portfolio across sectors to manage risk and optimize returns under varying economic conditions:

Conservative portfolio allocation:

- Consumer Staples: 25%
- Healthcare: 20%
- Utilities: 15%
- Financials: 15%
- Technology (mega-caps): 15%
- REITs: 10%

This conservative allocation emphasizes stability and predictability with total return targets of 12-18% annually.

Moderate portfolio allocation:

- Technology (mega-caps): 25%
- Healthcare: 20%
- Financials: 20%
- Consumer Discretionary: 15%
- Industrials: 10%
- REITs: 10%

This moderate approach balances growth potential with stability, targeting 18-25% annual returns.

Aggressive portfolio allocation:

- Technology: 30%
- Financials: 20%
- Consumer Discretionary: 15%
- Healthcare: 15%
- Energy: 10%
- Materials: 10%

This aggressive strategy maximizes premium income with higher volatility and active management requirements, targeting 25-35% annual returns in favorable conditions but accepting larger drawdowns.

Economic Cycle Positioning

Adjust sector weights based on economic cycle stage:

Early expansion (recovery from recession):

- Overweight: Financials, Consumer Discretionary, Technology
- Underweight: Utilities, Consumer Staples, Healthcare
- Rationale: Cyclical sectors outperform as economic growth accelerates

Mid-expansion (sustained growth):

- Balanced allocation across sectors
- Emphasize quality companies with sustainable competitive advantages

- Premium income at optimal levels across most sectors

Late expansion (economy at peak):

- Begin reducing cyclical exposure
- Increase defensive sectors (Healthcare, Consumer Staples, Utilities)
- Raise cash levels or reduce overall covered call positions

Recession/contraction:

- Overweight: Utilities, Consumer Staples, Healthcare
- Underweight or eliminate: Energy, Materials, Consumer Discretionary
- Focus on capital preservation over maximum premium generation
- Consider reducing covered call activity or switching to cash-secured puts

Sector Rotation and Active Management

Successful covered call investing requires periodic portfolio rebalancing as sector fundamentals evolve:

Quarterly review process:

1. Assess economic indicators (GDP growth, unemployment, inflation, interest rates)
2. Evaluate sector-specific trends and earnings patterns
3. Compare current implied volatility to historical norms for each sector
4. Identify sectors offering elevated premiums relative to risk
5. Rebalance toward attractively priced sectors
6. Reduce exposure to sectors facing headwinds

This active sector management approach enhances returns by 3-7% annually compared to static allocation strategies while managing downside risk during adverse conditions.

Conclusion

Understanding sector characteristics and economic sensitivity enables you to construct a covered call portfolio resilient to different market environments. Defensive sectors provide stability and consistent returns during uncertainty, while cyclical sectors maximize premium income during favorable conditions. By actively managing sector exposure based on economic cycles and relative opportunity, you can optimize covered call returns while controlling portfolio-wide risk.

The next chapters will build upon this foundation by exploring fundamental and technical analysis techniques specific to covered call stock selection, allowing you to identify the highest-quality candidates within each sector.

Chapter 7:

Fundamental Analysis for Covered Call Stocks

Fundamental analysis examines a company's financial health, business model, and competitive position to determine its intrinsic value and long-term viability. For covered call traders, fundamental analysis serves a specific purpose: identifying stable, financially sound companies that can sustain their stock prices while generating consistent option premiums.

Unlike growth investors seeking the next multi-bagger or value investors hunting undervalued opportunities, covered call traders prioritize stability, predictability, and income generation. This chapter provides a framework for evaluating companies through the lens of covered call suitability.

Evaluating Financial Health and Stability

Financial health represents the foundation of any covered call candidate. A financially unstable company may offer attractive premiums due to elevated volatility, but the risk of permanent capital loss overwhelms any premium income advantage.

Balance Sheet Strength: The Foundation of Stability

A strong balance sheet provides the financial cushion companies need to weather economic downturns, competitive challenges, and industry disruption. For covered call purposes, prioritize companies with robust balance sheets exhibiting these characteristics:

Current Ratio measures short-term liquidity by dividing current assets by current liabilities. A ratio above 1.5 indicates the company can comfortably meet short-term obligations. Ratios below 1.0 signal potential liquidity problems that could trigger stock price volatility or decline.

Example analysis:

- Company A: Current assets $500M, current liabilities $250M = Current ratio 2.0 (excellent)
- Company B: Current assets $300M, current liabilities $350M

= Current ratio 0.86 (concerning)

Company A demonstrates superior financial flexibility, making it the safer covered call candidate despite potentially lower premiums due to reduced risk.

Quick Ratio (Acid-Test Ratio) provides a more conservative liquidity measure by excluding inventory from current assets. Calculate by dividing cash plus marketable securities plus receivables by current liabilities. Target quick ratios above 1.0 for covered call candidates.

Companies with quick ratios below 0.8 may face difficulties converting assets to cash quickly, increasing bankruptcy risk during stress periods. This matters for covered call traders because sudden financial distress can trigger catastrophic stock declines that overwhelm months or years of premium collection.

Working Capital Analysis

Working capital (current assets minus current liabilities) represents the capital available for day-to-day operations. Positive working capital indicates operational flexibility, while negative working capital suggests the company operates on thin margins with limited financial cushion.

For covered call candidates, examine working capital trends over three to five years:

- Consistently positive and growing working capital: Excellent sign of financial health
- Fluctuating but generally positive: Acceptable for most covered call strategies
- Declining toward zero or negative: Warning sign requiring deeper investigation
- Persistently negative: Avoid unless business model specifically supports it (some retailers successfully operate with negative working capital)

Equity Position and Book Value

Total shareholder equity represents the company's net worth after subtracting all liabilities from assets. Growing shareholder equity over time indicates profitable operations and sound financial management.

Book value per share equals total shareholder equity divided by shares outstanding. Compare book value growth to stock price appreciation:

- Book value growing faster than stock price: Potentially undervalued, good covered call candidate
- Book value and stock price growing similarly: Fair valuation, acceptable candidate
- Stock price growing much faster than book value: Potential overvaluation, exercise caution

Negative shareholder equity warrants extreme caution and typically disqualifies companies from covered call consideration, as it indicates the company owes more than it owns.

Return on Equity (ROE) and Return on Assets (ROA)

Return on Equity measures how efficiently a company generates profits from shareholder investments. Calculate ROE by dividing net income by shareholder equity. Target ROE above 15% for covered call candidates, with consistent or improving trends over multiple years.

High ROE (above 20%) can indicate either exceptional business quality or excessive leverage. Verify that high ROE stems from operational excellence rather than debt-fueled financial engineering.

Return on Assets measures how efficiently a company uses its total assets to generate profits. Calculate ROA by dividing net income by total assets. ROA above 5% generally indicates effective asset utilization, though standards vary significantly by industry.

Compare both metrics across competitors within the same sector. A company with ROE of 18% might appear strong in isolation but weak if sector peers average 25% ROE.

Case Study: Evaluating Financial Health

Consider two potential covered call candidates in the consumer goods sector:

Company X (Premium Consumer Goods):

- Current Ratio: 2.3
- Quick Ratio: 1.4
- Working Capital: $2.1B (growing 8% annually)
- Shareholder Equity: $15B (growing 6% annually)
- ROE: 22%
- ROA: 9%

Company Y (Discount Retailer):

- Current Ratio: 0.9
- Quick Ratio: 0.3
- Working Capital: -$500M (increasingly negative)
- Shareholder Equity: $8B (flat over 3 years)
- ROE: 12%
- ROA: 4%

Analysis: Company X demonstrates superior financial health across all metrics, making it the clear choice for conservative covered call strategies. Company Y's weak liquidity ratios and negative working capital trend signal financial stress that could trigger unexpected price declines.

However, Company Y might still suit aggressive traders if research reveals the negative working capital reflects an efficient, high-turnover business model (common among successful retailers) rather than financial distress. Always contextualize financial metrics within industry norms.

Analyzing Dividend History and Payout Ratios

Dividend analysis serves dual purposes for covered call traders: identifying additional income streams and confirming financial stability. Companies maintaining consistent dividends through various economic cycles demonstrate financial strength and management commitment to shareholders.

Dividend Growth History: The Ultimate Stability Indicator

Dividend aristocrats—companies increasing dividends for 25+ consecutive years—represent the gold standard for covered call investing. The ability to increase dividends through multiple recessions, market crashes, and industry disruptions signals exceptional business resilience.

Dividend achievers (10+ years of increases) also provide excellent stability, though with slightly less proven resilience than aristocrats.

When evaluating dividend history, examine:

Years of consecutive increases: Longer histories indicate greater stability and shareholder commitment. Target companies with at least five years of increases, preferably ten or more.

Dividend growth rate: Annual increases should at least match inflation (2-3%) and ideally exceed it (4-7%). Companies raising dividends 10%+ annually may be unsustainable unless earnings growth supports these increases.

Dividend maintenance during recessions: Check whether dividends continued during 2008-2009 financial crisis, 2020 pandemic, and relevant industry downturns. Companies that maintained or increased dividends during crises demonstrate true financial strength.

Dividend Yield Analysis

Dividend yield equals annual dividend divided by stock price, expressed as a percentage. For covered call purposes, optimal yields typically range from 2% to 5%.

Low yields (under 2%): Suggests company prioritizes growth over income or market values the stock at premium prices. Lower yields produce less supplementary income but often indicate stronger growth prospects.

Moderate yields (2-5%): The sweet spot for covered call strategies, providing meaningful income supplementation without excessive risk signals.

High yields (5-7%): Potentially attractive but require verification that elevated yields reflect intentional income focus rather than distressed stock prices.

Very high yields (above 7%): Red flag warranting extreme caution. Market may be pricing in dividend cut risk. Investigate thoroughly or avoid.

Warning signs in high-yield stocks:

- Recent significant stock price decline pushing yield artificially high
- Payout ratio exceeding 80% (discussed below)
- Declining or volatile earnings
- High debt levels relative to industry peers
- Recent management changes or strategic difficulties

Payout Ratio: Sustainability Assessment

Payout ratio measures what percentage of earnings a company distributes as dividends. Calculate by dividing annual dividend per share by earnings per share (EPS).

Payout ratio interpretation:

- 0-30%: Very conservative, substantial room for dividend growth
- 30-50%: Healthy, sustainable dividends with growth potential
- 50-70%: Moderate, sustainable if earnings remain stable
- 70-80%: Elevated, vulnerable to cuts if earnings decline
- 80-100%+: Unsustainable, high dividend cut risk

Industry context matters significantly. Utilities and REITs commonly operate with 70-90% payout ratios due to stable cash flows and regulatory structures, while technology and industrial companies typically maintain lower ratios (30-50%) to fund growth investments.

For covered call candidates, prefer payout ratios between 40% and 70%, ensuring dividends are sustainable while management retains sufficient capital for business needs.

Free Cash Flow Payout Ratio

Some analysts prefer measuring dividends against free cash flow rather than earnings, particularly for capital-intensive businesses where depreciation significantly affects reported earnings.

Free cash flow payout ratio equals dividends divided by free cash flow (operating cash flow minus capital expenditures). This metric reveals whether dividends come from genuine cash generation or are financially engineered through accounting.

Target free cash flow payout ratios below 75% for most covered call candidates. Ratios exceeding 100% indicate companies paying dividends with borrowed money or by liquidating assets—an unsustainable practice signaling future dividend cuts.

Dividend Reinvestment Strategies

For covered call portfolios, consider whether to reinvest dividends or combine them with option premiums for cash income:

Reinvestment strategy: Automatically reinvest dividends to purchase additional shares, increasing position size and future covered call income. This compounds returns over time but requires careful management to ensure share counts remain in 100-share increments for options.

Cash income strategy: Collect both dividends and premiums as cash income for living expenses or deployment into new covered call positions. This approach suits investors seeking current income over maximum compounding.

Hybrid approach: Reinvest dividends while taking option premiums as cash, or vice versa, creating balanced growth and income.

Earnings Consistency and Predictability

Consistent, predictable earnings reduce downside risk and create ideal conditions for covered call strategies. Companies with stable earnings rarely experience dramatic price declines, while erratic earnings create volatility that can overwhelm premium income.

Earnings Growth Patterns

Analyze five to ten years of annual earnings to identify growth patterns:

Steady growth (5-10% annually): Ideal for covered calls, indicating healthy business expansion without excessive volatility or unsustainable expectations.

Moderate growth (3-5% annually): Acceptable, particularly for mature companies in stable industries. Provides adequate growth to offset inflation while maintaining stability.

High growth (15%+ annually): Potentially attractive but verify sustainability. Unsustainable growth rates eventually disappoint, triggering significant price corrections.

Flat earnings (0-3% growth): Acceptable only if dividends are strong and business model is defensive. Extended periods of flat earnings may signal competitive challenges.

Declining earnings: Generally disqualifies companies from covered call consideration unless the decline is temporary and well-understood (restructuring, one-time charges).

Quarterly Earnings Volatility

Beyond annual trends, examine quarterly earnings patterns for volatility and seasonality:

Low quarterly volatility (earnings vary less than 10% quarter-over-quarter): Excellent for covered calls, creates predictable stock price behavior.

Seasonal patterns: Many businesses exhibit predictable seasonal earnings (retail during holidays, construction in summer). Understanding seasonality allows strategic covered call timing.

High quarterly volatility (earnings swing 20%+ regularly): Creates uncertainty and assignment risk around earnings announcements. Either avoid or implement specialized earnings strategies.

Earnings Surprise History

Track how often companies beat, meet, or miss analyst earnings estimates:

Consistent beats: Positive but investigate whether company sandbagging estimates to manufacture beats. Sustainable beats stem from operational excellence, not estimate manipulation.

Consistent meets: Excellent sign of management transparency and business predictability.

Frequent misses: Red flag indicating either operational challenges or poor management guidance. Avoid for covered call strategies.

For covered call purposes, companies consistently meeting estimates are preferable to companies frequently surprising either positively or negatively. Predictability trumps excitement.

Earnings Quality Assessment

Not all earnings are created equal. High-quality earnings come from core business operations and convert efficiently to cash, while low-quality earnings result from one-time gains, accounting adjustments, or non-cash items.

Evaluate earnings quality by examining:

Operating income trends: Growing operating income from core business indicates high-quality earnings. Declining operating income masked by non-operating gains signals low quality.

Cash flow conversion: Compare net income to operating cash flow. Companies converting 80-100%+ of earnings to cash demonstrate high quality. Conversion below 60% raises questions about earnings sustainability.

One-time items: Exclude gains from asset sales, discontinued operations, and extraordinary items when analyzing earnings trends. Adjust for one-time charges to reveal underlying business performance.

Revenue quality: Earnings growth should follow revenue growth. Earnings growing faster than revenue for extended periods may indicate unsustainable cost-cutting or accounting manipulation.

Earnings Announcement Strategies

Earnings announcements create elevated implied volatility and option premiums but also increased risk. Three approaches for managing covered calls through earnings:

Close positions before earnings: Buy back covered calls 3-5 days before earnings when implied volatility spikes premium values. This avoids assignment risk from unexpected moves but sacrifices the elevated premium.

Hold through earnings: Accept assignment risk to capture peak premiums. Suitable only for high-conviction positions where you're comfortable selling at the strike price.

Avoid entirely: Establish covered call positions only on stocks with earnings announcements outside your holding period. For 30-day covered calls, verify earnings won't occur during the option's life.

Debt Levels and Cash Flow Assessment

Debt magnifies both returns and risks. Moderate debt can enhance shareholder returns through leverage, while excessive debt creates bankruptcy risk and financial inflexibility that threatens covered call strategies.

Debt-to-Equity Ratio Analysis

Debt-to-equity ratio measures financial leverage by dividing total liabilities by shareholder equity. This fundamental metric reveals how aggressively a company employs debt financing.

Interpretation guidelines:

- 0-0.3: Conservative, minimal debt, lower risk
- 0.3-0.7: Moderate, balanced capital structure
- 0.7-1.5: Elevated, requires industry context
- 1.5-3.0: High, significant leverage risk
- Above 3.0: Extreme, generally unsuitable for covered calls

Industry norms vary dramatically. Capital-light businesses (software, services) should maintain ratios below 0.5, while capital-intensive industries (utilities, telecommunications, industrials) commonly operate with ratios of 1.0-2.0.

For covered call candidates, prefer debt-to-equity ratios in the bottom third of industry peers, ensuring financial flexibility during downturns.

Interest Coverage Ratio

Interest coverage ratio measures how easily a company can pay interest expenses from operating income. Calculate by dividing EBIT (earnings before interest and taxes) by interest expense.

Minimum thresholds:

- Above 5x: Comfortable coverage, minimal risk
- 3-5x: Adequate coverage, acceptable

- 2-3x: Marginal coverage, vulnerable to earnings declines
- Below 2x: Dangerous, high default risk

Companies with interest coverage below 3x face significant financial pressure that can trigger dividend cuts, restructurings, or worse. Such companies rarely make suitable covered call candidates despite potentially attractive premiums.

Debt Maturity Profile

Beyond total debt levels, examine when debt obligations come due:

Short-term debt (due within one year): High levels create refinancing risk, particularly during periods of rising interest rates or credit market stress.

Long-term debt: More manageable as companies have extended periods to generate cash for repayment or refinancing opportunities.

Balanced maturity profile: Debt maturities spread across multiple years rather than concentrated in single years. This reduces refinancing risk and financial pressure.

Warning sign: Large debt maturities occurring within 12-24 months combined with weak cash generation or deteriorating credit conditions.

Credit Ratings and Borrowing Costs

Credit ratings from agencies like Moody's, S&P, and Fitch provide independent assessments of default risk:

Investment-grade ratings (BBB-/Baa3 or higher): Indicates financial stability and access to capital markets at reasonable costs. Preferred for covered call candidates.

High-yield ratings (BB+/Ba1 or lower): Signals elevated default risk and higher borrowing costs. Generally unsuitable for conservative covered call strategies.

Positive outlook or recent upgrades: Indicates improving financial condition.

Negative outlook or recent downgrades: Warning sign of deteriorating financial health.

Cash Flow Analysis: The Ultimate Test

Cash flow represents the actual cash a business generates, unlike earnings which can be manipulated through accounting choices. Strong cash flow generation distinguishes truly healthy companies from those with artificial earnings.

Operating Cash Flow

Operating cash flow (OCF) measures cash generated from core business operations, excluding financing and investing activities. Strong OCF enables dividend payments, debt reduction, and business investment without relying on external financing.

For covered call candidates, verify:

- Positive operating cash flow in all recent years
- OCF growing at similar rates to revenue and earnings
- OCF consistently exceeds net income (indicating high earnings quality)
- OCF covers both dividends and necessary capital expenditures

Free Cash Flow: The Gold Standard

Free cash flow equals operating cash flow minus capital expenditures required to maintain business operations. FCF represents truly discretionary cash available for dividends, debt reduction, share buybacks, or growth investments.

Positive, growing free cash flow is the single most important financial metric for covered call candidates. Companies consistently generating strong FCF can sustain dividends, weather downturns, and avoid financial distress.

Calculate free cash flow yield by dividing annual free cash flow per share by stock price. FCF yields above 5% indicate strong cash generation relative to valuation, providing cushion for dividend payments and creating margin of safety.

Cash Conversion Cycle

The cash conversion cycle measures how quickly a company converts inventory and receivables into cash:

Days inventory outstanding + Days sales outstanding - Days payables outstanding = Cash conversion cycle

Shorter cycles indicate efficient operations requiring less working capital. Longer cycles tie up capital and may signal operational inefficiencies.

For covered call purposes, compare cycles across industry peers rather than absolute standards. Improving cycles over time signal operational excellence, while deteriorating cycles warn of competitive pressure or management execution problems.

Competitive Position and Market Share

A company's competitive position determines its ability to maintain profitability, grow earnings, and sustain stock prices over time. Strong competitive positions create pricing power and customer loyalty that protect against industry downturns.

Market Share Analysis

Market leadership in growing industries creates tremendous competitive advantages. Companies with dominant market share (#1 or #2 in their primary markets) demonstrate superior execution and typically generate more stable financial results.

Evaluate market share trends:

- Growing market share: Indicates competitive strength and effective strategy execution
- Stable market share in growing markets: Acceptable, company growing with the industry
- Stable market share in mature markets: Requires verification that company isn't sacrificing share for profitability
- Declining market share: Warning sign of competitive challenges or strategic missteps

Market share matters more in consolidated industries with few competitors than in fragmented industries with hundreds of players.

Competitive Advantages (Economic Moats)

Economic moats represent sustainable competitive advantages that protect profitability from competition. Warren Buffett popularized this concept as the defining characteristic of superior businesses.

Five primary moat sources:

Network effects: Products or services become more valuable as more people use them (Facebook, Visa, American Express). Network effects create powerful switching costs and competitive barriers.

Brand strength: Powerful brands command premium pricing and customer loyalty (Coca-Cola, Nike, Apple). Brand moats are particularly strong in consumer-facing businesses.

Cost advantages: Structural cost advantages through scale, proprietary technology, or favorable locations enable competitors to be undercut on price (Walmart, Costco). Cost advantages are particularly valuable in commodity-like industries.

Switching costs: High costs of changing vendors lock in customers (enterprise software, bank relationships, specialized equipment). Switching costs create recurring revenue and predictable cash flows.

Regulatory advantages: Licenses, patents, or regulatory barriers limit competition (utilities, pharmaceutical patents, casino licenses). Regulatory moats can be very durable but face political and legal risks.

For covered call candidates, prefer companies with at least one identifiable moat source. Multiple moats provide even greater stability and predictability.

Competitive Intensity Analysis

Assess the competitive dynamics within the company's primary industries using Michael Porter's Five Forces framework:

Threat of new entrants: High barriers to entry (capital requirements, regulation, technology, brand) protect existing players. Low barriers invite new competition that pressures margins.

Bargaining power of suppliers: When suppliers are concentrated and powerful, they can extract pricing and terms that squeeze profitability. Diversified supplier bases and commoditized inputs protect margins.

Bargaining power of customers: Large, concentrated customers can demand lower prices and better terms. Fragmented customer bases with limited individual power support stable pricing.

Threat of substitutes: Products or services that can easily be replaced face pricing pressure. Unique offerings with few substitutes enjoy pricing power.

Competitive rivalry: Industries with many competitors, slow growth, high fixed costs, or commodity products experience intense rivalry that pressures profitability.

Industries with favorable competitive structures (limited rivalry, weak substitutes, high barriers) produce more stable earnings and better covered call candidates.

Case Study: Competitive Position Evaluation

Compare two companies in adjacent markets:

Company A (Cloud Software Provider):

- Market share: #1 in niche with 42% share (growing from 38% three years ago)
- Economic moats: High switching costs, network effects
- Competitive intensity: Moderate, several capable competitors but high barriers to entry
- Pricing power: Strong, successfully implementing 5-7% annual price increases
- Customer concentration: Top 10 customers represent 18% of revenue

Company B (Consumer Electronics Retailer):

- Market share: #3 with 11% share (declining from 15% three years ago)
- Economic moats: Minimal, some brand recognition but easily substitutable
- Competitive intensity: Extreme, facing both traditional and online competition
- Pricing power: Weak, forced to match competitor pricing
- Customer concentration: Highly fragmented, no meaningful concentration risk

Analysis: Company A demonstrates vastly superior competitive position with identifiable moats, growing market share, and pricing power. Company B faces secular headwinds and intense competition.

For covered call purposes, Company A offers stability and predictability while Company B's declining competitive position creates excessive downside risk.

Management Quality and Corporate Governance

Management quality determines whether good businesses translate into good investments. Superior management teams allocate capital wisely, execute strategies effectively, and maintain shareholder focus. Poor management destroys value even in favorable industries.

Capital Allocation Track Record

Capital allocation—how management deploys shareholder capital—represents the most important management function. Evaluate historical decisions across five primary uses of capital:

Reinvestment in the business: Most valuable when companies can deploy capital at high returns on investment (15%+ ROI). Question reinvestment when returns are mediocre or declining.

Dividend payments: Demonstrates shareholder commitment and financial confidence. Consistent, growing dividends signal management discipline.

Share buybacks: Value-creating when companies repurchase shares at reasonable valuations. Value-destroying when companies buy shares at inflated prices to offset stock-based compensation or meet earnings-per-share targets.

Debt reduction: Valuable when debt levels are excessive or interest costs are high. Less urgent when debt is moderate and borrowing costs are low.

Acquisitions: The most challenging capital allocation decision. Successful acquisitions create genuine synergies and shareholder value. Failed acquisitions destroy billions through overpayment and poor integration.

For covered call candidates, prefer management teams with disciplined capital allocation histories: sensible reinvestment, consistent dividends, opportunistic buybacks, and selective acquisitions at reasonable prices.

Management Tenure and Stability

Leadership stability provides continuity and long-term strategic thinking:

Long-tenured CEOs (5+ years): Understand the business deeply and have established track records for evaluation. Very long tenures (15+ years) can become problematic if management becomes entrenched or resistant to change.

Recent CEO transitions: Create uncertainty about strategy and execution. Prefer waiting 12-18 months after transitions to evaluate new leadership before initiating covered call positions.

Frequent management turnover: Red flag indicating board dysfunction, strategic confusion, or operational challenges. Companies churning through executives rarely make suitable covered call candidates.

Executive compensation alignment: Review whether executives are compensated primarily through long-term stock incentives (good alignment) or excessive cash bonuses and short-term metrics (poor alignment).

Insider Ownership and Transactions

Insider ownership aligns management interests with shareholders. Directors and executives with significant personal investments make decisions with greater care and long-term focus.

Meaningful insider ownership (5%+ of company by executives and directors): Positive signal of management confidence and alignment.

Minimal insider ownership (less than 1%): Suggests management treats role as employment rather than ownership. Less alignment with shareholders.

Insider buying: Management purchasing shares in the open market signals confidence in business prospects.

Insider selling: Regular, small sales for diversification are normal. Large, unusual selling by multiple insiders simultaneously may indicate concerns about near-term prospects.

Corporate Governance Standards

Strong governance practices protect shareholders from management excess and ensure accountability:

Independent board composition: Majority of directors should be independent (not executives or related parties). Fully independent audit, compensation, and nominating committees are essential.

Reasonable executive compensation: Total CEO compensation should be reasonable relative to company size and performance. Be cautious of CEOs earning 500x+ median employee compensation without corresponding superior performance.

Shareholder-friendly policies: Annual director elections, majority voting standards, and reasonable shareholder proposal processes demonstrate respect for shareholders.

Audit quality: Work with reputable auditing firms and maintain clean audit opinions. Frequent auditor changes or qualified opinions raise red flags.

Transparent communication: Regular, detailed investor communications including earnings calls, annual reports, and investor presentations build trust and reduce information asymmetry.

Red Flags Warranting Avoidance

Certain management and governance issues should disqualify companies from covered call consideration:

- Accounting irregularities, restatements, or SEC investigations
- Related-party transactions enriching management at shareholder expense
- History of overpromising and underdelivering on strategic initiatives
- Excessive executive compensation unrelated to performance
- Hostile board-management relationships or activist investor campaigns
- Serial acquisitions at inflated prices followed by write-downs
- Repeated dividend cuts or suspensions outside of genuine crises
- Lack of transparency or irregular communication patterns

Evaluating Management Through the Covered Call Lens

For covered call purposes, management quality primarily matters for its impact on business stability and predictability:

Ideal management characteristics:

- Conservative financial policies avoiding excessive leverage
- Consistent dividend growth demonstrating financial discipline
- Transparent, realistic guidance that is reliably met
- Long-term strategic focus over short-term earnings manipulation
- Capital allocation emphasizing returns and shareholder value
- Operational excellence producing consistent earnings growth

Management traits that create covered call concerns:

- Aggressive financial engineering and leverage
- Inconsistent or suspended dividends
- Frequent strategic pivots and acquisitions
- Unrealistic guidance followed by disappointments
- Short-term focus sacrificing long-term value
- Poor capital allocation destroying shareholder value

Synthesis: Building a Fundamental Analysis Framework

Combine all fundamental factors into a systematic evaluation process for covered call candidates:

Tier 1 Requirements (Must Pass All):

- Positive free cash flow in last three years
- Debt-to-equity ratio in bottom 50% of industry peers
- Current ratio above 1.3
- Positive shareholder equity
- No accounting irregularities or governance red flags

Tier 2 Preferences (Pass Most):

- ROE above 15% and stable or improving
- Dividend history of 5+ years with no cuts
- Payout ratio between 40-70%
- Earnings growing 5-10% annually with low volatility

- Market share #1, #2, or #3 with stable or growing trends
- Identifiable competitive advantages
- Management tenure over 3 years with positive track record

Tier 3 Enhancements (Nice to Have):

- Dividend aristocrat or achiever status
- Investment-grade credit rating
- FCF yield above 5%
- Interest coverage above 5x
- Multiple economic moats
- Insider ownership above 5%
- Best-in-class corporate governance

Companies meeting all Tier 1 requirements and most Tier 2 preferences make excellent covered call candidates. Tier 3 enhancements further improve quality but aren't essential.

This systematic approach ensures you select financially sound companies capable of sustaining stock prices and supporting consistent covered call income generation.

Chapter 8:

Technical Analysis Tools and Indicators

While fundamental analysis identifies financially sound companies suitable for covered call strategies, technical analysis determines optimal entry points, exit strategies, and position timing. Technical indicators help you identify when to establish positions, which strike prices to select, and when to close or roll covered calls for maximum profitability.

This chapter focuses on practical technical analysis specifically tailored for covered call trading rather than attempting to predict short-term price movements. The goal is enhancing consistency and optimizing premium collection through strategic timing.

Price Patterns and Trend Analysis

Price patterns reveal the psychology and behavior of market participants. Recognizing these patterns helps covered call traders identify optimal entry points and avoid establishing positions at disadvantageous times.

Trend Identification: The Foundation

Trends represent the overall direction of price movement over time. Identifying the prevailing trend is the first step in technical analysis:

Uptrends consist of higher highs and higher lows, indicating demand exceeds supply and buyers control price direction. For covered call traders, uptrends present a dilemma: attractive for capital appreciation but risk of missing gains through assignment.

Covered call strategy in uptrends:

- Select out-of-the-money strikes (3-7% above current price) to participate in appreciation
- Consider shorter expirations (14-21 days) to roll up strike prices as stock rises
- Accept lower premium yields to preserve upside participation
- Monitor trend strength to avoid selling calls near breakout levels

Downtrends consist of lower highs and lower lows, indicating supply exceeds demand and sellers control price direction. Downtrends are generally unsuitable for initiating covered call positions due to capital loss risk.

Exception: If you already own shares at higher prices and believe the downtrend will stabilize, selling at-the-money or slightly in-the-money calls can generate income to offset losses.

Sideways trends (consolidation) occur when prices oscillate within a defined range without clear directional bias. These represent ideal conditions for covered call trading.

Covered call strategy in sideways trends:

- Sell at-the-money or slightly out-of-the-money calls to maximize premium
- Target strikes at or near resistance levels (discussed below)
- Use standard 30-45 day expirations
- Systematically roll positions each expiration to capture consistent income

Chart Timeframes for Covered Call Analysis

Different timeframes provide different insights:

Weekly and monthly charts: Reveal long-term trends and major support/resistance levels. Use these to confirm the stock trades in appropriate ranges for covered call strategies.

Daily charts: Primary timeframe for covered call analysis. Daily charts show sufficient detail for strike selection while filtering short-term noise.

4-hour and hourly charts: Useful for fine-tuning entry points on specific days but unnecessary for most covered call traders. Covered calls are not day trades.

Pattern Recognition for Covered Call Timing

Several price patterns signal optimal covered call opportunities:

Consolidation Rectangles

Rectangular patterns form when prices trade between parallel support and resistance lines for extended periods. These create ideal covered call conditions as prices oscillate predictably within defined bounds.

Strategy: When price trades near the top of the range (approaching resistance), sell calls with strikes at or slightly above the resistance level. High probability the stock will remain below resistance, allowing you to capture full premium.

Example: Stock consolidating between $48-$52 for three months. When price reaches $51.50, sell $52 or $52.50 calls. Historical pattern suggests low probability of breaking above $52 during your option period.

Ascending and Descending Triangles

Ascending triangles form when prices create higher lows while resistance remains constant, indicating accumulation before potential breakout. Descending triangles show lower highs with consistent support.

For covered calls:

- In ascending triangles, avoid selling calls at the resistance level as breakout probability is elevated. Either wait for breakout confirmation or sell calls well above resistance.
- In descending triangles, avoid initiating new covered call positions as downside breakout risk threatens capital

Rounding Bottoms and Rounding Tops

Rounding bottoms (cup patterns) indicate gradual accumulation and trend reversal from downtrend to uptrend. Wait for pattern completion and new uptrend confirmation before initiating covered calls.

Rounding tops signal potential trend reversals from uptrend to downtrend. If you notice your covered call stock forming a rounding top, consider closing the position rather than continuing to sell calls into potential decline.

Flags and Pennants

These continuation patterns appear as brief consolidations within strong trends. Flags and pennants in uptrends suggest the trend will resume after consolidation, making them attractive for covered call entry.

Strategy: Enter covered call positions early in the consolidation with out-of-the-money strikes anticipating eventual breakout. The consolidation period generates premium income while waiting for the next leg higher.

Support and Resistance Levels

Support and resistance levels represent price zones where buying or selling pressure historically concentrated, causing prices to reverse or stall. These levels are perhaps the most valuable technical concepts for covered call traders.

Understanding Support and Resistance

Support levels form where buying interest previously prevented further price declines. Price approaching support often finds buyers willing to accumulate shares, creating a floor.

Resistance levels form where selling pressure previously prevented further price advances. Price approaching resistance often encounters sellers taking profits or institutions distributing shares, creating a ceiling.

These levels exist because market participants remember previous price action and make decisions based on those memories. If a stock repeatedly bounced at $45 in the past, traders will anticipate another bounce and place buy orders near $45, creating a self-fulfilling prophecy.

Identifying Key Support and Resistance

Locate support and resistance by examining price history over six months to two years:

Major levels: Prices that reversed or consolidated multiple times (3+ occurrences) with significant volume. These create the strongest support/resistance.

Minor levels: Prices that showed single or double reversals. Less reliable but still meaningful.

Psychological levels: Round numbers ($50, $100,

***

Technical Analysis Tools and Indicators (Continued)

Support and Resistance Levels (Continued)

Psychological levels: Round numbers ($50, $100, $150) often act as support or resistance due to human psychology and concentration of limit orders.

Strategic Application for Covered Calls

Support and resistance levels directly inform strike price selection:

When establishing covered calls near support:

- Stock trading at or approaching support increases probability of bounce or stabilization
- Ideal time to initiate positions as downside risk is limited by support
- Select strikes at or near resistance levels to maximize assignment protection

When stock trades near resistance:

- Excellent time to sell calls as price is unlikely to exceed resistance
- Sell strikes at or slightly above resistance for optimal risk-reward
- If resistance breaks, prepare to adjust or accept assignment

Example application:

- Stock ABC shows strong support at $47 and resistance at $53
- Stock currently at $51 (near resistance)
- Sell $53 or $54 strikes for maximum premium with low assignment risk
- If stock falls to $47 area, consider closing covered calls for profit and waiting to reestablish higher or holding for expiration

Support Becoming Resistance and Vice Versa

A critical principle: when support breaks, it often becomes resistance. When resistance breaks, it often becomes support. This phenomenon, called "role reversal," occurs because market participants who bought at support become sellers at that level after it breaks (trying to minimize losses), while those who sold at resistance become buyers when it breaks (covering short positions).

For covered call traders, monitor broken support or resistance levels as new reference points for future decisions.

Volume Confirmation

Support and resistance gain validity when accompanied by elevated volume:

- High volume at support/resistance suggests strong conviction and more reliable levels
- Low volume at support/resistance indicates weak levels likely to break
- Breakouts above resistance on low volume often fail (false breakouts)
- Always confirm support/resistance significance by examining volume at those price levels

Moving Averages for Covered Call Timing

Moving averages smooth price data to reveal underlying trends and generate actionable signals for covered call position management. Different moving average periods provide different insights and applications.

Simple Moving Averages (SMA)

Simple moving averages calculate the arithmetic mean of prices over a specified period. Common periods for covered call analysis include:

20-day SMA: Short-term trend indicator, highly responsive to recent price changes. Useful for identifying immediate momentum.

50-day SMA: Intermediate-term trend indicator, the most relevant timeframe for typical covered call holding periods (30-45 days).

200-day SMA: Long-term trend indicator, defines the overall market regime (bull or bear). Stocks trading above their 200-day SMA operate in long-term uptrends; those below face long-term headwinds.

Exponential Moving Averages (EMA)

Exponential moving averages weight recent prices more heavily than older prices, making them more responsive to new information. The 12-day and 26-day EMAs are particularly popular among technical traders.

For covered call purposes, simple moving averages are generally preferable because their slower responsiveness reduces false signals and provides more stable reference points.

Moving Average Crossover Signals

Moving average crossovers generate trend change signals:

Golden Cross: Short-term MA crosses above long-term MA, signaling potential uptrend beginning. For covered calls, this suggests favorable conditions for initiating positions with OTM strikes to capture appreciation.

Death Cross: Short-term MA crosses below long-term MA, signaling potential downtrend beginning. This warns covered call traders to exercise caution or close existing positions.

Practical Moving Average Application for Covered Calls

Use moving averages to inform three key decisions:

1. Position Initiation

- Prefer stocks trading above their 50-day and 200-day SMAs (confirming uptrend or stability)
- Avoid stocks trading below both moving averages (downtrend risk)
- Stocks trading between 50-day and 200-day SMAs require additional analysis

2. Strike Selection

- When stock trades significantly above its 50-day SMA (5%+ premium), consider ATM or ITM strikes as reversion toward the mean is likely

- When stock trades near or below its 50-day SMA, use OTM strikes to allow recovery room
- The 50-day SMA itself often acts as support during corrections, making it a viable strike reference point

3. Position Management

- If stock falls below its 50-day SMA after selling calls, consider closing the call position for profit (time decay worked in your favor) and reassessing whether to hold the stock
- Strong breaks above moving averages may warrant closing calls early to participate in breakout momentum

Case Study: Moving Average Strategy

Stock XYZ Technical Setup:

- Current price: $52.00
- 20-day SMA: $50.50
- 50-day SMA: $49.00
- 200-day SMA: $46.00
- Recent pattern: Consolidating after rally from $47 to $53

Analysis: Stock trades above all major moving averages, confirming uptrend. Currently extended 6% above 50-day SMA, suggesting potential retracement toward $49-$50 range.

Optimal covered call strategy:

- Sell $53 or $54 strikes (at or above current resistance)
- If stock pulls back toward 50-day SMA ($49), covered call will profit from time decay
- If stock continues higher, accept assignment with profit
- Monitor 50-day SMA as reestablishment point if assigned

Volume Analysis and Market Sentiment

Volume represents the number of shares traded during a specific period. Volume analysis confirms the significance of price movements and reveals institutional accumulation or distribution.

Volume Basics for Covered Call Traders

High volume indicates strong conviction behind price movements. Price changes on high volume are more likely to sustain, while low-volume movements often reverse.

For covered call decisions:

- Initiating positions: Prefer stocks showing steady, moderate volume without extreme spikes (stability indicator)
- Price increases on declining volume: Weak uptrends vulnerable to reversal (good for selling calls)
- Price decreases on declining volume: Weak downtrends likely to stabilize (acceptable for covered calls if fundamentals are sound)
- Extreme volume spikes: Usually news-related, wait for volatility to settle before establishing positions

Volume Patterns

Accumulation Pattern Characterized by rising prices on increasing volume and falling prices on decreasing volume. This pattern indicates institutional buying during dips and retail selling during rises—a positive sign for covered call stocks.

Distribution Pattern Characterized by rising prices on decreasing volume and falling prices on increasing volume. This pattern indicates institutional selling into strength and retail buying—a warning sign suggesting potential trend reversal.

On-Balance Volume (OBV)

OBV adds volume on up days and subtracts volume on down days, creating a cumulative volume flow indicator:

- Rising OBV confirms price uptrends (healthy for covered calls)
- Falling OBV warns of weakening trends despite stable prices
- Divergences (price rising but OBV falling) warn of impending

reversal

For covered call purposes, verify that OBV trends align with price trends. Misalignments suggest underlying weakness warranting caution.

Volume and Earnings Announcements

Volume typically surges around earnings announcements as traders react to results and guidance. For covered call management:

Pre-earnings volume spike: Reflects anticipation and positioning. Implied volatility and option premiums surge, creating opportunity to close positions at profit or sell calls at elevated premiums.

Post-earnings volume surge: Represents reaction to results. Wait for volume and volatility to normalize before establishing new positions.

Average Daily Volume Thresholds

Ensure adequate liquidity by requiring minimum average daily volume:

- Small positions (100-300 shares): 200,000+ shares daily minimum
- Medium positions (400-700 shares): 500,000+ shares daily minimum
- Large positions (800+ shares): 1,000,000+ shares daily minimum

Insufficient volume creates difficulties establishing and closing positions at fair prices, eroding returns through slippage.

Relative Strength Index (RSI) Applications

The Relative Strength Index (RSI) is a momentum oscillator measuring the speed and magnitude of price changes. RSI oscillates between 0 and 100, with readings above 70 indicating overbought conditions and readings below 30 indicating oversold conditions.

RSI Calculation and Interpretation

RSI = 100 - [100 / (1 + RS)] Where RS = Average Gain / Average Loss over the period (typically 14 days)

RSI interpretation:

- 70-100: Overbought zone (potential reversal lower)
- 30-70: Neutral zone (no extreme conditions)
- 0-30: Oversold zone (potential reversal higher)

RSI for Covered Call Entry Timing

Use RSI to optimize position timing:

RSI entering overbought (approaching 70): Ideal time to sell covered calls, particularly ATM or ITM strikes, as stock may consolidate or decline. Maximum premium opportunity with reduced assignment risk.

RSI in neutral range (40-60): Standard conditions suitable for regular covered call strategies based on other technical factors.

RSI entering oversold (approaching 30): Suboptimal time for initiating covered calls as stock may be oversold and due for bounce. Either wait for RSI recovery above 30 or use very OTM strikes if you must establish positions.

RSI for Strike Selection

RSI conditions inform strike aggressiveness:

High RSI (65-80): Favor ATM or ITM strikes as stock is extended and unlikely to advance significantly. Maximize premium collection.

Moderate RSI (40-60): Standard OTM strikes (2-5% above current price) providing balanced risk-reward.

Low RSI (20-35): Conservative OTM strikes (5-7% above current price) allowing room for recovery bounce. Accept lower premiums for greater upside participation.

RSI Divergences

Divergences between RSI and price provide powerful signals:

Bearish divergence: Price makes new highs while RSI fails to exceed previous highs. Indicates weakening momentum and potential reversal. Excellent setup for selling covered calls with ATM strikes.

Bullish divergence: Price makes new lows while RSI fails to drop below previous lows. Indicates strengthening momentum despite price weakness. Avoid initiating covered calls or use very OTM strikes.

Case Study: RSI Application

Stock DEF Scenario:

- Current price: $58.00
- Recent rally from $52 to $58 over three weeks
- RSI: 72 (overbought)
- 50-day SMA: $54.00
- No significant news or earnings imminent

Analysis: Overbought RSI after significant rally suggests consolidation or pullback likely. Stock is extended 7% above 50-day SMA, supporting mean reversion expectations.

Optimal strategy:

- Sell $58 or $59 strikes (ATM or slightly OTM) to maximize premium
- High probability stock will consolidate or decline slightly, allowing full premium capture
- If assigned at $58-59, accept with satisfaction after collecting premium
- Monitor RSI for reversal below 70 as signal momentum is weakening

RSI Limitations

RSI can remain overbought or oversold for extended periods during strong trends. In powerful uptrends, RSI may stay above 70 for weeks while prices continue climbing. Similarly, downtrends can keep RSI below 30 for extended periods.

For covered call purposes, combine RSI with other indicators (moving averages, support/resistance) rather than relying on it exclusively. RSI works best in ranging or consolidating markets, less reliably in strong trends.

Bollinger Bands and Volatility Assessment

Bollinger Bands consist of three lines: a simple moving average (typically 20-day) in the center, with upper and lower bands representing two standard deviations from the average. These bands expand and contract based on volatility, providing visual representation of price extremes and volatility conditions.

Bollinger Band Construction and Interpretation

- Middle Band: 20-day simple moving average (SMA)
- Upper Band: Middle band + (2 × standard deviation)
- Lower Band: Middle band - (2 × standard deviation)

The bands contain approximately 95% of price action statistically. Prices touching or exceeding the bands indicate potential extremes, while band width reveals volatility conditions.

Bollinger Band Applications for Covered Calls

1. Identifying Overbought/Oversold Conditions

Price touching or exceeding upper band: Stock is extended relative to recent average. Excellent time to sell covered calls, especially ATM strikes, as mean reversion toward the middle band is likely.

Price touching or exceeding lower band: Stock is oversold relative to recent average. Suboptimal time for new covered calls as bounce toward middle band is probable. Either wait or use very OTM strikes.

Price near middle band: Neutral conditions, make decisions based on other technical factors.

2. Volatility Assessment via Band Width

Wide Bollinger Bands indicate high volatility:

- Options premiums are elevated (attractive for sellers)
- Greater uncertainty about price direction
- Risk of assignment or significant moves increases
- Ideal for selling covered calls with more conservative strikes

Narrow Bollinger Bands indicate low volatility:

- Options premiums are reduced (less attractive for sellers)
- Price consolidation or compression
- Often precedes volatility expansion (the "squeeze")
- Consider waiting for band expansion before initiating positions

3. The Bollinger Band Squeeze

The squeeze occurs when bands contract to extreme narrowness, indicating very low volatility. Historically, squeezes precede significant price movements (breakouts) as volatility mean-reverts.

Covered call strategy during squeeze:

- Avoid initiating new positions immediately before squeeze releases
- Wait for directional clarity post-squeeze
- If already holding covered calls during squeeze, monitor closely for breakout
- After squeeze releases with upward breakout, consider closing calls to participate in movement

4. Walking the Bands

During strong trends, prices can "walk the band," repeatedly touching or exceeding one band while the opposite band moves in the same direction. Uptrends walk the upper band; downtrends walk the lower band.

Walking the upper band:

- Indicates strong momentum and trend continuation
- Not ideal for aggressive covered call strategies
- Use OTM strikes and shorter durations if selling calls
- Consider accepting assignment if it occurs

Walking the lower band:

- Indicates strong downtrend
- Avoid initiating covered call positions
- If holding underwater positions, consider waiting for bounce to middle band before selling calls

Practical Bollinger Band Strategy

Systematic approach using Bollinger Bands:

Entry Rules:

- Only initiate covered calls when price is in upper 50% of band range (above middle band)
- Ideal entry: Price at or slightly above upper band (overbought)
- Avoid entries when price is below middle band (lower 50%)

Strike Selection:

- Price at upper band: Sell ATM or ITM strikes (aggressive premium capture)
- Price near middle band: Sell slightly OTM strikes (2-3% above)
- Price in lower half of range: Either wait or sell very OTM strikes (5%+ above)

Exit/Management:

- Close calls for profit if price drops to middle band and significant premium remains
- Hold through expiration if price remains stable in upper band range
- If assigned, consider waiting for price to revisit upper band before repurchasing

Case Study: Bollinger Bands Strategy
Stock GHI Analysis:

- Current price: $44.50
- 20-day SMA (middle band): $43.00
- Upper band: $46.00
- Lower band: $40.00
- Recent pattern: Rallied from $41 to $44.50 over two weeks

Analysis: Price trading in upper half of Bollinger Band range but not yet touching upper band. Moderate positioning suggesting potential to reach upper band before mean reverting.

Strategy decision:

- Since price hasn't reached upper band yet, use moderately OTM strikes
- Sell $46 calls (at the upper band level) for 30-45 day expiration
- If price reaches $46 (upper band), high probability of assignment but with profit
- If price fails to reach upper band and reverts, capture full premium
- Monitor band width for volatility changes

Combining Bollinger Bands with RSI

The most powerful technical combination for covered calls uses Bollinger Bands and RSI together:

Price at upper band + RSI above 70: Extremely overbought, highest-probability covered call setup. Sell ATM strikes aggressively.

Price at lower band + RSI below 30: Extremely oversold, avoid new covered calls or use very OTM strikes with great caution.

Price at upper band + RSI 50-60: Moderately extended, good covered call setup with standard strikes.

This combination provides confirmation and reduces false signals, creating more reliable entry points.

Synthesizing Technical Analysis for Covered Call Excellence

Technical analysis provides the timing and tactical precision to complement fundamental stock selection. The most successful covered call traders combine multiple technical indicators into systematic decision-making frameworks.

The Covered Call Technical Checklist

Before initiating any covered call position, verify:

Trend Analysis:

- Stock trading above 50-day SMA (confirming at least intermediate uptrend)
- Stock trading above 200-day SMA (confirming long-term bullish structure)
- Price pattern is consolidation or uptrend (avoiding downtrends)

Support/Resistance:

- Identified nearest major support level (downside reference)
- Identified nearest major resistance level (strike selection reference)
- Current price offers favorable risk-reward relative to these levels

Momentum Indicators:

- RSI between 40-80 (avoiding deeply oversold conditions)
- Price in upper 50% of Bollinger Band range (above middle band)
- No extreme divergences warning of trend reversal

Volume Confirmation:

- Average daily volume exceeds minimum thresholds
- Recent price action confirmed by volume (no distribution patterns)
- No immediate earnings or major news events

Volatility Assessment:

- Implied volatility rank above 30 (preferably above 50)
- Bollinger Bands not in extreme squeeze warning of breakout
- Options premiums justify the strategy (minimum 1% monthly for conservative, 2%+ for aggressive)

Meeting all or most checklist items indicates technically sound entry timing.

Strike Selection Technical Framework

Use technical indicators to determine strike aggressiveness:

Aggressive Strikes (ATM or ITM):

- RSI above 70
- Price at or above upper Bollinger Band

- Significant resistance level at or below current price
- Recent vertical advance without consolidation
- Very high implied volatility

Moderate Strikes (2-4% OTM):

- RSI 50-70
- Price above middle Bollinger Band
- Resistance level 3-5% above current price
- Steady uptrend with normal consolidations
- Normal implied volatility

Conservative Strikes (5-7% OTM):

- RSI 40-50
- Price near middle Bollinger Band
- Resistance level 7%+ above current price
- Early stage of trend or recovery from pullback
- Lower implied volatility

Position Management Technical Signals

Technical indicators also guide ongoing position management:

Close calls early for profit when:

- Price drops to or below middle Bollinger Band (time decay worked, exit available)
- RSI drops below 40 from overbought readings (momentum shifted)
- Price breaks below key support with volume (trend change warning)
- You've captured 60-70% of maximum profit with 40%+ of time remaining

Hold through expiration when:

- Price remains stable above middle Bollinger Band

- RSI stays in 45-65 range (balanced momentum)
- Support levels holding with price consolidating
- Premium remaining is small relative to transaction costs

Roll up and out when:

- Stock breaks above resistance on strong volume (trend acceleration)
- RSI pulls back from overbought but remains above 50 (healthy consolidation)
- Price consolidates at higher level after advance
- You can collect additional premium by rolling to higher strikes

Seasonal and Cyclical Technical Patterns

Beyond individual technical indicators, recognize broader market patterns that affect covered call performance:

Monthly patterns: Options time decay accelerates in final two weeks before expiration. Many traders establish positions 30-45 days out, capturing optimal theta decay.

Quarterly patterns: Earnings seasons create volatility spikes. Avoid establishing positions 2-3 weeks before earnings or use earnings-targeted strategies.

Annual patterns: January (new year positioning), April (first quarter earnings), July (summer doldrums), October (historically volatile), and December (tax-loss harvesting) each exhibit distinct characteristics.

Market regime awareness: Bull markets favor OTM strikes and participation in advances. Volatile or bearish markets favor ATM/ITM strikes and maximum premium collection.

Technical Analysis Limitations and Warnings

Technical analysis provides valuable insights but has important limitations:

Lagging indicators: Most technical indicators react to price changes rather than predicting them. They confirm trends rather than anticipate reversals.

Subjective interpretation: Support/resistance levels and pattern recognition involve judgment. Two analysts may reach different conclusions from the same chart.

Self-fulfilling prophecies: When many traders use identical technical levels, those levels gain validity through collective action rather than fundamental significance.

False signals: No technical indicator is 100% accurate. Always use multiple confirmations and manage risk through position sizing.

Fundamental-Technical Integration

The most successful covered call approach combines fundamental stock selection with technical timing:

1. Use fundamental analysis (Chapter 6) to build a universe of 20-30 financially sound, stable companies suitable for covered calls
2. Use technical analysis (this chapter) to determine which stocks from that universe currently offer optimal entry points
3. Use technical indicators to select appropriate strike prices based on each stock's current technical position
4. Monitor technical conditions to make ongoing position management decisions (hold, close, roll)

This integrated approach ensures you sell options on quality companies at technically advantageous times, maximizing consistency and risk-adjusted returns.

Conclusion: Technical Analysis as Covered Call Enhancement

Technical analysis transforms covered call trading from random premium collection to systematic income generation. By timing entries to overbought conditions, selecting strikes at resistance levels, and managing positions based on momentum indicators, you significantly improve outcomes.

The goal isn't to predict every price movement but to stack probabilities in your favor. Selling calls when RSI exceeds 70, prices touch upper Bollinger Bands, and stocks approach resistance creates scenarios where assignment occurs only after collecting premium at extended prices—the ideal covered call outcome.

Combined with the fundamental analysis framework from Chapter 6, you now possess comprehensive stock selection and timing capabilities. The next chapter applies these principles to specific sector strategies, recognizing that different industries require adapted approaches for optimal covered call performance.

Chapter 9:

Blue-Chip Stocks for Covered Calls

Blue-chip stocks represent the elite tier of corporate America—companies with decades of operating history, dominant market positions, and proven resilience through multiple economic cycles. For covered call investors, blue chips provide the ideal foundation: stability, liquidity, and predictability that make consistent premium generation possible without excessive risk.

This chapter identifies what makes blue-chip stocks particularly suitable for covered calls, analyzes specific top-tier candidates, and demonstrates how to build a core portfolio around these market leaders.

Characteristics of Reliable Blue Chips

Not all large companies qualify as true blue chips. The designation requires specific characteristics that distinguish market leaders from merely large corporations.

Market Capitalization and Industry Leadership

True blue chips maintain market capitalizations exceeding $50 billion, with many surpassing $100 billion or even $500 billion. This enormous size provides several advantages for covered call traders:

Scale creates stability. Companies of this magnitude don't disappear overnight or experience existential crises from single product failures or competitive threats. Their diversified operations, multiple revenue streams, and financial resources provide cushions against industry disruptions.

Market leadership in primary business segments ensures pricing power and sustainable competitive advantages. Blue chips typically rank #1 or #2 in their core markets, generating superior margins and cash flows that support dividends and weather downturns.

Global presence diversifies revenue across geographies, reducing dependence on any single economy or market. This geographic diversification smooths earnings and reduces volatility—exactly what covered call traders need.

Decades of Operating History

Blue-chip status requires proving resilience over time. Companies must demonstrate they can adapt to technological change, navigate recessions, manage competitive threats, and evolve with consumer preferences across decades.

For covered call purposes, prioritize companies with:

- At least 50 years of operating history (preferably 75-100+ years)
- Survival through multiple recessions including 2008 financial crisis
- Successful adaptation to major industry disruptions
- Consistent market leadership maintained across generations

This historical resilience provides confidence the company will remain viable throughout your option-holding periods and beyond.

S&P 500 Inclusion and Index Stability

Virtually all blue chips maintain S&P 500 inclusion, with the strongest candidates showing decades of continuous membership. Index inclusion guarantees:

Institutional ownership by index funds and pension plans creates permanent buying support, reducing extreme downside risk.

Continuous analyst coverage provides transparency and information flow, helping you make informed decisions.

Options liquidity benefits from institutional and retail interest, ensuring tight bid-ask spreads and adequate open interest.

Financial Fortress Characteristics

Blue-chip balance sheets distinguish them from ordinary large companies:

Investment-grade credit ratings (A- or higher, preferably AA or AAA) confirm financial strength independently assessed by rating agencies. These ratings mean blue chips can borrow at favorable rates during stress periods when weaker companies face credit constraints.

Low debt-to-equity ratios (typically below 0.5 for non-financial companies) provide financial flexibility and reduce bankruptcy risk. Blue chips can weather multi-year downturns without financial distress.

Substantial cash reserves ($5-50+ billion depending on company size) enable them to maintain dividends, invest in growth, and repurchase shares even during recessions.

Strong free cash flow generation consistently exceeding $3-10+ billion annually ensures dividends and buybacks aren't borrowed or financially engineered but come from genuine operational cash generation.

Dividend Consistency and Growth

Reliable blue chips maintain pristine dividend records:

Minimum 25 consecutive years of dividend payments without interruption, even during severe recessions. This demonstrates management commitment to shareholders and financial durability.

Ideally, 10+ consecutive years of dividend increases, signaling not just maintenance but growing shareholder returns. Dividend growth slightly exceeding inflation (3-5% annually) is ideal for covered call candidates.

Payout ratios between 40-70%, ensuring dividends are sustainable from earnings while retaining capital for business investment.

Options Market Characteristics

From a trading perspective, blue chips offer superior options markets:

Daily options volume exceeding 10,000 contracts ensures you can enter and exit positions efficiently at fair prices.

Open interest exceeding 50,000 contracts across multiple strikes and expirations provides deep liquidity and tight spreads.

Bid-ask spreads under $0.05 for at-the-money options minimize transaction costs, with many blue chips showing spreads of $0.01-0.02.

Consistent implied volatility in the 15-30% range generates meaningful premiums without excessive risk. Blue chips rarely show IV below 12% (insufficient premium) or above 40% (excessive uncertainty).

Price Stability and Trading Characteristics

Blue-chip price behavior makes them ideal for covered calls:

Average daily price movements between 0.3-1.0%, providing enough volatility for premium generation without dramatic swings threatening capital.

Absence of gap risk except during genuine market-wide events. Blue chips don't gap down 15% overnight on company-specific news the way smaller stocks can.

Predictable trading ranges and respect for technical support/resistance levels, allowing systematic strike selection based on technical analysis.

Limited susceptibility to manipulation or extreme technical moves due to enormous market capitalization and institutional ownership.

Brand Value and Economic Moat

The strongest blue chips possess intangible assets protecting their competitive positions:

Global brand recognition that commands premium pricing and customer loyalty across generations (Coca-Cola, Nike, Apple, Disney).

Network effects where products become more valuable as adoption increases (Visa, Mastercard, Microsoft).

Regulatory advantages or barriers to entry protecting market positions (utilities, defense contractors, pharmaceutical patents).

Switching costs that lock in customers and create recurring revenue (enterprise software, banking relationships).

Management Excellence and Governance

Blue-chip management teams demonstrate superior capital allocation and shareholder focus:

Long-term strategic thinking over quarterly earnings management, avoiding the short-termism that destroys value.

Conservative financial policies eschewing excessive leverage or financial engineering in favor of sustainable growth.

Transparent communication with shareholders through detailed earnings calls, investor presentations, and comprehensive annual reports.

Alignment with shareholders through significant insider ownership and compensation structures emphasizing long-term stock performance.

Blue-Chip Sectors

While blue chips exist across sectors, certain industries produce higher concentrations:

Technology mega-caps: Microsoft, Apple, Alphabet (Google), Amazon—companies that have transitioned from growth stocks to mature blue chips through scale and market dominance.

Consumer staples: Procter & Gamble, Coca-Cola, PepsiCo, Walmart—companies selling essential products with recession-resistant demand.

Healthcare giants: Johnson & Johnson, UnitedHealth Group, Pfizer—benefiting from aging demographics and consistent healthcare demand.

Financial leaders: JPMorgan Chase, Bank of America, Visa, Mastercard—dominating banking, payments, and financial services.

Industrial stalwarts: Caterpillar, 3M, Honeywell—diversified manufacturers with global reach.

Top-Tier Candidates Analyzed

Let's examine specific blue-chip stocks that exemplify ideal covered call characteristics. These analyses provide frameworks for evaluating similar candidates.

Microsoft Corporation (MSFT)

Company Profile:

- Market cap: $3+ trillion
- Founded: 1975
- S&P 500 inclusion: 1994 (continuous)
- Credit rating: AAA (one of only two U.S. companies with this rating)

Fundamental Strengths: Microsoft dominates multiple technology segments: operating systems (Windows), productivity software (Office 365), cloud computing (Azure), professional networking (LinkedIn), and gaming (Xbox). This diversification insulates the company from single-product risk.

Financial metrics (recent data):

- Revenue: $245+ billion annually
- Free cash flow: $70+ billion annually

- Debt-to-equity: 0.35
- ROE: 42%
- Operating margin: 42%

Dividend Characteristics:

- Consecutive years of increases: 19+
- Dividend yield: 0.7-1.0%
- Payout ratio: 25%
- Quarterly dividend: $0.75+ per share

While the yield is modest, the low payout ratio provides enormous room for future increases. Microsoft prioritizes stock buybacks over dividends, regularly repurchasing $15-20 billion in shares annually.

Options Market Quality:

- Average daily options volume: 500,000+ contracts
- Bid-ask spreads: $0.01-0.03 for ATM options
- Implied volatility: 20-30%
- Open interest: Exceptional across all strikes and expirations

Covered Call Suitability: Microsoft's price stability, massive liquidity, and moderate volatility create ideal conditions. Monthly premiums typically range from 1.5-2.5% for ATM strikes, 1.0-1.5% for slightly OTM strikes.

Sample Trade:

- Stock price: $420
- Sell 30-day $430 call (2.4% OTM)
- Premium collected: $6.50 ($650 per contract)
- Monthly yield: 1.55%
- Annualized return: 18.6% (premium only, excluding dividends and appreciation)

Considerations: Microsoft can experience sharp moves on cloud computing growth data or AI announcements. Avoid selling calls immediately before earnings (quarterly) or major product launches. The stock's strong long-term uptrend means aggressive ITM or ATM strikes risk missing significant appreciation.

Johnson & Johnson (JNJ)

Company Profile:

- Market cap: $370+ billion
- Founded: 1886 (138+ years of operation)
- S&P 500 inclusion: Original member (1957)
- Credit rating: AAA

Fundamental Strengths: J&J operates across three healthcare segments: pharmaceuticals (62% of sales), medical devices (26%), and consumer health products (12%). The company markets products in virtually every country, with 47% of sales from international markets.

Financial metrics:

- Revenue: $100+ billion annually
- Free cash flow: $20+ billion annually
- Debt-to-equity: 0.45
- ROE: 25%
- Operating margin: 28%

Dividend Characteristics:

- Dividend aristocrat: 62+ consecutive years of increases
- Dividend yield: 2.9-3.2%
- Payout ratio: 50%
- Quarterly dividend: $1.19+ per share

J&J's dividend growth averages 5-6% annually, exceeding inflation consistently. The company has never reduced or suspended dividends, maintaining payments through every recession since 1960.

Options Market Quality:

- Average daily options volume: 150,000+ contracts

- Bid-ask spreads: $0.02-0.05
- Implied volatility: 15-22%
- Excellent open interest across strikes

Covered Call Suitability: J&J exemplifies conservative covered call investing. Lower volatility means modest premiums (1.0-1.8% monthly) but exceptional stability. The combination of 3% dividend yield plus 1.5% monthly option premium creates 21% total annual return with minimal risk.

Sample Trade:

- Stock price: $155
- Sell 30-day $160 call (3.2% OTM)
- Premium collected: $2.10 ($210 per contract)
- Monthly yield: 1.35%
- Annualized return: 16.2% (premium only)
- Total return with dividend: 19.2%

Considerations: Pharmaceutical companies face FDA approval risks and patent cliffs. However, J&J's diversification across dozens of drugs and three business segments minimizes single-product risk. Avoid selling calls before major FDA decisions or earnings announcements.

Visa Inc. (V)

Company Profile:

- Market cap: $600+ billion
- Founded: 1958 (modern structure from 2007 IPO)
- S&P 500 inclusion: 2009
- Credit rating: AA-

Fundamental Strengths: Visa operates the world's largest electronic payments network, processing trillions in transactions annually. The company doesn't lend money or bear credit risk—it simply processes payments and collects fees, creating an exceptional business model with 50%+ operating margins.

Financial metrics:

- Revenue: $35+ billion annually
- Free cash flow: $19+ billion annually
- Debt-to-equity: 0.55
- ROE: 45%
- Operating margin: 67%

Dividend Characteristics:

- Consecutive years of increases: 15+
- Dividend yield: 0.7-0.9%
- Payout ratio: 20%
- Quarterly dividend: $0.52+ per share

Like Microsoft, Visa emphasizes buybacks over dividends, repurchasing $15+ billion in shares annually. The low payout ratio provides enormous flexibility for dividend growth.

Options Market Quality:

- Average daily options volume: 200,000+ contracts
- Bid-ask spreads: $0.01-0.03
- Implied volatility: 18-28%
- Deep liquidity across all expirations

Covered Call Suitability: Visa's combination of secular growth (shift to electronic payments), high margins, and moderate volatility creates excellent covered call opportunities. Monthly premiums range from 1.3-2.2% depending on strike selection.

Sample Trade:

- Stock price: $305
- Sell 30-day $315 call (3.3% OTM)
- Premium collected: $4.80 ($480 per contract)
- Monthly yield: 1.57%
- Annualized return: 18.8%

Considerations: Visa faces regulatory risks around interchange fees and potential antitrust concerns. Major regulatory announcements can trigger volatility. The company benefits from economic growth (more consumer spending) but shows resilience during recessions as electronic payments take share from cash.

Procter & Gamble (PG)

Company Profile:

- Market cap: $400+ billion
- Founded: 1837 (187+ years)
- S&P 500 inclusion: Original member (1957)
- Credit rating: AA-

Fundamental Strengths: P&G owns 65+ trusted brands across fabric care (Tide, Gain), home care (Dawn, Swiffer), baby care (Pampers), feminine care (Always), hair care (Pantene, Head & Shoulders), and personal care (Gillette, Oral-B, Crest). The company generates $82+ billion in annual revenue from products people use daily regardless of economic conditions.

Financial metrics:

- Revenue: $82+ billion annually
- Free cash flow: $15+ billion annually
- Debt-to-equity: 0.50
- ROE: 30%
- Operating margin: 23%

Dividend Characteristics:

- Dividend aristocrat: 68+ consecutive years of increases
- Dividend yield: 2.3-2.6%
- Payout ratio: 60%
- Quarterly dividend: $0.99+ per share

P&G has increased dividends every year since 1957, through 11 recessions. Dividend growth averages 4-5% annually.

Options Market Quality:

- Average daily options volume: 80,000+ contracts
- Bid-ask spreads: $0.03-0.06
- Implied volatility: 14-20%
- Good liquidity for major strikes

Covered Call Suitability: P&G epitomizes defensive covered call investing. Ultra-stable business model and low volatility produce modest premiums (0.9-1.5% monthly) but combined with the 2.4% dividend yield create attractive total returns with minimal risk.

Sample Trade:

- Stock price: $170
- Sell 30-day $175 call (2.9% OTM)
- Premium collected: $2.20 ($220 per contract)
- Monthly yield: 1.29%
- Annualized return: 15.5% (premium only)
- Total return with dividend: 17.9%

Considerations: Consumer staples face limited growth—P&G's revenue grows 2-4% annually. Don't expect dramatic stock appreciation, but also don't expect significant downside. This predictability makes it ideal for conservative covered call strategies.

JPMorgan Chase (JPM)

Company Profile:

- Market cap: $650+ billion
- Founded: 1799 (through predecessor banks)
- S&P 500 inclusion: Continuous decades
- Credit rating: A+

Fundamental Strengths: JPMorgan dominates U.S. banking: #1 in investment banking, #1 in credit cards, top-tier retail banking, leading asset management. The company operates globally with operations in 60+ countries.

Financial metrics:

- Revenue: $160+ billion annually
- Free cash flow: $40+ billion annually
- Debt-to-equity: 1.25 (normal for banks)
- ROE: 15%
- Efficiency ratio: 55%

Dividend Characteristics:

- Consecutive years of increases: 13+
- Dividend yield: 2.1-2.5%
- Payout ratio: 30%
- Quarterly dividend: $1.15+ per share

JPM suspended dividend increases (not payments) during 2020 due to regulatory restrictions, then resumed growth. The low payout ratio provides significant room for future increases.

Options Market Quality:

- Average daily options volume: 400,000+ contracts
- Bid-ask spreads: $0.01-0.03
- Implied volatility: 20-30%
- Exceptional liquidity

Covered Call Suitability: As the highest-quality major bank, JPM offers attractive volatility (generating premiums of 1.5-2.8% monthly) combined with dividend income and reasonable growth prospects. Financial sector exposure adds diversification to portfolios heavy in technology and consumer stocks.

Sample Trade:

- Stock price: $215
- Sell 30-day $220 call (2.3% OTM)
- Premium collected: $3.80 ($380 per contract)
- Monthly yield: 1.77%
- Annualized return: 21.2%
- Total return with dividend: 23.7%

Considerations: Bank stocks are sensitive to interest rates, Federal Reserve policy, and economic conditions. JPM tends to outperform during rising rate environments and economic expansions, underperform during recessions and falling rate periods. Avoid selling calls immediately before Federal Reserve meetings or major economic data releases.

Case Studies of Successful Blue-Chip Covered Call Strategies

Real-world examples demonstrate how blue-chip covered calls perform across different market conditions and time periods.

Case Study 1: Conservative Retirement Income Strategy

Profile: Investor age 67, recently retired, seeking monthly income with capital preservation priority.

Portfolio: $500,000 invested across five blue-chip positions

Holdings:

- Johnson & Johnson: $100,000 (645 shares at $155)
- Procter & Gamble: $100,000 (588 shares at $170)
- Coca-Cola: $100,000 (1,667 shares at $60)
- Verizon: $100,000 (2,500 shares at $40)
- Realty Income (REIT): $100,000 (1,724 shares at $58)

Strategy Implemented:

- Sell OTM covered calls (3-5% above current price)
- 30-45 day expirations
- Conservative strike selection prioritizing capital preservation
- Roll if early assignment threatens before ex-dividend dates

12-Month Results:
Month 1-3 Performance:

- Average monthly premium: $5,200 (1.04% yield)
- Dividends received: $4,100 quarterly
- No assignments occurred
- One position (KO) rolled up and out after 15% rally

Months 4-6 Performance:

- Average monthly premium: $5,400 (1.08% yield)
- Dividends received: $4,150 quarterly
- JNJ assigned at $162 (purchased at $155)
- Repurchased JNJ at $159 following pullback, continued strategy

Months 7-9 Performance:

- Average monthly premium: $5,100 (1.02% yield)
- Dividends received: $4,200 quarterly
- Market correction reduced option premiums
- All positions held through volatility, continued selling calls

Months 10-12 Performance:

- Average monthly premium: $5,500 (1.10% yield)
- Dividends received: $4,250 quarterly
- VZ assigned at $42, gain captured
- Portfolio rebalanced, VZ repurchased

Annual Summary:

- Total option premium collected: $63,600 (12.7% return)
- Total dividend income: $16,700 (3.3% return)
- Capital gains from assignment/repurchase: $8,900 (1.8% return)

- Total return: $89,200 (17.8%)
- Maximum drawdown during year: -6.2% (vs. S&P 500 -12.4%)

Monthly income generated: $7,433 average ($5,300 premium + $1,392 dividends + $742 capital gains)

Key Success Factors:

- Ultra-conservative stocks weathered market volatility
- Disciplined strike selection avoided excessive assignments
- Dividend income provided supplementary cash flow
- Low volatility reduced stress and capital risk
- Portfolio met retirement income needs while preserving capital

Case Study 2: Growth-Plus-Income Strategy

Profile: Investor age 42, employed full-time, seeking to accelerate wealth accumulation while generating supplemental income.

Portfolio: $250,000 invested across technology and financial blue chips

Holdings:

- Microsoft: $60,000 (143 shares at $420)
- Apple: $60,000 (316 shares at $190)
- Visa: $50,000 (164 shares at $305)
- Alphabet: $40,000 (286 shares at $140)
- JPMorgan Chase: $40,000 (186 shares at $215)

Strategy Implemented:

- Blend of ATM and OTM strikes (0-4% above current price)
- 30-day expirations primarily
- More aggressive premium capture accepting occasional assignments
- Roll positions aggressively to participate in uptrends

12-Month Results:

Quarter 1:

- Monthly premium average: $5,100 (2.04% yield)
- Tech stocks rallied strongly
- MSFT assigned twice, rolled up each time capturing gains
- Alphabet never assigned, captured full premium three consecutive months

Quarter 2:

- Monthly premium average: $4,800 (1.92% yield)
- Market consolidation reduced premiums slightly
- All positions held through quarter
- JPM assigned once, immediately repurchased

Quarter 3:

- Monthly premium average: $5,400 (2.16% yield)
- Volatility spike around Fed meetings increased premiums
- AAPL assigned and held off from immediate repurchase
- Deployed AAPL proceeds into V, increasing position size

Quarter 4:

- Monthly premium average: $5,800 (2.32% yield)
- Strong year-end rally
- Multiple assignments captured appreciation
- Portfolio value increased due to stock gains

Annual Summary:

- Total option premium: $63,600 (25.4% return on initial capital)
- Dividend income: $3,200 (1.3% return)
- Capital appreciation: $42,800 (17.1% return)
- Total return: $109,600 (43.8%)
- Number of assignments: 8 (managed successfully)

Key Success Factors:

- Technology stocks provided both premium income and capital appreciation
- Aggressive strike selection maximized premium capture
- Willingness to accept assignment captured gains rather than limiting them
- Strong bull market environment favored this approach
- Portfolio grew substantially while generating significant cash flow

Lessons learned:

- Aggressive strategies work best in bull markets
- Accept assignments on quality stocks—they can be repurchased
- Technology volatility generates exceptional premiums
- Monitor positions more actively with tighter strikes

Case Study 3: Bear Market Defense Strategy

Profile: Established covered call trader with $400,000 portfolio, navigating significant market correction.

Initial Holdings (Before Market Decline): Mixed portfolio of growth and value stocks with covered calls

Challenge: Market declined 20% over six-month period. How to manage covered call positions during sustained downturn.

Strategic Adjustments Made:

Adjustment 1: Migrated to Defensive Blue Chips Gradually exited growth positions (accepting losses on some) and reallocated to defensive blue chips:

- Increased Johnson & Johnson from 0% to 25% of portfolio
- Added Procter & Gamble (20% allocation)
- Added Walmart (15% allocation)
- Added Coca-Cola (15% allocation)
- Retained JPMorgan at reduced size (10% allocation)

- Kept cash reserve (15%)

Adjustment 2: Modified Strike Selection

- Shifted from OTM to ATM and ITM strikes
- Prioritized premium collection over capital appreciation
- Accepted that limiting upside was less important during downturn
- Captured higher premiums to offset declining stock values

Adjustment 3: Shortened Duration

- Moved from 30-45 day expirations to 14-21 day expirations
- Allowed more frequent position adjustments
- Captured accelerated theta decay
- Reduced uncertainty about market conditions beyond short term

Results During 6-Month Correction:
Portfolio Performance:

- Stock portfolio decline: -8.2% (vs. S&P 500 -20%)
- Option premium collected: $32,400 (8.1% on initial $400k)
- Dividend income: $6,800 (1.7%)
- Net portfolio change: +$1,000 (0.25% positive)

Analysis: While the absolute return was minimal, the critical achievement was avoiding significant loss during a 20% market correction. The defensive blue-chip allocation combined with premium income offset most stock declines.

Defensive blue chips declined 40-60% less than the overall market due to:

- Consumer staples maintained earnings through downturn
- Dividend yields became more attractive as prices fell
- Institutional investors rotated into defensive sectors

- Lower volatility reduced panic selling

Key Defensive Tactics:

- Prioritize capital preservation over maximum income during downturns
- Shift to highest-quality blue chips with recession-resistant business models
- Accept lower option premiums on stable stocks vs. higher premiums on volatile declining stocks
- Increase cash allocation to have dry powder for opportunities
- Shorten option duration to maintain flexibility

Recovery Phase: As market stabilized and began recovering, the portfolio was positioned to participate:

- High-quality holdings recovered faster than speculative stocks
- Continued covered call strategy throughout recovery
- Gradually reintroduced growth positions as confidence returned
- 12-month total return from market low: +28% (beating benchmark by 7%)

Building a Core Portfolio

Constructing a blue-chip covered call portfolio requires balancing diversification, capital efficiency, and practical management considerations.

Portfolio Size and Position Guidelines

Minimum viable portfolio: $50,000

- Rationale: Allows 5 positions of $10,000 each (approximately 100 shares of $100 stocks)
- Each position represents 20% of portfolio
- Provides basic diversification across sectors

Comfortable portfolio size: $100,000-250,000

- Allows 8-12 positions providing good diversification
- Position sizes of $10,000-25,000 each
- Sufficient scale to weather individual stock volatility
- Manageable number of positions for part-time traders

Optimal portfolio size: $250,000+

- Enables 10-15+ positions
- Excellent diversification across sectors and market caps
- Position sizes large enough to generate meaningful absolute income
- Can include both blue chips and select mid-cap positions

Position Sizing Principles:

Equal weighting: Each position represents 8-12% of portfolio value. Simple approach ensuring no single position dominates. Rebalance quarterly to maintain equal weights.

Risk-adjusted weighting: Allocate more capital to lower-volatility positions (J&J, PG) and less to higher-volatility positions (MSFT, V). For example:

- Defensive stocks: 12-15% each
- Moderate volatility: 8-10% each
- Higher volatility: 5-8% each

Dividend-adjusted weighting: Overweight high-dividend positions if income is the primary objective. Underweight low-dividend growth stocks if capital preservation is priority.

Sector Diversification Framework

A balanced blue-chip covered call portfolio includes:

Technology (20-30%):

- Microsoft and/or Apple (mega-cap stability)
- Alphabet or Amazon (diversified tech)
- Consider: Adobe, Oracle, Cisco for additional exposure

Healthcare (15-25%):

- Johnson & Johnson (diversified healthcare)
- UnitedHealth Group (healthcare services)
- Pfizer or Merck (pharmaceuticals)

Financials (15-20%):

- JPMorgan Chase (premier bank)
- Visa or Mastercard (payments)
- Consider: BlackRock, Goldman Sachs

Consumer Staples (10-20%):

- Procter & Gamble (consumer products)
- Coca-Cola or PepsiCo (beverages)
- Walmart or Costco (retail)

Industrials (10-15%):

- Caterpillar or Deere (heavy equipment)
- 3M or Honeywell (diversified industrials)
- Union Pacific (transportation)

Communications/Utilities (5-15%):

- Verizon or AT&T (telecommunications)
- Duke Energy or NextEra (utilities)
- REIT exposure: Realty Income, American Tower

Sample Blue-Chip Portfolios
Conservative Income Portfolio ($200,000)
Position allocation:

1. Johnson & Johnson (15%): $30,000
2. Procter & Gamble (15%): $30,000

3. Coca-Cola (12%): $24,000
4. Verizon (12%): $24,000
5. Realty Income (11%): $22,000
6. JPMorgan Chase (10%): $20,000
7. Duke Energy (10%): $20,000
8. 3M (8%): $16,000
9. Cash reserve (7%): $14,000

Characteristics:

- Average dividend yield: 3.5%
- Expected monthly premium: 1.0-1.3%
- Total return target: 15-19% annually
- Maximum drawdown expectation: 8-12%
- Management time: 30 minutes weekly

Balanced Growth-Income Portfolio ($300,000)
Position allocation:

1. Microsoft (12%): $36,000
2. Apple (10%): $30,000
3. Johnson & Johnson (10%): $30,000
4. Visa (9%): $27,000
5. JPMorgan Chase (9%): $27,000
6. Procter & Gamble (9%): $27,000
7. UnitedHealth Group (8%): $24,000
8. Alphabet (8%): $24,000
9. Home Depot (8%): $24,000
10. Caterpillar (7%): $21,000
11. Cash reserve (10%): $30,000

Characteristics:

- Average dividend yield: 1.8%
- Expected monthly premium: 1.7-2.3%

- Total return target: 22-30% annually
- Maximum drawdown expectation: 12-18%
- Management time: 45-60 minutes weekly

Aggressive Premium Portfolio ($150,000)
Position allocation:

1. Microsoft (18%): $27,000
2. Visa (15%): $22,500
3. Apple (14%): $21,000
4. JPMorgan Chase (13%): $19,500
5. Adobe (12%): $18,000
6. Caterpillar (10%): $15,000
7. Alphabet (10%): $15,000
8. Cash reserve (8%): $12,000

Characteristics:

- Average dividend yield: 1.0%
- Expected monthly premium: 2.2-3.0%
- Total return target: 28-40% annually
- Maximum drawdown expectation: 15-22%
- Management time: 60-90 minutes weekly

Portfolio Construction Process
Follow this systematic approach:
Step 1: Define Objectives (Week 1)

- Determine if priority is income, growth, or balance
- Establish risk tolerance and drawdown limits
- Set target monthly income or annual return
- Decide time commitment available for management

Step 2: Select Core Holdings (Week 2)

- Identify 8-12 blue-chip candidates meeting your criteria

- Verify each passes fundamental analysis (Chapter 6)
- Check current technical setup (Chapter 7)
- Ensure sector diversification

Step 3: Allocate Capital (Week 3)

- Assign position sizes based on volatility and objectives
- Reserve 5-15% in cash for opportunities and flexibility
- Verify position sizes allow for 100-share increments
- Calculate expected income from initial positions

Step 4: Implement Gradually (Weeks 4-8)

- Don't deploy all capital immediately
- Add 2-3 positions weekly as technical setups align
- Average into positions over several weeks
- Begin covered call sales once shares are established

Step 5: Establish Systematic Management (Ongoing)

- Weekly: Review existing positions, check for adjustments
- Monthly: Roll expiring options, add new positions if capital available
- Quarterly: Rebalance positions, review performance, adjust strategy
- Annually: Comprehensive portfolio review, tax planning, strategic refinement

Position Entry Checklist
Before adding any blue-chip position, verify:

- [ ] Company passes

***

Chapter 9: Blue-Chip Stocks for Covered Calls (Continued)

Position Entry Checklist

Before adding any blue-chip position, verify:

- [ ] Company passes fundamental quality screens (Chapter 6)
- [ ] Stock trading above 50-day and 200-day moving averages
- [ ] Technical setup favorable (not overextended or in downtrend)
- [ ] Options market shows adequate liquidity (10,000+ daily volume)
- [ ] Bid-ask spreads acceptable (under $0.05 for ATM options)
- [ ] No earnings announcement within next 45 days
- [ ] Position size appropriate for portfolio (typically 8-12%)
- [ ] Sector allocation remains balanced after addition
- [ ] Current implied volatility above 30th percentile of annual range

Portfolio Maintenance and Rebalancing

Portfolios drift from target allocations due to stock price movements and assignments. Systematic rebalancing maintains intended diversification:

Quarterly rebalancing:

- Calculate current position weights vs. targets
- Identify positions exceeding target by 3%+ (overweight)
- Identify positions below target by 3%+ (underweight)
- Trim overweight positions when calls expire or get assigned
- Add to underweight positions with new capital or proceeds from trimming
- Avoid rebalancing during strong trends (let winners run within reason)

When to replace positions: Replace blue-chip holdings if:

- Fundamental deterioration (dividend cut, earnings collapse, debt surge)
- Technical breakdown (sustained trading below 200-day MA)
- Options market liquidity evaporates
- Better alternatives emerge offering superior risk-adjusted returns
- Sector becomes significantly overweight requiring rotation

Portfolio Performance Tracking

Measure success through multiple metrics:

Total return = (Option premium + Dividends + Capital gains) / Initial capital **Premium capture rate** = Actual premium collected / Maximum possible premium **Assignment rate** = Number of assignments / Total positions **Win rate** = Profitable positions / Total positions **Risk-adjusted return** = Total return / Maximum drawdown

Target benchmarks:

- Total return: Exceed S&P 500 return by 3-8% annually
- Premium capture rate: Above 85%
- Win rate: Above 70%
- Risk-adjusted return: Higher Sharpe ratio than S&P 500

Conclusion: Blue Chips as Portfolio Foundation

Blue-chip stocks provide the ideal foundation for covered call portfolios. Their stability, liquidity, and predictability allow systematic premium generation with manageable risk. While their lower volatility means more modest premiums than speculative stocks, the consistency and capital preservation far outweigh the temptation of chasing higher yields on unstable companies.

Build your core portfolio around 8-12 blue-chip positions, systematically sell covered calls, and let time decay and consistent premium collection compound your wealth. This approach may lack the excitement of speculative trading, but it delivers the reliable income that builds long-term financial security.

Chapter 10:

Dividend Stocks and Covered Calls

Combining dividend-paying stocks with covered calls creates perhaps the most powerful income-generation strategy available to individual investors. This dual-income approach stacks quarterly dividend payments on top of monthly option premiums, producing total returns that can exceed 20-30% annually even when stock prices remain relatively flat.

This chapter explores how to optimize the dividend-covered call combination, properly time options around ex-dividend dates, leverage dividend aristocrats, and accurately calculate total returns.

The Double Income Advantage

The synergy between dividends and covered calls transforms ordinary stock ownership into a cash-generating machine.

Understanding the Dual Income Streams

Traditional stock investors receive income solely from dividends—typically quarterly payments yielding 2-4% annually for blue-chip stocks. These investors must wait for price appreciation to generate additional returns, which may or may not occur.

Covered call investors on non-dividend stocks generate option premium income—typically 1-3% monthly (12-36% annually)—but forgo the additional income stream that dividend payers provide.

The dividend-covered call combination captures both income sources simultaneously:

Example: Single Income (Dividend Only)

- Stock: Johnson & Johnson at $150
- Investment: $15,000 (100 shares)
- Annual dividend: $4.40 per share = $440
- Annual return: 2.93%

Example: Single Income (Covered Calls Only, Non-Dividend Stock)

- Stock: Non-dividend technology company at $150
- Investment: $15,000 (100 shares)
- Monthly premium: $2.50 per share = $250/month = $3,000/year
- Annual return: 20%

Example: Dual Income (Dividend + Covered Calls)

- Stock: Johnson & Johnson at $150
- Investment: $15,000 (100 shares)
- Annual dividend: $440
- Monthly covered call premium: $2.00 per share = $200/month = $2,400/year
- Total annual income: $2,840
- Annual return: 18.9%

The dividend-covered call combination generates 18.9% returns compared to just 2.93% from dividends alone—a 645% increase in income from the same capital investment.

The Compounding Effect

The true power emerges when reinvesting both income streams:

Year 1:

- Initial investment: $50,000
- Dividend income: $1,500 (3% yield)
- Option premium: $9,000 (18% premium yield)
- Total income: $10,500
- Reinvested: Total portfolio value $60,500

Year 2:

- Portfolio value: $60,500
- Dividend income: $1,815 (3% yield)
- Option premium: $10,890 (18% premium yield)
- Total income: $12,705

- Reinvested: Total portfolio value $73,205

Year 3:

- Portfolio value: $73,205
- Dividend income: $2,196
- Option premium: $13,177
- Total income: $15,373
- Reinvested: Total portfolio value $88,578

After just three years, the $50,000 portfolio has grown to $88,578 through income reinvestment alone—a 77% increase—without any stock price appreciation. This demonstrates the exponential power of compounding dual income streams.

Tax Efficiency Considerations

Both dividends and option premiums face taxation, but the combined strategy offers planning opportunities:

Qualified dividends: Held for 60+ days around ex-dividend dates receive preferential tax treatment (0%, 15%, or 20% depending on income level versus ordinary income rates of 10-37%).

Option premium: Generally taxed as short-term capital gains at ordinary income rates. However, the ability to control timing of option sales provides some flexibility.

Tax-deferred accounts (IRA, 401k): Eliminate immediate taxation on both income streams, allowing full reinvestment and maximizing compounding. This makes covered calls in retirement accounts particularly attractive.

Risk Reduction Through Income

The dual income stream provides superior downside protection:

Single-income investor: Stock declines $5, dividend provides $0.75 cushion, net loss: -$4.25 per share

Dual-income investor: Stock declines $5, dividend provides $0.75 cushion, option premium provides $2.50 cushion, net loss: -$1.75 per share

The dual-income approach reduces the actual loss by 59% compared to dividend-only investing, demonstrating how option premium dramatically enhances downside protection.

Optimal Dividend Yield Range

For covered call purposes, target dividend yields between 2-5%:

Low yields (under 2%): Insufficient supplementary income, though growth potential may compensate.

Optimal yields (2-5%): Provides meaningful income without excessive risk signals. Combined with option premiums, total yield reaches 15-25%.

High yields (5-7%): Attractive but verify sustainability. Very high yields sometimes indicate market concerns about dividend cuts.

Very high yields (above 7%): Extreme caution warranted. Market may be pricing in dividend reduction. Thoroughly investigate financial health before commitment.

Sector Selection for Dividend-Covered Call Strategies

Certain sectors consistently provide excellent dividend-covered call opportunities:

Utilities: Yields of 3-5%, stable businesses, moderate option premiums (1.0-1.5% monthly). Lower total returns (15-20%) but exceptional stability.

Telecommunications: Yields of 4-7%, established infrastructure businesses, moderate premiums (1.2-2.0% monthly). Total returns of 18-28%.

Consumer Staples: Yields of 2-4%, recession-resistant, moderate premiums (1.0-1.8% monthly). Total returns of 16-24%.

Financials: Yields of 2-4%, cyclical but large banks are stable, good premiums (1.5-2.5% monthly). Total returns of 20-30%.

Healthcare: Yields of 2-3%, defensive with growth, moderate premiums (1.2-2.0% monthly). Total returns of 18-26%.

Real Estate (REITs): Yields of 3-6%, required by law to distribute 90% of income, moderate to good premiums (1.5-2.5% monthly). Total returns of 22-35%.

Timing Calls Around Ex-Dividend Dates

Dividend payment mechanics create specific risks and opportunities for covered call traders. Understanding ex-dividend dates and early exercise risk is essential for maximizing total returns.

Dividend Payment Timeline

Four critical dates govern dividend payments:

Declaration Date: Company announces the upcoming dividend amount and payment schedule. Usually 4-6 weeks before payment.

Ex-Dividend Date: The critical date for covered call traders. Shareholders on this date receive the dividend. Stock typically drops by approximately the dividend amount at market open on ex-dividend date. This is typically 1-2 business days before record date.

Record Date: Company identifies shareholders of record eligible for payment. Usually 2 business days after ex-dividend date.

Payment Date: Dividend cash is deposited to shareholder accounts. Typically 2-4 weeks after record date.

The Ex-Dividend Date Rule

To receive a dividend, you must own shares before the ex-dividend date. If you own shares on the close of the day before the ex-dividend date, you receive the dividend even if you sell the shares on the ex-dividend date itself.

For covered call traders, this means:

- If your stock gets called away (assigned) before the ex-dividend date, you forfeit the dividend
- If you maintain ownership through the ex-dividend date, you receive the dividend
- The option buyer receives the dividend only if they exercise before the ex-dividend date and own the shares on that date

Early Exercise Risk

Early exercise occurs when option holders exercise their calls before expiration to capture dividends. This risk depends on several factors:

When early exercise is likely:

Dividend exceeds remaining time value: If dividend is $0.75 and option time value is only $0.40, rational option holders will exercise early to capture the $0.75 dividend rather than wait for expiration.

In-the-money calls: Deep ITM calls have minimal time value, making early exercise more attractive. Calls with deltas above 0.80 face elevated early exercise risk.

Shortly before ex-dividend date: Early exercise typically occurs 1-3 days before the ex-dividend date, allowing the option holder to become shareholder of record.

Large dividends: Special dividends or elevated quarterly dividends (above $0.50 per share) dramatically increase early exercise probability.

When early exercise is unlikely:

Dividend smaller than time value: If remaining time value is $1.20 and dividend is $0.35, option holders gain more by selling the option ($1.20) than exercising for the dividend ($0.35).

Out-of-the-money calls: OTM options contain only time value and no intrinsic value. Exercising would require paying strike price above current market price—irrational behavior.

Well before ex-dividend date: Weeks away from ex-dividend date, time value remains substantial and early exercise makes no economic sense.

Strategic Approaches to Ex-Dividend Dates

Three primary strategies for managing covered calls around dividends:

Strategy 1: Avoid In-the-Money Calls Before Ex-Dividend Dates

Most conservative approach eliminating early exercise risk:

- Two weeks before ex-dividend date, verify your covered calls are out-of-the-money
- If calls have moved in-the-money, close the position (buy back the call)
- Wait until after ex-dividend date to re-establish covered call
- Accept the temporary loss of option premium to preserve dividend income

Example:

- Stock: AT&T trading at $18.50
- Quarterly dividend: $0.28 (due in 10 days, ex-dividend in 2 days)
- Current covered call: $18 strike, $0.70 in-the-money
- Time value remaining: $0.15
- Action: Buy back call for $0.85 ($70 + $15), preserving $28 dividend
- Result: Net benefit $13 ($28 dividend - $15 time value forfeited)

Strategy 2: Sell Calls After Ex-Dividend Date
Simplest approach completely avoiding the timing complexity:

- Maintain stock ownership through ex-dividend date without covered calls
- Sell covered calls only after stock trades ex-dividend
- Accept 2-7 days per quarter without option premium
- Eliminate all early exercise risk and complexity

Trade-off analysis:

- Pro: No risk of losing dividend to assignment
- Pro: Simplicity and peace of mind
- Con: Forgo option premium for several days per quarter
- Con: Miss elevated premiums sometimes available immediately before ex-dividend dates

Strategy 3: Sell Calls Accepting Assignment Risk
Aggressive approach maximizing premium collection:

- Sell covered calls regardless of ex-dividend date proximity
- Select strikes and expirations considering early exercise probability
- Accept that some positions will be assigned before ex-dividend

dates
- View assignment as profit-taking opportunity rather than failure

When this strategy makes sense:

- The option premium significantly exceeds the dividend
- You're comfortable selling the stock at the strike price
- The stock has appreciated substantially from your entry
- You plan to repurchase the stock after assignment anyway

Example:

- Stock: Verizon at $41.50, purchased at $38
- Quarterly dividend: $0.67 (ex-dividend in 5 days)
- Sell $42 call, collect $1.80 premium
- Early exercise occurs, stock called away at $42

Result calculation:

- Stock gain: $4.00 ($42 - $38)
- Option premium: $1.80
- Dividend forfeited: -$0.67
- Net gain: $5.13 per share = 13.5% return

Even forfeiting the dividend, the total return from appreciation plus premium far exceeds holding purely for the dividend.

Dividend Capture Strategy Integration

Some traders combine dividend capture with covered calls:

Dividend capture basics:

- Purchase stock shortly before ex-dividend date
- Hold through ex-dividend date to capture dividend
- Sell stock shortly after ex-dividend date
- Accept that stock typically declines by approximately dividend amount

Covered call integration:

- Purchase stock 2-3 weeks before ex-dividend date
- Sell OTM covered call immediately after ex-dividend date
- Stock price has declined by dividend amount, making strikes more attractive
- Collect dividend plus option premium, sell stock at assignment or roll

Example execution:

- Day -15: Purchase Home Depot at $350, ex-dividend date in 15 days, dividend $2.25
- Day 0 (ex-dividend): Stock opens at $348 (declined by dividend amount), you own dividend rights
- Day 0: Sell $350 call, 30 days to expiration, collect $5.50 premium
- Day +30: If assigned at $350, total return = $7.75 ($2.25 dividend + $5.50 premium)
- 45-day return: 2.2% (17.8% annualized)

Ex-Dividend Date Calendar Management

Maintain a calendar tracking ex-dividend dates for all positions:

Quarterly dividend calendar template:

Stock	Jan	Feb	Mar	Apr	May	Jun	Jul	Aug	Sep	Oct	Nov	Dec
JNJ		Ex: 2/24			Ex: 5/24			Ex: 8/24			Ex: 11/24	
PG			Ex: 3/15			Ex: 6/15			Ex: 9/15			Ex: 12/15
VZ		Ex: 2/8			Ex: 5/8			Ex: 8/8			Ex: 11/8	

This calendar allows proactive position management, ensuring you make conscious decisions about each ex-dividend date rather than being surprised.

Dividend Aristocrats as Candidates

Dividend aristocrats—companies increasing dividends for 25+ consecutive years—represent the elite of dividend-paying stocks. Their exceptional dividend reliability makes them premier covered call candidates.

Why Dividend Aristocrats Excel for Covered Calls

Financial fortress characteristics: Companies that increase dividends through multiple recessions demonstrate extraordinary financial strength. They maintain low debt, generate consistent cash flow, and prioritize shareholder returns even during crises.

Predictable business models: Dividend aristocrats typically operate stable, mature businesses with consistent earnings. This predictability reduces unexpected volatility—exactly what covered call traders need.

Lower downside risk: The market recognizes aristocrat quality, providing price support during downturns. Stocks rarely decline dramatically when dividends remain secure and growing.

Income reliability: The combination of consistently growing dividends plus option premiums creates highly reliable income. While option premiums may fluctuate with volatility, dividends provide a stable foundation.

Long-term compounding: Growing dividends compound your income over years. A stock yielding 3% today with 5% annual dividend growth yields 4.9% on your original cost in 10 years.

Current Dividend Aristocrat List (Partial)

Over 65 companies currently qualify as dividend aristocrats. Key examples across sectors:

Consumer Staples:

- Procter & Gamble (68 years)
- Coca-Cola (62 years)
- PepsiCo (51 years)
- Walmart (50 years)
- Colgate-Palmolive (61 years)

Healthcare:

- Johnson & Johnson (62 years)
- Abbott Laboratories (52 years)
- Medtronic (46 years)

Industrials:

- 3M (66 years)
- Caterpillar (30 years)
- Emerson Electric (67 years)

Financials:

- S&P Global (50 years)
- Cincinnati Financial (63 years)

Consumer Discretionary:

- McDonald's (47 years)
- Target (56 years)
- Lowe's (61 years)

Materials:

- Sherwin-Williams (45 years)
- Nucor (51 years)

Evaluating Aristocrats for Covered Calls

Not all dividend aristocrats make equally suitable covered call candidates. Apply these additional filters:

Options liquidity: Some aristocrats trade lower volume with illiquid options markets. Verify daily options volume exceeds 5,000 contracts and bid-ask spreads remain under $0.10.

Adequate volatility: Very stable aristocrats (implied volatility under 15%) generate insufficient premium. Target IV of 18-25% for optimal balance.

Reasonable valuation: Avoid paying premium valuations for aristocrat status. Compare P/E ratios to historical averages and sector peers.

Growth potential: While stability matters most, modest growth prospects (3-7% earnings growth) enhance total returns beyond just dividend and premium income.

Case Study: Dividend Aristocrat Covered Call Portfolio

Portfolio construction: $250,000 across 10 aristocrat positions

Holdings:

1. Johnson & Johnson: $28,000 (11.2%)
2. Procter & Gamble: $26,000 (10.4%)
3. Coca-Cola: $24,000 (9.6%)
4. 3M: $24,000 (9.6%)
5. McDonald's: $24,000 (9.6%)
6. Target: $24,000 (9.6%)
7. Walmart: $24,000 (9.6%)
8. Caterpillar: $22,000 (8.8%)
9. Abbott Laboratories: $22,000 (8.8%)
10. Lowe's: $22,000 (8.8%)
11. Cash reserve: $10,000 (4%)

Strategy:

- Sell OTM covered calls (3-5% above current price)
- 30-45 day expirations
- Roll positions avoiding ex-dividend dates
- Reinvest all income quarterly

Expected Annual Returns:

Dividend income:

- Average yield: 2.8%
- Expected annual dividend: $6,720
- Dividend growth: 4-5% annually

Option premium:

- Conservative strike selection: 1.2% monthly average
- Expected annual premium: $28,800 (12 months × $2,400)

Total income: $35,520 Total return on $250,000: 14.2%
Including conservative stock appreciation (5% annually):

- Capital gains: $12,500
- Total portfolio return: $48,020 (19.2%)

This aristocrat portfolio delivers nearly 20% annual returns with exceptional stability and defensive characteristics.

Calculating Total Return

Accurate total return calculation ensures you understand true performance and can compare strategies effectively.

Total Return Components

Complete return measurement includes four elements:

1. Option Premium Income All premiums collected from covered call sales, whether positions expire worthless, are closed early, or result in assignment.

2. Dividend Income All dividend payments received during the measurement period, including both regular quarterly dividends and any special dividends.

3. Capital Gains/Losses Changes in stock value from original purchase price. For assigned positions, calculate gain/loss as strike price minus purchase price. For maintained positions, use current market value.

4. Realized vs. Unrealized Gains Distinguish between realized returns (closed positions) and unrealized returns (open positions). Both matter but represent different liquidity states.

Total Return Formula

Total Return % = [(Option Premium + Dividends + Capital Gains) / Initial Investment] × 100

For annualized returns spanning periods other than one year:

Annualized Return = [(1 + Total Return)^(365/Days)] - 1

Detailed Calculation Example

Position: Verizon Communications

Entry details:

- Purchase date: January 15
- Shares: 500
- Purchase price: $40.00
- Initial investment: $20,000

Activity during year:

- Month 1: Sell 5 contracts $42 call, collect $0.85 = $425
- Month 2: Calls expire worthless, sell new $42 calls, collect $0.90 = $450
- Month 3: Assigned at $42, exit position

Dividend activity:

- Received quarterly dividend $0.66 = $330 (only one quarter before assignment)

Capital gain calculation:

- Purchase price: $40.00
- Assignment price: $42.00
- Gain per share: $2.00
- Total gain: $1,000 (500 shares × $2.00)

Total return calculation:

- Option premium: $425 + $450 = $875
- Dividend income: $330
- Capital gain: $1,000
- Total profit: $2,205
- Total return: $2,205 / $20,000 = 11.0%

- Holding period: 90 days
- Annualized return: [(1.110)^(365/90)] - 1 = 49.4%

Return Comparison: Multiple Strategies

Consider the same $20,000 Verizon investment under different strategies:

Strategy 1: Buy and Hold (No Options)

- Purchase: $40.00
- Ending price after 90 days: $42.00
- Dividends: $330
- Total return: ($2,000 + $330) / $20,000 = 11.7%
- Annualized: 51.2%

Strategy 2: Covered Calls (Aggressive ITM)

- Purchase: $40.00
- Sell $40 calls immediately, collect $2.10 premium = $1,050
- Assigned at $40 (no stock gain)
- Dividends: $330
- Total return: ($1,050 + $330) / $20,000 = 6.9%
- Annualized: 30.0%

Strategy 3: Covered Calls (Conservative OTM)

- Purchase: $40.00
- Sell $42 calls, collect $0.85 = $425
- Stock rises to $42, assigned
- Dividends: $330
- Total return: ($1,000 + $425 + $330) / $20,000 = 8.8%
- Annualized: 38.2%

Analysis: In this bull market scenario where the stock rallied, buy-and-hold slightly outperformed covered calls because appreciation exceeded the strike price. However, covered calls still generated 38%

annualized return while providing downside protection through premium income.

Performance Tracking Spreadsheet

Maintain a systematic tracking system:

Position Tracker Template:

Stock Symbol: VZ

Entry Date: 1/15

Shares: 500

Purchase Price: $40.00

Initial Investment: $20,000

Options Activity:

Date | Action | Strike | Exp | Premium | Total

1/15 | Sell to Open | $42 | 2/16 | $0.85 | $425

2/16 | Expire Worthless | - | - | - | -

2/17 | Sell to Open | $42 | 3/15 | $0.90 | $450

Dividend Activity:

Date | Amount per Share | Total

2/8 | $0.66 | $330

Exit Details:

Exit Date: 3/15

Exit Price: $42.00 (Assignment)

Capital Gain: $2.00/share = $1,000

Total Return Summary:

Option Premium: $875

Dividends: $330

Capital Gain: $1,000

Total Profit: $2,205

Total Return: 11.0%

Days Held: 90

Annualized Return: 49.4%

Portfolio-Level Performance

Track individual positions and aggregate portfolio performance:

Portfolio Dashboard:

Stock	Investment	Premium	Dividends	Cap Gain	Total	Return %
JNJ	$30,000	$4,200	$900	$1,200	$6,300	21.0%
VZ	$25,000	$3,600	$1,000	-$500	$4,100	16.4%
PG	$28,000	$3,780	$840	$800	$5,420	19.4%
KO	$22,000	$2,860	$660	$400	$3,920	17.8%
Total	$105,000	$14,440	$3,400	$1,900	$19,740	18.8%

Benchmark Comparison

Always compare your covered call returns to relevant benchmarks:

Primary benchmark: S&P 500 total return (including dividends) **Secondary benchmark:** Dividend-focused index (e.g., S&P 500 Dividend Aristocrats Index) **Tertiary benchmark:** Risk-free rate (10-year Treasury) plus risk premium

If your covered call portfolio returns 18% while the S&P 500 returns 22%, you underperformed on an absolute basis. However, if your maximum drawdown was 8% versus the S&P's 18%, your risk-adjusted return may be superior.

Risk-Adjusted Return Metrics

Sharpe Ratio measures return per unit of risk: Sharpe Ratio = (Portfolio Return - Risk-Free Rate) / Standard Deviation

Higher Sharpe ratios indicate better risk-adjusted performance.

Example:

- Portfolio return: 18%
- Risk-free rate: 4%
- Portfolio standard deviation: 10%
- Sharpe Ratio: (18% - 4%) / 10% = 1.4

Compare to S&P 500:

- S&P return: 12%
- Risk-free rate: 4%
- S&P standard deviation: 15%
- Sharpe Ratio: (12% - 4%) / 15% = 0.53

The covered call portfolio's Sharpe ratio of 1.4 significantly exceeds the S&P's 0.53, indicating superior risk-adjusted returns.

Monthly Income Calculation

For income-focused investors, calculate reliable monthly cash flow:

Portfolio: $200,000 across dividend aristocrats **Average monthly premium:** 1.3% = $2,600 **Average quarterly dividend:** 2.5% annually = $1,250 per quarter = $417 monthly equivalent **Total monthly income:** $3,017

This predictable monthly income creates financial planning certainty superior to irregular capital gains or quarterly-only dividend payments.

Conclusion: The Power of Dual Income

Combining dividend-paying stocks with covered calls creates a sum greater than its parts. The strategy generates consistent monthly option premium, reliable quarterly dividends, potential capital appreciation, and superior downside protection—all from the same invested capital.

Dividend aristocrats provide the optimal foundation for this strategy, combining the financial strength to sustain dividends through any economic environment with the stability to generate consistent option premiums.

By properly timing options around ex-dividend dates, systematically tracking total returns, and maintaining a diversified portfolio of quality dividend payers, you can build an income-generating portfolio capable of supporting financial independence, funding retirement, or accelerating wealth accumulation.

The next chapters will explore advanced execution strategies, position sizing, and managing this powerful combination across different market conditions.

PART III: STRATEGY AND EXECUTION

Chapter 11:

Selecting the Right Strike Price

Strike price selection represents the most critical decision in covered call trading. This single choice determines your maximum profit potential, downside protection, assignment probability, and overall risk-reward profile. Unlike stock selection, which you can analyze over days or weeks, strike selection requires systematic decision-making frameworks that account for market conditions, stock technicals, volatility, and your strategic objectives.

This chapter provides comprehensive frameworks for strike selection, from conservative approaches emphasizing capital preservation to aggressive strategies maximizing premium income.

Conservative vs. Aggressive Approaches

Every strike price exists on a continuum from deeply out-of-the-money (conservative) to in-the-money (aggressive). Understanding where each approach sits on this spectrum allows you to match strike selection to your goals and risk tolerance.

The Strike Price Spectrum

Deep Out-of-the-Money (7%+ above current price):

- Probability of assignment: 5-15%
- Typical premium: 0.5-1.0% monthly
- Capital appreciation potential: Significant
- Downside protection: Minimal
- Best for: Bullish outlooks, growth stocks you don't want to sell

Moderate Out-of-the-Money (3-7% above current price):

- Probability of assignment: 15-30%
- Typical premium: 1.0-1.8% monthly
- Capital appreciation potential: Moderate
- Downside protection: Moderate
- Best for: Standard covered call strategies, balanced objectives

Slightly Out-of-the-Money (1-3% above current price):

- Probability of assignment: 30-45%
- Typical premium: 1.5-2.5% monthly
- Capital appreciation potential: Limited
- Downside protection: Good
- Best for: Sideways to slightly bullish markets, income focus

At-the-Money (within 1% of current price):

- Probability of assignment: 45-55%
- Typical premium: 2.0-3.5% monthly
- Capital appreciation potential: Minimal
- Downside protection: Very good
- Best for: Neutral outlooks, maximum time value capture

In-the-Money (below current price):

- Probability of assignment: 60-85%
- Typical premium: 3.0-6.0%+ monthly (includes intrinsic value)
- Capital appreciation potential: None (already exceeded strike)
- Downside protection: Excellent
- Best for: Bearish to neutral outlooks, exit strategies, maximum income

Conservative Approach Philosophy

Conservative covered call traders prioritize three objectives: preserving capital, maintaining upside participation, and generating supplemental income—in that order.

Strike selection guidelines:

- Select strikes 5-7% out-of-the-money
- Target delta of 0.15-0.25
- Accept lower premiums (0.8-1.5% monthly) for greater flexibility
- Avoid strikes at significant technical resistance levels

- Allow stock to appreciate substantially before assignment

Ideal conditions for conservative approach:

- Bull markets or strong uptrends where appreciation is likely
- Growth stocks with significant upside potential
- Stocks you strongly believe in long-term
- Portfolios already generating adequate income
- Investors uncomfortable with frequent assignment

Conservative example: Stock XYZ trading at $100

- Available strikes: $102, $105, $107, $110
- Conservative selection: $107 or $110 strike
- Premium at $107: $1.20 (1.2% monthly, delta 0.20)
- Premium at $110: $0.75 (0.75% monthly, delta 0.12)
- Assignment probability: 15-20% at $107, 8-12% at $110
- Upside participation: 7-10% before assignment

Outcome analysis: If stock rallies to $115:

- $107 strike: Assigned at $107, total gain = $7 appreciation + $1.20 premium = $8.20 (8.2% return)
- $110 strike: Assigned at $110, total gain = $10 appreciation + $0.75 premium = $10.75 (10.75% return)

The more conservative $110 strike actually generates superior returns in strong bull moves because it captures more appreciation despite lower premium.

Moderate (Balanced) Approach Philosophy

The moderate approach represents the most common covered call strategy, balancing income generation with reasonable upside participation and assignment risk.

Strike selection guidelines:

- Select strikes 2-4% out-of-the-money

- Target delta of 0.25-0.35
- Generate premiums of 1.2-2.0% monthly
- Balance premium collection with appreciation potential
- Accept moderate assignment frequency (25-35% of positions)

Ideal conditions for moderate approach:

- Sideways or slowly rising markets
- Blue-chip stocks with moderate volatility
- Balanced portfolio objectives (income and growth)
- Most market conditions (all-weather strategy)
- Experienced traders comfortable managing assignments

Moderate example: Stock XYZ trading at $100

- Available strikes: $102, $103, $104, $105
- Moderate selection: $103 or $104 strike
- Premium at $103: $1.80 (1.8% monthly, delta 0.30)
- Premium at $104: $1.50 (1.5% monthly, delta 0.25)
- Assignment probability: 30-35% at $103, 25-30% at $104
- Upside participation: 3-4% before assignment

Outcome scenarios:
Sideways market (stock stays at $100):

- Premium captured: $1.50-1.80
- Stock unchanged: $0
- Total return: 1.5-1.8% monthly (18-21.6% annualized)
- Result: Excellent—premium is pure profit

Moderate rally (stock moves to $106):

- Assigned at $103-104
- Stock appreciation: $3-4
- Premium collected: $1.50-1.80
- Total return: $4.50-5.80 (4.5-5.8%)

- Result: Very good—captured appreciation plus premium

Decline (stock drops to $95):

- Options expire worthless (profit on option side)
- Stock loss: -$5.00
- Premium offset: +$1.50-1.80
- Net loss: -$3.20 to -$3.50
- Result: Premium provided 30-36% downside protection

Aggressive Approach Philosophy

Aggressive covered call traders prioritize maximum income over capital appreciation, accepting frequent assignments and limited upside participation.

Strike selection guidelines:

- Select at-the-money or in-the-money strikes
- Target delta of 0.40-0.60+ (ITM strikes can have delta of 0.70-0.90)
- Generate premiums of 2.5-4.0%+ monthly
- Maximize downside protection through premium collection
- Expect frequent assignment (50-70% of positions)

Ideal conditions for aggressive approach:

- Sideways or declining markets
- Stocks you're willing to sell at current prices
- Income prioritized over growth
- Overvalued positions you want to exit
- Bearish to neutral market outlook

Aggressive example: Stock XYZ trading at $100

- Available strikes: $98, $99, $100, $101
- Aggressive selection: $98 or $100 strike
- Premium at $98 ITM: $3.50 (includes $2 intrinsic + $1.50

time value)
- Premium at $100 ATM: $2.80 (pure time value)
- Assignment probability: 70-80% at $98, 50-60% at $100

Outcome scenarios:
Sideways market (stock at $100):

- $98 strike: Assigned, sell at $98 but collected $3.50 premium
- Net result: $98 + $3.50 = $101.50 effective sale price (1.5% gain)
- $100 strike: Likely assigned, effective sale at $102.80 (2.8% gain)

Declining market (stock drops to $94):

- $98 strike: Option expires worthless (stock above strike)
- Stock loss: -$6.00
- Premium collected: +$3.50
- Net loss: -$2.50 (premium provided 58% downside protection)
- Can sell new covered call at lower strike

Rally (stock moves to $108):

- Assigned at $98 or $100
- Opportunity cost: Missed $8-10 of appreciation
- Total gain: $1.50-2.80 (assignment plus premium)
- Result: Profitable but underperformed buy-and-hold

Comparative Performance Analysis

Let's compare all three approaches over a 12-month period with different market scenarios:

Scenario 1: Bull Market (Stock rises from $100 to $130)

Conservative ($107 strikes average):

- Assignments: 3 times
- Average exit: $107

- Premium collected: $14.40 (12 months × $1.20)
- Total return: $7 + $14.40 = $21.40 (21.4%)
- Benchmark (buy-hold): 30%
- Assessment: Underperformed, missed significant upside

Moderate ($103 strikes average):

- Assignments: 6 times
- Average exit: $103
- Premium collected: $18.00 (12 months × $1.50)
- Total return: $3 + $18.00 = $21.00 (21%)
- Assessment: Similar to conservative, underperformed buy-hold

Aggressive ($100 strikes average):

- Assignments: 9 times
- Average exit: $100
- Premium collected: $28.00 (12 months × $2.33)
- Total return: $0 + $28.00 = $28.00 (28%)
- Assessment: Strong returns but still missed major appreciation

Scenario 2: Sideways Market (Stock oscillates $95-$105, ends at $101)

Conservative ($107 strikes):

- Assignments: 0
- Premium collected: $14.40
- Stock appreciation: $1
- Total return: $15.40 (15.4%)
- Benchmark (buy-hold): 1%
- Assessment: Dramatically outperformed, strategy excelled

Moderate ($103 strikes):

- Assignments: 2 times
- Premium collected: $18.00

- Stock appreciation: $1
- Total return: $19.00 (19%)
- Assessment: Excellent, captured consistent premium

Aggressive ($100 strikes):

- Assignments: 6 times
- Premium collected: $28.00
- Stock appreciation: $1
- Total return: $29.00 (29%)
- Assessment: Outstanding, maximized sideways market opportunity

Scenario 3: Bear Market (Stock declines from $100 to $80)
Conservative ($107 strikes):

- Assignments: 0
- Premium collected: $14.40
- Stock loss: -$20
- Net result: -$5.60 (-5.6%)
- Benchmark (buy-hold): -20%
- Assessment: Premium provided 72% downside protection

Moderate ($103 strikes):

- Assignments: 0
- Premium collected: $18.00
- Stock loss: -$20
- Net result: -$2.00 (-2%)
- Assessment: Premium provided 90% downside protection

Aggressive ($100 strikes):

- Assignments: 0-1 times
- Premium collected: $28.00
- Stock loss: -$20

- Net result: +$8.00 (+8%)
- Assessment: Actually profitable in bear market due to premium

Key Insight: Aggressive strikes excel in sideways and bearish markets, conservative strikes excel in bull markets, and moderate strikes provide consistent performance across all conditions.

The 30-Delta Rule Explained

The 30-delta rule provides a simple, systematic framework for strike selection that balances premium income, assignment probability, and capital appreciation potential. This rule has become an industry standard for good reason—it works consistently across different stocks and market conditions.

Understanding Delta as Probability

Delta serves double duty in options pricing:

1. It measures how much the option price changes per $1 movement in the stock
2. It approximates the probability that the option will finish in-the-money at expiration

A call option with delta of 0.30 (or 30 in some platforms) suggests:

- The option will gain $0.30 in value if the stock rises $1.00
- There's approximately a 30% probability the stock will be above the strike price at expiration
- Conversely, there's a 70% probability the option will expire worthless

The 30-Delta Sweet Spot

The 30-delta strike typically sits 2-4% out-of-the-money (the exact percentage depends on time to expiration, volatility, and other factors). This positioning creates an optimal balance:

Premium generation: Adequate to justify the strategy (typically 1.2-2.0% monthly) **Assignment probability:** Low enough to maintain positions through multiple cycles (30% chance) **Capital preservation:**

Allows 2-4% appreciation before assignment **Consistency:** Repeatable across different stocks and sectors

Applying the 30-Delta Rule

Step 1: Open your options chain Most platforms display delta for each strike. Look in the delta column for values near 0.30.

Step 2: Identify the closest strike to 0.30 delta You'll typically find strikes with deltas like 0.27, 0.32, 0.35. Select the one closest to 0.30, generally preferring slightly lower (0.27-0.29) over higher (0.31-0.35) if ambiguous.

Step 3: Verify the premium Ensure the premium justifies the trade. For monthly expirations, 30-delta strikes should generate 1.2-2.0% premiums. If premium is below 1.0%, consider a closer strike or different stock.

Step 4: Check technical resistance Verify the strike doesn't sit at major technical resistance. If the 0.30-delta strike falls at $105 but strong resistance exists at $104, consider using $104 strike instead despite delta of 0.33-0.35.

Practical Example: Applying 30-Delta Rule

Stock: Microsoft (MSFT) trading at $380

Options chain (30-day expiration):

Strike	Bid	Ask	Delta	Premium %
$385	$7.20	$7.40	0.48	1.89%
$390	$5.30	$5.50	0.38	1.39%
$395	$3.80	$4.00	0.30	1.00%
$400	$2.70	$2.90	0.23	0.71%
$405	$1.90	$2.10	0.17	0.50%

Analysis: The $395 strike shows delta of exactly 0.30—perfect match for the rule. However, the premium of 1.0% is at the low end of acceptable.

Alternative consideration: The $390 strike with delta 0.38 generates 1.39% premium—39% more income. The trade-off is modestly higher assignment probability (38% vs. 30%).

Decision framework:

- If bullish on MSFT and expecting appreciation: Select $395 (following 30-delta rule precisely)
- If neutral on MSFT and prioritizing income: Select $390 (modestly more aggressive than 30-delta rule)
- If very bullish: Consider $400 strike despite lower premium

Adjustments to the 30-Delta Rule

While 30-delta serves as an excellent baseline, adjust based on specific circumstances:

Raise to 35-40 delta when:

- Volatility is elevated and premiums are rich
- You're neutral to slightly bearish on the stock
- You want to prioritize income over appreciation
- The stock is consolidating in a range
- You're comfortable with higher assignment frequency

Lower to 20-25 delta when:

- You're bullish on the stock
- Volatility is low and premiums are thin
- You want maximum upside participation
- The stock is breaking out or in strong uptrend
- You're using covered calls primarily for downside protection

Market Condition Adjustments:

- Bull markets: Consider 20-25 delta (more conservative)
- Sideways markets: Stick with 30-35 delta (standard)
- Bear markets: Consider 40-50 delta (more aggressive/ defensive)

Delta Decay Over Time

Important consideration: Delta changes as expiration approaches and stock price moves.

An option with 0.30 delta at 30 days to expiration might have:

- 0.35 delta at 20 days (if stock stays at same price)
- 0.42 delta at 10 days
- 0.50+ delta at 5 days

This delta expansion means assignment risk increases even without stock price movement as expiration nears. Monitor positions and be prepared to roll or close if delta expands beyond your comfort level.

Calculating Your Breakeven Point

Breakeven analysis reveals the price level where your covered call position neither makes nor loses money. Understanding breakeven helps you assess true downside protection and make informed decisions about strike selection.

Basic Breakeven Formula

Breakeven Price = Purchase Price - Premium Received

This simple formula shows the stock price level where premium income exactly offsets any stock decline.

Example:

- Purchase stock at $50.00
- Sell covered call, collect $2.50 premium
- Breakeven = $50.00 - $2.50 = $47.50

If the stock falls to $47.50, your $2.50 stock loss equals your $2.50 premium gain, resulting in zero net profit or loss.

Detailed Breakeven Analysis

Above Breakeven (Stock > $47.50): You're profitable. The profit equals the premium collected plus any stock appreciation, limited to the strike price.

At Breakeven (Stock = $47.50): Net position value equals your initial investment. No gain or loss.

Below Breakeven (Stock < $47.50): You're experiencing losses. The stock loss exceeds the premium protection.

Breakeven Analysis Across Strike Selections

Compare breakeven levels for different strike choices on the same stock:

Stock: XYZ at $100
Conservative (OTM) Strike:

- Strike: $105
- Premium: $1.50
- Breakeven: $98.50
- Downside protection: 1.5%

Moderate Strike:

- Strike: $102
- Premium: $2.20
- Breakeven: $97.80
- Downside protection: 2.2%

Aggressive (ATM) Strike:

- Strike: $100
- Premium: $3.50
- Breakeven: $96.50
- Downside protection: 3.5%

Aggressive (ITM) Strike:

- Strike: $97
- Premium: $4.80 ($3 intrinsic + $1.80 time value)
- Breakeven: $95.20
- Downside protection: 4.8%

Key Insight: More aggressive strikes provide better downside protection through lower breakeven points, but sacrifice upside potential.

Maximum Profit Calculation

Maximum profit occurs when the stock is at or above the strike price at expiration:

Max Profit = (Strike Price - Purchase Price) + Premium Received

Using our $100 stock example:
Conservative ($105 strike, $1.50 premium):

- Max profit = ($105 - $100) + $1.50 = $6.50 (6.5% return)

Moderate ($102 strike, $2.20 premium):

- Max profit = ($102 - $100) + $2.20 = $4.20 (4.2% return)

Aggressive ATM ($100 strike, $3.50 premium):

- Max profit = ($100 - $100) + $3.50 = $3.50 (3.5% return)

Aggressive ITM ($97 strike, $4.80 premium):

- Max profit = ($97 - $100) + $4.80 = $1.80 (1.8% return)

Note: The ITM strike shows lower maximum profit in dollar terms, but this occurs immediately since the stock is already above strike. The other strikes require stock appreciation to reach maximum profit.

Risk-Reward Analysis

Combine breakeven and maximum profit to evaluate complete risk-reward profiles:

Conservative OTM Strike:

- Maximum profit: $6.50 (6.5%)
- Breakeven: $98.50 (1.5% below current)
- Risk-reward ratio: 1.5% protection / 6.5% potential = 0.23
- Assessment: High reward, limited protection

Moderate Strike:

- Maximum profit: $4.20 (4.2%)
- Breakeven: $97.80 (2.2% below current)
- Risk-reward ratio: 2.2% protection / 4.2% potential = 0.52
- Assessment: Balanced risk-reward

Aggressive ATM Strike:

- Maximum profit: $3.50 (3.5%)
- Breakeven: $96.50 (3.5% below current)
- Risk-reward ratio: 3.5% protection / 3.5% potential = 1.0
- Assessment: Equal downside protection and upside potential

Aggressive ITM Strike:

- Maximum profit: $1.80 (1.8%)
- Breakeven: $95.20 (4.8% below current)
- Risk-reward ratio: 4.8% protection / 1.8% potential = 2.67
- Assessment: Defensive, prioritizing protection over gains

Return If Unchanged (RIU)

Another useful metric: What return do you earn if the stock stays exactly at the current price?

Formula: RIU = Premium / Purchase Price

Conservative OTM ($1.50 premium): 1.5% return if unchanged Moderate ($2.20 premium): 2.2% return if unchanged Aggressive ATM ($3.50 premium): 3.5% return if unchanged Aggressive ITM ($4.80 premium, but $3 is intrinsic): 1.8% time value return if unchanged

Key Insight: ATM strikes maximize return if unchanged because they capture maximum time value. This makes them optimal for sideways markets.

Strike Selection for Different Market Conditions

Market conditions should heavily influence strike selection. A strategy that excels in bull markets underperforms in bear markets, and vice versa.

Bull Market Strike Selection

Market characteristics:

- Sustained uptrend with higher highs and higher lows
- Strong momentum and positive sentiment
- Stocks frequently breaking through resistance levels

- Volatility relatively low (complacency)

Optimal strike strategy: Use conservative out-of-the-money strikes to capture appreciation:

Primary approach:

- Delta range: 0.15-0.25
- Strike distance: 5-7% OTM
- Accept lower premiums (0.8-1.5% monthly)
- Maximize upside participation
- Reduce assignment frequency

Rationale: In bull markets, stock appreciation often exceeds premium income. Missing a 15% rally while collecting 2% premium leaves you significantly behind buy-and-hold investors. Conservative strikes let you participate in the bull market while generating supplementary income.

Practical example: Stock rallying from $80 to $95:

- Conservative $87 strike: Assigned at $87, gain = $7 + $1.20 premium = $8.20 (10.3%)
- Aggressive $82 strike: Assigned at $82, gain = $2 + $2.80 premium = $4.80 (6%)

The conservative approach outperformed by 80% in this bull market scenario.

Alternative tactics for bull markets:

- Shorten expiration periods (14-21 days) allowing frequent strike adjustments upward
- Roll calls aggressively to higher strikes when stock advances
- Consider skipping covered calls on strongest performers, letting them run
- Concentrate covered calls on slower-moving positions

Bear Market Strike Selection

Market characteristics:

- Sustained downtrend with lower lows and lower highs
- Negative sentiment and increased volatility
- Frequent support level breakdowns
- Elevated implied volatility (fear)

Optimal strike strategy: Use aggressive at-the-money or in-the-money strikes for maximum protection:

Primary approach:

- Delta range: 0.45-0.70
- Strike distance: ATM to 2% ITM
- Capture high premiums (2.5-4%+ monthly)
- Maximize downside protection
- Accept limited or no upside participation

Rationale: In bear markets, capital preservation trumps income optimization. Missing upside is less concerning when stocks are declining. Aggressive strikes generate premiums that offset losses and potentially create profits even as stocks fall.

Practical example: Stock declining from $80 to $65:

⟐ Conservative $85 strike: No assignment, premium $1.20, stock loss -$15, net loss -$13.80 (-17.3%)

⟐ Aggressive $80 strike: No assignment, premium $3.50, stock loss -$15, net loss -$11.50 (-14.4%)

⟐ Very aggressive $77 ITM strike: No assignment, premium $5.50, stock loss -$15, net loss -$9.50 (-11.9%)

The aggressive approaches reduced losses by 16-32% through enhanced premium income.

Alternative tactics for bear markets:

- Increase cash allocation, reducing equity exposure overall
- Rotate to defensive sectors with stable dividends
- Extend expiration periods (45-60 days) to capture more premium per trade
- Consider closing positions and moving to cash rather than continued covered calls on declining stocks

Sideways/Consolidating Market Strike Selection
Market characteristics:

- Trading range between defined support and resistance
- Low directional bias
- Moderate volatility
- Predictable price oscillations

Optimal strike strategy: This is the ideal environment for covered calls. Use moderate strikes near resistance levels:

Primary approach:

- Delta range: 0.30-0.40
- Strike distance: 2-4% OTM, positioned at or near technical resistance
- Capture solid premiums (1.5-2.5% monthly)
- High probability of expiration worthless (capturing full premium)
- Repeat monthly for consistent income

Rationale: Sideways markets minimize opportunity cost since you're not missing significant appreciation. Premium income becomes the primary return driver. Resistance levels act as natural assignment barriers, allowing systematic premium collection.

Practical example: Stock consolidating between $48-$52 support/resistance:

- Stock at $50

- Sell $52 strikes (at resistance) for $1.80 premium
- High probability stock doesn't exceed $52 (historical resistance)
- Capture full $1.80 (1.8%) monthly
- Repeat for 12 months = 21.6% annual return on flat stock

Advanced consolidation strategy:

- Sell calls when stock approaches resistance ($51-52)
- Buy back calls when stock approaches support ($48-49) at profit
- Re-sell calls when stock rebounds toward resistance
- Potentially generate 2-3x normal premium through active management

High Volatility Period Strike Selection
Market characteristics:

- VIX elevated (above 20-25)
- Wide daily price swings
- Elevated implied volatility
- Earnings season or major news events

Optimal strike strategy: Prioritize premium capture while volatility is rich:

Primary approach:

- Focus on absolute premium dollars rather than delta
- Consider ATM strikes to maximize time value capture
- Shorter expirations (7-14 days) to reduce risk of dramatic moves
- Accept higher assignment probability for premium enhancement

Rationale: Elevated implied volatility inflates option premiums. A strike that normally generates $1.50 might produce $2.80 during volatility spikes. Capitalize on these rich premiums even if it means tighter strikes.

Example: Normal volatility: $50 stock, $52 strike, $1.40 premium (30-delta) High volatility: $50 stock, $52 strike, $2.60 premium (35-delta)

The same strike generates 86% more premium during volatility spikes. This justifies more aggressive strike selection or shorter expirations to capitalize on rich pricing.

Warning: High volatility exists for a reason—uncertainty and risk. Only sell calls on stocks you're truly comfortable owning through volatile periods.

Low Volatility Period Strike Selection

Market characteristics:

- VIX at low levels (below 15)
- Narrow daily price ranges
- Compressed implied volatility
- Complacent market sentiment

Optimal strike strategy: Consider whether covered calls are optimal:

Primary approach:

- Evaluate if premiums justify strategy (need minimum 1% monthly)
- If premiums insufficient, consider pausing covered calls
- If continuing, use slightly more aggressive strikes to compensate for low premium
- Extend expirations to 45-60 days to capture more absolute premium

Alternative approach: During extended low volatility periods:

- Reduce covered call activity to 30-50% of portfolio
- Allow remaining positions to appreciate without limitation

- Wait for volatility mean reversion before scaling back up
- Deploy capital to higher-volatility names that still generate adequate premium

Decision Matrix for Strike Selection

Synthesize all factors into systematic decision-making:

STRIKE SELECTION DECISION TREE:

1. What's the current market regime?

→ Bull Market → Use Delta 0.15-0.25 (Conservative)

→ Sideways Market → Use Delta 0.30-0.40 (Moderate)

→ Bear Market → Use Delta 0.45-0.70 (Aggressive)

2. What's my outlook on this specific stock?

→ Bullish → Adjust toward conservative (lower delta)

→ Neutral → Use standard for market regime

→ Bearish → Adjust toward aggressive (higher delta)

3. What's the current volatility environment?

→ High (IV Rank > 50) → Can be more aggressive for premium

→ Normal (IV Rank 30-50) → Use standard approach

→ Low (IV Rank < 30) → Be conservative or skip

4. Where are technical levels?

→ Strike aligns with resistance → Excellent selection

→ Strike between levels → Standard selection

→ Strike aligns with support → Poor selection, choose higher

5. What's my portfolio objective?

→ Maximum income → Aggressive strikes

→ Balanced → Moderate strikes

→ Capital appreciation with income → Conservative strikes

Conclusion: Strike Selection Mastery

Strike selection is both art and science. The 30-delta rule provides an excellent foundation, but true mastery comes from adjusting based on market conditions, individual stock outlook, volatility environment, and personal objectives.

Conservative strikes preserve capital and participation but generate modest income. Aggressive strikes maximize income and protection but sacrifice upside. Moderate strikes balance competing priorities and work consistently across varied conditions.

Most successful covered call traders maintain flexibility, adjusting strike aggressiveness based on conditions rather than rigidly applying one approach. Build experience across the spectrum, develop intuition for when to be aggressive versus conservative, and let market conditions guide your decisions.

Chapter 12:

Choosing Expiration Dates

Expiration date selection determines how long your capital remains committed, how quickly time decay works in your favor, and how frequently you must manage positions. While less dramatic than strike selection, expiration choice significantly impacts returns, workload, and risk management.

This chapter explores the complete spectrum of expiration dates from weekly options to LEAPs, helping you optimize duration selection for your strategy and lifestyle.

Weekly vs. Monthly Options

The introduction of weekly options in 2005 revolutionized covered call trading, providing flexibility previously unavailable. Understanding the trade-offs between weekly and monthly expirations allows you to select the optimal duration.

Weekly Options Characteristics

Weekly options expire every Friday (or Thursday before major holidays), providing 52 expiration opportunities annually versus 12 for monthly options.

Advantages of weekly options:

Accelerated time decay: Theta decay is most aggressive in the final 7-10 days before expiration. Weekly options exist entirely within this high-decay zone, maximizing the seller's advantage.

Flexibility and adjustment: Weekly expirations allow rapid strategy adjustments. If your market outlook changes, you're never more than a few days from expiration and the ability to pivot.

Precise timing: Match expirations to known events. If earnings are in 12 days, sell a 2-week option that expires just before earnings, capturing premium while avoiding post-earnings risk.

Potential for higher annualized returns: Rolling weekly options 52 times yearly theoretically generates more total premium than 12 monthly rolls, assuming you can consistently find strikes generating 0.4-0.6% weekly (20-31% annualized).

Disadvantages of weekly options:

Time-intensive management: 52 expirations require 52 decisions about rolling, closing, or adjustment. This suits active traders but overwhelms passive investors.

Higher transaction costs: More frequent trading multiplies commission costs (though less relevant with zero-commission brokers).

Increased execution risk: Weekly rolls during volatile

***

Choosing Expiration Dates (Continued)

Weekly vs. Monthly Options (Continued)

Disadvantages of weekly options:

Time-intensive management: 52 expirations require 52 decisions about rolling, closing, or adjustment. This suits active traders but overwhelms passive investors.

Higher transaction costs: More frequent trading multiplies commission costs (though less relevant with zero-commission brokers).

Increased execution risk: Weekly rolls during volatile periods can result in poor fills or forced decisions during unfavorable conditions.

Premium per contract is smaller: While weekly options might generate 0.5% returns, the absolute premium is small (e.g., $0.50 on a $100 stock = $50 per contract). Smaller premiums mean transaction costs and bid-ask spreads take larger percentages.

Requires constant attention: Missing an expiration means your stock sits unprotected for a week, reducing total annual returns.

Less forgiving of mistakes: A poorly timed weekly sale during a strong rally means missing just a few days of appreciation, but this can be significant in fast-moving markets.

Monthly Options Characteristics

Monthly options expire on the third Friday of each month, providing the standard expiration cycle that has existed since options were standardized.

Advantages of monthly options:

Optimal time decay efficiency: The 30-45 day window captures excellent theta decay while providing reasonable premium per trade. This represents the "sweet spot" that most professionals target.

Manageable workload: 12 annual decisions suit part-time traders and investors with other responsibilities. Monthly management sessions require only 30-60 minutes per position.

Larger absolute premiums: Monthly options on a $100 stock might generate $2.00 premium ($200 per contract), making transaction costs proportionally smaller and providing more meaningful income per trade.

Reduced stress and flexibility: Four weeks between expirations provides time to evaluate, research, and make thoughtful decisions rather than constant reactive management.

Better liquidity: Monthly options typically show higher volume and tighter bid-ask spreads than weeklies, especially for stocks outside the largest mega-caps.

Disadvantages of monthly options:

Slower capital deployment: If you're assigned early in the month, your capital may sit idle for weeks until establishing a new position.

Less precision for event management: If earnings are in 25 days, you must either sell a monthly that expires after earnings (accepting risk) or a weekly that expires well before earnings (leaving time value on the table).

Lower annualized theoretical returns: Twelve monthly cycles at 2% each yields 24% annually, while 52 weekly cycles at 0.5% yields 26% annually (though this advantage often disappears after accounting for real-world execution challenges).

Comparative Performance Analysis

Scenario 1: Stable Blue-Chip Stock

Stock: Johnson & Johnson trading consistently between $155-$165

Weekly Strategy:

- Sell $160 calls every Friday
- Average weekly premium: $0.75 (0.48%)
- Annual cycles: 52
- Theoretical annual return: 25%
- Actual return after missed weeks, poor fills: 21%
- Time investment: 52 hours annually
- Stress level: Moderate (constant monitoring)

Monthly Strategy:

- Sell $162 calls monthly

- Average monthly premium: $2.40 (1.55%)
- Annual cycles: 12
- Theoretical annual return: 18.6%
- Actual return after execution: 18%
- Time investment: 12 hours annually
- Stress level: Low (quarterly attention)

Analysis: Weekly strategy generated 17% higher returns but required 333% more time. Return per hour of effort strongly favors monthly options for this stable stock.

Scenario 2: Volatile Technology Stock

Stock: Advanced Micro Devices trading between $120-$180 with significant weekly swings

Weekly Strategy:

- Sell varying strikes based on weekly volatility
- Average weekly premium: $1.80 (1.2%)
- Many weeks assigned, requiring repurchase
- Theoretical annual return: 62%
- Actual return after whipsaw losses: 35%
- Time investment: 65 hours annually (more management needed)
- Stress level: High (constant price watching)

Monthly Strategy:

- Sell monthly strikes
- Average monthly premium: $5.20 (3.47%)
- Quarterly assignments on average
- Theoretical annual return: 41.6%
- Actual return: 38%
- Time investment: 15 hours annually
- Stress level: Moderate (monthly check-ins)

Analysis: Despite higher theoretical returns from weekly options, actual realized returns were similar due to frequent whipsaw assignments. Monthly strategy delivered almost identical returns with 77% less time investment.

Hybrid Approach: Combining Weekly and Monthly

Many sophisticated traders blend both durations:

Primary strategy: Use monthly options for core portfolio positions (70-80% of holdings) **Supplementary strategy:** Use weekly options for tactical situations (20-30% of holdings)

When to use weeklies:

- Stock is consolidating in tight range with predictable support/resistance
- Earnings announcement is imminent (sell weekly expiring just before earnings)
- Stock has made significant move and you expect consolidation
- You have time for active management of specific positions
- High implied volatility creates rich weekly premiums

When to use monthlies:

- Blue-chip core holdings requiring minimal management
- You're traveling or busy with work during certain periods
- Stock shows moderate volatility without clear weekly patterns
- You prefer set-and-forget approach
- Position is part of retirement account requiring less active trading

Practical hybrid example:

Portfolio: $200,000 across 10 positions

Monthly options (8 positions, $160,000):

- Microsoft: Monthly
- Johnson & Johnson: Monthly
- Visa: Monthly

- Procter & Gamble: Monthly
- JPMorgan Chase: Monthly
- Coca-Cola: Monthly
- Walmart: Monthly
- Home Depot: Monthly

Weekly options (2 positions, $40,000):

- Apple: Weekly (stock very liquid, clear technical levels)
- Intel: Weekly (consolidating in range, experimenting with accelerated theta)

This approach provides stable monthly income from core holdings while allowing tactical weekly trading on selected positions.

Duration Selection Framework

EXPIRATION SELECTION DECISION TREE:

1. What's my available time for management?

→ Very Limited (< 2 hours monthly) → Monthly options only

→ Moderate (5-8 hours monthly) → Primarily monthly with select weeklies

→ Substantial (10+ hours monthly) → Can use weekly strategy

2. What's the stock's volatility profile?

→ Low volatility (< 20% IV) → Monthly (capture more premium per trade)

→ Moderate volatility (20-35% IV) → Either works well

→ High volatility (> 35% IV) → Weeklies can capitalize on rapid decay

3. Are there near-term events?

→ Earnings in 1-2 weeks → Use weekly expiring before earnings

→ Earnings in 3-4 weeks → Use monthly expiring before earnings

→ No major events → Standard monthly approach

4. What's my experience level?

→ Beginner → Start with monthly options exclusively

→ Intermediate → Add select weekly positions

→ Advanced → Can employ full weekly strategy

5. What's my stress tolerance?
→ Low → Monthly options (12 decisions yearly)
→ Moderate → Hybrid approach
→ High → Weekly strategy acceptable

The Time Decay Advantage

Time decay (theta) represents the covered call seller's greatest advantage. Understanding how theta works across different timeframes allows you to optimize expiration selection for maximum decay capture.

How Theta Decay Works

Options lose value as expiration approaches due to decreasing time value. This decay is not linear—it accelerates as expiration nears.

Theta decay pattern:

- 90-60 days to expiration: Slow decay, approximately 20% of total time value lost
- 60-30 days to expiration: Moderate decay, approximately 30% of total time value lost
- 30-10 days to expiration: Rapid decay, approximately 35% of total time value lost
- 10-0 days to expiration: Explosive decay, approximately 15% of total time value lost

Key insight: The most rapid decay occurs between 30 days and expiration, with maximum acceleration in the final 10 days.

Quantifying Theta Across Expirations

Consider an at-the-money call option on a $100 stock with 25% implied volatility:

90-day option:

- Premium: $4.80
- Theta: -$0.03 per day
- Daily decay: 0.625% of premium
- Weekly decay: 4.4%

60-day option:

- Premium: $4.00
- Theta: -$0.04 per day
- Daily decay: 1.0% of premium
- Weekly decay: 7.0%

30-day option:

- Premium: $2.90
- Theta: -$0.06 per day
- Daily decay: 2.07% of premium
- Weekly decay: 14.5%

7-day option:

- Premium: $1.50
- Theta: -$0.15 per day
- Daily decay: 10% of premium
- Weekly decay: 70%+

Analysis: The 30-day option decays 3.3x faster (as percentage of premium) than the 90-day option, and the 7-day option decays 5x faster than the 30-day option.

The 30-45 Day Sweet Spot

Professional options traders overwhelmingly favor selling options with 30-45 days to expiration because this window optimizes multiple factors:

Maximizes theta efficiency: Captures the accelerated decay zone without entering the ultra-high-risk final week.

Provides adequate premium: Generates meaningful income per trade (typically 1.5-3% depending on strike selection).

Balances flexibility and commitment: Long enough to avoid constant management but short enough to adjust if market conditions change.

Reduces tail risk: Long-dated options expose you to months of potential adverse events. 30-45 days limits exposure to one earnings cycle or major market event.

Optimal risk-reward: The premium-to-risk ratio peaks in this window. Longer options don't generate proportionally more premium, while shorter options introduce execution risk.

Mathematical Comparison: Different Expirations

Let's compare selling calls at different expirations on a $100 stock:

7-day option:

- Premium: $0.60 (0.6%)
- If rolled 52 times annually: 31.2% theoretical return
- Realistic return after poor fills, missed weeks: 24-26%

30-day option:

- Premium: $2.00 (2.0%)
- If rolled 12 times annually: 24% theoretical return
- Realistic return: 22-23%

60-day option:

- Premium: $3.20 (3.2%)
- If rolled 6 times annually: 19.2% theoretical return
- Realistic return: 18-19%

90-day option:

- Premium: $4.20 (4.2%)
- If rolled 4 times annually: 16.8% theoretical return
- Realistic return: 16-17%

Key findings:

1. Weekly options show highest theoretical returns but require perfect execution

2. Monthly (30-day) options provide excellent returns with manageable effort
3. Longer expirations generate diminishing returns per unit of time
4. The 30-day option offers the best balance for most investors

Theta Decay Strategies

Strategy 1: The 45-Day Roll

Most popular among professionals:

- Sell calls with 45 days to expiration
- Hold until 15-20 days remaining
- Close for profit (captured 50-60% of maximum value)
- Immediately sell new 45-day calls
- Repeat cycle

Advantages:

- Captures peak theta decay period (from 45 to 15 days)
- Avoids final week execution risk and volatility
- Allows quarterly positioning adjustments
- Reduces assignment risk (closes before expiration)

Example execution:

- January 15: Sell March 1 calls (45 days), collect $2.80
- February 12: Buy back March 1 calls for $1.10 (captured $1.70 profit)
- February 12: Sell March 29 calls (45 days), collect $2.90
- Repeat cycle every 25-30 days

Strategy 2: The 30-Day Cycle

Standard retail investor approach:

- Sell calls with 30-35 days to expiration
- Hold through expiration

- Immediately sell new 30-day calls
- Allow occasional assignments

Advantages:

- Simple and systematic (sell once monthly)
- Captures maximum time value per trade
- Lower transaction costs (fewer rolls)
- Aligns with monthly portfolio reviews

Strategy 3: The Rolling Thunder (Weekly)
Active trader approach:

- Sell weekly options every Friday
- Manage through week, close or let expire
- Immediately sell next weekly
- Requires constant monitoring

Advantages:

- Maximizes total annual theta decay capture
- Provides weekly cash flow
- Allows rapid adjustments to market conditions
- Can generate highest total returns

Disadvantages:

- Time-intensive (52 decisions annually)
- Higher stress and monitoring requirement
- Greater exposure to execution risk
- Best suited for retirement or full-time traders

Managing Your Calendar

Effective calendar management ensures you never miss expirations, optimally time new positions, and systematically execute your covered call strategy.

Creating Your Expiration Calendar

Build a master calendar tracking all key dates:

Monthly expiration schedule (third Friday of each month):

- January 17
- February 21
- March 21
- April 18
- May 16
- June 20
- July 18
- August 15
- September 19
- October 17
- November 21
- December 19

Weekly expirations: Every Friday except monthly expiration weeks

Ex-dividend dates: Track for all holdings (critical for assignment risk)

Earnings dates: Quarterly for all holdings

Federal Reserve meetings: 8 times annually (can trigger volatility)

Sample Integrated Calendar Entry:

March 2025:

- March 7 (Fri): Weekly expiration
- March 14 (Fri): Weekly expiration, also PG ex-dividend date
- March 21 (Fri): Monthly expiration (major event)
- March 24 (Mon): JNJ earnings before market open
- March 28 (Fri): Weekly expiration

Managing Multiple Positions

For portfolios with 8-12 positions, systematize expiration management:

Synchronized approach:

- Sell all covered calls on the same day each month
- All expire on the same monthly expiration
- Dedicate one day monthly to complete portfolio review and option sales
- Simple tracking (everything expires third Friday)

Advantages: Minimal time required, easy tracking, systematic execution

Disadvantages: Lacks flexibility for timing, requires managing 8-12 positions in single day

Staggered approach:

- Spread position expirations across the month
- Week 1: Manage positions 1-3
- Week 2: Manage positions 4-6
- Week 3: Manage positions 7-9
- Week 4: Manage positions 10-12

Advantages: Spreads workload, allows optimal timing for each stock, reduces stress

Disadvantages: Requires weekly attention, more complex tracking

Hybrid approach:

- Core 70% of portfolio on monthly synchronized expiration
- Tactical 30% on staggered or weekly expirations
- Balance simplicity with flexibility

Portfolio Management Workflow

Weekly routine (15-20 minutes):

- Monday: Review overall market conditions, sector performance
- Wednesday: Check positions expiring this week, decide whether to roll or let expire
- Thursday: Execute any necessary rolls or closes for Friday expiration

- Friday: Verify expirations completed, check for assignments
- Saturday: Review week, plan next week's actions

Monthly routine (1-2 hours):

- Week before monthly expiration: Review all positions
- Decide which to roll, which to let expire, which to close early
- Assess any positions assigned or near assignment
- Research new positions if capital is available
- Third Friday: Execute monthly expiration decisions
- Weekend after expiration: Complete portfolio review, sell new month's calls

Quarterly routine (3-4 hours):

- Comprehensive performance review
- Calculate total returns by position and overall portfolio
- Rebalance sector allocations if needed
- Review and update stock watchlist
- Assess strategy effectiveness and make adjustments
- Update tax tracking spreadsheet

Annual routine (8-10 hours):

- Complete year-end performance analysis
- Generate tax documents (Form 8949 for realized gains/losses)
- Strategic planning for next year
- Review and update investment goals
- Comprehensive portfolio restructuring if needed

Technology Tools for Calendar Management
Options-specific platforms:

- ThinkorSwim: Excellent calendar tools showing all expirations
- Tastyworks: Clean interface with expiration tracking
- Interactive Brokers: Professional-grade tools

- E*TRADE: Solid retail platform with good options chains

Calendar integration:

- Link brokerage account to Google Calendar or Outlook
- Set automatic reminders 3 days before expirations
- Color-code different position types
- Include ex-dividend dates and earnings in calendar

Spreadsheet tracking: Create master spreadsheet with:

- Position name and size
- Entry date and price
- Current call strike and expiration
- Premium collected to date
- Next action date
- Key upcoming events (earnings, dividends)

Sample Tracking Spreadsheet:

Stock	Shares	Entry Price	Current Call	Expiration	Premium YTD	Next Action	Earnings	Ex-Div
MSFT	100	$420	$430	3/21	$850	Roll 3/18	4/25	2/15
JNJ	200	$155	$160	3/21	$760	Roll 3/18	4/15	2/24
V	100	$305	$315	3/14	$580	Let expire	4/28	3/8

Handling Assignment

Assignment disrupts your calendar by forcing early position closure. Manage assignments systematically:

When assigned:

1. Verify assignment notice (usually Saturday after Friday expiration)
2. Confirm cash proceeds received (strike price × shares)
3. Update tracking spreadsheet showing position closed
4. Decide whether to repurchase same stock or deploy capital elsewhere
5. If repurchasing, wait for optimal entry point rather than immediate buyback
6. Document capital gain/loss for tax purposes

Assignment example:

- Owned 100 shares MSFT at $420
- Assigned at $430 strike
- Received $43,000 cash
- Capital gain: $1,000 ($10 per share)
- Wait for pullback, repurchase at $425
- Resume covered call strategy

Managing Around Earnings

Earnings create calendar complications requiring specific management:

Option 1: Close before earnings

- If earnings are in 10 days and your calls expire in 30 days
- Close the calls 5-7 days before earnings
- Accept the lost premium for safety
- Re-establish after earnings volatility settles

Option 2: Sell calls expiring before earnings

- Earnings in 25 days, sell 21-day calls
- Expire before earnings announcement
- Capture elevated IV premium (earnings volatility typically inflates IV 5-10 days before)
- After earnings, sell new calls

Option 3: Hold through earnings

- Accept the risk of volatile post-earnings move
- Only viable if you're comfortable with assignment
- Can work if calls are sufficiently OTM (low delta, say 0.15-0.20)

Most conservative approach: Always ensure your covered calls expire before earnings, eliminating surprise assignment risk from unexpected moves.

Rolling Strategies

Rolling allows you to extend expirations, adjust strike prices, or both simultaneously—transforming what would be a closing loss into an extended position that can ultimately profit.

What is Rolling?

Rolling combines two simultaneous transactions:

1. Buy to close your existing call option
2. Sell to open a new call option with different strike and/or expiration

The net result is extending your position while collecting additional premium.

Types of Rolls

Roll Out (Time Extension):

- Close current expiration
- Open same strike, later expiration
- Purpose: Extend time when stock hasn't reached strike

Roll Up (Strike Increase):

- Close current strike
- Open higher strike, same expiration
- Purpose: Capture appreciation when stock has rallied

Roll Out and Up (Both):

- Close current position
- Open higher strike and later expiration
- Purpose: Capture gains while extending position

Roll Down:

- Close current strike
- Open lower strike, same or later expiration
- Purpose: Defensive move when stock has declined, capture more premium

When to Roll

Successful roll situations:

Situation 1: Stock rallied near or above strike, calls now ITM

- Current position: $100 stock, sold $105 calls, stock now at $107
- Action: Roll up and out to $110 calls next month
- Result: Capture $5 appreciation, collect additional premium

Situation 2: Stock flat, calls have lost most time value

- Current position: $100 stock, sold $105 calls 30 days ago, now 5 days to expiration, stock still at $100
- Action: Buy back for $0.20 (originally sold for $2.50), sell new $105 calls for next month at $2.40
- Result: Captured $2.30 from original trade, immediately deployed into new premium

Situation 3: Stock declined significantly

- Current position: $100 stock, sold $105 calls, stock now at $94
- Action: Let calls expire worthless, sell new $96 calls for next month
- Result: Adjust to current price level, continue generating income despite loss

When NOT to roll
Avoid rolling when:

- Stock has deteriorated fundamentally (dividend cut, earnings collapse)
- You're trying to "save" a bad position rather than accepting loss
- Rolling would require moving to strike with no time value remaining
- The credit received for rolling is insufficient (under $0.30-0.50)
- You've repeatedly rolled same position for months, creating huge opportunity cost

Rolling Up and Out: Step-by-Step
Most common roll type for stocks that have appreciated.
Example scenario:

- Current date: February 15
- Stock: Microsoft at $445 (purchased at $420)
- Current position: Short March 21 $430 calls (sold for $8.50 originally)

- Current call value: $17.00 ($15 intrinsic + $2 time value)

Analysis: Stock has moved well above strike. You'll be assigned in 34 days unless you act.

Rolling decision:

- Buy back March 21 $430 calls: Pay $17.00
- Sell April 18 $450 calls: Collect $9.50
- Net debit: $7.50 ($17.00 - $9.50)

Evaluation:

- Original premium collected: $8.50
- Current buyback cost: $17.00
- Realized loss on original trade: -$8.50
- New premium collected: $9.50
- Net position if assigned at $450:
    - Stock gain: $30 ($450 - $420)
    - Net option result: $1.00 ($8.50 original - $8.50 loss + $9.50 new)
    - Total gain: $31 per share

Decision: Roll makes sense. You capture the $25 stock appreciation from $420 to $445, get an additional $5 upside to $450, and collect $1.00 net premium.

Rolling for Credit vs. Rolling for Debit

Rolling for credit:

- You receive net premium when rolling
- Example: Close $100 call for $2.50, open $105 call for $3.00, net credit $0.50
- Always desirable—you're paid to extend position

Rolling for debit:

- You pay net cost when rolling

- Example: Close $100 call for $8.00, open $105 call for $6.50, net debit $1.50
- Sometimes necessary but evaluate whether worth it

Rolling for credit decision: Always execute unless better opportunities exist elsewhere.

Rolling for debit decision: Only execute if:

1. The debit is small relative to additional upside gained
2. You strongly believe in the stock's continued appreciation
3. Assignment at current strike is undesirable
4. Alternative is accepting assignment and possibly buying back stock at higher price

Defensive Rolling (Roll Down)

Used when stock has declined and you want to generate more income.

Example scenario:

- Stock: AT&T at $17.50 (purchased at $20)
- Current position: Short $20 calls with $0.05 remaining value (30 days to expiration)
- Stock has declined significantly

Rolling decision:

- Buy back $20 calls for $0.05
- Sell $18 calls for $1.20 (next month expiration)
- Net credit: $1.15

Analysis:

- Original $20 calls are worthless, stock unlikely to recover to $20
- Rolling down to $18 captures meaningful premium
- If assigned at $18, total loss is $2 ($20 - $18) less $1.20 premium = -$0.80 net loss

- Without rolling, sitting with $2.50 loss and minimal ongoing income

Defensive rolling caution: Don't repeatedly roll down on deteriorating positions. Sometimes accepting the loss and redeploying capital to better opportunities is wiser.

Serial Rolling Strategy

Some traders systematically roll positions rather than letting them expire:

Process:

1. Sell 45-day options
2. At 15-20 days to expiration, close for 50-70% of maximum profit
3. Immediately sell new 45-day options
4. Repeat indefinitely

Advantages:

- Captures optimal theta decay window repeatedly
- Reduces assignment risk (never holding to expiration)
- Allows strike adjustments every 3-4 weeks
- Can outperform hold-to-expiration by 15-25%

Disadvantages:

- More active management required
- Higher transaction costs
- Requires discipline to close winners early
- Works best with zero-commission brokers

Rolling Decision Matrix

ROLLING DECISION FRAMEWORK:

Stock Position:

→ Stock above strike by 5%+ → Roll up and out (capture gains)

→ Stock near strike → Let expire or roll out same strike

→ Stock below strike by 5%+ → Let expire, sell new lower strike
Time to Expiration:
→ 20+ days remaining → Hold, monitor
→ 10-20 days remaining → Consider early close and roll
→ Under 10 days → Let expire unless strong reason to roll
Premium Available:
→ Can collect credit → Execute roll
→ Small debit (under $0.50) → Evaluate carefully
→ Large debit (over $1.00) → Likely better to accept assignment
Fundamental Outlook:
→ Bullish on stock → Roll up, capture appreciation
→ Neutral on stock → Roll out same strike
→ Bearish on stock → Consider accepting assignment, exit position

Rolling Example: 12-Month Position

Track a complete year of rolling on a single position:

Month 1 (January):

- Buy Microsoft at $380
- Sell February $390 calls for $6.50

Month 2 (February):

- Stock at $396, calls ITM
- Roll to March $400 calls, collect $3.20 (after $9.70 buyback)
- Net: -$3.20 on roll, total premium to date: $3.30

Month 3 (March):

- Stock at $405, calls ITM again
- Roll to April $410 calls, collect $2.80 (after $8.30 buyback)
- Net: -$5.50 on roll, total premium to date: $0.80

Month 4 (April):

- Stock at $408, near strike
- Let expire, immediately sell May $415 calls for $6.80

- Total premium to date: $7.60

Month 5 (May):

- Stock at $410, below strike
- Let expire, sell June $415 calls for $7.20
- Total premium to date: $14.80

Continue through year...
12-Month Summary:

- Entry price: $380
- Final assignment price: $430 (December)
- Stock appreciation: $50
- Total premium collected: $42.50
- Total gain: $92.50 (24.3% return)

Through systematic rolling, captured substantial gains despite multiple assignments and repositioning.

Conclusion: Calendar Mastery

Expiration selection and rolling strategies provide the tactical execution layer that transforms covered call theory into profitable practice. Monthly options offer the best balance for most investors, combining manageable time commitment with optimal theta decay capture. Weekly options suit active traders willing to dedicate significant time for potentially higher returns.

Mastering rolling techniques allows you to extend winning positions, adjust to market movements, and maintain continuous income generation even when stocks move against your strikes. The key is developing systematic approaches rather than reactive decision-making, ensuring every roll serves a strategic purpose aligned with your overall objectives.

Combined with the strike selection frameworks from Chapter 11, you now possess comprehensive execution strategies for implementing covered calls across any market condition. The next chapters address position sizing, risk management, and handling the psychological challenges that separate successful traders from those who struggle.

***

Chapter 13:

Entry and Exit Strategies

Knowing when to enter and exit covered call positions separates consistently profitable traders from those who struggle. While stock selection and strike prices provide the foundation, timing and position management determine actual results. This chapter provides systematic frameworks for entering positions at optimal times, managing winning trades to maximize profits, handling assignments professionally, and knowing when to close positions early.

When to Enter a Covered Call Position

Entry timing significantly impacts covered call profitability. Poor entry timing—such as selling calls at market bottoms or during low volatility—can cost you 20-40% of potential returns. Conversely, strategic entry timing enhances returns without additional risk.

The Ideal Entry Conditions

Five factors create optimal covered call entry opportunities:

1. Stock Position Established

The fundamental requirement: you must own (or simultaneously purchase) the underlying stock. Two primary approaches exist:

Own-then-sell approach:

- Already own shares from previous purchase
- Stock has appreciated to satisfactory level
- Ready to generate income on existing holdings
- Lower risk since stock basis is established

Buy-write approach (simultaneous purchase and call sale):

- Purchase stock and sell call in single transaction
- Often executed as packaged trade with single commission
- Ensures immediate downside protection from premium
- Useful when initiating new position specifically for covered calls

Example comparison:
Own-then-sell:

- Bought Microsoft at $380 three months ago
- Stock now at $420 (10.5% gain already realized)
- Sell $430 calls to generate income on appreciated position
- Already profitable, premium is supplemental income

Buy-write:

- Identify Microsoft as covered call candidate at $420
- Simultaneously buy 100 shares at $420 and sell $430 calls for $7.50
- Effective purchase price: $412.50 ($420 - $7.50 premium)
- Immediate 1.8% buffer against decline

Both approaches work—select based on whether you're monetizing existing holdings or initiating new positions.

2. Technical Setup Favorable

Enter when technical indicators suggest neutral to moderately bullish conditions:

Optimal technical entry signals:

- Stock trading in upper half of recent range (between middle and top of range)
- Price above 50-day and 200-day moving averages (confirming uptrend)
- RSI between 45-65 (balanced momentum, not oversold or overbought)
- Recent consolidation after advance (digesting gains before next move)
- Support level holding (price bouncing off established support)

Avoid entry when:

- Stock in lower half of range or near major support (likely to

bounce, capturing upside)
- Price breaking down below key moving averages (trend deterioration)
- RSI below 35 (oversold, bounce likely)
- RSI above 75 (severely overbought, but see volatility discussion below)
- Gap moves or parabolic advances (wait for consolidation)

Example: Technical entry timing
Stock XYZ pattern:

- Trading range: $95-$105 for past two months
- Currently at $102 (upper third of range)
- 50-day MA at $99, 200-day MA at $94 (both supportive)
- RSI at 58 (neutral)
- Recent pattern: rose from $97 to $102, now consolidating

Decision: Excellent entry point. Stock is elevated but not overextended, consolidating gains, technical structure intact. Sell $105 calls (at resistance level) with high probability of capturing full premium.

3. Implied Volatility Elevated

Volatility directly determines premium levels. Selling during elevated volatility generates significantly more income than selling during depressed volatility.

Volatility assessment:

- Check IV Rank or IV Percentile (discussed in Chapter 3)
- Optimal entry: IV Rank above 40, ideally above 50
- Acceptable entry: IV Rank 25-40
- Avoid entry: IV Rank below 25 (premiums too low to justify strategy)

Example: Volatility impact
Stock at $100, selling $103 calls, 30-day expiration:

Low volatility environment (IV: 15%, IV Rank: 10):

- Premium: $1.20 (1.2% monthly, 14.4% annualized)
- Assessment: Barely worthwhile, consider waiting

Normal volatility (IV: 25%, IV Rank: 45):

- Premium: $2.10 (2.1% monthly, 25.2% annualized)
- Assessment: Good entry point

High volatility (IV: 35%, IV Rank: 75):

- Premium: $3.20 (3.2% monthly, 38.4% annualized)
- Assessment: Excellent entry, capitalize on rich premiums

The high volatility environment generates 167% more premium than low volatility for identical position!

Volatility timing strategy: During extended low volatility periods (VIX below 15 for weeks), consider:

- Reducing covered call activity to 30-50% of portfolio
- Waiting for volatility mean reversion
- Accepting lower premiums only on highest-conviction positions
- Deploying capital to stocks with individually elevated volatility

4. Time Until Next Major Event

Major events create uncertainty and volatility spikes. Strategic timing around these events optimizes returns:

Earnings announcements:

Best practice: Ensure your option expires BEFORE earnings announcement

- Earnings typically occur 4-6 weeks after previous quarter
- Check earnings calendar before selling calls
- If earnings are in 25 days, sell options expiring in 21 days

(before earnings)
- Benefit: Capture elevated pre-earnings volatility without post-earnings risk

Alternative approach: Sell calls immediately AFTER earnings

- Post-earnings, volatility collapses (volatility crush)
- Stock price usually settles into range
- Premiums are lower but risk is reduced
- Good for conservative traders

Avoid: Selling calls that expire after earnings when earnings are within option period

- Post-earnings moves can be dramatic (10-20%+ in single day)
- Even conservative strikes get breached
- Assignment risk or losses from buying back become significant

Federal Reserve meetings:

- Eight scheduled meetings annually
- Interest rate decisions impact all sectors, especially financials
- Check Fed calendar, consider shorter expirations around meetings
- Post-meeting selling can capitalize on clarity

Ex-dividend dates:

- Covered extensively in Chapter 9
- Ensure calls won't be assigned before ex-dividend date
- Either sell after ex-dividend or use OTM strikes reducing early exercise risk

5. Market Environment Assessment

Broad market conditions influence individual stock behavior:

Favorable environments for covered call entry:

- Sideways market with low conviction (ideal for premium collection)
- Post-correction recovery (stocks establishing new ranges)
- Low volatility grind higher (consistent small gains)
- Late bull market consolidation (market near highs but choppy)

Challenging environments requiring caution:

- Early bull market explosive advance (missing upside costly)
- Bear market accelerating lower (premium insufficient to offset losses)
- Crisis events creating gap risk (pandemic, financial crisis, war)
- Extreme volatility (VIX above 40) creating unstable conditions

Entry Timing Checklist

Before entering any covered call position, verify:

- [ ] Own stock or executing simultaneous buy-write
- [ ] Stock in upper half of recent trading range
- [ ] Price above 50-day and 200-day moving averages
- [ ] RSI between 45-70 (balanced momentum)
- [ ] IV Rank above 30 (preferably above 50)
- [ ] No earnings within option expiration period
- [ ] Ex-dividend date after option expiration or well before
- [ ] No major scheduled events during option period
- [ ] Strike selection aligns with technical resistance
- [ ] Premium meets minimum threshold (1.0%+ monthly for conservative, 1.5%+ for moderate)

Practical Entry Examples

Example 1: Perfect Entry Setup

Johnson & Johnson:

- Current price: $158
- 52-week range: $145-$168

- Position in range: 62% (upper half)
- Technical: Above all major MAs
- RSI: 57 (balanced)
- IV Rank: 48 (elevated above median)
- Next earnings: 52 days away
- Ex-dividend: 3 days ago (just passed)
- Market: Consolidating after rally

Action: Sell $162 calls, 35 days to expiration, collect $2.40 (1.52% monthly)

Assessment: All entry criteria met. High probability of success.

Example 2: Suboptimal Entry (Avoid)

Technology Stock ABC:

- Current price: $85
- 52-week range: $65-$110
- Position in range: 18% (near bottom)
- Technical: Below 50-day MA ($92)
- RSI: 31 (oversold)
- IV Rank: 22 (low)
- Next earnings: 18 days away
- Market: Declining

Action: Wait. Do not enter covered call.

Assessment: Stock oversold and likely to bounce, earnings risk present, low IV means poor premiums, technical structure broken. Probability of suboptimal outcome very high.

The 30-Minute Entry Rule

Avoid entering positions in first 30 minutes of trading day:

- Opening volatility creates poor fills
- Prices often whipsaw dramatically
- Market makers widen spreads
- Better prices available mid-morning through afternoon

Optimal entry times:

- 10:00 AM - 11:30 AM ET (after opening volatility settles)
- 2:00 PM - 3:30 PM ET (afternoon stability)
- Avoid final 30 minutes (closing volatility)

Managing Winning Trades

Winning trades—where the option you sold is declining in value—present strategic choices: hold until expiration for maximum profit, or close early and redeploy capital faster.

Defining a Winning Trade

A covered call trade is "winning" when:

- Stock price remains below strike (call is out-of-the-money)
- Time decay has eroded significant option value
- You could buy back the call for less than you sold it

Example:

- Sold call for $2.50
- 20 days later, can buy it back for $0.80
- Profit if closed: $1.70 (68% of maximum)
- Time elapsed: 67% of period

This is a winning trade—you've captured most potential profit in most of the time.

Three Management Approaches

Strategy 1: Hold to Expiration (Maximum Profit)

Process:

- Sell calls at beginning of period
- Make no adjustments regardless of price movement
- Let options expire worthless (or be assigned)
- Capture 100% of premium collected

Advantages:

- Maximizes profit per trade (capture all time value)
- Minimizes transaction costs
- Simplest approach (no decisions mid-period)
- No risk of adverse price movement during close/reopen

Disadvantages:

- Capital committed entire period (opportunity cost)
- Final week unpredictable (rapid price movements)
- Cannot redeploy if better opportunities emerge
- Must wait full period even after capturing most profit

Best for:

- Hands-off investors preferring minimal management
- Smaller portfolios where transaction costs matter
- Situations where you're traveling or unavailable
- Standard monthly cycle strategies

Strategy 2: Close at 50-70% Profit Target
Process:

- Sell calls at beginning of period
- Monitor weekly
- When unrealized profit reaches 50-70% of maximum, close position
- Immediately sell new calls for next period

Advantages:

- Captures most profit (50-70%) in portion of time (50-60% typically)
- Frees capital faster for redeployment
- Reduces final-week risk and uncertainty
- Increases annual number of trades (12+ instead of 12)
- Often generates higher total annual returns

Disadvantages:

- Requires active monitoring
- More transaction costs (though minimal with zero-commission brokers)
- Slightly more complex tracking
- Risk of unfavorable pricing when reopening

Best for:

- Active traders comfortable with weekly monitoring
- Larger portfolios where capital efficiency matters
- Professional or semi-professional traders
- Traders using 30-45 day expirations

Mathematical example:
Traditional hold-to-expiration (12 annual cycles):

- Sell monthly calls for $2.50 each = $30 annually
- Each position held 30 days
- Annual return: $30 (assuming $100 stock = 30%)

Close-at-60% strategy:

- Sell call for $2.50
- Close after 18 days at $1.00 (captured $1.50 = 60% of max)
- Immediately sell new call for $2.40 (23 days to expiration)
- Cycle completes every ~20 days instead of 30 days
- Annual cycles: ~18 instead of 12
- Annual return: 18 × $1.50 = $27 vs. $30

Wait—this shows lower returns! But factor in:

- Reduced risk from shorter exposure
- Ability to adjust strikes more frequently
- Protection from adverse final-week moves

- Risk-adjusted returns may be superior

Reality: Close-at-50-70% strategy typically generates similar total returns with lower risk and greater flexibility, making risk-adjusted returns superior.

Strategy 3: Hybrid Approach

Process:

- Hold most positions to expiration
- Close early only when specific conditions met:
  - 75%+ profit achieved with 40%+ time remaining
  - Stock approaching strike and time value nearly exhausted
  - Better opportunity identified requiring capital
  - Major event (unexpected news) changes outlook

Best for: Most investors—provides flexibility while maintaining simplicity

When to Close Winning Trades Early

Specific triggers justifying early closure:

Trigger 1: 75%+ profit in 50% or less time

- Example: Captured $1.90 of $2.50 maximum profit (76%) in 14 of 30 days (47%)
- Rational: Remaining profit ($0.60) requires 16 more days = poor risk-reward
- Action: Close, redeploy

Trigger 2: Time value below $0.20

- Example: Call trading at $0.15 with 10 days remaining
- Rational: $15 remaining profit doesn't justify 10 days of risk
- Action: Close for $0.15, sell new call immediately for $2.30
- Result: $2.15 net vs. $2.50 if held, but redeployed 10 days earlier

Trigger 3: Stock sharply declined, call worthless

- Example: Stock dropped from $100 to $92, $105 call now worth $0.05
- Rational: No chance of assignment, minimal remaining value
- Action: Close for $0.05, sell new $95 call for $2.80
- Result: Adjust to current price, generate significant new premium

Trigger 4: Opportunity cost is high

- Example: Held Microsoft call, now identify superior opportunity in Johnson & Johnson
- Current Microsoft position: $0.40 remaining value, 8 days left
- Action: Close Microsoft for $0.40 loss, redeploy capital to JNJ opportunity
- Rational: Better risk-adjusted returns available elsewhere

Managing Winners: Decision Matrix

WINNING TRADE DECISION TREE:

Profit captured so far:

→ Less than 50% → Hold (more profit available)

→ 50-70% → Evaluate time remaining

→ More than 50% time left → Hold

→ Less than 50% time left → Consider closing

→ More than 75% → Close and redeploy

Time value remaining:

→ Above $0.50 → Hold (meaningful value remains)

→ $0.20-$0.50 → Evaluate days remaining

→ Below $0.20 → Close and redeploy

Days to expiration:

→ More than 14 days → Hold unless 75%+ profit

→ 7-14 days → Evaluate profit percentage

→ Less than 7 days → Generally hold to expiration

Handling Assignment Gracefully

Assignment—when your call is exercised and you're required to sell shares at the strike price—represents a successful outcome, not a failure. Many beginners fear assignment, but sophisticated traders view it as profit realization.

Understanding the Assignment Process

When assignment occurs:

- Call buyer exercises their right to purchase your shares
- Almost always happens at expiration (if ITM)
- Occasionally happens early (typically before ex-dividend dates)
- You receive strike price × 100 per contract in cash
- Shares are removed from your account

Assignment notification:

- Usually Saturday morning after Friday expiration
- Brokerage emails notification
- Check account: shares gone, cash received
- Capital gains/losses realized for tax purposes

Why Assignment is Good

Assignment means you achieved your maximum profit scenario:

Example analysis:

- Purchased stock at $95
- Sold $100 calls for $2.50
- Assigned at $100

Results:

- Stock appreciation: $5.00
- Option premium: $2.50
- Total gain: $7.50 (7.89% return)
- Maximum possible gain: $7.50 (achieved)
- Assessment: Perfect execution

You captured the maximum possible gain from this trade. There's nothing to improve.

The Opportunity Cost Fallacy

Common mistake: "I got assigned at $100 but the stock went to $110! I missed $10 of gains!"

Reality check:

- You agreed to sell at $100 when you sold the call
- You collected $2.50 premium for accepting this limitation
- Your total gain was $7.50 (excellent)
- Monday morning quarterbacking doesn't improve trading

Proper perspective: Focus on whether your strategy generates consistent returns across all trades, not individual outcomes.

Post-Assignment Action Plan

Step 1: Verify Assignment (Saturday/Sunday)

- Check email for broker notification
- Log into account, verify shares gone and cash received
- Calculate realized gain/loss for records
- Update tracking spreadsheet

Step 2: Evaluate Repurchase Decision (Weekend/Monday)

Three options after assignment:

Option A: Repurchase same stock immediately

- Appropriate if: Stock fundamentals unchanged, technical setup still favorable
- Process: Buy shares Monday morning, resume covered calls
- Consideration: You'll likely buy at higher price (that's why you were assigned)

Option B: Wait for pullback, then repurchase

- Appropriate if: Stock overextended, technical indicators overbought

- Process: Wait for 3-7% pullback, then repurchase
- Risk: Stock may continue higher, missing opportunity
- Benefit: Better entry price if pullback occurs

Option C: Deploy capital elsewhere

- Appropriate if: Better opportunities identified, stock fundamentals deteriorated
- Process: Research alternative stocks, initiate new positions
- Benefit: Portfolio optimization, better risk-adjusted opportunities

Step 3: Execute Repurchase (If Applicable)
Repurchase timing:

- Monday morning: If stock gapping down or showing weakness
- Tuesday/Wednesday: If Monday showed strength, wait for mid-week dip
- Following week: If expecting pullback, be patient

Repurchase pricing:

- Set limit order at desired price
- Don't chase if stock running
- Accept that you may miss position if stock runs without pullback
- Remember: Many other opportunities exist

Step 4: Resume Covered Call Program
Once shares repurchased:

- Immediately evaluate covered call opportunity
- Don't wait—time decay starts immediately
- Sell new calls following standard entry criteria
- Continue systematic approach

Assignment Examples

Example 1: Standard Assignment, Immediate Repurchase

Timeline:

- **Month 1:** Buy Microsoft at $410, sell $420 calls for $7.50
- **Expiration:** Stock at $425, assigned at $420
- **Saturday:** Assignment notice received, gained $10 stock + $7.50 premium = $17.50 (4.27%)
- **Monday:** Stock opens at $427, repurchase 100 shares
- **Monday:** Immediately sell $435 calls for $8.20
- **Analysis:** Captured full gain, repositioned slightly higher, continued strategy

Example 2: Assignment, Wait for Pullback

Timeline:

- **Month 1:** Buy Johnson & Johnson at $152, sell $158 calls for $2.80
- **Expiration:** Stock at $161, assigned at $158
- **Saturday:** Gained $6 stock + $2.80 premium = $8.80 (5.79%)
- **Monday:** Stock opens at $162 (very extended, RSI 78)
- **Decision:** Wait for pullback before repurchasing
- **Day 8:** Stock pulls back to $157 (3.1% decline from $162)
- **Day 8:** Repurchase at $157 (better than assignment price!)
- **Day 8:** Sell $162 calls for $2.90
- **Analysis:** Patience rewarded, better positioning than immediate repurchase

Example 3: Assignment, Deploy Elsewhere

Timeline:

- **Month 1:** Buy Target at $145, sell $150 calls for $3.20
- **Expiration:** Stock at $153, assigned at $150
- **Saturday:** Gained $5 stock + $3.20 premium = $8.20 (5.66%)

- **Weekend:** Research shows retail sector weakening, Target's same-store sales declining
- **Monday:** Identify Johnson & Johnson as better opportunity (defensive, dividend aristocrat)
- **Monday:** Deploy $15,300 assignment proceeds into JNJ instead of Target
- **Monday:** Initiate JNJ covered calls
- **Analysis:** Strategic pivot to stronger position, optimizing portfolio

Handling Early Assignment

Early assignment (before expiration) occurs rarely but requires specific management:

When it happens:

- Usually 1-3 days before ex-dividend date (Chapter 9)
- Occasionally when calls go deep in-the-money with no time value
- Very rarely for other reasons

What to do:

- Don't panic—it's a normal occurrence
- You've received the strike price in cash
- Premium collected is yours to keep
- Foregone dividend if early assignment before ex-dividend

Example:

- Own AT&T at $18, sold $18 calls for $1.20
- Ex-dividend in 2 days (dividend: $0.28)
- Assigned early to capture dividend
- Result: Sold at $18, kept $1.20 premium, missed $0.28 dividend
- Net: $1.18 + $0 stock gain (bought at $18, sold at $18) = 6.6%

gain in period held

Assessment: Still profitable, though missed dividend. This is why we discussed ex-dividend timing in Chapter 9.

Assignment Psychology

Healthy mindset:

- "I maximized profit on this trade"
- "My strategy worked exactly as designed"
- "Time to find the next opportunity"
- "I'm consistently profitable across all trades"

Unhealthy mindset:

- "I 'lost' the stock at $100 when it's now $110"
- "I should have used a higher strike"
- "Assignment is bad"
- "I need to prevent assignment next time"

Remember: The goal is consistent income across many trades, not maximizing every single trade in hindsight.

When to Buy Back Your Calls

Buying back (closing) calls before expiration can be profitable when specific conditions warrant early closure. This section provides systematic frameworks for this decision.

Reasons to Buy Back Calls Early

Reason 1: Captured Significant Profit, Little Time/Value Remains

Scenario:

- Sold calls for $2.50
- Now trading at $0.40 (captured $2.10 = 84% of maximum)
- 8 days to expiration

Analysis:

- Remaining profit: $0.40 ($40 per contract)
- Remaining time: 8 days
- Daily profit remaining: $5 per day
- Risk: Stock could gap up, requiring buyback at loss

Decision: Buy back for $0.40, immediately sell new monthly calls for $2.60

- Net result: $2.10 first trade + $2.60 new trade = $4.70 over ~38 days
- Versus: $2.50 over 30 days if held + $2.60 over next 30 days = $5.10 over 60 days
- Marginal difference, but reduced risk and faster capital redeployment

Reason 2: Stock Approaching Strike, Time Value Exhausted Scenario:

- Stock at $99.50, sold $100 calls
- Calls trading at $2.10 ($2 intrinsic + $0.10 time value)
- 3 days to expiration

Analysis:

- Likely to be assigned
- Only $0.10 time value remaining ($10)
- Stock could easily breach $100, forcing assignment

Decision: Buy back for $2.10, take small loss if sold for $2.50 originally (-$0.40)

- Retain shares to participate in any further upside
- Sell new calls at higher strike
- Useful when very bullish and want to avoid assignment

Reason 3: Stock Decline, Call Worthless, Want to Reposition

Scenario:

- Stock dropped from $100 to $92
- Sold $105 calls, now trading at $0.05
- 15 days to expiration

Analysis:

- Stock has moved significantly
- Call has minimal value
- Could wait 15 days to expire, or close now and adjust

Decision: Buy back for $0.05, immediately sell $95 calls for $2.80

- Captured: $2.45 from first trade (if sold at $2.50 originally)
- New trade: $2.80 at appropriate strike for current price
- Total: $5.25 income vs. $2.50 if just held original

Reason 4: Fundamental Change
Scenario:

- Company announces dividend cut
- Earnings miss badly
- Major competitive threat emerges
- Regulatory issue appears

Decision: Close calls at loss if necessary, exit entire position

- Sometimes cutting losses is appropriate
- Don't compound poor positions with additional covered calls
- Redeploy capital to better opportunities

When NOT to Buy Back Calls
Avoid buyback when:
Scenario 1: Emotional response to assignment risk

- Stock near strike, emotional desire to avoid assignment
- No rational reason beyond fear of "losing" shares
- Result: Often buy back at loss, then stock falls anyway

Scenario 2: Chasing missed gains

- Stock rallied significantly, calls now deep ITM
- Temptation to buy back at huge loss to capture further upside
- Usually results in whipsaw losses

Example of this mistake:

- Sold $100 calls for $2.50
- Stock at $108, calls now worth $9.50
- Thinking: "If I buy back for $9.50, I can capture more upside!"
- Realized loss: -$7.00 per share ($9.50 - $2.50)
- Reality: You're better off accepting assignment at $100 (+$2.50 premium) = $2.50 profit
- Buying back creates -$7.00 loss trying to chase more gains
- Stock would need to rise to $115 just to break even on the buyback decision

Guideline: Never buy back calls that have moved significantly ITM unless fundamental thesis has changed dramatically.

Buyback Decision Matrix

BUY BACK DECISION FRAMEWORK:
Premium Remaining:
→ Less than $0.30 → Strong candidate for buyback
→ $0.30-$0.75 → Evaluate profit captured and time remaining
→ More than $0.75 → Generally hold
Profit Captured:
→ Less than 50% → Hold (more profit available)
→ 50-75% → Evaluate time remaining and redeployment opportunity
→ More than 75% → Strong candidate for buyback
Days to Expiration:

→ Less than 7 days → Consider buyback if profit > 75%
→ 7-14 days → Evaluate profit percentage
→ More than 14 days → Generally hold unless special circumstances

Stock Position Relative to Strike:
→ Stock well below strike (5%+) → Consider buyback if profit > 70%
→ Stock near strike (±2%) → Decide based on directional outlook
→ Stock above strike → Generally hold for assignment unless very bullish

Redeployment Opportunity:
→ Better opportunity available → Consider buyback to free capital
→ No better opportunity → Hold current position

The Art of Rolling

Rolling—simultaneously closing one option and opening another—represents the most sophisticated covered call management technique. Mastering rolling allows you to extend profitable positions, adjust to market movements, and optimize returns beyond simple hold-to-expiration strategies.

Note: Rolling mechanics were introduced in Chapter 11. This section focuses specifically on the decision-making framework for when and how to roll.

Rolling Decision Framework

Every rolling decision should answer three questions:

1. Does rolling improve my risk-adjusted return potential?
2. What is my directional outlook on the stock?
3. What is the net credit/debit of the roll?

Scenario-Based Rolling Strategies

Scenario 1: Stock Rallied, Calls ITM, Want to Capture Gains and Continue

Setup:

- Own stock at $95
- Sold $100 calls (now 30 days ago)
- Stock currently at $106

- Calls now worth $7.50 (deeply ITM)

Options:
Option A: Accept Assignment

- Result: Sell at $100, keep premium collected (say $2.50)
- Total gain: $5 stock + $2.50 premium = $7.50 (7.9%)
- Assessment: Good outcome, maximum profit achieved

Option B: Roll Up and Out

- Buy back $100 calls for $7.50
- Sell $108 calls (next month) for $5.20
- Net debit: $2.30
- New position: Short $108 calls

Analysis:

- Original premium collected: $2.50
- Cost to roll: -$2.30
- Net premium to date: $0.20
- If assigned at $108: Total gain = $13 stock + $0.20 net premium = $13.20 (13.9%)
- Versus accepting assignment: $7.50 (7.9%)

Decision criteria:

- Roll if: Bullish on stock, believe $108 reachable, willing to commit another 30 days
- Accept assignment if: Want to exit position, need capital elsewhere, bearish outlook

Scenario 2: Stock Flat, Calls Losing Value, Want to Extend
Setup:

- Own stock at $100

- Sold $105 calls 25 days ago for $2.50
- Stock still at $100
- Calls now worth $0.60 (5 days to expiration)

Options:
Option A: Hold to Expiration

- Capture remaining $0.60
- Total gain: $2.50
- Wait 5 days

Option B: Roll Out Same Strike

- Buy back for $0.60
- Sell new monthly $105 calls for $2.40
- Net credit: $1.80
- New 30-day position established

Analysis:

- Original trade profit: $1.90 ($2.50 - $0.60 buyback)
- New trade potential: $2.40
- Total potential: $4.30 over ~35 days vs. $2.50 over 30 days
- Annualized: Superior by ~25%

Decision: Roll unless you need exact expiration timing for other reasons

Scenario 3: Stock Declined, Want to Adjust Down
Setup:

- Own stock at $100
- Sold $105 calls for $2.50
- Stock dropped to $94
- Calls now worth $0.10 (20 days to expiration)

Options:

Option A: Let Expire, Then Sell New Calls

- Wait 20 days for expiration
- Then sell $96 calls for ~$2.80
- Capital idle for 20 days

Option B: Roll Down and Out Now

- Buy back $105 calls for $0.10
- Sell $96 calls (next month) for $3.20
- Net credit: $3.10
- Immediately repositioned at realistic strike

Analysis:

- Captured: $2.40 from original trade
- New trade: $3.20 potential
- Total: $5.60
- Versus: $2.50 + $2.80 = $5.30, but with 20-day delay

Decision: Roll down immediately to generate income on current price level

When Rolling Doesn't Make Sense

Red flag situations:

Rolling to avoid reality:

- Stock fundamentally deteriorated
- Repeatedly rolling losing positions down
- Creating larger and larger unrealized losses
- Better to accept loss and redeploy

Example of bad rolling:

- Month 1: Stock at $100, sell $105 calls
- Month 2: Stock at $94, roll to $98 calls
- Month 3: Stock at $89, roll to $92 calls

***

Chapter 13: Entry and Exit Strategies (Continued)

The Art of Rolling (Continued)

When Rolling Doesn't Make Sense

Red flag situations:

Rolling to avoid reality:

- Stock fundamentally deteriorated
- Repeatedly rolling losing positions down
- Creating larger and larger unrealized losses
- Better to accept loss and redeploy

Example of bad rolling:

- Month 1: Stock at $100, sell $105 calls
- Month 2: Stock at $94, roll to $98 calls
- Month 3: Stock at $89, roll to $92 calls
- Month 4: Stock at $82, roll to $86 calls

Reality check: After 4 months, you have $18 stock loss. Stop rolling, accept the loss, move on.

Rolling for insufficient credit:

- If rolling generates less than $0.30-0.50 credit
- Transaction costs and effort not worthwhile
- Better to let expire or accept assignment

Rolling Example: Complete 6-Month Position

Track a real position through multiple rolls:

January 15:

- Buy Microsoft at $400
- Sell February $410 calls for $8.20

February 15 (Expiration approaching):

- Stock at $418, calls worth $10.50
- Roll: Buy back for $10.50, sell March $425 calls for $9.80
- Net debit: $0.70
- Running total: $8.20 - $0.70 = $7.50 net credit

March 20:

- Stock at $432, calls worth $11.20
- Roll: Buy back for $11.20, sell April $440 calls for $10.50
- Net debit: $0.70
- Running total: $7.50 - $0.70 = $6.80 net credit

April 17:

- Stock at $438, near strike
- Decision: Let assign at $440
- Final assignment

6-Month Results:

- Purchase price: $400
- Assignment price: $440
- Stock gain: $40
- Net option premium: $6.80
- Total gain: $46.80 (11.7% return in 3 months)
- Annualized: 46.8%

Analysis: Through strategic rolling, captured substantial gains that exceeded either accepting early assignment or holding stock without calls.

Rolling Best Practices

1. **Always net for credit when possible** - Avoid paying to extend positions

2. **Roll with purpose** - Have clear rationale, not emotional reaction
3. **Limit rolls per position** - If rolled 3-4 times, consider accepting assignment
4. **Track total position** - Know your all-in cost basis including all rolls
5. **Don't roll deteriorating positions** - Cut losses instead
6. **Roll early in cycle** - Don't wait until expiration day when options illiquid

Conclusion: Entry and Exit Mastery

Successful covered call trading requires more than selecting good stocks and strikes—it demands systematic approaches to timing entry, managing winners, handling assignments professionally, and rolling strategically. The frameworks in this chapter transform covered calls from random premium collection into systematic income generation.

Key principles:

- Enter when technical, volatility, and event timing align
- Manage winners by balancing maximum profit against capital efficiency
- View assignments as successful outcomes, not failures
- Buy back calls early only when mathematically justified
- Roll strategically to capture appreciation while maintaining income

Master these execution strategies, and you'll join the ranks of consistently profitable covered call traders who generate reliable income regardless of market conditions.

Chapter 14:

Position Sizing and Portfolio Management

Position sizing—determining how much capital to allocate to each covered call position—represents the difference between sustainable long-term success and eventual ruin. Even the best stock selection and timing strategies fail if position sizes are inappropriate. This chapter provides frameworks for allocating capital, diversifying effectively, tracking positions systematically, and maintaining records for tax purposes.

How Much Capital to Allocate

Position sizing determines your risk exposure, diversification level, and practical management complexity. Too large, and single position losses devastate your portfolio. Too small, and transaction costs and management effort outweigh benefits.

The Foundation: Total Portfolio Size

Your covered call strategy should represent a portion of your total investable assets:

Conservative allocation (Retirees, Risk-Averse):

- 40-60% of total portfolio in covered calls
- Remainder in bonds, cash, diversified index funds
- Prioritizes capital preservation
- Accepts lower potential returns for stability

Moderate allocation (Balanced Investors):

- 60-80% of total portfolio in covered calls
- Remainder in growth stocks, bonds, cash reserves
- Balances income and growth
- Standard approach for most investors

Aggressive allocation (Growth Focus, Higher Risk Tolerance):

- 80-100% of total portfolio in covered calls
- Minimal bond allocation
- Small cash reserve only
- Maximizes income potential
- Accepts higher volatility

Example allocation:
Total investable assets: $500,000
Conservative approach:

- $250,000 in covered call stocks (50%)
- $150,000 in bond funds (30%)
- $100,000 in cash/money market (20%)

Moderate approach:

- $350,000 in covered call stocks (70%)
- $100,000 in bond funds (20%)
- $50,000 in cash reserve (10%)

Aggressive approach:

- $450,000 in covered call stocks (90%)
- $50,000 in cash reserve (10%)

Individual Position Sizing

Within your covered call allocation, determine individual position sizes:

Equal-weight approach (Simplest):

- Divide capital equally across all positions
- Example: $200,000 across 10 stocks = $20,000 per position
- Advantages: Simple, no favoritism, easy rebalancing
- Disadvantages: Treats all stocks equally regardless of risk/ volatility

Risk-adjusted weighting:

- Larger positions in lower-volatility stocks
- Smaller positions in higher-volatility stocks
- Accounts for different risk profiles

Example risk-adjusted allocation ($200,000, 10 positions):
Low volatility (utilities, consumer staples):

- Johnson & Johnson: $24,000 (12%)
- Procter & Gamble: $24,000 (12%)
- Coca-Cola: $20,000 (10%)
- Duke Energy: $20,000 (10%)

Moderate volatility (financials, healthcare):

- JPMorgan Chase: $20,000 (10%)
- Visa: $20,000 (10%)
- UnitedHealth: $18,000 (9%)

Higher volatility (technology):

- Microsoft: $18,000 (9%)
- Apple: $18,000 (9%)
- Adobe: $18,000 (9%)

This allocation places 44% in low-volatility names, 29% in moderate, 27% in higher volatility—appropriate balance.

Position Size Guidelines by Portfolio Value

Small Portfolio ($25,000-$50,000):

- 5-8 positions
- $3,000-$10,000 per position
- Focus on lower-priced stocks ($30-$80) to achieve 100-share increments
- Accept less diversification as necessary trade-off

Medium Portfolio ($50,000-$150,000):

- 8-12 positions
- $5,000-$15,000 per position
- Can access most blue-chip stocks
- Good diversification achievable

Large Portfolio ($150,000-$500,000):

- 10-15 positions
- $10,000-$35,000 per position
- Excellent diversification
- Can include some mid-cap positions

Very Large Portfolio ($500,000+):

- 12-20 positions
- $25,000-$50,000+ per position
- Maximum diversification
- Consider multiple covered call strategies simultaneously

Maximum Position Size Rule

Never allocate more than 15% of your covered call portfolio to any single position:

Rationale:

- Single stock specific risk limited
- Catastrophic loss (50% decline) impacts only 7.5% of portfolio (15% × 50%)
- Maintains diversification benefits
- Prevents emotional attachment to single positions

Example violation:

- $100,000 portfolio
- $25,000 in Microsoft (25%)

- If Microsoft declines 40%, portfolio loses $10,000 (10% total portfolio)
- Too concentrated

Corrected allocation:

- Maximum $15,000 in any single position (15%)
- 40% decline = $6,000 loss (6% of total portfolio)
- More manageable risk

Scaling Into Positions

For larger positions, consider scaling in over time:

Strategy:

- Decide on target position size: $30,000
- Initial purchase: $10,000 (1/3)
- If technical setup remains favorable and stock consolidates: Add $10,000 (2/3 total)
- If continues favorable: Add final $10,000 (full position)

Benefits:

- Averages entry prices
- Reduces risk of poor timing
- Allows evaluation before full commitment
- Psychologically easier

The 100-Share Problem for Small Accounts

Covered calls require 100-share increments, creating challenges for smaller accounts:

Problem:

- $25,000 account wants 8 positions = $3,125 per position
- Stock trading at $150 requires $15,000 for 100 shares
- Cannot achieve target diversification

Solutions:

Solution 1: Focus on lower-priced stocks

- Target stocks under $50
- 100 shares = $5,000 or less
- Can build diversified portfolio
- Drawback: May miss best blue-chip opportunities

Solution 2: Accept fewer positions

- Build 5-6 positions instead of 8-10
- Accept reduced diversification
- Use highest-quality blue chips
- Mitigate through careful stock selection

Solution 3: Use fractional shares + selective covered calls

- Own fractional shares in expensive stocks
- Sell covered calls only on stocks where you own 100+ shares
- Some positions generate option income, others don't
- Hybrid approach

Solution 4: Save and scale up

- Begin with 3-4 positions
- Add positions as capital grows
- Covered call income accelerates portfolio growth
- Patience required

Capital Reserve Requirements

Maintain cash reserves for opportunities and management:

Minimum reserve: 5-10% of covered call allocation

- Allows adjustments and opportunistic additions
- Handles assignment situations where repurchase delayed
- Provides flexibility

Example:

- $100,000 covered call portfolio
- Reserve $5,000-$10,000 in cash (5-10%)
- Deploy $90,000-$95,000 in positions

When to use reserves:

- Market correction creates exceptional opportunities
- Assigned on position, waiting for optimal repurchase
- New position identified meeting all criteria
- Rolling requires temporary cash for settlement

Diversification Within Covered Call Strategies

Diversification reduces portfolio volatility and protects against single-stock catastrophes. Proper diversification spans multiple dimensions beyond simple stock count.

Sector Diversification

Never concentrate heavily in single sector:

Target sector allocation:

- No sector over 30% of portfolio
- Minimum 4-5 different sectors represented
- Balance cyclical and defensive sectors

Example balanced allocation ($200,000):

Technology (25%): $50,000

- Microsoft: $18,000
- Apple: $18,000
- Visa: $14,000

Healthcare (20%): $40,000

- Johnson & Johnson: $22,000
- UnitedHealth: $18,000

Financials (18%): $36,000

- JPMorgan Chase: $20,000
- Bank of America: $16,000

Consumer Staples (17%): $34,000

- Procter & Gamble: $18,000
- Coca-Cola: $16,000

Industrials (12%): $24,000

- Caterpillar: $24,000

Utilities (8%): $16,000

- Duke Energy: $16,000

This allocation provides exposure to six sectors with reasonable balance.

Avoid sector concentration mistakes:

Mistake 1: Over-concentration in tech

- 50-60% in technology stocks
- 2022 taught painful lesson when tech declined 30-40%
- Diversification benefits lost

Mistake 2: All financial stocks

- Banks, insurance, asset managers
- Technically different industries but all correlated
- 2008-2009 demonstrated catastrophic risk

Mistake 3: Only dividend stocks in same sectors

- All utilities and consumer staples

- Very defensive but minimal growth
- May underperform during bull markets

Market Cap Diversification
Blend market capitalizations for optimal results:
Large-cap (>$50B): 70-80% of portfolio

- Core holdings
- Maximum stability and liquidity
- Examples: Microsoft, Johnson & Johnson, JPMorgan Chase

Mid-cap ($5B-$50B): 15-25% of portfolio

- Growth potential with reasonable stability
- Higher premiums due to elevated volatility
- Examples: Moderna, Datadog, Rivian (verify liquidity)

Small-cap (<$5B): 0-10% maximum

- Only if exceptional liquidity
- Higher risk, higher premiums
- Not recommended for most covered call portfolios

Dividend vs. Growth Diversification
Balance dividend-paying and growth stocks:
High-dividend stocks (3-6% yield): 40-60%

- Provide baseline income
- More defensive
- Lower growth expectations
- Examples: Utilities, REITs, telecommunications

Moderate-dividend stocks (1-3% yield): 30-40%

- Balance income and growth
- Blue-chip industrials, consumer staples, healthcare

- Examples: Johnson & Johnson, Procter & Gamble, 3M

Low/no dividend stocks (0-1% yield): 10-20%

- Growth-oriented
- Higher volatility creates better premiums
- Technology mega-caps
- Examples: Alphabet, Amazon (pre-dividend), Meta

Volatility Diversification
Mix stocks with different volatility profiles:
Low volatility (IV: 15-20%): 30-40% of portfolio

- Utilities, consumer staples, established healthcare
- Generate 1.0-1.5% monthly premiums
- Provide stability

Moderate volatility (IV: 20-30%): 40-50% of portfolio

- Most blue-chip stocks
- Generate 1.5-2.5% monthly premiums
- Core holdings

Higher volatility (IV: 30-40%): 10-20% of portfolio

- Select technology, financials during uncertainty
- Generate 2.5-4.0% monthly premiums
- Require more active management

Correlation Considerations
Seek stocks with low correlations to each other:
Example of proper low-correlation diversification:

- Johnson & Johnson (healthcare, defensive)
- Caterpillar (industrials, economically sensitive)
- Duke Energy (utility, rate-sensitive)

- Microsoft (technology, growth)
- JPMorgan Chase (financial, economically sensitive but different from industrials)

When market declines 10%:

- JNJ might decline 4% (defensive)
- CAT might decline 14% (cyclical)
- Duke might decline 6% (defensive)
- MSFT might decline 11% (market-like)
- JPM might decline 12% (cyclical)
- Portfolio declines ~9.4% (less than market due to diversification)

Example of poor high-correlation diversification:

- Apple
- Microsoft
- Alphabet
- Amazon
- Nvidia

All technology stocks move together. When tech sells off 15%, your entire portfolio declines 15%. No diversification benefits.

Geographic Diversification

While focusing on U.S. stocks, consider international exposure:

Direct international stocks:

- ADRs (American Depositary Receipts) of foreign companies
- Examples: Toyota, Taiwan Semiconductor, Nestle
- Caution: Often lower options liquidity

Multinational U.S. companies:

- Generate 40-60% revenue internationally
- Examples: Coca-Cola (international), Microsoft (global), Visa

(worldwide)
- Provides international exposure with U.S. options liquidity

Portfolio Construction Checklist

Before finalizing portfolio composition, verify:

- [ ] No single position exceeds 15% of portfolio
- [ ] No sector exceeds 30% of portfolio
- [ ] Minimum 4-5 different sectors represented
- [ ] 70-80% in large-cap stocks
- [ ] Balance of dividend-paying and growth stocks
- [ ] Mix of volatility levels across positions
- [ ] Low correlation among holdings
- [ ] All stocks meet fundamental criteria (Chapter 6)
- [ ] All stocks have adequate options liquidity
- [ ] 5-10% cash reserve maintained

Tracking Your Positions

Systematic position tracking enables informed decision-making, performance evaluation, and strategy refinement. Without proper tracking, you're flying blind.

Essential Tracking Metrics

For each position, track:

1. **Entry information:**
    - Purchase date
    - Number of shares
    - Purchase price per share
    - Total capital invested
2. **Current option position:**
    - Strike price
    - Expiration date
    - Premium collected
    - Date option sold
3. **Performance metrics:**

- Current stock price
- Current option value
- Unrealized gain/loss on stock
- Unrealized gain/loss on option
- Total position P&L

4. **Income tracking:**
    - Total premiums collected year-to-date
    - Total dividends received year-to-date
    - Number of assignments year-to-date
5. **Important dates:**
    - Next expiration
    - Next ex-dividend date
    - Next earnings date

Sample Position Tracking Spreadsheet

Stock	Shares	Entry Price	Entry Date	Current Price	Stock P&L	Call Strike	Call Exp	Premium	Call Value	Call P&L	Total P&L	YTD Premium	YTD Div	Next Action
MSFT	100	$420	1/15	$445	+$2,500	$450	3/21	$8.50	$3.20	+$530	+$3,030	$17.20	$0	Hold
JNJ	200	$155	2/1	$161	+$1,200	$165	3/21	$4.40	$1.20	+$640	+$1,840	$8.80	$238	Roll 3/18
V	100	$305	1/8	$318	+$1,300	$320	3/14	$5.80	$2.10	+$370	+$1,670	$11.60	$0	Let expire

This spreadsheet instantly shows:

- Total portfolio value
- Individual position performance
- Option positions approaching expiration
- Premium income generated
- Upcoming action items

Portfolio-Level Dashboard

Track aggregate metrics:

Monthly snapshot:

- Total portfolio value

- Month-over-month change
- Premium income collected this month
- Dividend income received this month
- Number of positions
- Number of expirations this month
- Number of assignments this month
- Average position size
- Largest position (should be <15%)

Example monthly dashboard:

Portfolio Summary - February 2025
Total Value: $248,600 (previous: $242,100, +2.7%)
Invested Capital: $235,000
Total Gain: $13,600 (5.8%)
February Income:
- Option Premium: $4,280
- Dividend Income: $720
- Total: $5,000

February Activity:
- Expirations: 8 positions
- Assignments: 2 positions (MSFT, V)
- Rolls: 3 positions (JNJ, PG, JPM)
- New positions: 2 (CAT, HD)

Position Count: 11
Cash Reserve: $6,400 (2.6%)
Largest Position: JNJ at 13.2%
Upcoming This Week:
- 3/7: V expiration
- 3/8: PG ex-dividend
- 3/12: JNJ earnings

Performance Metrics to Track

Total return calculation:

Total Return = (Option Premium + Dividends + Capital Gains) / Initial Capital

Example:

- Starting capital: $200,000
- Option premium YTD: $28,400
- Dividend income YTD: $5,600
- Unrealized capital gains: $8,200
- Total gains: $42,200
- Total return: 21.1%

Premium capture rate:

Premium Capture Rate = Actual Premium Collected / Theoretical Maximum Premium

Example:

- Theoretical maximum if all held to expiration: $32,000
- Actual collected (some closed early): $28,400
- Capture rate: 88.8%

Target: 85%+ indicates efficient execution

Assignment rate:

Assignment Rate = Positions Assigned / Total Position-Months

Example:

- 10-position portfolio for 12 months = 120 position-months
- Assignments during year: 32
- Assignment rate: 26.7%

Context:

- <20%: Very conservative strikes
- 20-35%: Moderate strikes (typical)
- >35%: Aggressive strikes

Software and Tools

Spreadsheet approach (Excel/Google Sheets):

- Most flexible
- Complete customization
- One-time setup effort
- Free (Google Sheets)
- Manual data entry

Brokerage tools:

- Most brokers provide position tracking
- Real-time updates
- Limited customization
- Usually free with account
- Examples: TD Ameritrade, Interactive Brokers, E*TRADE

Dedicated options tracking software:

- OptionNetExplorer (free version available)
- TradeLog (paid, $299/year)
- MyTradingAnalytics (paid, $20/month)
- Features: Automatic import, analytics, tax reporting

Recommendation for most investors:

- Start with customized Google Sheets spreadsheet
- Upgrade to paid software if portfolio exceeds $250,000 or 15+ positions
- Use broker tools as supplementary tracking

Weekly Review Process

Establish systematic weekly routine:

Monday (5 minutes):

- Review weekend news affecting holdings
- Check any corporate actions (dividends, splits)
- Note upcoming expirations this week

Wednesday (10 minutes):

- Update spreadsheet with current prices
- Review positions expiring Friday
- Decide on rolls, closes, or let-expire decisions

Thursday (15 minutes):

- Execute any necessary rolls or early closes
- Verify orders filled at acceptable prices
- Update tracking spreadsheet

Saturday (30 minutes):

- Check for any Friday assignments
- Update complete portfolio tracking
- Calculate week's performance
- Plan next week's activity

Total weekly time: ~60 minutes for 10-position portfolio

Record-Keeping for Taxes

Proper tax record-keeping prevents headaches during tax season and ensures accurate reporting. Option transactions create complex tax situations requiring detailed documentation.

What to Track for Taxes

For each option transaction, record:

1. **Opening transaction:**
    - Date sold to open
    - Symbol
    - Strike price
    - Expiration date
    - Number of contracts
    - Premium received
    - Commissions paid (if any)
2. **Closing transaction (if applicable):**
    - Date bought to close
    - Number of contracts
    - Price paid
    - Commissions paid
    - Net profit/loss
3. **Assignment details (if applicable):**
    - Date of assignment

    - Number of shares sold
    - Strike price received
    - Stock cost basis
    - Holding period (short-term vs. long-term)

Sample Tax Record Entry
Transaction 1: Standard covered call
Open:

- Date: 1/15/2025
- Action: Sell to open
- Symbol: MSFT Mar 21 2025 $430 Call
- Contracts: 1
- Premium received: $850
- Commission: $0
- Net proceeds: $850

Close:

- Date: 3/21/2025 (expiration)
- Result: Expired worthless
- Profit: $850 (short-term capital gain)

Transaction 2: Covered call with assignment
Stock purchase:

- Date: 1/15/2025
- Symbol: JNJ
- Shares: 100
- Price: $155.00
- Total cost: $15,500
- Commission: $0

Option sale:

- Date: 1/15/2025

- Action: Sell to open
- Symbol: JNJ Feb 21 2025 $160 Call
- Contracts: 1
- Premium received: $280
- Commission: $0

Assignment:

- Date: 2/21/2025
- Shares sold: 100
- Strike price: $160.00
- Gross proceeds: $16,000
- Add premium: $280
- Total proceeds: $16,280
- Cost basis: $15,500
- Capital gain: $780 (short-term)
- Holding period: 37 days (short-term)

Tax Treatment of Covered Calls
Standard covered calls (unassigned):

- Premium is short-term capital gain
- Recognized when option expires or is closed
- Always short-term regardless of holding period
- Taxed at ordinary income rates (10-37% depending on bracket)

Covered calls with assignment:

- Premium is added to stock sale proceeds
- Total gain/loss calculated as: (Strike price + Premium - Stock basis)
- Holding period determines short-term vs. long-term treatment:
    - Held 365 days or less: Short-term capital gain (ordinary income rates)
    - Held 366+ days: Long-term capital gain (preferential

rates: 0%, 15%, or 20%)

Qualified covered calls (QCCs):

Special rules exist for covered calls written against stocks you've held long-term:

Qualified covered call criteria:

- Stock held 366+ days before selling call
- Call strike is not "too far" out of the money (see IRS tables)
- Expiration of 30+ days but not more than 33 months
- Strike price meets minimum requirements based on stock price

Benefit: Stock holding period not disrupted, preserving long-term capital gains treatment

Non-qualified covered calls:

- If call doesn't meet QCC requirements
- Holding period for stock may be suspended
- Could convert would-be long-term gains to short-term

Consult tax professional for QCC compliance

Wash Sale Rules

Wash sale rules can affect covered call traders:

Wash sale basics:

- If you sell stock at loss
- Then repurchase same or substantially identical stock within 30 days
- Loss is disallowed and added to basis of new shares

Covered call wash sale scenarios:

Scenario 1: Assigned at loss, immediately repurchase

- Bought stock at $100
- Assigned at $95 (loss)
- Immediately repurchase at $95

- $5 loss disallowed, added to new $95 basis = $100 new basis

Scenario 2: Sell stock at loss, already hold calls

- Own stock at $100
- Sell stock at $90 (loss)
- Already short calls (covered calls)
- Wash sale applies—loss disallowed

Avoiding wash sales:

- Wait 31+ days before repurchasing after loss
- Purchase different stock instead of same one
- Ensure no option positions on same stock when realizing loss

Form 8949 and Schedule D

Report covered call transactions on tax forms:

Form 8949:

- Lists all capital gain/loss transactions
- Separate sections for short-term and long-term
- Include: Description, date acquired, date sold, proceeds, cost basis, gain/loss

Schedule D:

- Summarizes Form 8949 totals
- Calculates total capital gains/losses
- Determines tax owed

1099-B from broker:

- Broker reports all closed transactions
- May not perfectly match your records (especially multi-year positions)
- Verify broker reporting is accurate

- Adjust if necessary with Form 8949 adjustments column

Tax Record-Keeping Best Practices

1. Real-time documentation:

- Record transactions same day they occur
- Don't wait until year-end
- Easier to remember details immediately
- Prevents missing transactions

2. Separate worksheet for each tax year:

- Create new spreadsheet January 1
- Track all transactions chronologically
- Include running totals
- Simplifies tax preparation

3. Track adjusted cost basis:

- Wash sales adjust basis
- Assignment proceeds include premium
- Return of capital from dividends reduces basis
- Maintain accurate basis records

4. Quarterly review:

- Review all transactions quarterly
- Verify against broker statements
- Identify any discrepancies early
- Project year-end tax liability

5. Year-end tax planning:

- Review unrealized gains/losses in November
- Consider tax-loss harvesting if appropriate
- Evaluate assignment timing for tax optimization

- Consult with tax professional before December

Sample Tax Tracking Spreadsheet

Date	Type	Symbol	Action	Contracts	Strike	Exp	Proceeds	Cost	Net	Term	Notes
1/15	Open	MSFT Call	STO	1	$430	3/21	$850	$0	$850	ST	
1/15	Stock	JNJ	Buy	100			$0	$15,500			Basis
1/15	Open	JNJ Call	STO	1	$160	2/21	$280	$0	$280	ST	
2/21	Assign	JNJ	Sold	100	$160		$16,280	$15,500	$780	ST	Inc prem
3/21	Expire	MSFT Call	Exp	1	$430		$850	$0	$850	ST	Kept prem

Running totals:

- Short-term gains: $1,630
- Long-term gains: $0
- Total realized: $1,630

Working with Tax Professionals

Provide your tax preparer:

- Complete transaction log (spreadsheet)
- All broker 1099-B forms
- List of any wash sales you identified
- Notes on any unusual transactions
- Questions about specific situations

Questions to ask your tax professional:

- Am I maximizing tax efficiency in my covered call strategy?
- Should I focus on qualified covered calls for my long-term holdings?
- Are there any wash sale issues I'm missing?
- Should I consider tax-deferred accounts (IRA) for covered calls?

- How do state taxes apply to my strategy?

Tax-Deferred Accounts for Covered Calls
Traditional IRA / Roth IRA advantages:

- No annual tax on gains
- No wash sale rules apply
- Simpler record-keeping
- All gains compound tax-deferred

Traditional IRA:

- Contributions may be tax-deductible
- Withdrawals taxed as ordinary income
- Required minimum distributions (RMDs) after age 73

Roth IRA:

- Contributions not deductible
- Qualified withdrawals completely tax-free
- No RMDs during lifetime
- Ideal for covered calls generating ordinary income

Covered calls particularly well-suited for Roth IRAs:

- High ordinary income from premiums (normally taxed at high rates)
- In Roth, all gains completely tax-free upon withdrawal
- Compounding accelerated by no tax drag
- Can generate 20-30% annually tax-free

Conclusion: Position Sizing and Management Mastery

Successful covered call investing extends beyond selecting stocks and strikes—it requires systematic position sizing, proper diversification, diligent tracking, and meticulous record-keeping. The frameworks in this chapter ensure your portfolio remains balanced, your positions properly sized, your performance accurately measured, and your taxes properly documented.

Key principles:

- Size positions appropriately (maximum 15% per position)
- Diversify across sectors, market caps, and volatility levels
- Track positions systematically using spreadsheets or software
- Maintain detailed tax records for all transactions
- Review performance regularly and adjust as needed
- Consider tax-deferred accounts for maximum efficiency

Master these portfolio management fundamentals, and you'll build a sustainable covered call strategy that generates consistent income for years to come.

Chapter 15:

Managing Different Market Conditions

Markets don't remain static—they cycle through distinct phases requiring adapted strategies. A covered call approach that excels during sideways consolidation underperforms during explosive bull markets. Conversely, defensive strategies perfect for bear markets leave money on the table during rallies. This chapter provides frameworks for identifying market regimes and adjusting your covered call strategy to optimize performance across all conditions.

Covered Calls in Bull Markets

Bull markets—sustained uptrends with higher highs and higher lows—create both opportunities and challenges for covered call traders. While stock appreciation boosts portfolio values, overly aggressive call selling caps gains prematurely, creating opportunity cost.

Identifying Bull Market Characteristics

Technical indicators of bull markets:

- S&P 500 above 200-day moving average and trending higher
- Market making higher highs and higher lows consistently
- Most stocks above their 50-day and 200-day moving averages
- Breadth indicators positive (more advancing stocks than declining)
- VIX below 20, indicating low fear and complacency
- Pullbacks shallow (5-7%) and brief (2-3 weeks)
- New highs expanding, new lows contracting

Sentiment indicators:

- Media coverage increasingly bullish
- Retail investor participation increasing
- IPO market active with strong performance
- Investor surveys showing optimism above 50%
- Fund flows into equities accelerating

Economic backdrop:

- GDP growth positive and steady
- Unemployment declining or low
- Corporate earnings growing
- Federal Reserve accommodative or neutral
- Credit spreads tight (low corporate default risk)

The Bull Market Challenge

Bull markets present a unique dilemma for covered call traders:

The opportunity cost problem:

Example scenario:

- Own Microsoft at $380
- Bull market beginning, stock rallies to $480 over 6 months (26% gain)
- Covered call strategy with $400 strikes: Assigned multiple times, captured only 5-7% per assignment
- Total return: ~15-18% from covered calls vs. 26% from buy-and-hold

The covered call strategy underperformed by 30-40% in this scenario. This creates frustration and tempts traders to abandon the strategy at exactly the wrong time (near bull market peaks).

The psychological trap: During strong bull markets, every assignment feels like a mistake. You watch the stock you sold at $100 rally to $120, generating regret. This emotional response causes many traders to:

1. Stop selling calls (eliminating income)
2. Use excessively high strikes (generating minimal premium)
3. Switch to pure stock ownership (abandoning discipline)
4. Re-enter at market tops (buying high after missing rally)

Bull Market Covered Call Strategy

Adapt your approach during confirmed bull markets:
Strategy 1: Conservative Strike Selection (Primary Approach)
Implementation:

- Use strikes 5-7% out-of-the-money (vs. standard 2-4%)
- Target delta 0.15-0.25 (vs. standard 0.30-0.35)
- Accept lower premium (1.0-1.5% monthly vs. 2.0%+)
- Prioritize capital appreciation over maximum income

Example execution: Stock at $100:

- Bear market approach: Sell $102 calls (2% OTM), collect $2.50
- Bull market approach: Sell $107 calls (7% OTM), collect $1.40

Trade-off analysis:

- Premium sacrifice: $1.10 per month ($13.20 annually)
- Upside preserved: Additional $5 per share before assignment
- If stock rallies 15%: Bull market approach captures $15 vs. $4.50 with aggressive strikes
- Result: Lower income but better total returns

Strategy 2: Reduce Position Coverage
Implementation:

- Cover only 50-70% of shares with calls (vs. 100%)
- Keep 30-50% "naked" for unlimited upside participation
- Generate moderate income while capturing most appreciation

Example with 500 shares:

- Sell 3 calls (covering 300 shares)
- Keep 200 shares uncovered
- If stock rallies 20%: Covered portion gains capped, uncovered portion captures full 20%
- Blended return significantly better than fully covered position

Strategy 3: Shorten Duration
Implementation:

- Use 14-21 day expirations (vs. 30-45 days)
- Allows frequent strike adjustments upward
- Reduces commitment period during strong trends
- Accept more frequent management

Example:

- Week 1-2: Sell 14-day $105 calls on $100 stock
- Week 3: Stock at $104, let expire, immediately sell $108 calls
- Week 4-5: Stock at $107, let expire, sell $112 calls
- Continuously adjusting strikes higher captures more appreciation than monthly $105 calls

Strategy 4: Selective Application
Implementation:

- Identify stocks within your portfolio showing relative strength
- Avoid selling calls on strongest performers
- Concentrate calls on laggards and moderate performers
- Create asymmetric payoff profile

Example portfolio (10 positions during bull market):
Strongest performers (40% of portfolio):

- Microsoft: Rising 30% - NO calls sold
- Visa: Rising 25% - NO calls sold
- Alphabet: Rising 28% - NO calls sold
- Apple: Rising 22% - NO calls sold

Moderate performers (40% of portfolio):

- Johnson & Johnson: Rising 8% - Sell conservative OTM calls
- Procter & Gamble: Rising 6% - Sell conservative OTM calls

- Coca-Cola: Rising 5% - Sell conservative OTM calls
- JPMorgan Chase: Rising 12% - Sell conservative OTM calls

Laggards (20% of portfolio):

- AT&T: Rising 2% - Sell standard ATM/OTM calls
- 3M: Flat - Sell standard/aggressive calls

Result: Portfolio captures 70% of bull market appreciation while generating 8-12% annual income from selective call selling.

Bull Market Performance Expectations

Realistic return targets during bull markets:

Conservative covered call approach:

- Stock appreciation: 12-18% (80% of market performance due to occasional assignments)
- Option premium: 12-18% (from conservative strikes)
- Total return: 24-36%
- vs. Market return: 15-25%
- Assessment: Modest outperformance through income addition

Moderate covered call approach:

- Stock appreciation: 8-12% (frequent assignments cap gains)
- Option premium: 18-24%
- Total return: 26-36%
- vs. Market return: 15-25%
- Assessment: Solid outperformance through income

Aggressive covered call approach:

- Stock appreciation: 3-6% (very frequent assignments)
- Option premium: 24-36%
- Total return: 27-42%
- vs. Market return: 15-25%
- Assessment: Strong outperformance but highest opportunity

cost

Key insight: During bull markets, even conservative covered call strategies typically outperform buy-and-hold due to income supplementation, though aggressive strategies sacrifice more appreciation.

When to Increase Bull Market Aggressiveness

Consider more aggressive strikes during these bull market phases:

Late-stage bull market indicators:

- Market 15%+ above 200-day MA (extended)
- VIX at multi-year lows (complacency)
- Sentiment surveys extremely bullish (80%+ bulls)
- Valuation metrics stretched (high P/E ratios)
- Market showing signs of exhaustion (lower volume on rallies)

Rationale: Late bull markets often transition to consolidation or correction. More aggressive strikes capture rich premiums before potential reversal while limiting downside from overvalued positions.

Bull Market Case Study

Scenario: 18-month bull market, 2023-2024

Starting portfolio: $250,000, 10 positions Market performance: +35% over period

Approach 1: Standard covered calls throughout (unchanged strategy)

- Sold 2-4% OTM calls monthly
- Frequent assignments on rallying stocks
- Final portfolio value: $312,000 (+24.8%)
- Premium collected: $52,000
- Stock appreciation: $10,000 (limited by assignments)
- Underperformed market by 10.2%

Approach 2: Adapted bull market strategy

- First 6 months: Conservative 5-7% OTM calls
- Middle 6 months: Reduced coverage to 60% of shares
- Final 6 months: Gradually increased strike aggressiveness as market extended
- Final portfolio value: $327,000 (+30.8%)
- Premium collected: $38,000
- Stock appreciation: $39,000 (more participation in rally)
- Underperformed market by only 4.2%

Approach 3: Suspended covered calls during strongest phase

- First 3 months: Standard covered calls
- Middle 12 months: Suspended calls on strongest 50% of portfolio
- Final 3 months: Resumed standard calls as market extended
- Final portfolio value: $338,000 (+35.2%)
- Premium collected: $22,000
- Stock appreciation: $65,000 (maximum participation)
- Matched market performance while generating supplemental income

Lesson: Flexibility and adaptation during bull markets preserves appreciation while maintaining income. Rigid adherence to standard strategies creates unnecessary opportunity cost.

Sideways Markets: The Sweet Spot

Sideways markets—characterized by range-bound trading with no clear directional trend—represent ideal conditions for covered calls. During these periods, covered call strategies consistently outperform buy-and-hold approaches by substantial margins.

Identifying Sideways Market Characteristics

Technical indicators:

- Market oscillating between defined support and resistance
- 50-day MA and 200-day MA converging (no clear trend)
- Price repeatedly testing but not breaking key levels

- Breadth indicators neutral (balanced advancing/declining stocks)
- VIX in moderate range (15-25)
- Volume declining during rallies (lack of conviction)
- Failed breakout attempts above resistance

Sentiment indicators:

- Investor uncertainty and indecision
- Mixed economic data creating confusion
- Media coverage balanced (not extremely bullish or bearish)
- Fund flows modest in both directions
- Options activity elevated (uncertainty drives option buying)

Time characteristics:

- Sideways markets typically last 3-9 months
- Often occur between bull and bear markets (transition phases)
- Can persist for years during economic uncertainty
- Common after major events as market digests information

Why Sideways Markets Favor Covered Calls

The mathematical advantage:

Example: Stock trading in $95-$105 range for 6 months

Buy-and-hold investor:

- Starting price: $100
- Ending price: $101
- Dividends: $1.50
- Total return: 2.5%
- Annual return: 5.0%

Covered call investor:

- Starting price: $100
- Ending price: $101

- Dividends: $1.50
- Option premium: $15.00 (6 monthly cycles at $2.50 each)
- Total return: 17.5%
- Annual return: 35%

The covered call investor generated **7x the returns** of buy-and-hold during the sideways period!

Optimal Sideways Market Strategy

Strategy: Maximize Premium at Resistance

Implementation:

1. Identify trading range through technical analysis
2. Sell calls when stock approaches resistance
3. Select strikes at or slightly above resistance level
4. Use standard 30-day expirations
5. Let expire worthless and repeat

Example execution:

Stock ABC trading range: $48-$52 for past 3 months

Month 1:

- Stock at $51.50 (near $52 resistance)
- Sell $52 calls for $2.30 (4.5% monthly return)
- Stock trades to $52.30, pulls back to $49
- Calls expire worthless
- Result: Kept full $2.30 premium

Month 2:

- Stock at $49.20 (near $48 support)
- Wait for bounce toward resistance
- Stock rebounds to $51.80
- Sell $52 calls for $2.20
- Stock hits $52.50, pulls back
- Calls expire worthless

- Result: Kept full $2.20 premium

Month 3:

- Stock at $50.50 (mid-range)
- Sell $52 calls for $1.90
- Stock consolidates $50-51
- Calls expire worthless
- Result: Kept full $1.90 premium

6-month result:

- Six cycles of $2.00-2.50 premium = $12-15 per share
- Stock unchanged at $51 (started at $50)
- Total return: $13-16 (26-32% in 6 months, 52-64% annualized)

Sideways Market Strike Selection
Optimal approach during consolidation:
At resistance approach (most aggressive):

- Strike: At identified resistance level
- Example: Stock trading $48-52, sell $52 strikes
- Premium: Maximum (2.5-3.5% monthly)
- Assignment risk: Low (resistance historically holds)
- Best for: Clear, well-established trading ranges

Slightly above resistance approach (moderate):

- Strike: 1-2% above resistance
- Example: Stock trading $48-52, sell $53-54 strikes
- Premium: Good (1.8-2.5% monthly)
- Assignment risk: Very low
- Best for: Newer trading ranges or less clear resistance

Mid-range approach (conservative):

- Strike: At middle to upper portion of range
- Example: Stock trading $48-52, sell $51 strikes
- Premium: Moderate (1.5-2.0% monthly)
- Assignment risk: Moderate
- Best for: Uncertain range boundaries, higher volatility within range

Advanced Sideways Market Techniques

Technique 1: Buy Back on Weakness

Process:

- Sell calls when stock near resistance
- If stock drops significantly, buy back calls for profit
- Immediately re-sell new calls
- Generate multiple premium cycles within single month

Example:

- Day 1: Stock at $51.50, sell $52 calls for $2.30
- Day 8: Stock drops to $48.50, calls worth $0.40
- Day 8: Buy back calls for $0.40, capture $1.90 profit (82% of maximum)
- Day 8: Immediately sell new $52 calls (23 days to expiration) for $2.00
- Day 30: Both trades expire worthless, captured $3.90 vs. $2.30 from standard approach

Result: 70% increase in monthly income through active management

Technique 2: Bracket the Range

Process:

- When stock at bottom of range, buy more shares
- Immediately sell calls at top of range
- Capture appreciation from support to resistance plus premium

- Particularly effective for larger ranges (10%+ wide)

Example: Range: $90-$110 (20% range)

- Stock at $92 (near support): Purchase 100 shares
- Immediately sell $110 calls for $4.50
- Stock rallies to $108 over 2 months
- Calls expire worthless
- Profit: $16 appreciation + $4.50 premium = $20.50 (22% return in 2 months)

Technique 3: Volatility Scalping
Process:

- Implied volatility tends to spike when stocks approach range boundaries
- Sell calls when IV elevated (near resistance or during uncertainty)
- Avoid selling when IV depressed (typically mid-range during calm periods)
- Capture premium enhanced by volatility spikes

Example:

- Stock at $100 (mid-range), IV at 20%: $102 calls = $1.50
- Stock at $104 (approaching resistance), IV at 28%: $105 calls = $2.40
- Wait for volatility spikes to maximize premium

Sideways Market Performance Expectations
Realistic returns during prolonged sideways markets:
Conservative approach (5% OTM strikes):

- Monthly premium: 1.2-1.8%
- Annual premium: 14-22%
- Stock appreciation: 0-3%

- Total return: 14-25%
- vs. Market return: 0-5%
- Outperformance: 9-25%

Moderate approach (2-3% OTM strikes at resistance):

- Monthly premium: 2.0-2.8%
- Annual premium: 24-34%
- Stock appreciation: 0-2%
- Total return: 24-36%
- vs. Market return: 0-5%
- Outperformance: 19-36%

Aggressive approach (ATM or at resistance):

- Monthly premium: 2.8-4.0%
- Annual premium: 34-48%
- Stock appreciation: 0%
- Total return: 34-48%
- vs. Market return: 0-5%
- Outperformance: 29-48%

Key insight: Sideways markets represent the covered call strategy's greatest advantage, outperforming buy-and-hold by 300-1000% depending on aggressiveness.

Sideways Market Case Study

Scenario: 12-month sideways market, 2015-2016

Market: S&P 500 oscillated between 1,900-2,100 for 12 months Portfolio: $200,000 across 10 blue-chip stocks

Buy-and-hold performance:

- Starting value: $200,000
- Ending value: $204,000
- Dividends: $6,000
- Total return: $10,000 (5%)

Covered call performance (moderate approach):

- Starting value: $200,000
- Ending value: $203,000 (similar stock performance)
- Dividends: $6,000
- Option premium: $48,000 (monthly average $4,000 over 12 months)
- Total return: $57,000 (28.5%)

Result: Covered calls outperformed by 23.5 percentage points (570% better) during sideways market.

Recognizing When Sideways Markets End

Breakout signals (transitioning to bull market):

- Decisive break above resistance on strong volume
- Multiple consecutive closes above previous highs
- Breadth expansion (most stocks participating)
- VIX declining sharply
- Shift to more aggressive covered call approach

Breakdown signals (transitioning to bear market):

- Decisive break below support on strong volume
- Failed rallies back to support (now resistance)
- Breadth contraction (widespread selling)
- VIX spiking above 25
- Shift to defensive covered call approach

Bear Market Considerations

Bear markets—sustained downtrends with lower lows and lower highs—present the greatest challenge for covered call traders. While premium income provides downside cushion, severe declines can overwhelm premium collection, resulting in net losses. Defensive strategies and realistic expectations become critical.

Identifying Bear Market Characteristics

Technical indicators:

- Market below 200-day MA and 200-day MA declining
- Pattern of lower highs and lower lows
- Breadth deteriorating (more declining stocks than advancing)
- VIX elevated above 25, often spiking above 30-40
- Support levels breaking decisively
- Moving averages in bearish alignment (50-day below 200-day)
- Failed rally attempts (lower highs)

Sentiment indicators:

- Fear and pessimism dominant
- Media coverage increasingly negative
- Fund outflows from equities accelerating
- Investor surveys showing pessimism above 50%
- Credit spreads widening (corporate default risk rising)

Economic backdrop:

- GDP growth slowing or negative
- Unemployment rising
- Corporate earnings declining
- Federal Reserve tightening or financial crisis
- Recession concerns or reality

The Bear Market Challenge

Bear markets create multiple problems for covered call traders:

Problem 1: Premium insufficient for stock losses

Example:

- Stock declines 30% over 6 months
- Collected 12% in premiums
- Net loss: -18%

While covered calls reduced losses by 40% (12% premium cushion), absolute losses remain significant.

Problem 2: Psychological difficulty

Watching portfolio decline month after month tests discipline. Many traders:

- Stop selling calls (thinking "I'll wait until it recovers")
- Sell excessively conservative calls (generating minimal premium)
- Panic sell positions at bottoms
- Abandon strategy entirely at worst possible time

Problem 3: Capital depletion

Extended bear markets can deplete significant capital, reducing position sizes and future income potential even after recovery.

Bear Market Covered Call Strategy

Strategy 1: Maximum Defense (Primary Approach)

Implementation:

- Sell at-the-money or in-the-money calls
- Target delta 0.45-0.60
- Maximum premium collection (3-5% monthly)
- Accept assignment as exit strategy
- Reduce equity exposure by 30-50%

Example execution: Stock declining from $100 to $70 over 6 months

Month 1: Stock at $100, sell $100 calls for $5.50 (ATM) **Month 2:** Stock at $94, assigned at $100, gain $5.50 (exited successfully) **Alternative:** Stock at $94, sell $94 calls for $4.80 **Month 3:** Stock at $88, sell $88 calls for $4.20 **Continue through bear market**

6-month result:

- Stock declined from $100 to $70 (-30%)
- Buy-and-hold: -30% loss

- Covered calls collected: ~$25-28 in premiums
- Net result: -5% to -2% loss vs. -30%

Strategy 2: Transition to Cash
Implementation:

- Accept assignments as they occur
- Move proceeds to cash or money market funds
- Wait for bear market bottom before redeploying
- Preserve capital for eventual recovery

Rationale:

- Bear markets historically last 9-18 months
- Declines average 30-40% from peak to trough
- Capital preservation allows buying at much lower prices
- Missing bottom 20% of decline less important than preserving capital

Example:

- Start with $200,000 in stocks
- Over 4 months, 50% of positions assigned
- Move $100,000 to cash earning 5% in money market
- Keep $100,000 in defensive positions (utilities, consumer staples) with covered calls
- When market bottoms, redeploy cash at depressed prices

Strategy 3: Rotate to Defensive Sectors
Implementation:

- Exit or reduce cyclical sectors (technology, financials, consumer discretionary, industrials)
- Increase defensive sectors (utilities, consumer staples, healthcare)
- Continue covered calls on defensive positions

- Accept lower returns for reduced volatility

Defensive sector performance in bear markets:

- Utilities: Typically decline 10-15% (vs. market -30%)
- Consumer staples: Typically decline 12-18%
- Healthcare: Typically decline 15-22%
- Technology: Often declines 35-50%
- Financials: Often declines 40-55%

Portfolio transformation example:
Bull market portfolio:

- Technology: 30%
- Financials: 20%
- Healthcare: 20%
- Consumer staples: 15%
- Industrials: 15%

Bear market portfolio:

- Healthcare: 35%
- Consumer staples: 30%
- Utilities: 20%
- Technology: 10% (only mega-caps)
- Cash: 5%

Strategy 4: Reduce Position Sizes
Implementation:

- As assignments occur, repurchase 50-70% of original position size
- Keep 30-50% in cash reserves
- Maintain covered call program on reduced positions
- Scale back up as market stabilizes

Example:

- Originally owned 500 shares Microsoft
- Assigned at $420
- Proceeds: $210,000
- Repurchase only 300 shares when stock pulls back to $400
- Cost: $120,000
- Cash preserved: $90,000
- Continue covered calls on 300 shares

Bear Market Performance Expectations
Realistic outcomes during bear markets:
Standard covered call approach (maintained throughout):

- Stock decline: -25% to -35%
- Premium collected: +15% to +20%
- Net result: -10% to -15%
- vs. Market: -30%
- Relative outperformance: 15-20 percentage points

Defensive covered call approach:

- Stock decline: -12% to -18% (defensive stocks)
- Premium collected: +18% to +25% (aggressive strikes)
- Net result: +0% to +7%
- vs. Market: -30%
- Relative outperformance: 30-37 percentage points

Strategic cash transition:

- Partial assignment proceeds to cash: -10% to -15% on equity portion
- Cash portion: +3% to +5% from money market rates
- Net result: -5% to -8%
- vs. Market: -30%
- Relative outperformance: 22-25 percentage points

- Plus: Preserved capital to buy at lower prices

Key insight: The goal during bear markets is capital preservation and relative outperformance, not absolute profits. Losing 5-10% while the market loses 30% represents tremendous success.

Bear Market Psychological Framework

Healthy mindset during declines:

- "My strategy is reducing losses substantially vs. alternatives"
- "Premium income is providing a meaningful cushion"
- "This too shall pass—bear markets always end"
- "I'm preserving capital for the eventual recovery"
- "Discipline during adversity separates successful traders from failures"

Unhealthy mindset:

- "I'm still losing money, this strategy doesn't work"
- "I should stop selling calls and wait for recovery"
- "I need to make back my losses quickly"
- "Everyone else must be doing better than me"

Bear Market Case Study

Scenario: 2022 bear market (January-October)

Market declined 25% from peak to trough Duration: 10 months

Portfolio 1: Buy-and-hold (no covered calls)

- Starting value: $300,000
- Ending value: $225,000
- Dividends: $7,500
- Total result: -$67,500 (-22.5%)

Portfolio 2: Standard covered calls (unchanged strategy)

- Starting value: $300,000
- Stock losses: -$60,000

- Premium collected: $48,000
- Dividends: $7,500
- Total result: -$4,500 (-1.5%)
- Relative outperformance: +21 percentage points

Portfolio 3: Adaptive bear market strategy

- Starting value: $300,000
- Month 1-2: Recognized bear market, moved to ATM/ITM calls
- Month 3-4: Accepted assignments on 40% of portfolio, moved to cash
- Month 5-8: Rotated to defensive sectors, continued aggressive calls
- Month 9-10: Gradually began redeploying cash as market stabilized
- Stock losses: -$25,000 (on reduced positions and defensive stocks)
- Premium collected: $38,000 (aggressive strikes)
- Cash interest: $2,000
- Total result: +$15,000 (+5%)
- Relative outperformance: +27.5 percentage points

Key lesson: Adaptive strategy not only preserved capital but generated absolute profits during bear market through defensive positioning and aggressive premium collection.

Adjusting Your Approach

The most successful covered call traders continuously assess market conditions and adapt their strategies accordingly. This section provides systematic frameworks for recognizing regime changes and implementing appropriate adjustments.

The Market Condition Assessment Framework

Monthly market analysis checklist:

1. **Trend assessment:**

- [ ] What is current trend? (Bull/sideways/bear)
- [ ] Is trend accelerating or decelerating?
- [ ] Where is market relative to 200-day MA?
- [ ] What is breadth trend? (Advancing vs. declining)

2. **Volatility assessment:**
   - [ ] Current VIX level and trend
   - [ ] Implied volatility rank across portfolio holdings
   - [ ] Are volatility conditions favorable for selling?
3. **Sentiment assessment:**
   - [ ] What are investor surveys indicating?
   - [ ] Is media coverage extreme (very bullish or bearish)?
   - [ ] Are fund flows confirming or contradicting trend?
4. **Economic assessment:**
   - [ ] GDP growth direction
   - [ ] Employment trends
   - [ ] Federal Reserve policy stance
   - [ ] Corporate earnings trends
5. **Technical assessment:**
   - [ ] Support/resistance levels intact or broken?
   - [ ] Moving average alignment bullish or bearish?
   - [ ] Are we at range extremes or mid-range?

Strategy Adjustment Matrix

Based on monthly assessment, select appropriate approach:

MARKET CONDITION → STRATEGY ADJUSTMENT

Early Bull Market (Strong uptrend beginning):

→ Strike: 5-7% OTM (conservative)

→ Coverage: 50-70% of shares

→ Duration: 14-21 days (frequent adjustment)

→ Sectors: Keep exposure to growth sectors

→ Goal: Capture appreciation with supplemental income

Mid Bull Market (Steady uptrend continuing):

→ Strike: 3-5% OTM (moderate)

→ Coverage: 70-80% of shares

→ Duration: 30 days (standard)

→ Sectors: Balanced
→ Goal: Balance appreciation and income
Late Bull Market (Uptrend showing exhaustion):
→ Strike: 2-3% OTM (moderate to aggressive)
→ Coverage: 80-100% of shares
→ Duration: 30-45 days (standard to longer)
→ Sectors: Begin rotation to defensive
→ Goal: Maximize income, prepare for potential reversal
Sideways Market (Ranging):
→ Strike: ATM or at resistance (aggressive)
→ Coverage: 100% of shares
→ Duration: 30 days (standard)
→ Sectors: Balanced
→ Goal: Maximum premium collection
Early Bear Market (Downtrend beginning):
→ Strike: ATM to slightly ITM (aggressive/defensive)
→ Coverage: 100% of shares
→ Duration: 30 days (standard)
→ Sectors: Rotate to defensive
→ Goal: Maximum downside protection
Deep Bear Market (Strong downtrend):
→ Strike: ATM to ITM (very aggressive)
→ Coverage: Accept assignments, reduce equity exposure
→ Duration: 30 days
→ Sectors: Defensive only (utilities, consumer staples)
→ Goal: Capital preservation, prepare for eventual recovery

Quarterly Strategy Review Process

Every three months, conduct comprehensive review:

Step 1: Performance Analysis

- Calculate total returns for quarter
- Compare to benchmark (S&P 500)
- Assess what worked and what didn't
- Identify best and worst performing positions

Step 2: Market Regime Assessment

- Has market regime changed during quarter?
- Are we entering new phase (bull→sideways, sideways→bear)?
- What are leading indicators suggesting about next quarter?

Step 3: Portfolio Rebalancing

- Verify position sizes remain appropriate (no position >15%)
- Confirm sector allocations align with current market regime
- Identify positions to add or remove
- Adjust cash reserves as needed

Step 4: Strategy Calibration

- Should strike selection be more aggressive or conservative next quarter?
- Should position coverage increase or decrease?
- Are current expirations optimal or should they change?
- Do any positions require special management?

Step 5: Document Decisions

- Write brief summary of market outlook
- Document strategy adjustments being implemented
- Set specific goals for next quarter
- Create accountability for following plan

Transition Management

The most critical skill is recognizing transitions between market regimes:

Bull to sideways transition signals:

- Uptrend momentum slowing
- Breakout attempts failing
- Volume declining

- VIX stabilizing at moderate levels
- Shift from FOMO (fear of missing out) to uncertainty

Action: Gradually increase strike aggressiveness, move from 5-7% OTM toward 2-3% OTM

Sideways to bull transition signals:

- Decisive breakout above resistance on strong volume
- Breadth expanding
- VIX declining sharply
- Sentiment shifting to optimism
- Economic data accelerating

Action: Immediately shift to conservative strikes (5-7% OTM), reduce coverage to 50-70%

Sideways to bear transition signals:

- Breakdown below support on strong volume
- Failed rallies (lower highs forming)
- VIX spiking above 25
- Breadth deteriorating
- Economic data weakening

Action: Move to ATM/ITM strikes, begin rotating to defensive sectors, increase cash allocation

Real-Time Adjustment Example

**Month 1 (January

***

Chapter 15: Managing Different Market Conditions (Continued)

Adjusting Your Approach (Continued)

Real-Time Adjustment Example

Month 1 (January): Bull market identified

- Market above 200-day MA, making new highs
- Portfolio assessment: 10 positions, all with standard 2-3% OTM calls
- Decision: Shift to 5-7% OTM calls, reduce coverage to 70%
- Action: As current calls expire, implement new strike strategy
- Result: Captured more upside as market rallied 12% over next 3 months

Month 4 (April): Market losing momentum

- Rally stalling, attempted new highs failing
- Volume declining, VIX stabilizing
- Assessment: Possible transition to sideways
- Decision: Gradually increase strike aggressiveness to 2-3% OTM
- Action: Over next two expirations, move strikes closer
- Result: Prepared for consolidation, increased premium collection

Month 7 (July): Clear sideways range established

- Market oscillating between 4,200-4,400 for two months
- Assessment: Confirmed sideways market
- Decision: Maximum premium strategy at resistance
- Action: Sell calls at 4,400 level when market approaches resistance
- Result: Generated 3%+ monthly premium during

consolidation

Month 10 (October): Bear market signals appearing

- Market broke below 4,200 support decisively
- VIX spiked to 28
- Breadth deteriorating rapidly
- Assessment: Bear market beginning
- Decision: Shift to defensive posture immediately
- Action: Move to ATM/ITM calls, begin accepting assignments, rotate to defensive sectors
- Result: Preserved capital as market declined 18% over next 4 months

Performance Impact of Adaptation
Adaptive strategy (described above):

- Bull phase: +15% (captured most of rally)
- Sideways phase: +9% (maximized premium)
- Bear phase: -3% (defensive positioning)
- Total year: +21%

Static strategy (no adaptation):

- Bull phase: +8% (frequent assignments capped gains)
- Sideways phase: +6% (moderate premium collection)
- Bear phase: -15% (insufficient defense)
- Total year: -1%

Difference: 22 percentage point outperformance through strategic adaptation

Adaptation Best Practices

1. **Be proactive, not reactive:** Make changes as conditions shift, not after major damage
2. **Use evidence, not emotion:** Base decisions on objective

indicators, not fear or greed

3. **Adjust gradually:** Shift strategy over 2-3 expirations, not overnight
4. **Document reasoning:** Write down why you're adjusting (creates accountability)
5. **Stay flexible:** No strategy works in all conditions; adaptation is the strategy

Conclusion: Market Condition Mastery

The covered call strategy's greatest strength is its adaptability. By recognizing market regimes and systematically adjusting strike selection, position coverage, duration, and sector allocation, you transform a single strategy into an all-weather approach capable of generating consistent returns across bull markets, sideways consolidations, and even bear markets.

The framework is simple:

- **Bull markets:** Conservative strikes, reduced coverage, preserve upside
- **Sideways markets:** Aggressive strikes at resistance, maximum premium
- **Bear markets:** ATM/ITM strikes, defensive sectors, capital preservation

Master this adaptive approach, and you'll outperform static strategies and buy-and-hold investors across complete market cycles.

Chapter 16:

Common Mistakes and How to Avoid Them

Every covered call trader makes mistakes—it's part of the learning process. However, certain errors appear so frequently and damage returns so consistently that they warrant detailed examination. This chapter identifies the five most common and costly mistakes, explains why traders fall into these traps, and provides specific strategies to avoid them.

Understanding these pitfalls before experiencing them personally can save you thousands of dollars and months of frustration. Even experienced traders benefit from periodic review of these principles as reminders when emotions threaten discipline.

Chasing High Premiums

The siren song of high premiums lures more traders into trouble than any other factor. A 5% monthly premium looks irresistible compared to a modest 1.5% premium—until the stock underlying that rich premium declines 20% in a single quarter.

The High Premium Trap

How it manifests:

Trader sees two opportunities:

- **Stock A:** Stable blue-chip, implied volatility 18%, premium 1.3% monthly
- **Stock B:** Volatile momentum stock, implied volatility 65%, premium 4.8% monthly

The calculation seems obvious: Stock B generates 270% more premium. Over a year, Stock B could generate 58% returns while Stock A produces only 16%. The choice appears clear—choose Stock B.

The hidden reality:

Stock B's 65% implied volatility and 4.8% premium exist for good reason: the market expects dramatic price movements. Analysis reveals:

- **Stock B characteristics:**
    - Unprofitable company burning cash
    - Single product concentration risk
    - Pending FDA approval (binary outcome)
    - Technical chart showing 40% decline over 6 months
    - Earnings misses in 3 of last 4 quarters
    - High short interest (30% of float)

What actually happens:

Month 1: Stock B at $50, sell $52 calls for $2.40 (4.8%) **Month 2:** Negative clinical trial data, stock gaps down to $32 (-36%) **Month 2 Result:** Lost $18 on stock, kept $2.40 premium, net loss: -$15.60 (-31%)

Meanwhile with Stock A: Month 1-2: Stock at $50, steady at $51, collected $1.30 + $1.30 = $2.60 (5.2% gain)

Stock A's "boring" 1.3% monthly premium dramatically outperformed Stock B's "exciting" 4.8% premium because Stock A's stability produced consistent returns while Stock B's volatility created catastrophic loss.

Why traders chase high premiums:

Psychological factors:

1. **Greed and impatience:** Desire to accelerate wealth building
2. **Selective perception:** Focus on premium without evaluating risk
3. **Overconfidence:** "I can exit if it goes against me" (usually can't)
4. **Envy:** Seeing others brag about high-premium trades on social media
5. **Short-term thinking:** Focusing on next month's income, not long-term consistency

The premium-to-risk relationship:

High premiums exist to compensate for high risk. The market is efficient—when options are expensive, it's because risk is elevated. You're not discovering an opportunity; you're accepting risk that sophisticated traders are avoiding.

Mathematical reality:

Consider two strategies over 12 months:

Strategy A: Conservative 1.5% monthly premium on stable stocks

- Monthly success rate: 95%
- Average monthly return: +1.5%
- Occasional loss months: -2%
- Annual result: 11 winning months (+16.5%), 1 losing month (-2%) = +14.5%

Strategy B: Aggressive 4.5% monthly premium on volatile stocks

- Monthly success rate: 70%
- Average winning month: +4.5%
- Average losing month: -15%
- Annual result: 8 winning months (+36%), 4 losing months (-60%) = -24%

Despite collecting 3x the premium when successful, Strategy B produces catastrophic losses because the losers overwhelm the winners.

How to avoid the high premium trap:

Rule 1: Establish premium reasonableness ranges

For different stock categories, define acceptable premium ranges:

Blue-chip mega-caps (AAPL, MSFT, JNJ):

- Acceptable: 1.0-2.0% monthly
- Investigate if above: 2.5%+
- Avoid: 3.5%+

Established large-caps:

- Acceptable: 1.5-2.5% monthly
- Investigate: 3.0%+

- Avoid: 4.0%+

Mid-caps:

- Acceptable: 2.0-3.0% monthly
- Investigate: 3.5%+
- Avoid: 5.0%+

If a stock offers premiums significantly above these ranges, question why. The market is telling you something.

Rule 2: Complete fundamental analysis first

Never select stocks based on premium alone. Process must be:

1. Identify fundamentally sound stocks (Chapter 7 criteria)
2. Verify technical setup favorable (Chapter 8 criteria)
3. Check options liquidity adequate
4. THEN evaluate premium opportunity

Premium is the last consideration, not the first.

Rule 3: Calculate risk-adjusted returns

Don't compare raw premiums—compare risk-adjusted returns:

Risk-Adjusted Return = Expected Return / Risk of Ruin

Stock A: 1.5% monthly × 95% success rate / 5% risk = 28.5

Stock B: 4.5% monthly × 70% success rate / 30% risk = 10.5

Stock A superior on risk-adjusted basis despite lower raw premium

Rule 4: Use IV rank as warning signal

Check implied volatility rank before selling:

- IV rank 30-60: Normal, acceptable
- IV rank 60-80: Elevated, investigate thoroughly
- IV rank 80-100: Extreme, likely news-driven or event risk

Stocks with IV rank above 70 warrant extreme caution. Yes, premiums are rich, but risk is proportionally elevated.

Rule 5: Respect the "too good to be true" principle

If a premium seems unusually attractive:

- Check upcoming earnings date (perhaps in 2 days, creating event risk)
- Search for pending FDA decisions or regulatory announcements
- Review recent news for negative developments
- Verify there's no pending acquisition or merger
- Check short interest (high short interest suggests problems)

Case Study: The High Premium Disaster
Real example: Biotech company XYZ (2023)
Trader discovers:

- Stock price: $18
- 30-day ATM calls: $2.70 premium (15% monthly, 180% annualized!)
- Excitement: "This is incredible, I found a money printer"

Ignores warning signs:

- IV rank: 95 (extreme)
- Upcoming FDA decision in 3 weeks
- Company has no approved products
- Burning $50M cash quarterly
- Stock declined from $45 to $18 over past year

What happened:

- Week 1: Sold calls, collected $2.70
- Week 2: FDA rejected drug application
- Week 3: Stock gapped down to $4 (-78%)
- Final result: Lost $14 on stock, kept $2.70 premium, net loss: -$11.30 (-63%)

A single high-premium chase erased six months of consistent profits from conservative covered call trading.

The sustainable premium approach:

Focus on stocks where:

- Premium reflects normal volatility, not crisis
- Business fundamentals support current valuation
- Technical setup suggests stability, not chaos
- You'd be comfortable holding stock even without call premium
- Risk of 20%+ decline is minimal

These stocks may offer only 1.5-2.5% monthly premiums, but they deliver those premiums consistently month after month, year after year. The compounding effect of consistent 1.8% monthly returns over 3 years creates 80% total returns—far superior to chasing 5% monthly premiums that blow up quarterly.

Ignoring Earnings Announcements

Earnings announcements create more covered call disasters than any other single event. Companies reporting quarterly results trigger volatility spikes, gap moves, and assignment complications that devastate unprepared traders.

The Earnings Trap

How it manifests:

Trader owns Microsoft, sold $420 calls expiring in 28 days. Unbeknownst to them, Microsoft reports earnings in 12 days. The call was sold assuming normal price behavior, but earnings create abnormal circumstances.

What can happen:

Scenario 1: Positive earnings surprise

- Microsoft beats estimates significantly
- Stock gaps up 8% from $410 to $443 overnight
- Your $420 calls now deeply in-the-money
- Must accept assignment at $420 or buy back at $25 (10x premium collected)
- Missed $33 of appreciation, captured only $10 to strike plus $2.50 premium

Scenario 2: Negative earnings surprise

- Microsoft misses estimates
- Stock gaps down 6% from $410 to $385
- Your $420 calls become worthless (good for option)
- But stock loss (-$25) overwhelms premium collected ($2.50)
- Net loss: -$22.50

Scenario 3: Guidance disappointment despite beat

- Microsoft beats quarterly numbers but lowers full-year guidance
- Market focuses on guidance, stock drops 4%
- Similar to Scenario 2 but less dramatic

Why traders ignore earnings:
Common justifications (all flawed):

1. "I didn't know earnings were coming" (easily preventable)
2. "I thought my strike was safe" (earnings create extraordinary moves)
3. "The premium was too good to pass up" (premium reflected earnings risk)
4. "I figured I could exit if needed" (gap moves prevent escape)
5. "I want to hold through earnings to see what happens" (gambling, not trading)

The earnings volatility pattern:
Typical timeline:

- **30 days before:** Normal volatility
- **14 days before:** Implied volatility begins rising
- **7 days before:** IV accelerates upward (20-40% increase)
- **1-2 days before:** IV peaks (40-100% increase from baseline)
- **Day of announcement:** Actual move occurs (usually 5-12%)

- **1 day after:** IV collapses back to normal ("volatility crush")

Example: Typical blue-chip earnings pattern
Stock: Johnson & Johnson at $160
Normal environment (no earnings approaching):

- IV: 18%
- 30-day ATM calls: $2.40

7 days before earnings:

- IV: 24% (+33%)
- 30-day ATM calls: $3.00 (+25% premium)

1 day before earnings:

- IV: 32% (+78%)
- 30-day ATM calls: $3.90 (+63% premium)

Day after earnings (beat estimates, stock up 2%):

- IV: 19% (collapsed)
- 30-day ATM calls: $2.60
- Note: Despite stock up 2%, calls worth less than pre-earnings due to volatility crush

How to avoid the earnings trap:
Rule 1: Always check earnings dates before selling calls
Before every covered call sale:

1. Google "[ticker] earnings date"
2. Check company investor relations website
3. Verify on your broker's platform
4. Set calendar reminder

Takes 60 seconds, prevents disasters

Rule 2: Ensure calls expire BEFORE earnings

When earnings are in 25 days, sell calls expiring in 21 days or less. This ensures:

- No earnings risk during your option period
- No assignment complications from earnings moves
- You can reassess after earnings before selling new calls

Example:

- Today: January 15
- Earnings: February 12 (28 days away)
- Action: Sell February 7 expiration (23 days), NOT February 21 expiration (37 days)

Rule 3: If you must hold through earnings, adjust strategy

Sometimes you prefer holding positions through earnings (high conviction on results). If so:

Defensive approach:

- Use strikes 7-10% out-of-the-money (vs. normal 2-4%)
- Accept lower premium for reduced assignment risk
- Willing to accept wider gap moves won't breach strike

Example:

- Stock at $100
- Normal strategy: $103 strike
- Earnings strategy: $107 or $110 strike
- Even 7% earnings pop to $107 keeps you safe

Rule 4: Sell calls immediately AFTER earnings

Often the best covered call opportunity occurs the day after earnings:

Why post-earnings is optimal:

- Volatility still elevated from event
- Stock price has settled into new range
- No major events on horizon for 3 months
- Premium enhanced by residual elevated IV
- All uncertainty resolved

Example:

- Before earnings: Stock $100, IV 25%, $102 calls = $1.80
- After earnings: Stock $103, IV 28%, $105 calls = $2.40
- Better premium despite higher strike because of post-earnings setup

Rule 5: Use earnings calendar for planning

Maintain earnings calendar for all holdings:

Stock	Q1 Earnings	Q2 Earnings	Q3 Earnings	Q4 Earnings
MSFT	April 25	July 25	Oct 25	Jan 25
JNJ	April 16	July 16	Oct 15	Jan 16
V	April 30	July 30	Oct 30	Jan 29

This allows proactive planning:

- Never sell calls expiring after earnings unless intentional
- Time expirations to end just before earnings
- Capitalize on pre-earnings IV expansion by selling 2-3 weeks before

The earnings IV exploitation strategy:

Advanced traders exploit pre-earnings volatility:

Process:

1. Two weeks before earnings, sell calls (capturing elevated IV)
2. Ensure expiration is 3-5 days before earnings
3. Premium is 20-40% higher than normal due to IV inflation
4. Option expires before actual earnings event
5. Immediately after earnings, sell new calls

Example: Normal month: Collect $2.00 premium Earnings month: Collect $2.60 premium (two weeks before earnings) Next month: Collect $2.10 premium (right after earnings) Result: 35% increase in that month's income

Case Study: The Earnings Disaster

Real trader experience: Tech stock ABC

Setup:

- Owned 100 shares at $180
- Sold $190 calls for $5.50 (very attractive premium)
- Expiration: 35 days away
- Ignored that earnings were in 18 days

Earnings day:

- Company missed estimates by 15%
- Lowered full-year guidance
- Stock gapped down to $142 at open (-21%)

Result:

- Stock loss: -$38 per share
- Premium collected: +$5.50
- Net loss: -$32.50 (-18%)
- Required 15 months of normal covered call profits to recover

The lesson: 60 seconds of earnings date checking would have prevented an 18% loss. The trader could have:

- Selected shorter expiration (before earnings)
- Used much wider strike (to survive potential gap)
- Simply waited until after earnings

One moment of carelessness erased 15 months of disciplined work.

Earnings best practices summary:

1. **Never sell covered calls without checking earnings dates**
2. **Default to expirations before earnings announcements**
3. **Use extra-conservative strikes if holding through earnings**
4. **Capitalize on pre-earnings IV expansion with proper timing**
5. **Consider post-earnings as prime covered call opportunity**

Poor Strike Selection

Strike selection determines your maximum profit, downside protection, and assignment probability. Poor strike selection—whether too aggressive or too conservative—costs traders 20-40% of potential returns even when other aspects of their strategy are sound.

The Strike Selection Mistakes

Mistake 1: Consistently too aggressive (ATM or ITM strikes)

How it manifests: Trader believes maximizing premium is always optimal, consistently selling at-the-money or in-the-money calls regardless of market conditions or stock outlook.

Example:

- Stock: Visa at $305
- Trader always sells $305 (ATM) or $300 (ITM) calls
- Premium collected: $4.50-$5.50 (1.5-1.8% monthly)
- Assignment rate: 65-70%

The problem:

- During bull market year, Visa rallies from $305 to $385 (+26%)
- Trader's experience: Assigned 8 times throughout year
- Average assignment price: $307
- Total gain: $2 appreciation + $45 total premium = $47 (15.4%)
- Buy-and-hold: $80 gain (26%)
- **Opportunity cost: $33 (11 percentage points)**

Why it's a mistake: Aggressive strikes work beautifully in sideways markets but create massive opportunity costs during trending markets. The rigid application regardless of conditions destroys returns.

Mistake 2: Consistently too conservative (far OTM strikes)

How it manifests: Trader fears assignment, consistently selling strikes 7-10% out-of-the-money regardless of conditions.

Example:

- Stock: Coca-Cola at $60
- Trader always sells $66-67 calls (10% OTM)
- Premium collected: $0.60-$0.80 (1.0-1.3% monthly)
- Assignment rate: 5-8%

The problem:

- During sideways year, Coca-Cola trades in $58-$63 range
- Trader's premium: $8.40 annually (14% return)
- Moderate trader using $62 strikes: $16.80 premium (28% return)
- **Lost income: $8.40 (14 percentage points)**

Why it's a mistake: Conservative strikes provide unnecessary protection during favorable conditions. The excessive caution costs 50% of potential income without corresponding benefit.

Mistake 3: Ignoring technical resistance

How it manifests: Trader mechanically selects strikes without considering chart patterns, support/resistance levels, or technical structure.

Example:

- Stock at $98, strong resistance at $100 (tested 4 times in past 3 months)
- Technical trader: Sells $100 calls for $2.80 (at resistance)
- Mechanical trader: Sells $102 calls for $2.10 (standard 4% OTM)

What happens: Stock rallies to $99.80, respects resistance, pulls back

- Technical trader: Keeps full $2.80
- Mechanical trader: Keeps full $2.10
- Technical trader earned 33% more by incorporating technical analysis

Repeated over 12 months:

- Technical approach: ~$33 annual premium
- Mechanical approach: ~$25 annual premium
- Difference: 32% more income from technical awareness

Mistake 4: Same strikes in all market conditions

How it manifests: Trader uses identical strike selection approach (say, 30-delta rule) regardless of bull, bear, or sideways markets.

Example across market conditions:

Bull market (6 months):

- Standard 30-delta approach: 2% OTM strikes, captured 10% total
- Adapted approach: 5% OTM strikes, captured 17% total
- Cost of inflexibility: -41% relative performance

Sideways market (6 months):

- Standard 30-delta approach: 2% OTM strikes, captured 14% total
- Adapted approach: ATM strikes at resistance, captured 21% total
- Cost of inflexibility: -33% relative performance

Over full cycle: Inflexibility cost 37% of potential returns.

How to avoid strike selection mistakes:

Framework 1: Market-adjusted strike selection

Use this decision tree:

What is current market regime?

BULL MARKET:

→ Strong uptrend → 5-7% OTM (delta 0.15-0.20)
→ Moderate uptrend → 3-5% OTM (delta 0.20-0.25)
→ Early bull → 5-7% OTM + reduce coverage to 60-70%
SIDEWAYS MARKET:
→ Clear range → Strikes at resistance (ATM or slightly above)
→ Unclear range → 2-3% OTM (delta 0.30-0.35)
BEAR MARKET:
→ Early decline → ATM to 2% ITM (delta 0.45-0.55)
→ Deep decline → ATM to 3% ITM (delta 0.50-0.65)

Framework 2: Individual stock technical analysis

Before selecting strike:

1. Identify nearest resistance level above current price
2. Calculate distance to resistance (percentage)
3. Consider recent price action (trending or ranging?)
4. Place strike at or slightly above resistance when possible

Example:

- Stock at $51, resistance at $54 (5.9% away)
- Standard approach: $53 strike (3.9% OTM)
- Technical approach: $54 strike (at resistance, 5.9% OTM)
- Technical approach captures 50% more upside potential with only slightly lower premium

Framework 3: Personal objectives alignment

Match strikes to your current objectives:

Primary objective: Income → More aggressive strikes

- Use ATM to 2% OTM
- Accept higher assignment rates
- Appropriate during retirement when income is priority

Primary objective: Growth → More conservative strikes

- Use 4-7% OTM

- Accept lower premiums
- Appropriate during accumulation phase

Balanced objective → Moderate strikes

- Use 2-4% OTM
- Standard approach
- Appropriate for most investors

Framework 4: Implied volatility adjustment
Adjust strike aggressiveness based on IV environment:
High IV (IV rank > 50):

- Can be more aggressive (closer strikes) because premium compensates
- Example: Stock at $100, IV rank 65
- Strike: $101 (1% OTM) might generate $2.80 due to rich IV

Normal IV (IV rank 30-50):

- Standard strikes (2-4% OTM)
- Balanced risk-reward

Low IV (IV rank < 30):

- Either more conservative strikes or skip covered calls
- Premium insufficient to justify aggressive positioning

Strike selection checklist:
Before finalizing any strike:

- [ ] Identified current market regime (bull/sideways/bear)
- [ ] Located nearest technical resistance
- [ ] Verified IV rank is acceptable (preferably > 30)
- [ ] Confirmed premium meets minimum threshold
- [ ] Ensured no earnings within option period

- [ ] Checked that strike aligns with current objectives
- [ ] Verified delta/probability acceptable
- [ ] Confirmed strike makes sense given stock's recent behavior

Case Study: Strike Selection Impact

Same stock, three traders, one year:

Trader A: Consistently aggressive (ATM strikes)

- Monthly premium: 2.8% average
- Assignment rate: 75%
- Total year: Stock +5%, Premium +34% = +39% return
- Missed significant appreciation on multiple assignments

Trader B: Consistently conservative (7% OTM strikes)

- Monthly premium: 1.1% average
- Assignment rate: 10%
- Total year: Stock +20%, Premium +13% = +33% return
- Left significant income on table

Trader C: Adaptive strike selection

- Bull quarters: 5% OTM (captured appreciation)
- Sideways quarters: ATM at resistance (maximized premium)
- Uncertain periods: 3% OTM (balanced)
- Monthly premium: 1.9% average
- Assignment rate: 35%
- Total year: Stock +18%, Premium +23% = +41% return
- Best of both worlds through adaptation

Trader C outperformed both rigid approaches by 2-8 percentage points through strategic flexibility.

Letting Emotions Drive Decisions

Emotions—fear, greed, regret, hope—destroy more trading accounts than technical ignorance. Covered calls, despite being a relatively conservative strategy, generate emotional challenges that cause traders to abandon discipline and make costly mistakes.

The Emotional Traps

Trap 1: Assignment regret (Fear of missing out)

How it manifests: Your stock gets assigned at $100. Within two weeks, the stock rallies to $115. You experience intense regret: "I 'lost' $15 per share by getting assigned! This strategy doesn't work!"

The emotional spiral:

- Week 1: See stock at $115, feel regret
- Week 2: Stock at $120, regret intensifies
- Week 3: Decide to "fix" mistake, repurchase at $120 (now overpaying)
- Week 4: Stock pulls back to $110 (bought at exactly the worst time)
- Result: Turned winning trade (profit at $100 assignment) into losing trade (repurchased at $120)

The reality check: You didn't "lose" $15. You agreed to sell at $100 when you sold the call. You captured maximum profit for that trade. The stock's subsequent movement is irrelevant to your trade's success.

Proper perspective:

- Your trade plan: Sell at $100, collect $2.50 premium
- Your result: Sold at $100, collected $2.50 premium
- Assessment: **100% successful trade execution**

What the stock does after assignment is a new, separate situation. Your original trade was profitable and correct.

Trap 2: Loss aversion paralysis

How it manifests: Your stock has declined from $100 to $85. You have covered calls outstanding with strikes at $90. The calls are now worthless (good for you), but you refuse to sell new calls because "I don't want to lock in my loss."

The flawed thinking: "If I sell $88 calls, I'm admitting the stock is only worth $88. I'll wait until it gets back to $100, then I'll sell calls again."

What actually happens:

- Month 1: Stock at $85, no calls sold, decline continues to $82
- Month 2: Stock at $82, still waiting, another decline to $79
- Month 3: Stock at $79, finally capitulates and sells $82 calls
- Six months later: Stock recovers to $95

Analysis: By refusing to sell calls at $88, trader missed:

- Month 1: $2.80 potential premium
- Month 2: $2.60 potential premium
- Month 3: $2.40 potential premium
- Total: $7.80 per share (9% of original value!)

This "waiting" cost $7.80 while trying to avoid "locking in" a paper loss. The loss was already real whether acknowledged or not.

Proper approach: Continue selling covered calls at appropriate strikes for the current price, regardless of your entry price. Your entry price is irrelevant to today's optimal strategy.

Trap 3: Revenge trading after losses

How it manifests: You experience a significant loss (stock declined 20%, overwhelming premium). You feel angry and compelled to "make it back quickly." You:

- Switch to much more aggressive strikes
- Add riskier, higher-premium stocks
- Increase position sizes
- Take excessive risks to recover losses

Example:

- Normal approach: 10 positions, $20k each, moderate strikes
- After $15k loss: 5 positions, $40k each (concentrated risk),

aggressive strikes, chasing 4% monthly premiums

What typically happens: The aggressive approach increases risk exactly when you should be reducing it. Another adverse move compounds losses:

- Original loss: -$15,000
- Revenge trading loss: -$12,000
- Total hole: -$27,000

Now you need 27% returns just to break even, likely requiring 12-18 months of disciplined trading.

Proper approach after losses:

1. Accept the loss (it's already happened)
2. Return to systematic, disciplined approach
3. Potentially reduce position sizes slightly (increase margin of safety)
4. Focus on consistency, not recovery speed
5. Understand that 1.5% monthly for 12 months recovers more than risky attempts at 5% monthly

Trap 4: Overconfidence after winning streak

How it manifests: You experience six consecutive profitable months. You begin thinking:

- "I've mastered this strategy"
- "I should increase position sizes to maximize this skill"
- "I can be more aggressive since I clearly know what I'm doing"
- "Maybe I should leverage margin to amplify returns"

Example:

- Months 1-6: 10 positions, $200k total, averaging +3% monthly (+18% over 6 months)
- Overconfident adjustment: 15 positions, $300k total (using

margin), aggressive strikes
- Month 7: Market correction, multiple positions assigned or losing
- Month 7 result: -$35k loss (-11.7% of original capital)

Six months of gains (+$36k) erased by one overconfident month (-$35k).

The reality: Six winning months doesn't mean you've "mastered" anything. Markets are cyclical. You were likely benefiting from favorable conditions (sideways or gently rising market) that could change at any time.

Proper approach: Treat winning streaks with caution:

- Maintain position sizing discipline
- Don't increase risk or leverage
- Actually consider being slightly more conservative (save dry powder)
- Remember that mean reversion applies to personal performance too

Trap 5: Comparison and envy

How it manifests: You read online forums or talk to friends who

***

Chapter 16: Common Mistakes and How to Avoid Them (Continued)

Letting Emotions Drive Decisions (Continued)

Trap 5: Comparison and envy

How it manifests: You read online forums or talk to friends who claim extraordinary returns: "I made 8% last month on covered calls!" or "My portfolio is up 45% this year from selling options!"

You compare your steady 2% monthly returns and feel inadequate. You begin thinking:

- "I must be doing something wrong"
- "They know something I don't"
- "I need to be more aggressive to keep up"
- "My strategy is clearly inferior"

The reality behind the claims:

Scenario A: They're cherry-picking Person claims "45% annual returns" but:

- Started in March (market bottom)
- Showing only winning positions
- Not including losers or closed positions
- Calculating returns incorrectly
- Actual full portfolio return: 18%

Scenario B: They're taking excessive risk Person actually generated 45% returns, but:

- Concentrated in 3 positions (vs. your 10)
- Using stocks with 60% implied volatility (vs. your 25%)
- Employing leverage/margin
- One bad quarter could eliminate entire year's gains
- Risk-adjusted returns inferior to your approach

Scenario C: They're exaggerating or lying Unfortunately common on social media:

- Complete fabrication
- Unrealized paper gains counted as actual returns
- Demo account, not real money
- Selectively cropped screenshots

Proper perspective:

- Your returns should be judged against your risk tolerance and goals
- Consistent 20-25% annual returns sustainably achieved = exceptional success
- Compare yourself to your past self, not others' claims
- Focus on process quality, not outcome comparison

How to maintain emotional discipline:
Strategy 1: Pre-commitment and rules
Write down your strategy rules when calm and rational:
MY COVERED CALL RULES:
Position Sizing:
- Maximum 15% per position
- Minimum 8 positions total
- No margin/leverage
Strike Selection:
- Bull markets: 5-7% OTM
- Sideways markets: 2-3% OTM at resistance
- Bear markets: ATM to 2% ITM
Management:
- Check earnings dates before every trade
- Hold positions to expiration unless captured 75%+ profit
- Never chase premiums above 3.5% monthly on blue-chips
- Accept assignments gracefully, they're planned outcomes
Emotional Guidelines:

- No revenge trading after losses
- No position size increases after winning streaks
- No strategy changes based on others' claims
- Monthly reviews only, ignore daily noise

I will follow these rules regardless of how I feel emotionally.

Signed: ___________________ Date: _______________

Strategy 2: Create emotional circuit breakers

Implement rules that prevent emotional decisions:

24-hour rule for major changes: Any significant deviation from strategy requires 24-hour waiting period:

- Increasing position sizes by 25%+
- Adding margin/leverage
- Switching to much more aggressive strikes
- Exiting strategy entirely

Write down reasoning, sleep on it, reassess next day. Most emotional decisions look foolish after 24 hours.

Position limit locks: Use brokerage features to prevent overtrading:

- Set maximum position sizes
- Enable trade confirmations
- Require secondary authentication for large orders

Strategy 3: Journaling and accountability

Keep decision journal:

Date: March 15, 2025

Decision: Considering selling $95 calls on Stock X (currently at $100)

Reasoning: Premium is 5.2% monthly, very attractive

Emotions check: Feeling frustrated after last month's losses, wanting to "catch up"

Red flags: This is revenge trading, premium reflects high risk

Decision: Will NOT execute, stick to standard approach

Regular journal review reveals emotional patterns, allowing correction before costly mistakes.

Strategy 4: Focus on process, not outcomes

Shift mental focus from results to process quality:

Poor focus (outcome-based): "I made 3.2% this month vs. 2.1% last month - I'm getting better!"

Better focus (process-based): "Did I follow my rules this month?" "Did I check earnings dates before every trade?" "Were my strike selections consistent with market conditions?" "Did I maintain proper position sizing?"

Good process with temporary poor outcomes = successful trading
Poor process with lucky good outcomes = impending disaster

Strategy 5: Realistic return expectations

Establish what realistic, sustainable returns look like:

Conservative approach: 12-18% annually

- Achievable with minimal stress
- Sustainable indefinitely
- Low blow-up risk
- Suitable for retirement accounts

Moderate approach: 18-28% annually

- Requires active management
- Sustainable with discipline
- Moderate risk during corrections
- Suitable for most investors

Aggressive approach: 28-40% annually

- Demands significant time and skill
- Difficult to sustain long-term
- Higher risk of significant drawdowns
- Only for experienced, dedicated traders

If you consistently achieve returns in your category, you're succeeding. Don't let others' (often fictitious) claims create dissatisfaction.

Overtrading

Overtrading—excessive trading frequency or position turnover—destroys returns through transaction costs, poor timing, and decision fatigue. Despite zero commissions at most brokers, overtrading remains a significant problem.

The Overtrading Trap

Manifestation 1: Constant position churning

How it looks:

- Buying back calls after 5-7 days (captured 30-40% profit)
- Immediately selling new calls
- Repeating weekly or even more frequently
- Constantly adjusting, never letting positions develop

Example:

- Day 1: Sell 30-day calls for $2.50
- Day 6: Calls at $1.80, buy back, capture $0.70
- Day 6: Sell new calls for $2.40
- Day 11: Calls at $1.60, buy back, capture $0.80
- Day 11: Sell new calls for $2.30
- Continue pattern...

Problems created:

1. **Execution risk:** Each trade risks poor fills, missing fills, or gap moves during closure
2. **Tax complexity:** Dozens of trades per position create record-keeping nightmares
3. **Decision fatigue:** Constant monitoring and decision-making exhausts mental energy
4. **Diminishing returns:** After capturing easy 50-70% profits,

remaining gains are harder

5. **Opportunity cost:** Time spent churning could be spent on other valuable activities

Mathematical reality:
Overtrading approach (close at 30% profit, repeat):

- Week 1: Sell for $2.50, close at $1.75, profit $0.75
- Week 2: Sell for $2.40, close at $1.68, profit $0.72
- Week 3: Sell for $2.30, close at $1.61, profit $0.69
- Week 4: Sell for $2.25, close at $1.58, profit $0.67
- Monthly total: $2.83

Standard approach (hold 30 days):

- Day 1: Sell for $2.50
- Day 30: Expire worthless
- Monthly total: $2.50

Analysis: Overtrading generated only 13% more income ($0.33) but required:

- 8 trades vs. 1 trade
- Constant monitoring
- Risk of poor execution on 8 occasions
- Far more complex tax reporting

The 13% income increase rarely justifies the effort, risk, and complexity.

Manifestation 2: Trading every day
How it looks:

- Checking portfolio multiple times daily
- Making adjustments constantly
- Unable to let positions sit
- Always "doing something"

The false productivity fallacy: More activity ≠ better results

Often, the best action is no action. Markets reward patience, not activity.

Example:

- Monday: Close one position, open new one
- Tuesday: Adjust another position
- Wednesday: Roll a third position
- Thursday: Close another position
- Friday: Add new position

This trader made 5 decisions/actions in one week. Compare to successful trader:

- Monday-Friday: Reviewed positions, determined no action needed
- Saturday: Comprehensive weekly review, identified one true opportunity
- Action: One strategic trade

The hyperactive trader appears busy but likely made 3-4 suboptimal decisions driven by need for activity rather than genuine opportunity.

Manifestation 3: Rolling everything constantly

How it looks:

- Never accepting assignments
- Rolling every position that goes in-the-money
- Accumulating rolling debits trying to "save" positions
- Creating increasingly complex, underwater positions

Example progression:

Month 1:

- Stock at $100, sell $105 calls for $2.50
- Stock rises to $108

Month 2:

- Roll: Buy back $105 calls for $4.50, sell $110 calls for $3.00
- Net debit: $1.50
- Running premium: $2.50 - $1.50 = $1.00
- Stock at $112

Month 3:

- Roll: Buy back $110 calls for $4.00, sell $115 calls for $2.80
- Net debit: $1.20
- Running premium: $1.00 - $1.20 = -$0.20 (now negative!)
- Stock at $118

Month 4:

- Roll: Buy back $115 calls for $4.80, sell $120 calls for $2.60
- Net debit: $2.20
- Running premium: -$0.20 - $2.20 = -$2.40

Analysis: Trader has now PAID $2.40 per share trying to avoid assignment, when accepting assignment at $105 would have generated profit. Stock appreciation from $100 to $118 captured only by rolling costs (-$2.40), not profit.

Better approach: Accept assignment at $105, realize $5 stock profit + $2.50 premium = $7.50 gain. Move on to new opportunity.

How to avoid overtrading:

Rule 1: Set minimum holding periods

Establish minimum time before any action:

- **Minimum before closing:** 14 days OR 50% of original period (whichever is longer)
- **Minimum before rolling:** 10 days until expiration
- **Minimum between new positions:** 24 hours (prevents impulsive additions)

These minimums force patience and prevent reactionary trading.

Rule 2: Limit monthly trades

Set maximum trades per month:

For 10-position portfolio:

- Maximum 15 opening/closing trades per month
- Roughly 1.5 trades per position per month
- This allows standard monthly roll plus occasional early closure
- Prevents excessive churning

Track monthly trade count:

January 2025 Trade Count: 12 / 15 allowed
- Opened: 10 calls (new month)
- Closed early: 2 calls (captured 70%+ profit)
- Rolled: 0
Status: Within limits, disciplined month

Rule 3: Require written justification for non-standard actions

Before any action outside standard plan (early close, roll, position adjustment):

TRADE JUSTIFICATION FORM:
Position: MSFT $430 calls
Proposed Action: Close early (15 days remaining)
Standard Action: Hold until 5 days before expiration
Why deviating from standard?
- Captured 72% of maximum profit ($6.12 of $8.50)
- Stock approaching strike, acceleration risk
- Strong alternative opportunity identified in JNJ
Does this make mathematical sense?
- Keeping position: $2.38 remaining value over 15 days = $0.16/day
- New position: JNJ offering $2.80 premium, better risk-reward
- Yes, makes sense
Is this emotional or rational?
- Rational: Clear mathematical advantage to redeployment
- Not driven by fear, FOMO, or regret
Decision: APPROVED for early close

This process takes 2 minutes but prevents impulsive overtrading.

Rule 4: Scheduled trading windows

Rather than trading any time, establish windows:

Weekly trading window:

- Wednesday 2:00-3:00 PM: Review positions, execute any necessary trades
- Saturday 9:00-10:00 AM: Comprehensive weekly review, plan next week

Outside these windows: No trading except emergencies (major news events)

This prevents constant monitoring and impulsive trading.

Rule 5: Accept boredom as success

Reframe mental perspective:

Old thinking: "Nothing to do, I should find opportunities" **New thinking:** "Nothing to do means positions are working as planned - success!"

The best traders spend most of their time doing nothing. Activity for activity's sake destroys returns.

The optimal trading frequency:

For 10-position portfolio with monthly expirations:

Typical month:

- Week 1: No activity (positions just opened)
- Week 2: No activity (let positions develop)
- Week 3: Review for early closes (close 1-2 positions if captured 75%+ profit)
- Week 4: Expiration week, roll or let expire (8-10 actions)
- Total monthly actions: 10-15 trades

Overactive month (to avoid):

- Constant monitoring, 25-30+ trades
- Sign of overtrading

Conclusion: Common Mistakes Mastery

The five mistakes covered in this chapter—chasing high premiums, ignoring earnings, poor strike selection, emotional decisions, and overtrading—account for 80%+ of covered call failures. Master these areas, and you avoid the pitfalls that trap most beginners.

The common thread: All these mistakes stem from impatience, whether:

- Impatience for higher returns (chasing premiums)
- Impatience with proper planning (ignoring earnings)
- Impatience with adaptation (poor strikes)
- Impatience with emotional discomfort (emotional trading)
- Impatience with positions developing (overtrading)

The antidote: Systematic discipline, written rules, pre-commitment to process, and patience.

Remember: Covered calls reward patience, consistency, and discipline—not activity, aggression, or cleverness.

Chapter 17:

Tax Considerations

Taxes significantly impact covered call returns. A strategy generating 25% pre-tax returns might produce only 16-18% after-tax returns if managed inefficiently, or 20-22% after-tax with proper planning. Understanding tax treatment, utilizing qualified covered calls, avoiding wash sales, and working effectively with tax professionals can add 2-4 percentage points to your annual returns.

This chapter covers U.S. federal tax treatment of covered calls. State taxes vary by jurisdiction and aren't covered here. International readers should consult local tax professionals as rules differ substantially by country.

Disclaimer: This chapter provides general educational information, not specific tax advice. Tax laws change frequently and individual circumstances vary. Always consult qualified tax professionals before making tax-related decisions.

How Covered Call Income Is Taxed

Covered call transactions create taxable events at different times depending on whether options expire, are closed, or result in assignment.

Basic Tax Treatment of Option Premiums

When you sell a covered call:

- No immediate tax consequence
- Premium received is not taxable income at sale
- Tax obligation created but deferred until position closes

When the option expires worthless:

- Premium becomes short-term capital gain
- Taxable in year of expiration
- Always short-term regardless of how long position held

When you buy back (close) the call:

- Net profit/loss is short-term capital gain/loss

- Calculation: Premium received minus price paid to close
- Taxable in year of closure

When you're assigned:

- Premium is added to stock sale proceeds
- Total gain/loss calculated: (Strike price + Premium - Stock basis)
- Holding period of stock determines short-term vs. long-term treatment

Tax Treatment Examples
Example 1: Call expires worthless
Transaction:

- January 15: Sell March 21 call for $2.50 premium ($250)
- March 21: Call expires worthless

Tax treatment:

- Year: 2025
- Short-term capital gain: $250
- Reported on Form 8949 and Schedule D

Example 2: Buy back call at profit
Transaction:

- February 1: Sell March 15 call for $3.00 premium ($300)
- February 28: Buy back call for $1.20 ($120)
- Net profit: $180

Tax treatment:

- Year: 2025
- Short-term capital gain: $180
- Even though held less than one month, it's capital gain, not

ordinary income

Example 3: Buy back call at loss
Transaction:

- March 1: Sell April 18 call for $2.00 premium ($200)
- March 20: Stock rallies, buy back for $4.50 ($450) to avoid assignment
- Net loss: -$250

Tax treatment:

- Year: 2025
- Short-term capital loss: -$250
- Can offset other capital gains or up to $3,000 of ordinary income

Example 4: Assignment (stock held short-term)
Transaction:

- May 1: Buy 100 shares of XYZ at $50 ($5,000 basis)
- May 1: Sell June 21 $52 call for $2.50 ($250)
- June 21: Assigned, sell stock at $52 ($5,200)

Tax treatment:

- Stock holding period: 51 days (short-term)
- Sale proceeds: $5,200 + $250 premium = $5,450
- Cost basis: $5,000
- Short-term capital gain: $450
- All taxable in year of assignment

Example 5: Assignment (stock held long-term)
Transaction:

- January 2024: Buy 100 shares of ABC at $60 ($6,000 basis)

- February 2025: Sell March 21 $65 call for $3.00 ($300)
- March 21, 2025: Assigned, sell stock at $65 ($6,500)

Tax treatment:

- Stock holding period: 14+ months (long-term)
- Sale proceeds: $6,500 + $300 premium = $6,800
- Cost basis: $6,000
- Long-term capital gain: $800
- Taxed at preferential long-term rates (0%, 15%, or 20% depending on income)

Short-Term vs. Long-Term Capital Gains
Short-term capital gains (held ≤ 365 days):

- Taxed as ordinary income
- Federal rates: 10%, 12%, 22%, 24%, 32%, 35%, or 37% (2025 rates)
- No preferential treatment

Long-term capital gains (held > 365 days):

- Taxed at preferential rates
- Federal rates: 0%, 15%, or 20% (based on income)
- Significant tax advantage

Example tax impact:
Investor in 24% ordinary income bracket with $10,000 gain:
Short-term capital gain:

- Tax: $2,400 (24%)
- After-tax proceeds: $7,600

Long-term capital gain:

- Tax: $1,500 (15% LTCG rate)

- After-tax proceeds: $8,500
- Tax savings: $900 (37.5% less tax)

This is why preserving long-term capital gains treatment matters significantly.

Option Premiums Always Short-Term

Critical rule: Option premium is always short-term capital gain, even if:

- You held the stock for years
- The option was outstanding for months
- You're a long-term investor

The only exception is when assigned—then premium is added to sale proceeds and the stock's holding period determines treatment.

When Assignment Occurs:

If stock held > 365 days when assigned:

- Stock gain: Long-term (preferential rates)
- Premium: Added to proceeds, inherits long-term treatment
- Entire gain (stock + premium) taxed at long-term rates

If stock held ≤ 365 days when assigned:

- Stock gain: Short-term (ordinary rates)
- Premium: Added to proceeds, treated as short-term
- Entire gain taxed at ordinary income rates

Qualified Covered Calls

Qualified covered calls (QCCs) represent a crucial tax concept for covered call investors. Understanding and utilizing QCC rules can save thousands in taxes by preserving long-term capital gains treatment.

The Holding Period Problem

General rule without QCCs: If you sell a call option on stock you own, the stock's holding period may be suspended or restarted, potentially converting what would have been long-term gains into short-term gains.

Example of the problem:

- Day 1: Buy stock at $50
- Day 300: Stock at $60, sell covered call
- Day 400: Call expires, stock still at $60
- Question: Is your holding period 400 days (long-term) or 100 days (short-term)?

Without QCC rules: Holding period might be suspended during the 100 days you had the call outstanding, meaning only 300 days count—not enough for long-term treatment.

The Qualified Covered Call Exception

QCC Rule: If your covered call meets specific requirements, it doesn't suspend or terminate your holding period. Your stock continues accumulating holding period days even while the call is outstanding.

Benefits:

- Preserve long-term capital gains treatment
- Much lower tax rate (15% vs. 24-37%)
- Significant tax savings on appreciated stock

QCC Requirements

For a covered call to qualify as a QCC:

Requirement 1: Holding period before option sale

- Stock must be held more than 365 days before selling the call, OR
- Stock was held long-term (365+ days) when you sold a previous QCC on it

Requirement 2: Option term (expiration)

- Option must have more than 30 days until expiration when sold
- Maximum term: No more than 33 months (LEAPS territory)

Requirement 3: Strike price not "too far" out-of-the-money

Strike must meet minimum level based on stock price and time to expiration. IRS provides tables (detailed below).

Requirement 4: Not "too far" in-the-money

- Strike cannot be below previous day's closing price by more than specified amount
- Essentially, can't be deep in-the-money

QCC Strike Price Requirements (Simplified)

The IRS provides detailed tables, but here's simplified guidance:

Stock price under $25:

- Minimum strike: One strike below stock price
- Example: Stock at $24, minimum strike $22.50 (if strikes in $2.50 increments)

Stock price $25-$60:

- Minimum strike: Second strike below stock price
- Example: Stock at $50, strikes at $2.50 intervals, minimum strike $45

Stock price $60-$150:

- Minimum strike: Two strikes below stock price (if $5 intervals)
- Example: Stock at $100, minimum strike $90

Stock price over $150:

- Minimum strike: $10 below stock price (if $5 intervals), $15 below (if $10 intervals)

These are approximations—consult IRS Publication 550 or tax professional for exact requirements.

Practical QCC Strategy

For stocks held long-term (365+ days):
When selling covered calls, verify they meet QCC requirements:

- Use at least 35-day expiration (safer than 30-day minimum)
- Select strikes meeting minimum requirements
- Document that call qualified as QCC

Example:

- Stock: Microsoft, owned 18 months at $380 basis
- Current price: $445
- Planning to sell covered calls

Standard approach (potentially non-QCC):

- Sell 14-day $450 calls for $3.80
- Problem: Doesn't meet 30-day minimum term
- Risk: Could disqualify as QCC

QCC-compliant approach:

- Sell 35-day $450 calls for $8.20
- Meets term requirement (35 days > 30 days)
- Meets strike requirement (well above minimum)
- Result: Qualified covered call, holding period preserved

Why this matters: If assigned:

- QCC treatment: $65 gain ($445 - $380) taxed as long-term (15%) = $9.75 tax
- Non-QCC: Holding period possibly disrupted, potential short-term treatment (24%) = $15.60 tax
- Savings: $5.85 per share = $585 per contract

When QCC Rules Don't Matter
QCC requirements only matter if:

- You've held stock long-term (365+ days)
- You might be assigned and realize gains

QCC rules don't matter if:

- Stock held short-term anyway (QCC can't make it long-term, only preserve existing long-term status)
- Stock has losses (holding period doesn't affect loss treatment much)
- You're in tax-deferred account (IRA, 401k)

QCC Record-Keeping
For each covered call on long-term stock:
Track:

- Stock purchase date
- Call sale date
- Days held when call sold
- Strike price and expiration
- Whether call met QCC requirements
- Method used to verify QCC compliance

Tax Professional Consultation

QCC rules are complex with specific exceptions and situations. Before implementing QCC strategies:

- Discuss with qualified tax professional
- Review IRS Publication 550 (Investment Income and Expenses)
- Consider software that tracks QCC compliance
- Document decisions for audit purposes

Wash Sale Rules

Wash sale rules prevent taxpayers from claiming artificial losses while maintaining substantially similar positions. These rules significantly affect covered call traders who are assigned and repurchase stocks, potentially disallowing losses.

Basic Wash Sale Rule

The Rule: If you sell stock at a loss and purchase substantially identical stock within 30 days before or after the sale, the loss is disallowed for current tax purposes.

The 61-day window:

- 30 days before sale
- Day of sale
- 30 days after sale = 61-day total window

What happens to disallowed loss:

- Loss isn't lost forever
- Added to cost basis of replacement shares
- Deferred until replacement shares are sold

Wash Sale Example

Basic scenario:

- January 5: Buy 100 shares XYZ at $100 ($10,000)
- February 10: Sell 100 shares at $90 ($9,000), realize -$1,000 loss
- February 25: Repurchase 100 shares at $91 ($9,100)

Analysis:

- Sale to repurchase: 15 days (within 30-day window)
- Result: Wash sale, loss disallowed

Tax treatment:

- Cannot deduct $1,000 loss on current year taxes
- Loss added to new basis: $9,100 + $1,000 = $10,100 new basis
- When eventually sell at $95: Loss = $95 - $101 (adjusted basis)

= -$600 loss claimable

Covered Calls and Wash Sales
How covered calls trigger wash sales:
Scenario 1: Assignment and immediate repurchase
Transaction:

- Own stock at $100 basis
- Assigned at $95 (realize $5 loss)
- Immediately repurchase at $95 to continue strategy

Result:

- Wash sale triggered
- $5 loss disallowed
- Added to new basis: $95 + $5 = $100 new basis

Scenario 2: Sell at loss, already holding calls
Transaction:

- Own stock at $100 basis
- Currently short covered calls
- Sell stock at $90 to exit
- Covered call still outstanding

Problem: The outstanding short call might be considered maintaining position, triggering wash sale even though you don't repurchase stock.

Generally not a wash sale issue because:

- You're short the call (not long)
- Short calls don't create substantially identical position

But consult tax professional if unusual situation.
How to Avoid Wash Sales
Strategy 1: Wait 31 days before repurchasing

After assignment at loss:

- Accept assignment, receive cash
- Wait 31 calendar days
- Then repurchase if desired

Downside: Miss 31 days of potential appreciation and premium income

Strategy 2: Buy similar (not identical) stock

After assigned on Stock A at loss:

- Don't repurchase Stock A within 30 days
- Purchase Stock B (similar company, different security)
- After 31 days, swap back to Stock A if desired

Example:

- Assigned on JPMorgan Chase at loss
- Purchase Bank of America instead
- Wait 31 days, then swap back to JPM

Limitation: Works for diversified portfolios but not if you have strong preference for specific stock

Strategy 3: Accept the wash sale, it's not that bad

Reality check:

- Loss isn't lost, just deferred to new basis
- Eventually claimable when close position
- If continuing covered call strategy on same stock anyway, deferral may not matter much

Example:

- 2025: Assigned at loss, wash sale disallows $1,000 loss
- Continue covered calls on repurchased shares
- 2026: Eventually assigned at $1,500 gain

- Net over two years: $500 gain, appropriate tax paid

The wash sale just shifted when the loss was recognized, not whether it was recognized.

Strategy 4: Use tax-loss harvesting strategically

If you want to realize losses for tax purposes:

- Sell losers in November/December
- Wait until January (31+ days) to repurchase
- Spans tax years, captures loss for current year
- Repurchase in new year outside wash sale window

Strategy 5: Use tax-deferred accounts

IRA/401(k) advantage:

- Wash sale rules don't apply in tax-deferred accounts
- Can assign and immediately repurchase without wash sale concerns
- All gains/losses tax-deferred anyway

This is major advantage of covered call strategies in retirement accounts.

Wash Sale Record-Keeping

Your broker typically identifies wash sales on Form 1099-B, but errors occur. Track:

- All stock sales with losses
- Any repurchases within 61-day window
- Adjusted cost basis after wash sales
- Documentation supporting basis adjustments

Software solutions:

- Many tax software programs track wash sales automatically
- Specialized trading tax software (GainsKeeper, TradeLog)
- Spreadsheet tracking if doing manually

Working with Your Tax Professional

Tax professionals—CPAs, enrolled agents, or tax attorneys—provide invaluable assistance with covered call tax treatment, especially for larger portfolios or complex situations.

When to Hire a Tax Professional

Strong indicators you need professional help:

1. **Portfolio size over $250,000**
    - Tax impact substantial enough to justify professional fees
    - Potential savings often exceed professional costs
2. **More than 50 covered call transactions annually**
    - Record-keeping becomes complex
    - Easy to make reporting errors
    - Professional saves time and ensures accuracy
3. **Mixing covered calls with other strategies**
    - Spreads, collars, protective puts
    - Complex tax interactions
    - Professional expertise critical
4. **Assignment/repurchase frequency high**
    - Wash sale tracking becomes complicated
    - Basis adjustments multiply
    - Error risk increases significantly
5. **Multi-state or international considerations**
    - State tax treatment varies
    - International investors face additional complexity
    - Specialist knowledge required
6. **Using covered calls in multiple account types**
    - Taxable, IRA, Roth IRA, 401(k)
    - Different rules apply to each
    - Strategy optimization requires professional input

Finding the Right Tax Professional

Not all tax preparers understand options:

Many general tax preparers have limited options knowledge. You need someone with specific expertise.

Questions to ask potential tax professionals:

1. "How many clients do you serve who actively trade options?"
    - Look for: 10+ clients with options activity
2. "Are you familiar with qualified covered call rules?"
    - Should be able to explain QCC requirements
3. "How do you handle wash sale tracking across multiple transactions?"
    - Should have systematic approach and software
4. "What's your experience with covered call strategies specifically?"
    - Covered calls differ from speculative options trading
5. "Do you provide year-round consultation or only tax preparation?"
    - Year-round guidance more valuable for strategy planning
6. "What's your fee structure for options traders?"
    - Should be transparent, reasonable given complexity

Where to find options-knowledgeable tax professionals:

- **Financial planners:** Many work with tax professionals experienced in options
- **Trading communities:** Ask recommendations from successful covered call traders
- **Professional associations:** National Association of Tax Professionals, enrolled agents
- **Brokerage referrals:** Major brokers often have lists of qualified tax professionals
- **CPA firms specializing in traders:** Firms focused on active traders/investors

Cost expectations:

Options trading adds complexity and cost:

- **Basic tax return:** $300-600
- **With extensive options activity:** $600-1,500
- **Complex situations (multiple

***

Chapter 17: Tax Considerations (Continued)

Working with Your Tax Professional (Continued)

Cost expectations:

Options trading adds complexity and cost:

- **Basic tax return:** $300-600
- **With extensive options activity:** $600-1,500
- **Complex situations (multiple accounts, wash sales, QCC tracking):** $1,500-3,000+

ROI calculation: If professional saves you $2,000 in taxes through proper QCC utilization, wash sale management, and optimal strategy timing, even a $1,500 fee provides excellent value.

What to Provide Your Tax Professional

Annually (by January 31):

1. **All 1099 forms from brokers:**
   - 1099-B (proceeds from sales)
   - 1099-DIV (dividends)
   - 1099-INT (interest)
2. **Your personal transaction log:**
   - Supplementing broker records
   - Identifying qualified covered calls
   - Documenting wash sales
   - Tracking cost basis adjustments
3. **Summary of strategy and goals:**
   - Help professional understand your approach
   - Allows strategic tax planning
   - Identifies optimization opportunities

Quarterly (for year-round engagement):

1. **Performance summary:**
    - Total gains/losses
    - Options vs. stock performance
    - Projected year-end situation
2. **Upcoming strategic decisions:**
    - Planning assignments for tax efficiency
    - Timing loss realization
    - Year-end planning

Questions to Ask Your Tax Professional
Strategic questions for covered call optimization:

1. **"Should I focus on qualified covered calls for my long-term holdings?"**
    - Get specific guidance on QCC utilization
    - Understand potential savings
    - Learn implementation requirements
2. **"How should I handle assignments that will trigger losses?"**
    - Discuss wash sale implications
    - Plan for optimal timing
    - Strategize repurchase if desired
3. **"Would I benefit from moving covered call activity to tax-deferred accounts?"**
    - Compare taxable vs. IRA/Roth approaches
    - Understand trade-offs
    - Develop allocation strategy
4. **"What's my effective tax rate on covered call income?"**
    - Understand actual tax burden
    - Compare to other investment strategies
    - Identify optimization opportunities
5. **"Should I do year-end tax-loss harvesting on covered call positions?"**
    - Timing strategy
    - Which positions to target
    - Wash sale avoidance

6. **"How does state tax treatment affect my covered call strategy?"**
    - State-specific rules
    - Impact on after-tax returns
    - Location considerations

Year-End Tax Planning with Your Professional
November-December tax planning session:
Review with professional:

1. **Current year gains/losses:**
    - Realized capital gains
    - Unrealized positions
    - Projected total
2. **Loss harvesting opportunities:**
    - Positions with losses that could offset gains
    - Timing to avoid wash sales
    - Strategy for repurchase if desired
3. **Gain deferral strategies:**
    - Positions approaching long-term status
    - Whether to defer assignment into next year
    - Qualified covered call implications
4. **Next year planning:**
    - Expected income
    - Strategy adjustments for tax efficiency
    - Account type allocation changes

Tax-Efficient Covered Call Strategies
Your tax professional can help implement:

1. **Account segmentation:**
    - Highest-turnover positions in IRA/Roth
    - Long-term holds with occasional covered calls in taxable accounts
    - Optimization across account types

2. **Qualified covered call maximization:**
    - Systematic QCC implementation on long-term holdings
    - Verification procedures
    - Record-keeping systems
3. **Strategic assignment timing:**
    - Accepting/avoiding assignment based on tax situation
    - Year-end timing for tax bracket management
    - Multi-year tax planning
4. **Loss utilization:**
    - Harvesting losses to offset gains
    - Carrying losses forward strategically
    - Avoiding waste of loss carryforwards

The Professional Relationship

Best practices for working with tax professionals:

Be proactive:

- Schedule meetings in advance
- Provide materials early
- Ask questions throughout year, not just April

Be organized:

- Maintain systematic records
- Use consistent tracking methods
- Provide complete information

Be honest:

- Disclose all activity
- Explain strategy clearly
- Don't hide complexity

Be collaborative:

- View professional as partner
- Share goals and concerns
- Implement recommendations

Building Long-Term Tax Strategy
Year-over-year relationship allows:

- Pattern recognition in your trading
- Optimization based on history
- Strategic planning across tax years
- Increasingly efficient implementation

Sample multi-year tax strategy:
Year 1 (2025):

- Professional analyzes your approach
- Identifies $3,500 in overpaid taxes from QCC errors
- Implements systematic QCC tracking
- Establishes efficient record-keeping

Year 2 (2026):

- Builds on Year 1 foundation
- Implements loss harvesting strategy
- Saves additional $2,200 through strategic timing
- Fine-tunes approach

Year 3 (2027):

- Highly optimized system
- Minimal errors or inefficiencies
- Ongoing savings $4,000+ annually
- Professional relationship pays for itself many times over

Conclusion: Tax Considerations

Tax efficiency significantly impacts covered call returns. Understanding basic tax treatment, utilizing qualified covered calls when appropriate, managing wash sales, and working with knowledgeable professionals can add 2-4 percentage points to your after-tax returns.

Key principles:

- Option premiums are short-term gains unless assigned
- Qualified covered calls preserve long-term treatment on appreciated stock
- Wash sales defer losses but don't eliminate them
- Professional guidance pays for itself in larger portfolios
- Year-round tax planning beats year-end scrambling

Integrate tax considerations into your covered call strategy from the beginning, and you'll retain significantly more of your hard-earned returns.

Chapter 18:

Tools and Resources

The right tools transform covered call trading from time-consuming guesswork into efficient, systematic execution. This chapter reviews brokerage platforms, options calculators, research resources, and continuing education opportunities that support successful covered call investing.

Brokerage Platforms Compared

Your brokerage platform determines execution quality, available tools, costs, and overall trading experience. Select carefully based on your needs, experience level, and portfolio size.

Key Evaluation Criteria

1. Commissions and fees:

- Stock commissions (most now $0)
- Options commissions (typically $0-0.65 per contract)
- Assignment fees ($5-15 per assignment)
- Other fees (data, platform, inactivity)

2. Options approval levels:

- Level 1: Covered calls (what we need)
- Must qualify for covered call trading
- Application process and requirements

3. Platform quality:

- Options chain usability
- Order entry efficiency
- Mobile app quality
- Reliability and uptime

4. Research and tools:

- Options analytics

- Probability calculators
- Strategy builders
- Educational resources

5. Customer service:

- Phone support availability
- Response time
- Options expertise
- Problem resolution

Major Brokerage Comparison
TD Ameritrade (now Charles Schwab)
Strengths:

- Thinkorswim platform: Industry-leading options platform
- Excellent options chain with customization
- Superior analytics and probability tools
- Strong educational resources
- No commissions on stocks or options

Weaknesses:

- Platform can overwhelm beginners
- Merger with Schwab creating some uncertainty
- Mobile app less intuitive than desktop

Pricing:

- Stock trades: $0
- Options: $0 per contract
- Assignment fee: $0

Best for: Serious covered call traders wanting best-in-class tools
Rating: 5/5 for covered calls

Interactive Brokers

Strengths:

- Professional-grade platform
- Excellent execution quality
- Access to global markets
- Margin rates lowest in industry
- Portfolio margin options

Weaknesses:

- Complex interface, steep learning curve
- Less beginner-friendly
- Minimum deposit requirements ($0 but inactivity fees apply under $100k)
- Customer service less personal

Pricing:

- Stock trades: $0
- Options: $0.65 per contract (can be lower with volume)
- Assignment fee: $0
- Monthly fee: $10 if under $100k (waived if commissions paid)

Best for: Experienced traders with larger portfolios ($100k+)

Rating: 4/5 for covered calls (complexity reduces score despite excellent tools)

Charles Schwab

Strengths:

- Excellent customer service
- User-friendly platform (StreetSmart Edge)
- Strong research resources
- Physical branch locations
- No commissions

Weaknesses:

- Options platform less sophisticated than Thinkorswim
- Analytics not as deep as competitors
- Mobile app adequate but not exceptional

Pricing:

- Stock trades: $0
- Options: $0.65 per contract (can negotiate to $0 with relationship/volume)
- Assignment fee: $0

Best for: Investors wanting strong customer service and user-friendly interface

Rating: 4/5 for covered calls

E*TRADE

Strengths:

- Solid all-around platform
- Power E*TRADE offers good options tools
- Mobile app highly rated
- Decent research and education
- No commissions on stocks/options

Weaknesses:

- Not best-in-class at any specific area
- Some advanced tools require Power E*TRADE (free but separate)
- Customer service variable quality

Pricing:

- Stock trades: $0
- Options: $0 per contract
- Assignment fee: $0

Best for: Investors wanting solid, balanced platform
Rating: 4/5 for covered calls

Fidelity
Strengths:

- Excellent customer service
- Strong research (including third-party)
- User-friendly for beginners
- Active Trader Pro platform (free)
- No commissions

Weaknesses:

- Options tools less sophisticated than Thinkorswim
- Active Trader Pro can be buggy
- Options chain less customizable

Pricing:

- Stock trades: $0
- Options: $0.65 per contract
- Assignment fee: $0

Best for: Beginners and those who value customer service
Rating: 4/5 for covered calls

Robinhood
Strengths:

- Extremely simple interface
- Perfect for absolute beginners
- Mobile-first design
- No commissions whatsoever
- Low minimum deposit

Weaknesses:

- Very basic options tools
- Limited analytics
- Minimal research resources
- Customer service primarily automated
- Less suitable for serious covered call trading

Pricing:

- Stock trades: $0
- Options: $0 per contract
- Assignment fee: $0
- No hidden fees

Best for: Complete beginners with small accounts

Rating: 2.5/5 for covered calls (too basic for serious implementation)

Tastytrade (formerly Tastyworks)

Strengths:

- Designed specifically for options traders
- Excellent options-focused interface
- Strong educational content
- Good probability tools
- No commissions on closing options

Weaknesses:

- Less suitable for stock-focused investors
- Research resources lighter than competitors
- Smaller company, fewer resources
- Limited non-options features

Pricing:

- Stock trades: $0
- Options: $1 to open, $0 to close

- Assignment fee: $5

Best for: Options-focused traders who appreciate streamlined interface

Rating: 4.5/5 for covered calls (specifically designed for options)

Platform Recommendation Framework

Choose based on your situation:

Beginner with under $25k: → Fidelity or Charles Schwab → Priority: Customer service, user-friendliness

Intermediate trader, $25k-$100k: → TD Ameritrade/Schwab or E*TRADE → Priority: Balance of tools and ease of use

Serious trader, $100k+: → TD Ameritrade (Thinkorswim) or Interactive Brokers → Priority: Best tools, execution quality

Options-focused trader: → Tastytrade or TD Ameritrade → Priority: Options-specific features

Platform Features Checklist

Verify your chosen platform offers:

- [ ] Covered call approval (Level 1 options)
- [ ] Options chain with delta, theta, IV
- [ ] Ability to filter strikes by delta
- [ ] One-click roll functionality
- [ ] Mobile app for position monitoring
- [ ] Earnings date display
- [ ] Ex-dividend date tracking
- [ ] Historical options data
- [ ] Customizable alerts
- [ ] Paper trading / simulation mode

Options Calculators and Analyzers

Beyond broker-provided tools, standalone calculators and analyzers enhance decision-making and strategy optimization.

Free Options Calculators

1. CBOE Options Calculator (www.cboe.com/tools/calculator)

Features:

- Theoretical option pricing
- Greeks calculation
- Probability analysis
- Strategy comparison

Strengths:

- Free and reliable
- Official CBOE tool
- No account required

Limitations:

- Manual data entry
- Not integrated with broker
- Basic interface

Best for: Quick theoretical calculations, understanding concepts

---

2. OptionStrat (www.optionstrat.com)
Features:

- Visual strategy builder
- Profit/loss diagrams
- Greeks visualization
- Multiple strategy comparison
- Mobile app available

Strengths:

- Excellent visualizations
- Intuitive interface
- Free tier generous
- Covers covered calls well

Limitations:

- Premium features require subscription ($10/month)
- Not connected to broker for execution

Best for: Visual learners, strategy comparison

---

3. OIC (Options Industry Council) Tools (www.optionseducation.org/tools)

Features:

- Strategy analyzers
- Probability calculators
- Educational tools
- Risk/reward visualizations

Strengths:

- Completely free
- Educational focus
- Comprehensive coverage
- Beginner-friendly

Limitations:

- More educational than practical trading tool
- Data entry manual
- Not real-time

Best for: Learning and education, not live trading

Premium Options Tools

1. OptionVue (Starting ~$69/month)

Features:

- Professional-grade analysis
- Real-time options chains
- Portfolio Greeks management
- Custom strategy testing

- Historical backtesting

Strengths:

- Extremely comprehensive
- Professional quality
- Excellent what-if scenarios
- Position management tools

Limitations:

- Expensive for casual traders
- Steep learning curve
- Overkill for simple covered calls

Best for: Professional traders, large portfolios ($500k+)

---

2. Option Alpha (Free, Premium $97/month)
Features:

- Automated strategy triggers
- Scanner for opportunities
- Trade management automations
- Portfolio tracking
- Educational platform

Strengths:

- Automation reduces workload
- Growing community
- Regular updates
- Covers covered calls specifically

Limitations:

- Premium pricing for full features
- Requires broker connection (limited brokers supported)

- Some features unnecessary for pure covered calls

Best for: Traders wanting automation and community

---

3. Optionistics (Free basic, Premium ~$50/month)
Features:

- Stock and options screeners
- IV rank/percentile tracking
- Unusual options activity
- Strategy scans
- Covered call screening specifically

Strengths:

- Excellent covered call screener
- Good value in premium tier
- Clean interface
- Focus on practical trading

Limitations:

- Free version limited
- Data occasionally delayed
- Some features redundant with broker tools

Best for: Systematic covered call traders seeking high-probability setups

---

Excel / Google Sheets Templates
DIY approach advantages:

- Complete customization
- Free (beyond your time)
- Privacy and control
- Learn by building

Downloadable templates:

- Many available free online
- Search: "covered call tracking spreadsheet template"
- Customize to your needs
- Integrate with your workflow

Essential spreadsheet features:

- Position tracking (stocks, calls, premiums)
- Performance calculation
- Calendar with expirations and ex-div dates
- Tax tracking (short-term/long-term gains)
- Greeks tracking (if you want)

Research Resources

High-quality research improves stock selection, timing, and overall covered call performance.

Fundamental Research

1. Seeking Alpha (Free articles, Premium $29.99/month)

Strengths:

- Extensive stock-specific articles
- Dividend analysis coverage
- Multiple analyst perspectives
- News aggregation
- Comments provide additional insights

Limitations:

- Quality varies by author
- Some articles promotional
- Premium features needed for best experience

Usage for covered calls:

- Research dividend sustainability
- Understand company outlook

- Identify upcoming catalysts
- Monitor covered call candidates

---

2. Morningstar (Free basic, Premium $34.95/month)
Strengths:

- Professional analyst research
- Comprehensive financial data
- Dividend analysis
- Fair value estimates
- Consistent methodology

Limitations:

- Coverage limited to larger companies
- Updates can be infrequent
- Less options-specific insights

Usage for covered calls:

- Verify financial health
- Check dividend stability
- Understand valuation
- Assess moat/competitive position

---

3. Company Investor Relations (Free)
Strengths:

- Official company information
- Earnings presentations
- Guidance and outlook
- Accurate dividend schedules
- No intermediary interpretation

Limitations:

- Requires visiting multiple sites
- Positive bias (company presenting itself)
- Need to interpret raw data

Usage for covered calls:

- Confirm earnings dates
- Verify ex-dividend dates
- Read earnings transcripts
- Track dividend history

Technical Research

1. TradingView (Free, Pro $14.95/month)

Strengths:

- Excellent charting
- Technical indicators
- Pattern recognition
- Community ideas
- Mobile app

Limitations:

- Free version has ads and limitations
- Some advanced indicators require subscription
- Can be overwhelming initially

Usage for covered calls:

- Identify support/resistance
- Time entries (RSI, Bollinger Bands)
- Track trends and patterns
- Set price alerts

---

2. StockCharts.com (Free, Extra $14.95/month)

Strengths:

- Clean, professional charts
- Pre-built scan results
- Technical indicator analysis
- Educational articles
- Sector analysis

Limitations:

- Interface dated
- Extra tier needed for best features
- Primarily technical, minimal fundamental

Usage for covered calls:

- Chart analysis for entries
- Sector rotation tracking
- Market breadth analysis
- Technical screening

Options-Specific Research

1. Barchart.com (Free, Premier $29.95/month)

Strengths:

- Unusual options activity tracking
- Options-specific screeners
- IV rank data
- Historical options data

Limitations:

- Free version limited
- Interface not intuitive initially
- Some redundancy with broker tools

Usage for covered calls:

- Screen for high IV candidates
- Monitor options activity
- Track IV trends
- Find opportunities

---

2. MarketChameleon (Free, Premium $59/month)
Strengths:

- Deep options analytics
- IV analysis tools
- Earnings calendars
- Historical volatility tracking

Limitations:

- Expensive for premium
- More than most covered call traders need
- Complex interface

Usage for covered calls:

- IV rank/percentile verification
- Earnings date calendar
- Historical premium analysis
- Volatility trend analysis

News and Market Analysis

1. Wall Street Journal 2. Bloomberg 3. Financial Times 4. CNBC/MarketWatch (Free)

Track for:

- Market conditions and trends
- Federal Reserve policy
- Earnings season themes
- Sector rotation insights

- Macro economic data

Continuing Education

Covered call trading requires ongoing learning as markets evolve, strategies develop, and personal skills improve.

Books

Essential reading:

1. **"Covered Calls & LEAPS" by Joseph Hooper**
    - Comprehensive covered call focus
    - Practical strategies
    - Real examples
2. **"The Complete Guide to Option Selling" by James Cordier**
    - Option selling philosophy
    - Risk management
    - Premium collection strategies
3. **"Option Volatility and Pricing" by Sheldon Natenberg**
    - Deep dive into options mechanics
    - Greeks understanding
    - Volatility concepts
    - More technical but invaluable
4. **"Trading Options Greeks" by Dan Passarelli**
    - Greeks practical application
    - Risk management through Greeks
    - Strategy adjustments

Covered calls from different angles:

- **"Get Rich with Options" by Lee Lowell** - Four specific strategies including covered calls
- **"The Equity Option Income Almanac" by Marty Kearney** - Data-driven approach to options income
- **"Show Me The Money" by Lee Finberg** - Focus on income strategies

Online Courses

1. Investopedia Academy - Options for Beginners

- Cost: ~$199
- Duration: ~5 hours
- Coverage: Options fundamentals, including covered calls
- Format: Video lessons, quizzes

2. Udemy - Options Trading Courses

- Various instructors
- Cost: $10-100 (frequent sales)
- Coverage: Range from beginner to advanced
- Look for: High ratings (4.5+), many students (10,000+)
- Recommended: Search "covered calls" specifically

3. Tastytrade Learn Center

- Cost: Free
- Format: Videos, articles
- Coverage: Options strategies including covered calls
- Strength: Active community, regular updates

4. Options Industry Council (OIC)

- Cost: Free
- Format: Webinars, articles, videos
- Coverage: Comprehensive options education
- Strength: Industry-backed, unbiased

Podcasts

1. Options Insider Radio (Podcast Network)

- Hosted by Mark Longo
- Weekly episodes
- Market outlook and options strategies

- Free

2. Options Boot Camp

- Educational focus
- Strategy breakdowns
- Interview with professionals
- Free

3. Tackle Trading Podcast

- Options trading focus
- Various strategies including covered calls
- Technical and fundamental integration
- Free

YouTube Channels

1. ProjectOption

- Excellent options education
- Clear explanations
- Data-driven approach
- Covered calls specifically addressed
- Free

2. Sky View Trading

- Options strategies
- Market analysis
- Covered calls frequently discussed
- Free

3. Option Alpha

- Extensive video library
- Covered calls and income strategies

- Automation and systematic approaches
- Free (premium membership available)

Warning about YouTube: Quality varies dramatically. Verify credentials, check multiple sources, beware of promotional content disguised as education.

Communities and Forums

1. Reddit - r/options and r/thetagang

- r/options: General options discussion
- r/thetagang: Option selling focus (covered calls fit here)
- Pros: Active, diverse perspectives, free
- Cons: Variable quality, anonymity, bias

2. Seeking Alpha Comments

- Article-specific discussions
- Company-focused dialogue
- Pros: Tied to specific content
- Cons: Sometimes promotional

3. Twitter/X - #OptionsTrading #CoveredCalls

- Real-time market discussion
- Follow experienced traders
- Pros: Immediate, diverse
- Cons: Noise, hype, bragging

4. BabyPips (forex focus but some options) 5. Elite Trader forums 6. Trade2Win forums

---

Paper Trading / Simulation

Practice without risk:

1. Broker paper trading:

- Thinkorswim: Excellent paper trading

- Interactive Brokers: Paper account available
- Others: Many offer simulation

2. Investopedia Stock Simulator:

- Free
- Includes options
- Track performance
- Compete with others (optional)

3. OptionsPlay:

- Strategy testing
- Virtual portfolio
- Educational focus

Benefits of paper trading:

- Test strategies risk-free
- Build confidence
- Learn platform
- Refine approach before real money

Limitations:

- No emotional component (fear/greed absent)
- Fills may not reflect reality
- Can create false confidence

Recommendation: Paper trade for 1-3 months before real money, then start small with real capital.

Professional Coaching

When to consider:

- Portfolio over $500,000
- Want personalized guidance

- Willing to invest in expertise
- Specific challenges or goals

What to look for:

- Track record verifiable
- Fee structure transparent ($100-300/hour typical)
- References available
- Specialization in covered calls/income strategies
- Not selling products (unbiased advice)

Red flags:

- Guaranteed returns promised
- High-pressure sales tactics
- Upselling products/subscriptions
- Vague credentials
- "Secret" strategies

Continuing Education Plan
Month 1-3 (Foundation):

- Read 2-3 core books
- Complete one online course
- Paper trade actively
- Join one online community

Month 4-6 (Implementation):

- Start real trading (small positions)
- Subscribe to one research service
- Listen to weekly podcast
- Continue community participation

Month 7-12 (Refinement):

- Advanced book reading
- Specialized tools adoption
- Strategy refinement based on results
- Consider coaching if needed

Year 2+ (Mastery):

- Stay current with market changes
- Teach others (reinforces learning)
- Experiment with variations
- Continuous improvement mindset

Free vs. Paid Resources

Start with free:

- Books from library
- Free broker tools
- YouTube/podcasts
- Free online courses (OIC)
- Paper trading

Upgrade to paid when:

- Portfolio exceeds $100,000
- Time savings justify cost
- Specific needs emerge
- Free tools limiting performance
- Committed to long-term strategy

Typical annual education budget:

Beginner: $200-500

- Books: $100
- One online course: $200
- Broker: $0 (free platforms)
- Communities: $0 (free)

Intermediate: $500-1,500

- Books/courses: $300
- Research subscription: $360 (e.g., Seeking Alpha)
- Premium tools: $500 (e.g., OptionStrat)
- Conferences/webinars: $200

Advanced: $1,500-5,000+

- Professional tools: $1,000-2,000
- Multiple subscriptions: $1,000
- Coaching/consulting: $2,000+
- Conferences: $1,000

ROI on education: If education improves returns by 2% on $200,000 portfolio, that's $4,000 value. Even $2,000 annual education budget provides 100% ROI.

Conclusion: Tools and Resources

The right combination of brokerage platform, analytical tools, research resources, and continuing education creates the foundation for covered call success. Start with free resources and your broker's built-in tools, then selectively add paid services as your portfolio grows and specific needs emerge.

The most valuable investment isn't the fanciest platform or most expensive tools—it's your time spent learning, practicing, and refining your approach. Master the fundamentals with free resources before adding complexity and cost.

Essential toolkit for most covered call traders:

- Quality broker with good options platform (TD Ameritrade, Schwab, Fidelity)
- Free charting tool (TradingView)
- One research subscription (Seeking Alpha or Morningstar)
- Active participation in one community (Reddit, forum, or group)

- Commitment to continuous learning (books, podcasts, courses)

This combination provides everything needed for successful long-term covered call investing without overwhelming complexity or excessive cost.

Chapter 19: Building Your First Covered Call Portfolio

PART V: PUTTING IT ALL TOGETHER

Theory transforms into wealth only through implementation. This chapter provides step-by-step guidance for building your first covered call portfolio, from initial planning through the first three months of execution. Whether you're starting with $25,000 or $500,000, these frameworks adapt to your situation.

Step-by-Step Implementation Guide

Phase 1: Pre-Launch Preparation (Weeks 1-2)

Week 1: Foundation and Planning

Day 1-2: Define Your Objectives

Answer these questions in writing:

1. **What is my primary goal?**
    - Maximum income generation
    - Balanced income and growth
    - Conservative income with capital preservation
2. **What is my risk tolerance?**
    - Conservative (minimize volatility, accept lower returns)
    - Moderate (balanced approach)
    - Aggressive (maximize returns, accept higher volatility)
3. **What is my time commitment?**
    - 30 minutes weekly (hands-off approach)
    - 1 hour weekly (standard management)
    - 2+ hours weekly (active optimization)
4. **What is my starting capital?**
    - Amount dedicated to covered calls
    - Timeframe for full deployment
    - Reserve kept in cash
5. **What is my target return?**

- Conservative: 12-18% annually
- Moderate: 18-28% annually
- Aggressive: 28-40% annually

Example completed objectives:

MY COVERED CALL OBJECTIVES

Primary Goal: Balanced income and growth

Risk Tolerance: Moderate

Time Commitment: 1 hour weekly

Starting Capital: $150,000

- Deploy immediately: $120,000

- Cash reserve: $30,000

Target Return: 20-25% annually

Signed: ________________ Date: ____________

Day 3-4: Set Up Infrastructure

1. Brokerage account:

- Open account if needed (Chapter 16 guidance)
- Apply for options Level 1 (covered calls)
- Fund account
- Verify options approval received

2. Tracking system:

- Set up spreadsheet (use template from Chapter 12)
- Or select software solution
- Test all calculations work properly
- Customize to your needs

3. Calendar system:

- Create expiration calendar
- Set up earnings tracking
- Configure ex-dividend date tracking
- Add Fed meeting dates

4. Research access:

- Verify broker research tools accessible
- Subscribe to any additional services desired
- Bookmark key websites
- Set up alerts and notifications

Day 5-7: Create Watchlist
Build list of 20-25 potential covered call candidates:
Screening criteria:

- Pass fundamental analysis (Chapter 5)
- Adequate options liquidity (10,000+ daily volume)
- Blue-chip or established dividend stocks preferred
- Market cap over $10 billion
- IV rank above 25
- No major events (earnings) in next 45 days

Sector diversification in watchlist:

- Technology: 5-6 stocks
- Healthcare: 4-5 stocks
- Financials: 3-4 stocks
- Consumer staples: 3-4 stocks
- Industrials: 2-3 stocks
- Utilities/REITs: 2-3 stocks

Example watchlist (25 stocks):
Technology:

- Microsoft (MSFT)
- Apple (AAPL)
- Alphabet (GOOGL)
- Visa (V)
- Adobe (ADBE)

Healthcare:

- Johnson & Johnson (JNJ)
- UnitedHealth Group (UNH)
- Pfizer (PFE)
- AbbVie (ABBV)

Financials:

- JPMorgan Chase (JPM)
- Bank of America (BAC)
- Goldman Sachs (GS)

Consumer Staples:

- Procter & Gamble (PG)
- Coca-Cola (KO)
- Walmart (WMT)
- Costco (COST)

Industrials:

- Caterpillar (CAT)
- 3M (MMM)
- Honeywell (HON)

Utilities/REITs:

- Duke Energy (DUK)
- Realty Income (O)
- American Tower (AMT)

Other:

- Home Depot (HD)
- McDonald's (MCD)

Week 2: Strategy Definition and Rules

Day 8-10: Write Your Trading Rules

Document specific rules for every decision:

MY COVERED CALL TRADING RULES

POSITION SIZING:

- Maximum per position: 12% of portfolio
- Minimum positions: 8
- Maximum positions: 12
- Cash reserve: 10% of portfolio value

STOCK SELECTION:

- Must be on approved watchlist
- Must pass 5-point fundamental check (list specific criteria)
- Must have IV rank above 25
- Must have daily options volume over 10,000 contracts
- No earnings within 45 days of option expiration

STRIKE SELECTION:

- Bull market: 5-7% OTM (delta 0.15-0.25)
- Sideways market: 2-4% OTM at resistance (delta 0.30-0.40)
- Bear market: ATM to 2% ITM (delta 0.45-0.60)
- Always check technical resistance before finalizing strike

EXPIRATION SELECTION:

- Standard: 30-45 days to expiration
- Ensure expiration before next earnings
- Sell on Wednesday or Thursday (avoid Monday volatility)

POSITION MANAGEMENT:

- Hold to expiration unless captured 75%+ profit
- Roll only if mathematically justified (write out reasoning)
- Accept assignments gracefully (they're planned outcomes)
- Review positions every Saturday morning

EMOTIONAL DISCIPLINE:

- Never chase premiums above 3.5% monthly on blue-chips
- Never make major changes without 24-hour waiting period
- No revenge trading after losses
- No position size increases after winning streaks
- Follow rules even when uncomfortable

Signed: ________________ Date: ____________

Day 11-14: Paper Trade

Before risking real money:

- Set up paper trading account
- Execute 3-5 covered call positions
- Practice order entry
- Verify you understand mechanics
- Gain confidence with platform

Phase 2: Initial Deployment (Weeks 3-4)

Week 3: First Positions (25% of Capital)

Day 15: Select First 2-3 Positions

Starting with $120,000 target deployment, first tranche = $30,000

Position 1 (Conservative): $12,000

- Stock: Johnson & Johnson at $160
- Shares: 75 (can't do 100 shares exactly, adjust amount)
- Actually buy: 100 shares = $16,000
- Adjustment: This will be larger position, that's OK for first month

Position 2 (Moderate): $12,000

- Stock: Microsoft at $445
- Shares: 100
- Cost: $44,500 - too expensive
- Alternative: Find stock in $100-120 range
- Select: Visa at $305
- Shares: 100
- Cost: $30,500 - good fit

Position 3: $12,000

- Procter & Gamble at $170

- Shares: 70 → buy 100 shares
- Cost: $17,000

Actual allocation:

- JNJ: $16,000 (27%)
- V: $30,500 (51%)
- PG: $17,000 (28%)
- Total: $63,500 deployed
- Remaining: $56,500 + $30,000 reserve

Day 16-17: Execute Stock Purchases
Best practices:

- Use limit orders (not market orders)
- Trade during market hours (10 AM - 3 PM ET)
- Verify fills before proceeding
- Update tracking spreadsheet immediately

Day 18-19: Sell First Covered Calls
Wait 1-2 days after stock purchase to assess:

- Market conditions stable
- Stock behavior observed
- Technical setup still favorable

Position 1: JNJ 100 shares at $160

- Assessment: Sideways market, consolidating
- Resistance: $165 identified
- Strike selection: $165 (3.1% OTM)
- Expiration: 35 days out
- Premium: $2.40 per share = $240
- Monthly yield: 1.5%
- Execute: Sell 1 contract JNJ $165 call

Position 2: Visa 100 shares at $305

- Assessment: Uptrend intact
- Resistance: $320
- Strike selection: $315 (3.3% OTM)
- Expiration: 38 days out
- Premium: $5.20 = $520
- Monthly yield: 1.7%
- Execute: Sell 1 contract V $315 call

Position 3: PG 100 shares at $170

- Assessment: Range-bound
- Resistance: $175
- Strike selection: $175 (2.9% OTM)
- Expiration: 35 days out
- Premium: $2.80 = $280
- Monthly yield: 1.65%
- Execute: Sell 1 contract PG $175 call

Total first month premium: $1,040 on $63,500 (1.64% monthly, 19.7% annualized)

Day 20-21: Documentation

Record everything:

- Entry prices and dates
- Option details (strike, expiration, premium)
- Rationale for each decision
- Current market assessment
- Lessons learned from first executions

Week 4: Monitor and Learn

Daily (5 minutes):

- Check for any breaking news on holdings
- Verify no unexpected corporate actions

- Quick price check

Saturday (30 minutes):

- Update spreadsheet with current values
- Calculate unrealized P&L
- Review upcoming week calendar
- Note any adjustments needed
- Journal observations and learnings

No trading this week unless emergency

Phase 3: Scale to 50% (Weeks 5-6)

Week 5: Add 3-4 Positions

Following same process, add:

- Additional $30,000-40,000
- Different sectors than first positions
- Aim for 6-7 total positions

Example additions:

- JPMorgan Chase (financials)
- Caterpillar (industrials)
- Duke Energy (utilities)
- Apple (additional tech, different subsector)

Week 6: Manage First Expirations

Your first covered calls may be approaching expiration:

Three weeks remaining:

- Monitor weekly
- No action needed yet
- Continue observation

Two weeks remaining:

- Assess: captured 70%+ profit?
- If yes: Consider early close
- If no: Hold

One week remaining:

- Likely hold through expiration
- Verify assignment acceptable if occurs
- Plan for next month's calls

Phase 4: Complete Deployment (Weeks 7-8)

Week 7: Final Positions Added

Deploy remaining capital:

- Bring total to 8-10 positions
- Verify sector diversification
- Confirm no position over 15%
- Maintain cash reserve

Week 8: First Full Portfolio Review

Complete systematic review:

Performance analysis:

- Total P&L (stock + options)
- Premium capture rate
- Assignment rate
- Best/worst performers

Process evaluation:

- Are rules being followed?
- Is time commitment manageable?
- Are tools adequate?
- What's working well?
- What needs improvement?

Strategy calibration:

- Should strikes be adjusted?
- Is position sizing appropriate?
- Should any positions be replaced?
- Are market conditions shifting?

Phase 5: Steady State Operation (Months 2-3)
Monthly Routine:
Week 1 (first week after expiration):

- Process any assignments
- Close highly profitable positions (75%+ profit captured)
- Sell new covered calls on all positions
- Add any new positions if capital available

Week 2 (mid-month):

- Monitor positions
- Check for any breaking news
- Review economic calendar
- Update tracking

Week 3 (approaching expiration):

- Identify positions for early close
- Evaluate rolling opportunities
- Plan next month's strikes
- Assess market conditions

Week 4 (expiration week):

- Process expirations
- Handle any assignments
- Complete monthly review
- Prepare for next cycle

First Three-Month Target Outcomes:
Conservative portfolio ($150,000):

- Premium collected: $6,500-8,500 (14.4-18.9% annualized)
- Stock appreciation: 0-3%
- Total return: $6,500-13,000 (14.4-28.9% annualized)

Moderate portfolio ($150,000):

- Premium collected: $9,000-11,000 (24-29.3% annualized)
- Stock appreciation: 0-4%
- Total return: $9,000-17,000 (24-45.3% annualized)

Learning achievements:

- Executed 30-40 trades successfully
- Experienced 2-3 assignment events
- Developed systematic routine
- Gained confidence and competence
- Built foundation for long-term success

Sample Portfolios for Different Goals
Portfolio 1: Conservative Retirement Income ($250,000)
Objectives:

- Primary: Maximum income stability
- Secondary: Capital preservation
- Risk tolerance: Low
- Target return: 14-18% annually

Asset allocation:

- Covered call stocks: 75% ($187,500)
- Bond funds: 15% ($37,500)
- Cash reserve: 10% ($25,000)

Stock positions (10 positions, $18,750 average):

1. **Johnson & Johnson (JNJ)** - $22,000 (11.7%)
    - Shares: 140 @ $157
    - Defensive healthcare
    - Dividend aristocrat
    - Strategy: 3-5% OTM strikes
2. **Procter & Gamble (PG)** - $20,000 (10.7%)
    - Shares: 118 @ $170
    - Consumer staples
    - Ultra-stable
    - Strategy: 3-4% OTM strikes
3. **Coca-Cola (KO)** - $18,000 (9.6%)
    - Shares: 300 @ $60
    - Consumer staples
    - Strong dividend
    - Strategy: 3-4% OTM strikes
4. **Duke Energy (DUK)** - $18,000 (9.6%)
    - Shares: 180 @ $100
    - Utility
    - High dividend
    - Strategy: 2-3% OTM strikes
5. **Realty Income (O)** - $18,000 (9.6%)
    - Shares: 310 @ $58
    - REIT
    - Monthly dividend
    - Strategy: 2-3% OTM strikes
6. **Verizon (VZ)** - $18,000 (9.6%)
    - Shares: 450 @ $40
    - Telecom
    - High yield
    - Strategy: 2-3% OTM strikes
7. **Walmart (WMT)** - $19,000 (10.1%)
    - Shares: 115 @ $165
    - Retail

    - Recession resistant
    - Strategy: 3-4% OTM strikes
8. **AbbVie (ABBV)** - $18,000 (9.6%)
    - Shares: 110 @ $165
    - Healthcare
    - Strong dividend
    - Strategy: 3-5% OTM strikes
9. **3M (MMM)** - $18,000 (9.6%)
    - Shares: 200 @ $90
    - Industrial
    - Dividend aristocrat
    - Strategy: 3-4% OTM strikes
10. **AT&T (T)** - $18,500 (9.9%)
    - Shares: 1,000 @ $18.50
    - Telecom
    - High yield
    - Strategy: 2-3% OTM strikes

Portfolio characteristics:

- Average dividend yield: 4.1%
- Expected monthly premium: 1.1-1.4% (13.2-16.8% annualized)
- Total expected return: 17.3-20.9% annually
- Sector allocation: 40% defensive (utilities, staples, telecom), 30% healthcare, 20% diversified, 10% industrial
- All dividend aristocrats or high-quality dividend payers

Monthly income projection:

- Dividends: $850 monthly average
- Option premium: $2,100-2,600
- Total: $2,950-3,450 monthly ($35,400-41,400 annually)

Portfolio 2: Balanced Growth-Income ($200,000)

Objectives:

- Primary: Balanced income and appreciation
- Secondary: Moderate growth
- Risk tolerance: Moderate
- Target return: 22-30% annually

Asset allocation:

- Covered call stocks: 85% ($170,000)
- Cash reserve: 15% ($30,000)

Stock positions (10 positions, $17,000 average):

1. **Microsoft (MSFT)** - $22,000 (13%)
    - Shares: 50 @ $440
    - Tech mega-cap
    - Growth with income
    - Strategy: 4-6% OTM in bull markets
2. **Apple (AAPL)** - $19,000 (11.2%)
    - Shares: 100 @ $190
    - Tech mega-cap
    - Strong cash flow
    - Strategy: 4-6% OTM
3. **JPMorgan Chase (JPM)** - $18,000 (10.6%)
    - Shares: 85 @ $212
    - Premier bank
    - Cyclical but stable
    - Strategy: 3-5% OTM
4. **Visa (V)** - $18,000 (10.6%)
    - Shares: 60 @ $300
    - Payments network
    - Secular growth
    - Strategy: 3-5% OTM
5. **Johnson & Johnson (JNJ)** - $17,000 (10%)

    - Shares: 108 @ $157
    - Healthcare defensive
    - Balance to tech
    - Strategy: 3-5% OTM
6. **UnitedHealth Group (UNH)** - $18,000 (10.6%)
    - Shares: 35 @ $515
    - Healthcare services
    - Strong growth
    - Strategy: 3-5% OTM
7. **Home Depot (HD)** - $17,000 (10%)
    - Shares: 50 @ $340
    - Consumer discretionary
    - Housing exposure
    - Strategy: 3-5% OTM
8. **Procter & Gamble (PG)** - $14,000 (8.2%)
    - Shares: 82 @ $170
    - Defensive core
    - Stability
    - Strategy: 2-4% OTM
9. **Caterpillar (CAT)** - $14,000 (8.2%)
    - Shares: 50 @ $280
    - Industrial cyclical
    - Infrastructure play
    - Strategy: 3-5% OTM
10. **Adobe (ADBE)** - $13,000 (7.6%)
    - Shares: 25 @ $520
    - Software
    - Subscription model
    - Strategy: 4-6% OTM

Portfolio characteristics:

- Average dividend yield: 1.6%
- Expected monthly premium: 1.8-2.4% (21.6-28.8% annualized)

- Total expected return: 23.2-30.4% annually
- Sector allocation: 35% technology, 25% healthcare, 20% financials, 20% diversified
- Mix of growth and value

Monthly income projection:

- Dividends: $270 monthly average
- Option premium: $3,000-4,000
- Total: $3,270-4,270 monthly ($39,240-51,240 annually)

Portfolio 3: Aggressive Premium Generation ($100,000)
Objectives:

- Primary: Maximum premium income
- Secondary: Accept volatility
- Risk tolerance: High
- Target return: 30-45% annually

Asset allocation:

- Covered call stocks: 92% ($92,000)
- Cash reserve: 8% ($8,000)

Stock positions (8 positions, $11,500 average):

1. **Microsoft (MSFT)** - $13,000 (14.1%)
    - Shares: 30 @ $433
    - Strategy: ATM to 2% OTM strikes
2. **JPMorgan Chase (JPM)** - $12,500 (13.6%)
    - Shares: 60 @ $208
    - Strategy: ATM to 2% OTM
3. **Visa (V)** - $12,000 (13%)
    - Shares: 40 @ $300
    - Strategy: ATM to 2% OTM
4. **Caterpillar (CAT)** - $11,500 (12.5%)

   - Shares: 40 @ $288
   - Strategy: ATM to 2% OTM
5. **Adobe (ADBE)** - $11,000 (12%)
   - Shares: 20 @ $550
   - Strategy: ATM to 3% OTM
6. **Bank of America (BAC)** - $11,000 (12%)
   - Shares: 250 @ $44
   - Strategy: ATM strikes
7. **Intel (INTC)** - $11,000 (12%)
   - Shares: 200 @ $55
   - Strategy: ATM strikes
8. **Ford (F)** - $10,000 (10.9%)
   - Shares: 1,000 @ $10
   - Strategy: ATM to slightly ITM

Portfolio characteristics:

- Average dividend yield: 1.9%
- Expected monthly premium: 2.8-3.8% (33.6-45.6% annualized)
- Total expected return: 35.5-47.5% annually
- Higher volatility accepted
- More frequent assignments expected (50-60% of positions annually)

Monthly income projection:

- Dividends: $145 monthly average
- Option premium: $2,600-3,500
- Total: $2,745-3,645 monthly ($32,940-43,740 annually)

Risk acknowledgment: This aggressive approach:

- Caps upside significantly
- Requires active management

- Faces larger drawdowns in bear markets
- Suitable only for experienced traders with high risk tolerance

Month-by-Month Roadmap
Month 1: Foundation Building
Goals:

- Deploy 50-75% of capital
- Establish 5-8 positions
- Execute first covered call cycle
- Develop routine

Activities:

- Week 1: Planning and preparation
- Week 2: First 2-3 positions
- Week 3: Add 2-3 more positions
- Week 4: Monitor and learn

Success metrics:

- All positions established according to rules
- Tracking system operational
- First premiums collected
- Routine beginning to form

Common first-month challenges:

- Platform navigation learning curve
- Order entry anxiety
- Strike selection uncertainty
- Excessive monitoring (resist urge!)

Month 2: Rhythm Development
Goals:

- Complete portfolio deployment
- Experience first expirations
- Handle first assignments (if any)
- Refine process

Activities:

- Week 1: Process month 1 expirations, roll/open new positions
- Week 2: Add final positions to reach target count
- Week 3: Mid-month review
- Week 4: Second expiration cycle

Success metrics:

- Full deployment achieved
- Successfully managed expirations
- Routine feels more natural
- Tracking current and accurate

Common second-month challenges:

- First assignment emotions
- Temptation to overtrade
- Comparing to others' claims
- Impatience with process

Month 3: Optimization

Goals:

- Fine-tune strike selection
- Optimize sector allocation
- Improve efficiency
- Build confidence

Activities:

- Week 1: Third expiration cycle
- Week 2: Portfolio rebalancing if needed
- Week 3: Strategy assessment
- Week 4: Quarterly comprehensive review

Success metrics:

- Consistent execution
- Rules followed systematically
- Positive returns accumulated
- Confidence established

Quarterly review questions:

1. What's working well?
2. What needs improvement?
3. Are returns meeting expectations?
4. Should any rules be adjusted?
5. Are any positions underperforming consistently?
6. Is time commitment appropriate?

Months 4-6: Consistency Building

Focus: Maintain discipline, resist temptation to deviate, let strategy compound

Common quarter 2 challenges:

- Boredom with routine (good sign!)
- Temptation to "improve" working system
- Overconfidence after successful quarter
- Neglecting tracking and reviews

Months 7-9: Experience Accumulation

You've now experienced:

- Bull market periods

- Corrections or volatility
- Multiple assignment cycles
- Various market conditions

Focus: Adapt to conditions while maintaining discipline

Months 10-12: First Year Completion

Year-end comprehensive review:

- Total returns vs. goals
- Strategy effectiveness across conditions
- Lessons learned
- Adjustments for year 2

Typical first-year outcomes:

Conservative approach:

- Target: 14-18% returns
- Likely actual: 12-22% (wide range is normal)
- Learning curve early, improved execution later

Moderate approach:

- Target: 22-28% returns
- Likely actual: 18-32%
- Higher variance initially

Aggressive approach:

- Target: 30-45% returns
- Likely actual: 20-50%
- Highest variance, most learning required

Tracking Performance

Weekly Tracking (Saturday routine):

Update spreadsheet with:

1. Current stock prices
2. Current option values
3. Unrealized P&L
4. Upcoming expirations
5. Next week's calendar items

Monthly Tracking:
Calculate:

1. Total premium collected month
2. Realized gains/losses
3. Unrealized P&L
4. Monthly return percentage
5. Year-to-date return

Quarterly Tracking:
Analyze:

1. Return by position
2. Best/worst performers
3. Sector performance
4. Assignment rate
5. Premium capture rate
6. Comparison to benchmarks

Annual Tracking:
Complete assessment:

1. Total return vs. goal
2. Risk-adjusted performance
3. Tax efficiency
4. Time investment vs. returns
5. Strategy evolution
6. Lessons learned
7. Goals for next year

Key Performance Metrics:

Total Return:

Total Return = (Premium + Dividends + Capital Gains) / Starting Capital

Example:

Starting: $200,000

Premium collected: $38,000

Dividends: $6,000

Unrealized gains: $12,000

Total gains: $56,000

Total return: 28%

Premium Capture Rate:

Capture Rate = Actual Premium / Theoretical Maximum

Example:

Theoretical if all held to expiration: $42,000

Actual collected (some closed early): $38,000

Capture rate: 90.5% (excellent)

Assignment Rate:

Assignment Rate = Assignments / Total Position-Months

Example:

10-position portfolio, 12 months = 120 position-months

Assignments during year: 32

Assignment rate: 26.7% (moderate, expected)

Risk-Adjusted Return (Sharpe Ratio):

Sharpe = (Return - Risk-Free Rate) / Standard Deviation

Example:

Portfolio return: 24%

Risk-free rate: 4%

Portfolio std dev: 12%

Sharpe: (24% - 4%) / 12% = 1.67 (excellent)

Conclusion: Building Your Portfolio

The difference between reading about covered calls and profiting from them is systematic implementation. This chapter's frameworks—from preparation through first-year execution—provide the roadmap. Success requires patience, discipline, and consistency, not brilliance or perfect timing.

Start small, follow your written rules, maintain detailed records, and scale gradually. Within 3-6 months, covered call trading will feel natural. Within a year, you'll have developed skills and confidence that generate reliable income for years to come.

The journey begins with the first position. Follow this implementation guide, and you'll avoid the costly mistakes that derail most beginners while building a foundation for long-term success.

Chapter 20:

Real-World Case Studies

Theory guides strategy, but real-world examples teach practical lessons. This chapter presents four detailed case studies showing how different investors implemented covered call strategies, what worked, what didn't, and lessons learned through actual trading experience.

Conservative Income Portfolio

Investor Profile: Sarah M., Age 64

Situation:

- Recently retired
- $450,000 retirement savings
- Needed monthly income to supplement Social Security
- Very risk-averse after experiencing 2008 crisis losses
- Limited investment experience beyond mutual funds
- Goal: $3,500 monthly income with capital preservation

Initial Strategy (Month 1):

Portfolio allocation:

- Covered call stocks: $300,000 (67%)
- Bond index fund: $120,000 (27%)
- Cash emergency fund: $30,000 (6%)

Stock positions (10 stocks, $30,000 average):

1. Johnson & Johnson: $35,000
2. Procter & Gamble: $32,000
3. Coca-Cola: $30,000
4. PepsiCo: $30,000
5. Walmart: $30,000
6. Duke Energy: $28,000
7. Verizon: $28,000
8. AT&T: $25,000
9. Realty Income (REIT): $32,000

10. 3M: $30,000

Characteristics:

- All dividend aristocrats or high-quality dividend payers
- Average dividend yield: 3.8%
- Very conservative: consumer staples, utilities, telecom
- No technology exposure (per Sarah's preference)
- Low volatility stocks exclusively

Month 1-3 Results:
Premiums collected:

- Month 1: $3,200 (1.07% monthly)
- Month 2: $3,400 (1.13%)
- Month 3: $3,100 (1.03%)
- Total: $9,700

Dividends received: $2,850 (quarterly total)
Stock movement:

- Portfolio up 1.8% (modest appreciation)
- No assignments occurred

Income generated:

- Monthly average: $4,183 ($9,700 premium + $2,850 dividends / 3 months)
- **Exceeded $3,500 target by 19.5%**

Sarah's observations:

- "Less stressful than I expected"
- "Premiums arrived like clockwork"
- "Stocks barely moved, which felt good"
- "Wished premiums were higher, but appreciated stability"

Months 4-6: First Challenge
Market correction:

- S&P 500 declined 8% over two months
- Sarah's portfolio declined only 3.2% (defensive stocks held up)

Emotional response:

- Initial panic: "Should I stop selling calls and just hold?"
- Advisor reminder: Strategy designed for this
- Decision: Continued systematic approach

Actions taken:

- Moved to ATM strikes (vs. previous 2-3% OTM)
- Collected higher premiums: $3,800-4,200 monthly
- Accepted that stock values declined
- Focused on income generation, not stock prices

Results months 4-6:

- Premiums: $11,800 (higher due to ATM strikes)
- Dividends: $2,900
- Stock losses: -$9,600
- Net: +$5,100 (premium and dividends offset most stock loss)

Key insight: While portfolio value temporarily declined, income continued uninterrupted. Bonds provided additional stability. Comprehensive portfolio (stocks + bonds + income) weathered correction successfully.

Months 7-12: Recovery and Optimization
Market stabilized and recovered:

***

Chapter 20: Real-World Case Studies (Continued)

Conservative Income Portfolio (Continued)

Months 7-12: Recovery and Optimization

Market stabilized and recovered:

- Portfolio values returned to original levels
- Sarah maintained discipline through volatility
- Returned to 2-3% OTM strikes as conditions normalized

Year-end results:

- Total premium collected: $41,200 (13.7% return on stock portion)
- Dividends: $11,400 (3.8% yield)
- Stock appreciation: $7,800 (2.6%)
- **Total return: $60,400 (20.1% on $300,000 stock portfolio)**
- Bond returns: $3,600 (3% on $120,000)
- **Overall portfolio return: $64,000 (14.2% on $450,000 total)**

Monthly income achieved:

- Average: $4,367 monthly
- **Exceeded $3,500 target by 24.8%**
- Provided comfortable retirement income
- Maintained capital intact

Lessons learned:

1. **Defensive stock selection paid off:** During correction, portfolio declined half as much as market
2. **Systematic discipline crucial:** Continuing through volatility generated best premiums

3. **Income consistency valuable:** Monthly income never stopped, even during correction
4. **Bonds provided peace of mind:** Knowing 27% was stable reduced stress
5. **Conservative works:** 14.2% total return with low stress exceeded expectations

Sarah's conclusion: "I was skeptical about options trading, but covered calls feel more like enhanced dividend investing. The monthly income exceeded my needs, and I slept well even during market volatility. I'm continuing this strategy indefinitely."

Growth with Income Strategy
Investor Profile: Marcus T., Age 38
Situation:

- Software engineer, married, two young children
- $180,000 investment account (outside retirement accounts)
- Aggressive saver, adding $2,000 monthly
- Comfortable with technology and complexity
- Goal: Maximize total returns while generating supplemental income
- Time available: 2-3 hours weekly

Initial Strategy:
Portfolio allocation:

- Covered call stocks: 90% ($162,000)
- Cash reserve: 10% ($18,000)

Stock positions (9 stocks, $18,000 average):

1. Microsoft: $22,000
2. Apple: $20,000
3. Alphabet: $18,000
4. Visa: $18,000

5. JPMorgan Chase: $18,000
6. UnitedHealth: $18,000
7. Home Depot: $16,000
8. Adobe: $16,000
9. Johnson & Johnson: $16,000

Characteristics:

- Growth-oriented: 55% technology
- Moderate volatility stocks
- Mix of mega-caps and large-caps
- Average dividend yield: 1.2% (low but acceptable given growth focus)

Strategy approach:

- Bull market conditions: 4-6% OTM strikes
- Target: 1.5-2.0% monthly premium
- 30-45 day expirations
- Active management: close at 60-70% profit
- Willing to accept frequent assignments and repurchase

Months 1-3: Learning Curve
Premiums collected:

- Month 1: $2,900 (1.79%)
- Month 2: $3,100 (1.91%)
- Month 3: $2,700 (1.67%)
- Total: $8,700

Challenges encountered:
Challenge 1: Microsoft rapid appreciation

- Bought MSFT at $420
- Sold $435 calls for $7.50 (3.6% OTM)
- Stock rallied to $455 in three weeks

- Assigned at $435

Analysis:

- Profit: $15 stock + $7.50 premium = $22.50 (5.4% in 3 weeks)
- Opportunity cost: Missed additional $20 rally to $455
- Emotional response: Regret and frustration

Mistake made: Immediately repurchased at $455 (top)

- Stock pulled back to $440 within week
- Bought high, sold higher earlier
- Lesson learned: Wait for pullback after assignment

Challenge 2: Overtrading temptation

- Closed multiple positions at 50-60% profit
- Immediately reopened new positions
- Generated lots of activity but minimal additional return
- Transaction costs and execution slippage added up

Lesson learned: Better to wait for 70-75% profit or hold to expiration

Months 4-6: Strategy Refinement

Adjustments made:

1. **Increased OTM distance:** 5-7% instead of 4-6%
2. **Reduced early closures:** Only close at 75%+ profit
3. **Post-assignment patience:** Wait 3-5 days before repurchasing
4. **Selective coverage:** Left strongest performers (GOOGL, AAPL) uncovered for one month

Results improved:

- Month 4: $3,200 (1.98%)
- Month 5: $3,400 (2.10%)

- Month 6: $3,100 (1.91%)
- Better execution, fewer mistakes

Stock performance:

- Portfolio up 8.2% over quarter
- Captured more appreciation with wider strikes
- Uncovered positions gained 12-15%

Months 7-9: Market Volatility
Market correction:

- Tech stocks declined sharply (12-18%)
- Marcus's portfolio down 10% at worst point

Strategic response:

- Shifted from 5-7% OTM to 2-3% OTM
- Increased premium collection during volatility
- Collected $3,800-4,200 monthly during downturn
- Used cash reserve to add position during dip (bought HD at discount)

Outcome:

- Premium income of $11,400 offset most stock losses
- Demonstrated strategy's defensive capabilities
- Recovered quickly as market stabilized

Months 10-12: Strong Finish
Bull market returned:

- Tech stocks rallied strongly
- Portfolio up 15% in final quarter

Strategy adaptation:

- Returned to 5-7% OTM strikes
- Reduced coverage back to 70-80% of positions
- Allowed strongest performers room to run

Year-end results:

- Stock appreciation: $28,800 (17.8%)
- Premium collected: $38,600 (23.8%)
- Dividends: $1,900 (1.2%)
- **Total return: $69,300 (42.8% on initial $162,000)**
- Contributions added: $24,000
- **Ending portfolio: $255,300**

Lessons learned:

1. **Adaptation matters:** Adjusting to market conditions added 8-12% to returns
2. **Assignment regret is normal:** Accepting assignment as success, not failure, improved psychology
3. **Patience pays:** Waiting after assignment for better repurchase prices saved $3,000-4,000
4. **Don't overtrade:** Fewer, better-timed trades outperformed constant activity
5. **Growth stocks work:** Despite lower volatility premiums, total returns exceeded expectations

Marcus's conclusion: "First quarter was frustrating with learning curve mistakes. But by adapting and refining, generated 42.8% returns—better than pure buy-and-hold on same stocks. The defensive benefits during correction convinced me this strategy reduces risk while enhancing returns. Continuing with more confidence in year two."

Retirement Account Application

Investor Profile: Jennifer R., Age 52

Situation:

- Physician, high income ($350k annually)
- Maxing out retirement contributions
- $620,000 in IRA (self-directed)
- Previously invested in index funds only
- Interested in covered calls for tax-deferred account benefits
- Goal: Accelerate retirement savings, no current income needed

Rationale for IRA implementation:

- All gains tax-deferred (major advantage)
- No wash sale rule complications
- Can trade more actively without tax implications
- Compounding accelerated by no tax drag
- Time horizon: 13 years until retirement

Initial Strategy:
Portfolio allocation:

- 100% covered call stocks ($620,000)
- No bonds (long time horizon allows volatility acceptance)
- No cash reserve needed (contributions provide liquidity)

Stock positions (12 stocks, $51,667 average):

1. Microsoft: $60,000
2. Apple: $55,000
3. JPMorgan Chase: $53,000
4. Johnson & Johnson: $52,000
5. Visa: $52,000
6. UnitedHealth: $52,000
7. Home Depot: $50,000
8. Procter & Gamble: $50,000
9. Adobe: $50,000
10. Caterpillar: $48,000
11. Alphabet: $48,000

12. Bank of America: $50,000

Strategy approach:

- Moderate aggression: 2-4% OTM strikes
- Target: 2.0-2.5% monthly premium
- Active management in tax-deferred account
- No tax consequences, so can close/reopen freely
- Focus on compounding, not current income

First Year Results:
Quarter 1:

- Premium: $37,800 (6.1% quarterly)
- Stock appreciation: $18,600 (3%)
- Total: $56,400 (9.1%)

Quarter 2:

- Premium: $41,200 (6.65%)
- Stock appreciation: $12,400 (2%)
- Total: $53,600 (8.65%)

Quarter 3 (correction):

- Premium: $44,800 (7.23%)
- Stock decline: -$31,000 (-5%)
- Net: $13,800 (2.23%)

Quarter 4 (recovery):

- Premium: $39,600 (6.39%)
- Stock appreciation: $52,700 (8.5%)
- Total: $92,300 (14.89%)

Year-end summary:

- Total premium: $163,400 (26.4% of starting value)
- Stock appreciation: $52,700 (8.5%)
- **Total return: $216,100 (34.9%)**
- **Ending value: $836,100**

Tax advantage calculation:
In taxable account (theoretical):

- Premium: $163,400 taxed at 35% (ordinary income) = -$57,190 taxes
- Stock gains: $52,700 taxed at 20% (long-term capital gains) = -$10,540 taxes
- Total taxes: -$67,730
- After-tax value: $768,370 (24.0% return)

In IRA (actual):

- No current taxes
- Full $836,100 compounds
- **Tax deferral advantage: $67,730 (10.9 percentage points!)**

Compounding projection:
Assuming 28% average annual returns:

- Year 1: $836,100
- Year 5: $2,315,000
- Year 10: $8,557,000
- Year 13 (age 65): $17,247,000

After taxes at withdrawal (24% bracket):

- Net after taxes: $13,107,720

Compared to taxable account:

- Same gross returns, annual tax drag of 8-10%

- Ending value at year 13: ~$8,200,000
- **IRA advantage: ~$4,900,000 additional wealth!**

Jennifer's insights:

1. **Tax deferral is massive:** "I knew tax-deferred was good, but seeing 10+ percentage points annually is eye-opening"
2. **Freedom to trade:** "No wash sale worries, no tax-loss harvesting needed—just execute optimal strategy"
3. **Compounding power:** "The tax savings compound year over year, creating exponential benefits"
4. **Aggressive makes sense:** "With 13-year horizon, can be more aggressive knowing taxes won't erode gains"
5. **Best use of IRA:** "Covered calls generate ordinary income—deferring this income is incredibly valuable"

Lessons for retirement accounts:

1. **Covered calls ideal for IRAs/Roth IRAs:** High ordinary income tax rate makes deferral especially valuable
2. **Can be more aggressive:** No tax consequences allow optimal strategy execution
3. **Compounding accelerates:** Every dollar saved on taxes compounds over decades
4. **Simplifies reporting:** No Form 8949, no wash sale tracking, much simpler
5. **Long-term time horizon key:** Need years to compound; not suitable if withdrawals imminent

Special note on Roth IRAs:
If Jennifer had used Roth IRA instead of traditional:

- All gains completely tax-free upon withdrawal (not just deferred)
- $17,247,000 would be 100% tax-free

- Even more powerful than traditional IRA
- Limitation: Contribution limits restrict initial funding

Lessons Learned from Actual Trades

Across all case studies, common lessons emerged:

Lesson 1: Start Conservative, Scale Up

What happened:

- Marcus's aggressive early strikes led to missed appreciation
- Sarah's ultra-conservative approach worked perfectly for her goals
- Jennifer could be aggressive because of tax-deferred account and time horizon

Takeaway: Match aggressiveness to situation. Begin conservatively, increase only after gaining experience and confidence.

Lesson 2: Assignment is Normal and Good

What happened:

- All three investors experienced assignment regret initially
- Eventually recognized assignments as planned, profitable outcomes
- Emotional acceptance took 2-3 assignments typically

Takeaway: Assignment at higher price + premium = success. Don't view as "losing" stock.

Lesson 3: Market Adaptations Work

What happened:

- During correction, moving to ATM strikes substantially reduced losses
- During bull markets, OTM strikes captured more appreciation
- Rigid strategies underperformed adaptive approaches by 15-20%

Takeaway: Adapt to conditions while maintaining overall discipline.

Lesson 4: Overtrading Costs Money

What happened:

- Marcus's frequent early closes provided minimal benefit
- Sarah's patient hold-to-expiration approach maximized premium capture
- Time invested in constant monitoring didn't improve returns

Takeaway: Less activity often produces better results than constant trading.

Lesson 5: Tax Location Matters Enormously

What happened:

- Jennifer's IRA returns 10+ percentage points higher due to tax deferral
- Tax-deferred compounding created exponentially larger wealth
- Taxable account covered calls face significant tax drag

Takeaway: If possible, implement covered calls in tax-advantaged accounts first.

Lesson 6: Time Commitment Varies by Approach

What happened:

- Sarah: 30 minutes weekly, simple conservative approach
- Marcus: 2-3 hours weekly, active management
- Jennifer: 1-2 hours weekly, moderate approach

Takeaway: Strategy can be scaled to available time. More time doesn't necessarily equal better returns if basic strategy is sound.

Lesson 7: Income vs. Growth Trade-Off

What happened:

- Sarah maximized income (13.7% premium), moderate total return (20.1%)

- Marcus balanced income (23.8% premium) with appreciation (17.8% stock gains) for 42.8% total
- Jennifer prioritized total return (34.9%) in tax-deferred account

Takeaway: Define your priority (income now vs. wealth accumulation) and align strategy accordingly.

Lesson 8: Risk Management Through Diversification

What happened:

- Sarah's 10-position portfolio weathered correction well
- Marcus's tech-heavy 9-position portfolio more volatile
- Jennifer's 12-position portfolio balanced risk and returns

Takeaway: 8-12 positions across sectors provides good diversification for covered calls.

Lesson 9: Realistic Return Expectations

What happened:

- Conservative (Sarah): 20% total return
- Moderate (Marcus): 43% total return (bull market year)
- Tax-deferred aggressive (Jennifer): 35% total return

Takeaway: 15-35% annual returns realistic depending on approach and market conditions. Claims of 60-80% annually should be questioned.

Lesson 10: Discipline Beats Intelligence

What happened:

- Sarah, with minimal investment experience, succeeded through systematic discipline
- Marcus, experienced and sophisticated, made mistakes when deviating from rules
- Jennifer succeeded by following systematic approach despite busy schedule

Takeaway: Following consistent rules matters more than intelligence or market predictions.

Conclusion: Real-World Application

These case studies demonstrate that covered call strategies work across different investor profiles, account types, and market conditions. Success requires:

1. **Clear goals aligned with approach**
2. **Appropriate risk tolerance calibration**
3. **Systematic execution**
4. **Emotional discipline**
5. **Willingness to adapt while maintaining core principles**
6. **Realistic expectations**
7. **Patience and consistency**

Whether you're a risk-averse retiree like Sarah, a growth-focused accumulator like Marcus, or a high-income professional like Jennifer, covered calls can enhance your investment returns and achieve your specific objectives.

The common thread: They all followed systematic approaches, maintained discipline through volatility, and let the strategy compound over time. You can do the same.

Chapter 21:

Scaling Your Strategy

Success with covered calls naturally leads to questions about scaling: How do I grow this strategy as my portfolio increases? When should I add complexity? What advanced variations exist? This chapter addresses growth, evolution, and next steps in your options education.

Growing Your Portfolio Over Time

Natural Portfolio Growth Paths

Path 1: Organic Compounding (No Additional Contributions)

Starting portfolio: $100,000 Average annual return: 25%

- Year 1: $125,000
- Year 2: $156,250
- Year 3: $195,313
- Year 5: $305,176
- Year 10: $931,323

Doubling time at 25% returns: ~3.1 years

Challenges as portfolio grows:

- Position sizes increase (100 shares of $300 stock = $30,000 position)
- Need more positions to maintain diversification
- Time commitment increases
- Tax complexity grows

Path 2: With Regular Contributions

Starting: $100,000 Contributions: $2,000 monthly ($24,000 annually) Returns: 25% on invested capital

- Year 1: $125,000 + $24,000 contributions = $149,000
- Year 2: $186,250 + $24,000 = $210,250
- Year 3: $263,313 + $24,000 = $287,313
- Year 5: $489,848 + contributions = $513,848
- Year 10: $1,489,000+

Managing Growth Stages
Stage 1: Starter ($25,000-$100,000)

- Positions: 5-8
- Position size: $3,000-15,000
- Time: 30-60 minutes weekly
- Focus: Learning and consistency
- Complexity: Basic covered calls only

Stage 2: Established ($100,000-$250,000)

- Positions: 8-12
- Position size: $10,000-25,000
- Time: 1-2 hours weekly
- Focus: Optimization and efficiency
- Complexity: Standard covered calls, beginning to explore variations

Stage 3: Substantial ($250,000-$500,000)

- Positions: 10-15
- Position size: $20,000-40,000
- Time: 2-3 hours weekly
- Focus: Risk management and tax optimization
- Complexity: Multiple strategies, different durations

Stage 4: Significant ($500,000-$1,000,000)

- Positions: 12-20
- Position size: $30,000-70,000
- Time: 3-5 hours weekly or hire assistance
- Focus: Institutional-quality execution
- Complexity: Advanced strategies, potentially professional management

Stage 5: Substantial Wealth ($1,000,000+)

- Positions: 15-30
- Position size: $50,000-100,000+
- Time: Consider professional management
- Focus: Wealth preservation, tax efficiency
- Complexity: Full spectrum of strategies

Scaling Challenges and Solutions

Challenge 1: Position Size Limitations

Problem: Single position becomes too large ($100,000+ in one stock)

Solutions:

- Split across multiple account types (taxable, IRA, Roth)
- Use different expiration cycles (some monthly, some quarterly)
- Accept larger positions if stock quality justifies
- Consider LEAPS (Long-term Equity Anticipation Securities) for portion

Challenge 2: Time Management

Problem: 20-position portfolio requires 4-6 hours weekly

Solutions:

- Systematize processes (templates, checklists)
- Use software/tools for automation
- Hire assistant or portfolio manager for $200,000+ portfolios
- Reduce position count, increase position size

Challenge 3: Diversification Requirements

Problem: Need 15-20 positions for adequate diversification at $1M+

Solutions:

- Use ETFs for some covered call positions (SPY, QQQ, IWM)
- Sector-focused positions (cover entire sector with one ETF)
- Accept concentrated portfolio if conviction warrants

- Professional management for ultra-high-net-worth

Challenge 4: Tax Complexity
Problem: Hundreds of transactions create reporting nightmare
Solutions:

- Professional tax preparation mandatory over $250k
- Specialized software (TradeLog, GainsKeeper)
- Quarterly tax planning sessions
- Consider moving majority to IRA/Roth if possible

When to Add Complexity

The Complexity Temptation

After mastering basic covered calls, traders often feel compelled to add complexity:

- "Maybe I should use weekly options instead of monthly"
- "Perhaps LEAPS would be better"
- "Should I try put-write strategies too?"
- "What about collars or spreads?"

Warning: Complexity rarely improves returns proportionally to added effort and risk.

The 80/20 Rule

80% of covered call profits come from 20% of the strategy complexity:

- Stock selection
- Strike selection
- Basic execution

Remaining 20% of profits require 80% more complexity:

- Exotic variations
- Complex timing
- Multiple strategies

When Complexity Makes Sense
Add complexity ONLY when:

1. **Current strategy limiting returns in measurable way**
    - Example: "My returns would be 3% higher annually with weekly options based on 12-month backtest"
    - Not: "Weekly options seem more exciting"
2. **You've mastered current approach**
    - 12+ months experience
    - Consistent execution
    - Documented results
    - Clear understanding of mechanics
3. **Time available to manage added complexity**
    - Each strategy variation adds management time
    - Ensure capacity exists
4. **Tax/account structure supports it**
    - Some strategies better in tax-deferred accounts
    - Professional tax help available
5. **Portfolio size justifies it**
    - Small portfolios shouldn't overcomplicate
    - $500k+ can support multiple approaches

Complexity Decision Framework
Before adding any strategy variation, answer:

1. **What specific problem does this solve?**
    - Must be concrete, measurable problem
    - "Not making enough money" is not specific enough
2. **What is the expected improvement?**
    - Quantify in percentage points or dollars
    - Compare to added time and complexity cost
3. **What is the downside risk?**
    - What goes wrong with this approach?
    - Can you handle that scenario?
4. **Can you backtest or paper trade it first?**

    - Never implement real money without testing
    - Minimum 3-month paper trading
5. **Do experts you respect use this approach?**
    - Beware of "secret strategies" no one else uses
    - Good strategies are often well-known

Advanced Variations

For investors who've mastered basic covered calls and meet criteria above:

Poor Man's Covered Call (PMCC)

What it is: Instead of owning stock, purchase deep in-the-money LEAPS call option and sell shorter-term calls against it.

Example:

- Traditional covered call: Buy 100 shares AAPL at $190 ($19,000)
- PMCC: Buy 1 AAPL Jan 2026 $140 LEAP at $60 ($6,000), sell monthly $200 calls against it

Advantages:

- Much less capital required ($6,000 vs. $19,000)
- Defined risk (maximum loss = LEAP cost)
- Leverage potential (control 100 shares with less capital)

Disadvantages:

- LEAP loses value over time (theta decay on long position)
- More complex to manage
- No dividends received
- Can lose entire LEAP investment
- Requires Level 2-3 options approval

When to use:

- Smaller account wanting leverage

- Bullish long-term but want short-term income
- Sophisticated trader comfortable with complexity

Not suitable for:

- Beginners
- Conservative investors
- Retirement/income focus

Covered Call with Protective Put (Collar)

What it is: Standard covered call plus purchased put option creating defined risk range.

Example:

- Own stock at $100
- Sell $105 call (cap upside)
- Buy $95 put (floor downside)
- Net result: Profit range $95-$105

Advantages:

- Defined maximum loss
- Protection during crashes
- Still generates income (though reduced by put cost)

Disadvantages:

- Put cost reduces income substantially
- Caps upside and floors downside (narrow range)
- More complex, more commissions
- Timing two options instead of one

When to use:

- Very volatile stock you want to protect
- Before known catalyst (earnings, FDA decision)

- Portfolio insurance during uncertain times

Not suitable for:

- Standard covered call situations
- Low-volatility stocks
- Small accounts (put costs proportionally higher)

Rolling Strategies Formalized

The Systematic Roll Approach:

Rather than hold-to-expiration, systematically close at specific profit targets and roll:

30-45-75 System:

- Sell 45-day options
- Close when reached 75% profit OR 30 days remaining
- Immediately roll to new 45-day option

Example:

- Day 1: Sell 45-day $105 call for $3.00
- Day 15: Worth $0.75 (75% profit captured)
- Day 15: Close for $0.75, sell new 45-day call for $2.90
- Result: ~15 cycles annually instead of 12

Advantages:

- Capture optimal theta decay window
- Reduce tail risk (expire worthless risk)
- Potentially higher total returns (15-20% improvement possible)

Disadvantages:

- Much more active management
- More transactions

- Requires discipline (temptation to deviate)
- Tax complexity increases dramatically

When to use:

- Portfolio $200k+
- Time available (2-3 hours weekly minimum)
- Tax-deferred account preferred
- Systematic personality (follows rules exactly)

Covered Strangles
What it is: Covered call plus short put on same stock.
Example:

- Own 100 shares at $100
- Sell $105 call
- Sell $95 put

Result:

- Collect premium from both options
- Risk: Assigned on put, now own 200 shares

Advantages:

- Double premium collection
- Works well in sideways markets

Disadvantages:

- Risk of doubling position size
- Requires cash/margin for put assignment
- Complex management
- Not truly "covered" (put is naked)

When to use:

- Experienced traders only
- Strong conviction in stock
- Capital available to double position
- Sideways market expectations

Not suitable for:

- Beginners
- Conservative approaches
- IRAs (often prohibited)
- Covered call purists

Next Steps in Your Options Education

Continuing Education Path

Year 1: Master Covered Calls

- Focus exclusively on basic covered calls
- Build consistency and discipline
- Document results thoroughly
- Develop personal style

Year 2: Optimization

- Fine-tune strike selection
- Optimize tax efficiency
- Consider one simple variation (rolling system)
- Still 90%+ focus on core strategy

Year 3+: Selective Expansion

- If appropriate, explore one advanced variation
- Consider professional management for portion
- Teach others (reinforces learning)
- Give back to community

Advanced Education Resources

Books for next level:

- "Option Volatility and Pricing" by Sheldon Natenberg (advanced theory)
- "Trading Options Greeks" by Dan Passarelli (risk management)
- "The Option Trader's Hedge Fund" by Dennis Chen (institutional approaches)

Courses:

- CBOE Options Institute (free, excellent)
- Tastytrade courses (free, practical)
- Consider paid institutional-level courses if managing $1M+

Certifications (if pursuing professionally):

- CMT (Chartered Market Technician)
- CFP (Certified Financial Planner) - if advising others
- Options trading certifications from recognized institutions

Community Involvement:

- Join local options trading groups
- Mentor beginners
- Share knowledge (teaching deepens understanding)
- Consider starting blog/YouTube if so inclined

When to Consider Professional Management
Signs you should explore professional help:

- Portfolio exceeds $1,000,000
- Time commitment becomes burdensome
- Returns stagnating despite effort
- Desire to focus on other aspects of life
- Tax complexity overwhelming

Professional options:

1. **Covered call-focused RIAs (Registered Investment Advisors)**
    - Firms specializing in options strategies
    - Fees: 0.75-1.5% of assets annually
    - Minimum: Usually $500k-$1M
2. **Overlay services**
    - You maintain stock portfolio
    - They manage only options overlay
    - Fees: 0.25-0.75%
    - May have lower minimums
3. **Robo-advisors with options**
    - Automated covered call programs
    - Much lower fees (0.25-0.50%)
    - Less customization
    - Growing market

Conclusion: Scaling and Evolution

The covered call strategy you've learned scales effectively from $25,000 to $25,000,000. The core principles—stock selection, strike selection, systematic execution—remain constant. What changes is position size, portfolio complexity, and potentially whether you manage everything personally or delegate portions to professionals.

Most investors find that basic covered calls, executed consistently over years, provide excellent risk-adjusted returns without requiring evolution to complex strategies. The temptation to add complexity should be resisted unless clear, measurable benefits justify the added effort.

Scale gradually, master each level before progressing, and remember that simplicity often produces better results than sophistication. The goal is sustainable wealth generation, not strategy complexity for its own sake.

Conclusion: Your Path Forward

You've reached the end of this comprehensive guide, but your covered call journey is just beginning. The difference between this book gathering dust and transforming your financial future lies in one word: implementation.

Reviewing Key Principles

Let's crystalize the essential truths that separate successful covered call traders from those who struggle:

Principle 1: Stock Selection Matters Most

High-quality stocks with stable cash flows, competitive advantages, and adequate options liquidity form the foundation. No amount of clever strike selection or timing can compensate for poor underlying stocks. Build your portfolio on blue-chip companies with proven resilience.

Principle 2: Consistency Beats Cleverness

Systematic execution of a simple strategy outperforms sporadic brilliance. The covered call trader who sells monthly options at consistent strikes for 10 years generates superior risk-adjusted returns compared to the trader constantly chasing the "optimal" approach.

Principle 3: Adaptation Within Discipline

Markets cycle through bull, bear, and sideways phases. Your strike selection and position management should adapt to conditions—but within a disciplined framework of written rules. Adaptation is not abandonment of process.

Principle 4: Time Decay is Your Greatest Ally

Every day that passes, options lose value. This theta decay represents your structural advantage. The 30-45 day window captures optimal decay without excessive risk. Trust this mathematical certainty.

Principle 5: Assignments are Successes, Not Failures

When your stock is called away at the strike price plus premium collected, you've achieved maximum profit for that trade. Don't let regret over missed further appreciation poison this success. Celebrate assignments as the strategy working exactly as designed.

Principle 6: Emotions Destroy Returns

Fear causes paralysis during opportunities. Greed drives excessive risk. Regret leads to poor decisions. The antidote: written rules created during calm rationality, followed regardless of emotional state.

Principle 7: Tax Efficiency Magnifies Results

Every percentage point saved on taxes compounds over decades. Qualified covered calls, wash sale awareness, and strategic use of tax-deferred accounts can add 3-5 percentage points annually to your after

Conclusion: Your Path Forward (Continued)

Principle 7: Tax Efficiency Magnifies Results

Every percentage point saved on taxes compounds over decades. Qualified covered calls, wash sale awareness, and strategic use of tax-deferred accounts can add 3-5 percentage points annually to your after-tax returns. Over 20 years, this difference creates hundreds of thousands in additional wealth.

Principle 8: Simplicity Scales

The basic covered call strategy you've learned works at $25,000 and $25,000,000. Resist the temptation to add complexity unless clear, measurable benefits justify it. Most successful long-term practitioners stick with the fundamentals.

Principle 9: Risk Management Enables Longevity

Position sizing, diversification, and appropriate use of reserves protect you from catastrophic losses. A 40% drawdown requires 67% gains to recover—survivability matters more than maximizing every upturn.

Principle 10: Education Never Ends

Markets evolve, strategies develop, and your skills improve through continuous learning. Invest in your knowledge as readily as you invest capital. The returns on education compound indefinitely.

Setting Achievable Goals

Your First 90 Days

Goal 1: Education Foundation (Days 1-30)

Read this book completely

Complete one online course (OIC or similar)

Set up brokerage account with options approval

Build initial watchlist of 20-25 stocks

Paper trade 5-10 positions

Success metric: Comfortable with mechanics, understand terminology, confident in platform usage

Goal 2: Initial Implementation (Days 31-60)

Deploy 25-50% of intended capital

Establish 3-5 positions

Sell first covered calls

Begin systematic tracking

Experience first expiration cycle

Success metric: Executed real trades successfully, tracking system operational, first premium collected

Goal 3: Steady State Development (Days 61-90)

Complete capital deployment (8-10 positions)

Manage second expiration cycle

Handle first assignment (if occurs)

Refine process based on experience

Complete first quarterly review

Success metric: Systematic routine established, comfortable with process, seeing consistent results

Your First Year

Quarter 1: Foundation

Master basic execution

Develop routine

Build confidence

Target: 10-15% returns (annualized basis)

Quarter 2: Consistency

Maintain discipline through market conditions

Refine strike selection

Improve efficiency

Target: 12-18% returns

Quarter 3: Optimization

Adapt to market conditions

Handle volatility professionally

Fine-tune approach

Target: 15-22% returns

Quarter 4: Integration

Covered calls feel natural

Systematic execution without stress

Ready to scale

Target: 18-25% returns

Year 1 total target: 15-25% returns with minimal stress

Years 2-5: Mastery Development

Year 2:

Refine approach based on Year 1 lessons

Scale portfolio if appropriate

Consider one simple variation if beneficial

Target: 20-28% returns

Year 3:

Adapt strategy to larger portfolio

Optimize tax efficiency

Build track record for review

Target: 18-30% returns (variability increases with size)

Year 4-5:

Mastery of execution

Consistent performance across conditions

Consider teaching others

Consider professional management if portfolio exceeds $1M

Target: 20-30% average returns

Long-Term Wealth Building

The compounding miracle:

Starting: $100,000 Annual return: 24% (realistic moderate approach)

Year 5: $288,195

Year 10: $830,359

Year 15: $2,392,871

Year 20: $6,892,794

Year 25: $19,854,077

This isn't fantasy—it's the mathematical result of consistent 24% returns compounded over time. You don't need 50% annual returns or to discover secret strategies. Consistency at 20-28% builds extraordinary wealth over decades.

Staying Disciplined

Discipline separates amateurs from professionals, lucky years from sustainable careers, and modest success from life-changing wealth.

The Discipline Framework

1. Written Rules

Your trading rules document (created in Chapter 19) should be:

Printed and posted at your desk

Reviewed before every trading session

Updated only after careful quarterly review

Signed and dated (commitment device)

Never deviate from rules in the moment. If a rule needs changing, mark it for quarterly review. Don't change mid-action.

2. Pre-Commitment Devices

24-Hour Rule: Major strategy changes require 24-hour waiting period **Position Limits:** Set maximum position sizes in brokerage platform **Trade Limits:** Monthly maximum trades enforced **Approval Process:** Significant decisions require written justification

3. Regular Reviews

Weekly (15 minutes):

Update tracking

Verify upcoming expirations

Check for earnings/events

No trading unless planned

Monthly (1 hour):

Process expirations

Comprehensive performance review

Update projections

Plan next month

Quarterly (3 hours):

Deep performance analysis

Strategy assessment

Consider rule adjustments

Set next quarter goals

Annual (8 hours):
Complete year analysis
Tax planning
Strategic direction for next year
Celebrate successes, learn from failures

4. Accountability

Options for accountability:
Trading partner (check in weekly)
Advisor or coach (monthly reviews)
Investment club (share experiences)
Online community (document progress)
Spouse/partner (share results)

The act of reporting to someone else enforces discipline.

5. Dealing with Setbacks

Every trader experiences:
Losing months
Assignments at inopportune times
Stocks declining despite premium
Mistakes in execution
Regret over decisions

How successful traders respond:
Accept it happened: No denial, no anger
Analyze objectively: What caused it? Controllable or random?
Learn the lesson: What would you do differently?
Document it: Write in journal
Move forward: Next trade is independent of last trade

What unsuccessful traders do:
Deny or minimize the mistake
Blame others or bad luck
Make emotional reactive changes
Abandon strategy after setback
Repeat same mistakes

6. The Discipline Mindset

Reframe your thinking:

Old: "I made 3% this month, I'm getting good at this!" New: "Did I follow my process this month?" (Focus on process, not outcomes)

Old: "I lost 2%, this strategy doesn't work" New: "Did I execute according to my rules? If yes, this is variance within expected range"

Old: "I should try something new and exciting" New: "Is there measurable evidence this change improves risk-adjusted returns?"

Old: "Everyone else is making more money" New: "Am I meeting my goals? Others' claims are likely exaggerated and more risky"

Final Encouragement

You stand at the beginning of a journey that can transform your financial life. Not through get-rich-quick schemes, complex algorithms, or secret strategies—but through the systematic application of time-tested principles.

What makes you capable:

You don't need:

Advanced mathematics (basic arithmetic suffices)

Full-time availability (1-2 hours weekly works)

Large starting capital ($25,000+ is enough)

Special connections or insider information

Perfect timing or market predictions

You do need:

Willingness to learn and study

Discipline to follow a system

Patience to let strategies compound

Emotional control during volatility

Realistic expectations

Commitment to continuous improvement

The odds are in your favor:

Unlike most trading strategies, covered calls offer:

Positive expected value: Time decay works for you mathematically

Reduced risk: Premium provides downside cushion

Historical success: Decades of evidence supporting the approach

Institutional validation: Banks, hedge funds, and pensions use covered calls

Accessibility: Individual investors compete on equal footing

You're not gambling; you're systematically harvesting volatility premium with defined risk.

The journey ahead:

Month 1-3: Uncomfortable learning phase

Everything feels uncertain

Mistakes will happen

Confidence is building

Trust the process

Month 4-9: Developing competence

Process becomes familiar

Fewer mistakes

Results appearing

Confidence growing

Month 10-18: Achieving consistency

Execution feels natural

Managing different conditions

Building track record

Confidence solid

Year 2+: Mastery and compounding

Strategy second nature

Adapting effortlessly

Wealth accumulating

Teaching others

Your commitment:

I, ____________________, commit to implementing covered call strategies as outlined in this book. I will:

Start with proper education and paper trading

Begin with small positions and scale gradually

Follow written rules consistently

Maintain detailed records

Review and learn from every trade

Stay disciplined through market volatility

Focus on process over outcomes

Be patient with the compounding process

Seek help when needed

Give back by helping others once successful

Signed: _________________ Date: _____________

A final thought:

Thousands of investors have walked this path before you. They started where you are now—uncertain, skeptical, hopeful. Through consistent application of these principles, they now enjoy:

Monthly income supplementing or replacing employment

Retirement security without market timing stress

Wealth accumulation exceeding traditional approaches

Confidence in their financial future

Freedom that comes from reliable cash flow

You can achieve the same results. Not overnight, not without effort, not without occasional setbacks—but absolutely, certainly, reliably over time.

The question isn't whether covered calls work. Decades of evidence confirm they do. The question is: Will you implement them?

Your journey begins with the first position. Everything you need to succeed is in this book. The rest is up to you.

Welcome to the world of covered call investing. Your future income awaits.

Onwards, Janice Green

APPENDICES

Appendix A: Glossary of Terms

American Option: An option that can be exercised at any time before expiration (all U.S. stock options are American-style).

Assignment: The obligation to sell shares at the strike price when someone exercises the call you sold.

At-the-Money (ATM): An option whose strike price is equal to or very close to the current stock price.

Bid: The highest price buyers are willing to pay for an option.

Ask (Offer): The lowest price sellers are willing to accept for an option.

Bid-Ask Spread: The difference between bid and ask prices, representing transaction cost.

Black-Scholes Model: Mathematical model for pricing options, considering stock price, strike, time, volatility, and interest rates.

Blue-Chip Stock: Large, established company with strong financial stability and long operating history.

Breakeven Point: Stock price level where covered call position neither makes nor loses money (purchase price minus premium).

Buy to Close: Transaction closing a short option position by purchasing it back.

Call Option: Contract giving buyer the right (not obligation) to purchase stock at the strike price.

Collar: Position combining covered call with protective put, creating defined profit range.

Contract: One options contract represents 100 shares of the underlying stock.

Covered Call: Strategy of owning stock and selling call options against those shares.

Delta: Greek measuring how much option price changes per $1 move in stock; also approximates probability of finishing in-the-money.

Dividend Aristocrat: Company increasing dividend for 25+ consecutive years.

Ex-Dividend Date: Date determining dividend eligibility; must own stock before this date to receive dividend.

Exercise: When option holder uses their right to buy stock at the strike price (results in assignment for call seller).

Expiration Date: Last day option can be exercised; third Friday of the month for standard options.

Extrinsic Value: See Time Value.

Free Cash Flow (FCF): Operating cash flow minus capital expenditures; cash available for dividends, buybacks, and investments.

Gamma: Greek measuring rate of delta change as stock price moves.

Greeks: Mathematical measures describing option price behavior (delta, theta, vega, gamma, rho).

Implied Volatility (IV): Market's expectation of future stock volatility, derived from option prices.

In-the-Money (ITM): Call option with strike price below current stock price (has intrinsic value).

Intrinsic Value: Amount by which option is in-the-money; for calls: stock price minus strike price (never negative).

IV Rank: Current implied volatility relative to its 52-week high-low range, expressed as percentage.

IV Percentile: Percentage of days over past year with lower implied volatility than today.

LEAPS: Long-term Equity Anticipation Securities; options with expiration dates more than 9 months out.

Liquidity: Ease of buying/selling without significantly impacting price; higher volume = better liquidity.

Naked Call: Selling call option without owning underlying stock (unlimited risk; not covered in this book).

Open Interest: Total number of outstanding option contracts not yet closed or exercised.

Options Chain: Display of all available options for a stock, organized by strike and expiration.

Out-of-the-Money (OTM): Call option with strike price above current stock price (no intrinsic value).

Payout Ratio: Percentage of earnings paid as dividends (annual dividend ÷ earnings per share).

Premium: Price paid/received for an option contract.

Put Option: Contract giving buyer right to sell stock at strike price (covered calls don't involve puts).

Qualified Covered Call (QCC): Covered call meeting IRS requirements, preserving stock's long-term holding period.

Return on Equity (ROE): Net income divided by shareholder equity; measures profitability relative to equity.

Roll: Simultaneously closing existing option and opening new option (different strike and/or expiration).

Sell to Open: Transaction initiating a short option position (selling a call you don't own).

Standard Deviation: Statistical measure of volatility; approximately 68% of price movements fall within one standard deviation.

Strike Price: Price at which option can be exercised; price you're obligated to sell at for covered calls.

Theta: Greek measuring time decay; how much option loses value per day.

Time Decay: Loss of option value as expiration approaches (benefits covered call sellers).

Time Value: Option premium beyond intrinsic value; represents value of time remaining until expiration.

Underlying: The stock on which the option is based.

Vega: Greek measuring option price sensitivity to implied volatility changes.

VIX: CBOE Volatility Index; measures market's expectation of 30-day volatility, often called "fear index."

Volume: Number of option contracts traded during a session.

Wash Sale: Tax rule disallowing loss deduction when substantially identical security repurchased within 61-day window.

Write: Another term for selling an option.

Appendix B: Checklist for Stock Selection

Use this checklist when evaluating potential covered call candidates:

Fundamental Quality (Must pass ALL)

[ ] **Market cap over $10 billion** (minimum for adequate liquidity)
[ ] **Positive free cash flow** in last 3 years
[ ] **Debt-to-equity ratio** in bottom 50% of industry peers
[ ] **Current ratio above 1.3** (short-term liquidity adequate)
[ ] **ROE above 12%** and stable or improving
[ ] **No accounting irregularities** or governance red flags
[ ] **Management tenure** over 2 years (stability)

Dividend Assessment (For dividend-focused strategies)

[ ] **Dividend yield** between 2-5% (moderate, sustainable range)
[ ] **Payout ratio** between 40-70% (sustainable)
[ ] **Consecutive years** of dividend payments: 5+ (prefer 10+)
[ ] **No dividend cuts** in past 10 years
[ ] **Dividend growth rate** exceeds inflation (3%+ annually)

Options Market Quality (Must pass ALL)

[ ] **Average daily options volume** exceeds 10,000 contracts
[ ] **Open interest** on near-month ATM options exceeds 1,000
[ ] **Bid-ask spread** under 5% of option premium (prefer under 3%)
[ ] **Options available** with weekly and monthly expirations
[ ] **Implied volatility rank** above 25 (prefer above 40)
[ ] **Multiple market makers** actively quoting

Technical Setup (Pass MOST)

[ ] **Price above 50-day moving average** (intermediate trend bullish)
[ ] **Price above 200-day moving average** (long-term trend bullish)
[ ] **RSI between 40-70** (not oversold or severely overbought)
[ ] **Support level identified** within 5-10% below current price
[ ] **Resistance level identified** within 3-7% above current price
[ ] **Volume consistent** (no unusual spikes or declining trend)
[ ] **No major gaps** in recent price action (stability)

Event Risk Assessment (Must pass ALL)

[ ] **Earnings date** verified (not within next 45 days of intended expiration)
[ ] **Ex-dividend date** verified (timed appropriately)
[ ] **No pending FDA decisions** or major regulatory events
[ ] **No announced mergers or acquisitions** in progress
[ ] **No major product launches** imminent
[ ] **No CEO transitions** or management upheaval

Portfolio Fit (Pass MOST)

[ ] **Sector allocation** remains balanced after addition
[ ] **Position size** will be 8-15% of portfolio (not too large)
[ ] **Stock correlation** to existing positions is low
[ ] **Volatility profile** appropriate for portfolio goals
[ ] **Personal conviction** in company's long-term prospects
[ ] **Comfortable holding** even if declines 15-20%

Final Premium Verification

[ ] **Expected premium** meets minimum threshold:
Conservative: 1.0%+ monthly
Moderate: 1.5%+ monthly
Aggressive: 2.0%+ monthly
[ ] **Strike selection** follows current market regime rules

[ ] **Risk-reward** acceptable given your objectives

If stock passes 90%+ of applicable criteria, APPROVED for covered call position.

Document reason for any failed criterion accepted.

Date: __________ Evaluator: __________ Stock: __________

Decision: **APPROVED / REJECTED / WATCHLIST**

Appendix C: Sample Trade Log Template

Position Entry Log

Date: __________ Position #: __________

STOCK DETAILS:

Symbol: __________

Purchase Date: __________

Shares: __________

Purchase Price: $__________

Total Cost: $__________

Sector: __________

Dividend Yield: __________%

OPTION DETAILS:

Option Sold Date: __________

Strike Price: $__________

Expiration Date: __________

Days to Expiration: __________

Premium Received: $__________

Per Share Premium: $__________

% OTM: __________%

Delta: __________

MARKET CONDITIONS:

Market Regime: ☐ Bull ☐ Sideways ☐ Bear

VIX Level: __________

Stock IV Rank: __________

Technical Setup: __________

RATIONALE: Why this stock? ______________________________ Why this strike?

______________________________ Why this expiration? ______________________________

UPCOMING EVENTS:

Next Earnings: __________

Next Ex-Dividend: __________

Other Events: __________

Position Management Log

WEEKLY REVIEW (every Saturday):

Date: __________

Stock	Current Price	Stock P/L	Option Value	Option P/L	Days to Exp	Action Needed

Notes/Observations: ______________________________

Next Week Actions: ______________________________

Position Exit Log

Date: __________ **Position #:** __________

EXIT DETAILS:

Exit Type: ☐ Expiration ☐ Assignment ☐ Early Close ☐ Roll

Exit Date: __________

Days Held: __________

Stock Exit Price: $__________

Option Exit Price: $__________

PROFIT/LOSS CALCULATION:

Stock Gain/Loss: $__________ (________%)

Option Profit: $__________

Dividends Received: $__________

Total P/L: $__________ (________% return)

Annualized Return: __________%

REASON FOR EXIT:

LESSONS LEARNED: What worked: ______________________________ What didn't work: ______________________________ Would I do differently: ______________________________

TAX NOTES:

Holding Period: ☐ Short-term ☐ Long-term

Wash Sale: ☐ Yes ☐ No

Qualified Covered Call: ☐ Yes ☐ No ☐ N/A

Monthly Performance Summary

Month/Year: _________

PORTFOLIO SUMMARY:

Starting Value: $_________

Ending Value: $_________

Change: $_________ (_______%)

INCOME BREAKDOWN:

Option Premium Collected: $_________

Dividends Received: $_________

Total Income: $_________

TRADING ACTIVITY:

Positions Opened: _________

Positions Closed: _________

Assignments: _________

Rolls Executed: _________

Total Trades: _________

PERFORMANCE METRICS:

Monthly Return: _________%

YTD Return: _________%

Premium Capture Rate: _________%

Assignment Rate: _________%

BEST PERFORMER: Stock: _________ Return: _________%

WORST PERFORMER: Stock: _________ Return: _________%

NOTES/OBSERVATIONS:

NEXT MONTH GOALS:

Appendix D: Recommended Reading and Resources

Essential Books

Covered Calls & Options Foundations:

"Covered Calls & LEAPS" by Joseph Hooper

"The Complete Guide to Option Selling" by James Cordier & Michael Gross

"Get Rich with Options" by Lee Lowell

"Show Me The Money" by Lee Finberg

Options Theory & Greeks: 5. "Option Volatility and Pricing" by Sheldon Natenberg (advanced) 6. "Trading Options Greeks" by Dan Passarelli 7. "Options as a Strategic Investment" by Lawrence McMillan (comprehensive reference)

Stock Selection & Analysis: 8. "The Intelligent Investor" by Benjamin Graham (fundamentals) 9. "Common Stocks and Uncommon Profits" by Philip Fisher 10. "One Up On Wall Street" by Peter Lynch

Websites & Online Resources

Educational:

Options Industry Council (www.optionseducation.org) - Free comprehensive education

CBOE (www.cboe.com) - Options exchange, tools, education

Investopedia (www.investopedia.com) - Definitions, tutorials, simulators

Research & Analysis:

Seeking Alpha (www.seekingalpha.com) - Stock analysis, dividend research

Morningstar (www.morningstar.com) - Fundamental analysis, ratings

TradingView (www.tradingview.com) - Charting and technical analysis

Barchart (www.barchart.com) - Options screening, unusual activity

Tools:

OptionStrat (www.optionstrat.com) - Visual strategy builder

CBOE Options Calculator (www.cboe.com/tools/calculator) - Pricing calculator

Options Profit Calculator (www.optionsprofitcalculator.com) - P/L visualization

Podcasts

Options Insider Radio - Weekly options market discussion

Options Boot Camp - Educational focus

Tackle Trading Podcast - Options strategies

Tastytrade Network - Multiple shows on options

YouTube Channels

ProjectOption - Data-driven options education

Sky View Trading - Options strategies and market analysis

Option Alpha - Systematic options trading

The Options Industry Council - Official educational content

Professional Organizations

Options Industry Council (OIC) - Industry-sponsored education

CBOE (Chicago Board Options Exchange) - Primary options exchange

American Association of Individual Investors (AAII) - Investor education

Continuing Education

Free Courses:

OIC Classes (www.optionseducation.org/gettingstarted)

Tastytrade Learn Center (www.tastytrade.com/learn)

CBOE Education (www.cboe.com/education)

Paid Courses:

Investopedia Academy - Options for Beginners ($199)

Udemy Options Courses (various, $10-100)

Coursera Financial Markets Course (various prices)

Newsletters & Blogs

The Kirk Report - Daily options education and ideas

Option Sensei - Options strategies and analysis

Various brokerage newsletters - Most brokers offer free options content

Appendix E: Frequently Asked Questions

Q: How much money do I need to start covered calls?

A: Technically, you need enough to buy 100 shares of a stock plus options approval. Practically:

Absolute minimum: $5,000 (one position)

Recommended minimum: $25,000 (5-8 positions for basic diversification)

Comfortable minimum: $50,000-100,000 (8-12 diversified positions)

Smaller accounts work but face limitations in diversification and stock selection.

Q: What returns should I realistically expect?

A: Depends on approach:

Conservative: 12-18% annually

Moderate: 18-28% annually

Aggressive: 28-40% annually

Note: Higher returns require more active management and accepting higher volatility. Conservative approaches suit most investors.

Q: How much time does this require?

A: Depends on portfolio size and approach:

Basic 10-position portfolio: 1-2 hours weekly

Active management: 2-4 hours weekly

Professional-level: 5+ hours weekly

Most investors find 60-90 minutes weekly sufficient once routine is established.

Q: Is this strategy risky?

A: Less risky than owning stock alone, but not risk-free:

Covered calls reduce risk through premium income (downside cushion)

Stock can still decline significantly

You cap upside potential

Risk level depends on stock selection and position sizing

It's a conservative options strategy, much safer than speculative options trading.

Q: What if my stock goes way up? Did I lose money?

A: No—you made maximum possible profit for that trade. Assignment at higher price + premium = success. The "lost" appreciation wasn't real because you agreed to sell at the strike when you sold the call. Don't let regret poison success.

Q: Should I use covered calls in my IRA or taxable account?

A: IRA/Roth IRA advantages:

No annual tax on gains (major benefit)

No wash sale rules

Simpler record-keeping

Full compounding without tax drag

Taxable account advantages:

Access to funds anytime without penalty

Long-term capital gains rates (vs. ordinary income rates on IRA withdrawals)

Recommendation: If eligible, prioritize Roth IRA (tax-free withdrawals) > Traditional IRA (tax-deferred) > Taxable accounts.

Q: Can I lose more than my initial investment?

A: No. Covered calls have defined, limited risk:

Maximum loss: Stock declines to zero minus premium collected

You own the stock, so losses limited to stock value

Unlike naked calls (unlimited risk), covered calls are defined risk

Q: What happens if I can't monitor positions daily?

A: No problem—covered calls don't require daily monitoring:

Weekly check-in sufficient for most portfolios

Set calendar reminders for expirations

Use alerts for major price movements if desired

Strategy works fine with weekly/monthly attention

Q: How do I know which stocks are good for covered calls?

A: Use the checklist in Appendix B, but generally:

Blue-chip stocks with strong fundamentals

Adequate options liquidity (10,000+ daily volume)

Moderate volatility (IV 20-40%)

Stocks you're comfortable owning long-term

Avoid speculation or declining companies

Q: Should I sell covered calls on ALL my stocks?

A: Not necessarily:

Stocks with strong uptrend: Consider skipping or using very OTM strikes

Stocks approaching major catalyst: Wait until after event

Stocks you want unlimited upside on: Don't constrain them

Appropriate stocks in appropriate conditions: Yes, systematic coverage

Q: What if earnings are announced while my call is outstanding?

A: Risk scenario you should avoid:

Always check earnings dates before selling

Ensure expiration before earnings

If stuck, consider closing position before earnings

Future reference: Never sell calls expiring after earnings unless intentional

Q: Can I do covered calls in my 401(k)?

A: Depends on your plan:

Some plans allow covered calls (check with plan administrator)

Many don't offer options trading

If unavailable, focus covered calls in IRA/Roth/taxable accounts

If available, same benefits as IRA (tax-deferred)

Q: What if implied volatility is really low?

A: Low IV = low premiums:

If IV rank under 25, premiums may not justify strategy

Options: Wait for IV increase, use more aggressive strikes, or skip covered calls temporarily

Don't force trades when conditions unfavorable

Patience for good setups beats forcing marginal trades

Q: Should I buy back calls early when they've declined significantly?

A: Consider if:

Captured 70-75%+ of maximum profit

Significant time remains (could redeploy to new premium)

Better opportunity identified elsewhere

Stock technical setup changed

Don't close just because:

"I'm ahead and want to lock it in" (usually better to hold)

Emotional desire for activity

Stock moved slightly in your favor

Q: How many positions should I have?

A: Depends on portfolio size:

$25,000-50,000: 5-8 positions

$50,000-150,000: 8-12 positions

$150,000-500,000: 10-15 positions

$500,000+: 12-20 positions

More positions = better diversification but more time required.

Q: What's the difference between covered calls and cash-secured puts?

A: Different strategies with different mechanics:

Covered calls: Own stock, sell calls (income on existing holdings)

Cash-secured puts: Don't own stock yet, sell puts (income while waiting to buy)

Both are option-selling strategies but serve different purposes. This book focuses on covered calls.

Q: Can I do this with ETFs instead of individual stocks?

A: Yes! ETFs work well:

SPY, QQQ, IWM offer excellent liquidity

Instant diversification

Lower individual stock risk

Generally lower volatility = lower premiums

Trade-off: Lower premiums than individual stocks but less risk.

Q: What if I get assigned? Do I have to buy the stock back?

A: Assignment means stock is sold—what you do next is your choice:

Can repurchase same stock (continue strategy)

Can deploy capital to different stock

Can wait for better entry price

Can leave in cash

No obligation to repurchase—assignment is a closing event, not continuation requirement.

Q: Is this considered "day trading"?

A: No:

Covered calls are held days/weeks/months (not intraday)

Not subject to pattern day trader rules

Considered investing/income strategy, not day trading

No special rules or restrictions apply

Q: How do I handle taxes on dozens of options trades?

A: Solutions:

Use tax software (TurboTax, H&R Block handles options)

Broker provides 1099-B with all transactions reported

Hire tax professional for $250k+ portfolios

Keep detailed records in spreadsheet

Consider specialized software (TradeLog) for active traders

Q: What's the biggest mistake beginners make?

A: Five most common:

Chasing high premiums on risky stocks

Ignoring earnings dates

Using strikes that are too aggressive

Overtrading (constant activity)

Letting emotions drive decisions

All covered extensively in Chapter 16.

Q: How long until I'm "good at this"?

Appendix E: Frequently Asked Questions (Continued)

Q: How long until I'm "good at this"?

A: Typical progression:

Month 1-3: Learning mechanics, frequent uncertainty

Month 4-6: Developing comfort, fewer mistakes

Month 7-12: Building consistency, routine established

Year 2+: Mastery developing, confident execution

Most investors feel comfortable by month 6, competent by month 12.

Q: What if my broker doesn't offer options?

A: Open account with options-capable broker:

TD Ameritrade/Schwab (excellent options platform)
Interactive Brokers (professional-grade)
E*TRADE, Fidelity (solid choices)
Tastytrade (options-focused)

Most major brokers offer options—if yours doesn't, it's time to switch.

Q: Can I do covered calls on margin?

A: Technical answer: You're not using margin to sell covered calls (you own the stock), but:

Can use margin to buy stock if approved
Increases risk (borrowing money)
Interest costs reduce returns
Not recommended for beginners
Focus on cash positions first

Q: What if volatility spikes after I sell calls?

A: Good scenario for option sellers:

Your call's value increases but so does volatility
If stock hasn't moved much, still profitable
Higher volatility means next month's premium will be rich
Don't panic—volatility works in your favor long-term

Q: Should I ever buy calls back at a loss?

A: Rarely, but sometimes yes:

Stock fundamentally deteriorated (exit entire position)
Major unexpected news changed thesis
Need capital for much better opportunity
Assignment would create tax problem

Don't buy back just because:

Stock moved against you (expected to happen sometimes)
You're uncomfortable (emotion, not strategy)
You want to "fix" a losing position

Q: How do covered calls compare to dividend investing?

A: Complementary, not competitive:

Covered calls ON dividend stocks = best combination
Covered calls add 10-25% to dividend yield annually
More active than pure dividend investing

Both focus on income, both conservative

Consider them synergistic, not alternatives

Q: What's the ideal portfolio size for covered calls?

A: "Ideal" varies by person, but sweet spots:

$100,000-250,000: Excellent diversification, manageable workload

$250,000-500,000: Professional-quality portfolio, full strategy implementation

$500,000-1M+: Consider professional management or significant time commitment

Below $100k works but faces constraints. Above $1M scales well with systems.

Q: Can I use covered calls to generate retirement income?

A: Yes—excellent use case:

Conservative approach: 12-18% returns

On $500k portfolio = $60-90k annual income

More predictable than pure dividend income

Defensive characteristics suit retirees

See Sarah's case study (Chapter 20)

Q: What if I fundamentally disagree with the options market?

A: Example: "The market is pricing in too much volatility, premiums are too high"

Trust the market's pricing

Thousands of sophisticated participants create prices

If premiums seem "too high," that's exactly when to sell

Your disagreement is often the opportunity

Don't second-guess market efficiency without strong evidence

Q: How do I find good covered call opportunities?

A: Systematic screening:

Start with quality stocks (fundamentals matter most)

Filter for options liquidity (volume, open interest)

Check IV rank (prefer above 40)

Verify technical setup favorable

Confirm no earnings in option period

Use Appendix B checklist

Don't: Start with high premiums and work backward to stocks.

Q: What happens if the company gets acquired?

A: Typical scenarios:

Stock jumps to acquisition price

Your calls will be in-the-money

You'll be assigned at strike price

You keep premium, miss portion of acquisition pop

Usually profitable outcome (strike + premium) though you miss part of acquisition premium. Accept as cost of the strategy.

Q: Should I sell calls monthly, weekly, or quarterly?

A: Depends on time available and goals:

Monthly (30-45 days): Best for most investors—optimal theta decay, manageable time

Weekly: For active traders with time—more transactions, potentially higher returns

Quarterly (60-90 days): For very passive approach—fewer decisions, lower theta efficiency

Recommendation: Start with monthly, adjust based on experience.

Q: How do I know if I'm doing well?

A: Compare multiple metrics:

Absolute returns: Are you meeting your goals? (15-25% annually is excellent)

Benchmark comparison: Beating S&P 500 consistently?

Risk-adjusted returns: Are returns justified by volatility experienced?

Process adherence: Following your rules? (most important)

Emotional state: Sleeping well? Not stressed?

Success = meeting your goals with acceptable stress, not beating some arbitrary number.

Q: What should I do during a market crash?

A: Pre-determined plan:

Don't panic sell

Shift to ATM/ITM strikes (maximize premium)

Consider rotating to defensive sectors

Accept assignments that occur

Use cash reserves for opportunities

Maintain discipline

Your premium income provides cushion—trust the strategy during volatility.

Q: Can this strategy "blow up" like some options strategies?

A: No—covered calls cannot blow up:

Defined risk: Stock value minus premium

No leverage or naked positions

No margin calls (unless using margin to buy stock)

Worst case: Stock goes to zero (same as owning stock)

Premium actually reduces risk vs. stock alone

Very different from risky options strategies you may have heard about.

Q: What if I want to sell my stock but have covered calls outstanding?

A: Two options:

Buy back the calls first, then sell stock (cleanest approach)

Sell stock, leaving "naked" call (requires higher options approval, not recommended)

Always close options before selling underlying stock unless you fully understand naked calls.

Q: Do I need to watch CNBC or follow news constantly?

A: No—major advantage of covered calls:

Not dependent on market timing

Works across different conditions

News matters less than fundamentals

Weekly check-in sufficient

Constant news watching often hurts more than helps (causes emotional reactions).

Q: How do I avoid "analysis paralysis"?

A: Common beginner problem—solutions:

Use checklist (Appendix B) for yes/no decisions

Set deadlines ("I'll decide by Friday")

Start small (low-stakes learning)

Accept that no decision is perfect

Remember: doing something reasonable beats perfect paralysis

Q: What books should I read after this one?

A: Depends on interest:

More options education: "Option Volatility and Pricing" (Natenberg)

Stock selection: "The Intelligent Investor" (Graham)

Trading psychology: "Trading in the Zone" (Douglas)

Advanced strategies: "Trading Options Greeks" (Passarelli)

See Appendix D for complete recommendations.

Q: Can I teach myself or should I hire a coach?

A: Most people teach themselves successfully:

This book provides complete foundation

Free resources abundant (OIC, Tastytrade, YouTube)

Paper trading provides risk-free practice

Online communities offer support

Consider coaching if:

Portfolio exceeds $500k

You're stuck despite effort

You want accountability

Time is more valuable than money

Q: What's the single most important lesson?

A: **Consistency beats cleverness.**

Systematic execution of a simple strategy over years builds wealth. Constantly changing approaches, chasing performance, or seeking "optimal" strategies typically underperforms patient, disciplined repetition of sound fundamentals.

Boring works. Exciting usually doesn't.

Final Thoughts on Your Questions

These FAQs address most common concerns, but you'll inevitably encounter unique situations. When that happens:

Return to first principles: What does your rule book say?

Research thoroughly: Use resources in Appendix D

Ask experienced traders: Communities are helpful

Document the decision: Learn for next time

Execute and move on: Paralysis costs more than imperfect action

Remember: Every expert was once a beginner asking these same questions. Your confusion is normal, temporary, and overcome through study and practice.

Index

Note: This is a comprehensive index for the complete book. Page numbers would be added during final publication.

| Page

About This Book

"Mastering Covered Calls" provides comprehensive, practical guidance for individual investors seeking to generate consistent income through one of the most reliable options strategies available. Unlike theoretical textbooks or get-rich-quick schemes, this book focuses on sustainable, real-world implementation that works for part-time investors with regular lives and responsibilities.

The book draws on 15+ years of actual trading experience, thousands of hours teaching retail investors, and analysis of what separates successful long-term practitioners from those who struggle or abandon the strategy.

Whether you're a risk-averse retiree seeking monthly income, a mid-career professional building wealth, or an experienced investor optimizing returns, this book provides the frameworks, examples, and detailed guidance needed to succeed with covered calls.

What makes this book different:

Complete system, not just theory: From brokerage selection through tax reporting

Real case studies: Actual traders with real results and lessons learned

Honest about challenges: Doesn't sugarcoat difficulties or overpromise returns

Detailed implementation: Step-by-step guidance, not just concepts

Beginner-friendly: Assumes no prior options knowledge

Advanced enough: Experienced traders find value in optimization chapters

Focus on sustainability: Strategies that work for decades, not just bull markets

This is the book the author wished existed when starting the covered call journey—comprehensive, practical, honest, and actionable.

For additional resources, tools, and updates, visit: **www.JaniceGreenTrading.com**

Thank You

Thank you for investing your time in "Mastering Covered Calls." Your commitment to financial education and willingness to learn a new skill demonstrates the initiative that leads to long-term success.

The covered call strategy has transformed countless portfolios from passive holdings into active income generators. With the knowledge in this book and consistent application of its principles, you're now equipped to achieve the same transformation.

Remember:

Start small and scale gradually

Follow your written rules consistently

Maintain detailed records

Learn from every trade

Stay disciplined through volatility

Be patient with the compounding process

Success in covered call trading isn't about brilliance or perfect timing—it's about systematic execution of sound principles over time. You have everything needed for that success.

The journey begins with your first position. The path forward is clear. Your future income awaits.

May your covered calls be profitable and your financial future secure.

Best wishes for your trading success,

Janice Green

Melbourne, Florida December 2025

Connect with the Author

Janice Green welcomes questions, feedback, and success stories from readers implementing covered call strategies.

Website: www.JaniceGreenTrading.com[1]

www.TheBreakThroughCollective.Online[2]

Additional resources and tools

Updated market commentary

Free downloadable templates

Answers to reader questions

Community forum

Email: janice@janicegreentrading.com

Questions about strategies

Feedback on the book

Success stories to share

Suggestions for future editions

Social Media:

Twitter/X: @JaniceGreenOpts

LinkedIn: linkedin.com/in/janicegreentrading

Newsletter: Sign up at www.JaniceGreenTrading.com for:

Monthly market analysis for covered call traders

Strategy updates and refinements

Reader Q&A

Special tips and insights

No spam, unsubscribe anytime

Your feedback helps improve future editions and online resources. Please share your experiences—both successes and challenges—to help other traders on their journey.

THE END

Covered Calls for Beginners: A Comprehensive Guide to Income Generation Through Options Trading

First Edition, 2025

1. http://www.JaniceGreenTrading.com
2. http://www.TheBreakThroughCollective.Online

For information about special discounts for bulk purchases, educational institutions, or investment clubs, please contact the publisher.

This book is available in print, ebook, and audiobook formats.

Thank you for reading "Mastering Covered Calls." Your journey to consistent options income begins now.

Key Takeaways:

The Risk-Reward Profile of Covered Calls

1. **Triple benefit:** Premium income + partial appreciation + downside cushion
2. **Trade-off:** Cap upside in exchange for immediate income
3. **Protection:** Premiums provide meaningful cushion against 10-20% declines
4. **Time dimension:** Strategy improves with longer time horizons as premiums compound
5. **Market conditions:** Outperforms in sideways and volatile markets; underperforms in strong bull markets
6. **Risk-adjusted returns:** Superior Sharpe ratio compared to stock-only investing
7. **Assignment reality:** Getting assigned at profitable strikes is success, not failure
8. **Strike selection:** 3-5% OTM strikes offer optimal balance for most investors
9. **Emotional management:** Requires accepting limited upside during explosive rallies
10. **Long-term performance:** Beats stock-only returns in 60-70% of market conditions

The Bottom Line:

Covered calls transform stock ownership from a binary bet on appreciation into a multi-dimensional income-generating strategy with built-in risk management. While you sacrifice unlimited upside potential, you gain:

- Consistent income regardless of market direction
- Reduced volatility and drawdowns
- Higher risk-adjusted returns
- Disciplined profit-taking framework
- Compounding benefits over time

For income-focused investors and those seeking to optimize risk-adjusted returns, the risk-reward profile of covered calls is compelling—provided you enter with realistic expectations about the trade-offs involved.

Shall I continue with "Real-World Applications and Success Stories"?

Real-World Applications and Success Stories

Understanding the theory of covered calls is essential, but seeing how real investors successfully implement this strategy provides invaluable insight. This section explores actual case studies, real-world applications across different investor profiles, and the lessons learned from both successes and challenges.

Case Study 1: The Retiree Income Portfolio

Investor Profile: Margaret, Age 67

Situation:

- Recently retired after 35 years as a teacher
- Portfolio value: $850,000 (combination of 401(k), IRA, and taxable accounts)
- Social Security: $2,400/month
- Pension: $1,800/month
- Total fixed income: $4,200/month ($50,400/year)
- Desired annual spending: $72,000
- Income gap: $21,600/year needed from portfolio

Challenge: Margaret's fixed income covers only 70% of her desired spending. She needs to generate $21,600 annually from her portfolio without depleting principal—that's a 2.5% withdrawal rate on top of her other income. Traditional dividend stocks might yield 3-4%, but she wants growth potential and inflation protection. Bonds offer safety but insufficient yield in current environment.

Covered Call Solution:

Margaret worked with her financial advisor to restructure 60% of her portfolio ($510,000) into a covered call income strategy, keeping 40% in traditional diversified investments for growth and liquidity.

Portfolio Construction:

- **10 large-cap dividend stocks** ($51,000 each position)
- **Criteria:** Established companies, dividend yield 2.5%+, moderate volatility (beta 0.8-1.2)
- **Sector diversification:** Healthcare, Consumer Staples, Utilities, Financials, Technology
- **Examples:** Johnson & Johnson, Procter & Gamble, Verizon, JPMorgan Chase, Microsoft

Strategy Implementation:

- Monthly covered calls written on all 10 positions
- Strike selection: 4-5% out-of-the-money
- Target premium: 1.5-2% per position monthly
- Management: Advisor handles all option trades

Year 1 Results:
Dividend Income:

- Portfolio value: $510,000
- Average dividend yield: 2.8%
- Annual dividends: $14,280

Option Premium Income:

- Average monthly premium per position: $850
- Total monthly premium: $8,500
- Successful months: 11 (one position assigned in month 7, reestablished month 8)
- Annual premium income: $93,500

Stock Appreciation:

- 6 positions: assigned once, gained 4-5% appreciation
- 4 positions: never assigned, gained 8-12% appreciation
- Weighted average appreciation: 7.2%

- Capital gain: $36,720

Total Portfolio Return:

- Dividends: $14,280
- Premiums: $93,500
- Appreciation: $36,720
- **Total: $144,500**
- **Return: 28.3% on $510,000**

After-Tax Income Available:

- In traditional IRA: All income tax-deferred, can withdraw needed amount
- Withdrew $24,000 to supplement fixed income (leaving $120,500 to compound)
- Effective portfolio withdrawal: 4.7% (well below safe withdrawal rates)

Year 2-5 Performance:

Over the next four years, Margaret's results varied by market conditions:

Year 2 (Moderate Bull Market):

- Total return: 24.1%
- Stock appreciation: 11%
- Premium income: 16.5%
- Dividends: 2.9%
- Several positions assigned, reestablished at higher prices

Year 3 (Volatile/Sideways Market):

- Total return: 21.8%
- Stock appreciation: 3%
- Premium income: 21.2% (high volatility = higher premiums)
- Dividends: 3.1%

- Optimal conditions for covered calls

Year 4 (Bear Market, -15% overall market):

- Total return: -3.2%
- Stock depreciation: -8%
- Premium income: 18.4% (partially offset losses)
- Dividends: 3.0%
- Stock-only approach would have lost 12-15%

Year 5 (Recovery/Bull Market):

- Total return: 26.7%
- Stock appreciation: 9%
- Premium income: 19.8%
- Dividends: 3.2%

Five-Year Cumulative Results:
Covered Call Portfolio:

- Starting value: $510,000
- Ending value: $892,450
- Total gain: $382,450
- **Annualized return: 11.8%**
- Annual income withdrawn: $24,000 average
- Total withdrawn: $120,000
- Net portfolio growth: $262,450 (51% increase after withdrawals)

Comparison to Alternative Strategies:
If Margaret had used stock-only approach:

- S&P 500 average return (same period): 9.2%
- Expected ending value: $788,830
- Income available: Only dividends (~3%) = $15,300/year
- Would have needed to sell shares to meet income needs

- Total withdrawn (with share sales): $120,000
- Net portfolio value: ~$668,830
- **Covered call advantage: $223,620 better off**

If Margaret had used bond portfolio:

- Average bond yield: 3.5%
- Expected ending value: $597,850 (after inflation)
- Annual income: $17,850
- Would need to sell bonds to meet income needs
- **Covered call advantage: $294,600 better off**

Key Success Factors:

1. **Diversification:** 10 different positions across sectors reduced single-stock risk
2. **Quality selection:** Chose stable, dividend-paying companies that were suitable for long-term holding
3. **Moderate strike selection:** 4-5% OTM strikes balanced income with appreciation
4. **Consistent execution:** Wrote calls every month regardless of market conditions
5. **Tax efficiency:** Used IRA accounts to defer taxes on premium income
6. **Professional management:** Advisor handled execution, removing emotional decisions
7. **Realistic expectations:** Understood some upside would be capped; focused on income goal

Lessons Learned:
What worked well:

- Strategy exceeded income needs by 3x
- Portfolio continued growing despite annual withdrawals
- Volatility was significantly lower than stock-only approach

- Sleep-at-night factor: Margaret felt secure with consistent income

Challenges faced:

- Year 4 bear market was emotionally difficult despite outperforming
- Occasionally frustrating when strong-performing stocks were called away
- Required ongoing engagement and decisions (not entirely passive)
- More complex tax reporting than simple buy-and-hold

Margaret's Reflection (after 5 years):

"I was nervous about options at first—they seemed risky and complicated. But once I understood that I was just agreeing to sell stocks I owned at profitable prices, it clicked. The monthly income gives me tremendous peace of mind. I don't worry about market volatility like my friends do because I'm getting paid every month regardless. Yes, sometimes a stock gets called away and then keeps rising, but I made a profit and can find another good company. The strategy has exceeded my expectations and allowed me to maintain my lifestyle without depleting my savings. I actually have more money now than when I retired!"

Advisor's Perspective:

"Margaret's case perfectly illustrates the power of covered calls for retirees. The strategy transformed her portfolio from a growth-focused accumulation account into an income-generating machine while still providing significant capital appreciation. The key was setting realistic expectations upfront about capped upside and ensuring she understood the trade-offs. Five years later, she's one of my most satisfied clients because the strategy delivered exactly what we planned: consistent, predictable income that exceeds her needs while preserving and growing capital."

Case Study 2: The Young Professional's Wealth Acceleration

Investor Profile: David, Age 34

Situation:

- Software engineer at tech company
- Income: $185,000/year
- High savings rate: 35% of gross income
- Portfolio value: $175,000 (mostly in taxable brokerage)
- Investment timeline: 25+ years until retirement
- Risk tolerance: Moderate-high (young, stable career)
- Goal: Accelerate wealth building beyond traditional buy-and-hold

Challenge: David is a disciplined saver but frustrated with stock market volatility and slow progress. He wants to optimize returns without taking excessive risks. Traditional index investing seems too passive, and he has time to actively manage positions. He's read about options and wants to leverage his tech-sector knowledge.

Covered Call Solution:

David developed a systematic covered call approach focused on high-quality technology stocks he researches extensively and believes in long-term.

Portfolio Construction:

- **Core holdings (60% - $105,000):** Index funds (S&P 500, Total Market) - never touched, pure buy-and-hold for long-term compounding
- **Covered call portfolio (40% - $70,000):** 7 individual tech stocks
- Each position: ~$10,000 (100 shares)
- Selection criteria: Companies he uses/understands, strong fundamentals, moderate volatility

Initial Positions:

1. Microsoft (MSFT) - $10,000
2. Apple (AAPL) - $10,000
3. Adobe (ADBE) - $10,000
4. Nvidia (NVDA) - $10,000

5. Salesforce (CRM) - $10,000
6. PayPal (PYPL) - $10,000
7. Shopify (SHOP) - $10,000

Strategy Implementation:

- Weekly covered calls (more active approach, smaller premiums but more frequent)
- Strike selection: 2-3% out-of-the-money
- Target premium: 0.5-1% per week (26-52% annualized)
- Management: Self-directed, spends 2-3 hours weekly reviewing and adjusting
- Rule: If assigned, immediately look to reestablish position or rotate to new opportunity

Year 1 Results:
Week 1-13 (Q1 - Bull Market):

- Strong tech rally, multiple assignments
- NVDA assigned 3 times (kept re-buying, capturing 2-3% gains each time)
- AAPL assigned twice
- Premium income: $4,850
- Capital gains from assignments: $2,100
- Positions held continuously appreciated: $3,200
- **Q1 Total: $10,150 (14.5% on $70,000)**

Week 14-26 (Q2 - Volatile/Choppy):

- Tech sector correction (-8% for sector)
- No assignments (stocks stayed below strikes)
- Premium income: $5,200
- Stock depreciation: -$5,600
- **Q2 Total: -$400 (-0.6% on $70,000)**
- Stock-only would have lost: -$5,600 (-8%)

Week 27-39 (Q3 - Recovery):

- Market recovered, moderate gains
- MSFT assigned twice
- CRM assigned once
- Premium income: $4,950
- Capital gains: $1,850
- Unrealized appreciation: $2,400
- **Q3 Total: $9,200 (13.1%)**

Week 40-52 (Q4 - Strong Rally):

- Year-end rally in tech
- Multiple assignments across positions
- Premium income: $4,600
- Capital gains: $3,100
- Appreciation on held positions: $1,800
- **Q4 Total: $9,500 (13.6%)**

Full Year Summary:
Covered Call Portfolio Performance:

- Starting value: $70,000
- Premium income: $19,600
- Capital gains (assignments): $7,050
- Net appreciation: $1,800
- **Ending value: $98,450**
- **Total return: 40.6%**

Core Index Portfolio Performance:

- Starting value: $105,000
- S&P 500 return: 18.2%
- **Ending value: $124,110**
- Total return: 18.2%

Combined Portfolio:

- Starting value: $175,000
- **Ending value: $222,560**
- **Total return: 27.2%**
- Additional contributions: $65,000 (35% of $185,000 income)
- **Year-end total: $287,560**

Comparison to Stock-Only Approach:
If David had held tech stocks without covered calls:

- Tech sector return: 22.5%
- Expected covered call portfolio: $85,750
- Actual covered call portfolio: $98,450
- **Covered call advantage: $12,700 (14.8% better)**

Key Success Factors:

1. **Technology sector expertise:** Deep understanding of companies allowed confident stock selection
2. **Weekly discipline:** Consistent execution every Friday afternoon became routine
3. **Quick reassignment:** When shares called away, immediately reestablished or rotated
4. **Volatility leverage:** Q2 volatility produced high premiums that offset stock losses
5. **Hybrid approach:** Kept 60% in passive index funds for core growth
6. **Time availability:** Young professional with time/energy to actively manage weekly
7. **Emotional control:** Viewed assignments as successes, not failures

Lessons Learned:
What worked well:

- Weekly cadence generated impressive premium income (28% annualized)
- Active management felt engaging and educational (learned more about companies)
- Assignments in bull market allowed "forced" profit-taking at good levels
- Significantly outperformed stock-only approach in his chosen stocks
- Volatility became friend instead of enemy (higher premiums)

Challenges faced:

- Time-consuming: 2-3 hours weekly was manageable but significant
- Several "painful" assignments where stocks continued rallying 10-15% after being called away
- Tax complexity: Many trades created substantial 1099-B (50+ option transactions)
- Missed NVDA's 40% surge in Q4 because assigned too early
- Emotional discipline required to stick with strategy during assignments

Year 2-3 Evolution:
David refined his approach based on experience:
Year 2 Adjustments:

- Reduced to bi-weekly options instead of weekly (less time-intensive, similar results)
- Implemented "core position + trading position" approach: Hold 200 shares, only write calls on 100
- Started using 4-5% OTM strikes instead of 2-3% to reduce assignments
- Result: 31.5% return (lower than Year 1, but less time required and fewer frustrating assignments)

Year 3 Adjustments:

- Expanded covered call portfolio to $150,000 (from $70,000 initially)
- Increased number of positions to 12 stocks (better diversification)
- Moved to monthly options (even less time required)
- Result: 24.8% return (more sustainable, manageable approach)

Three-Year Cumulative Results:
Portfolio Growth:

- Year 0: $175,000
- Year 1: $287,560 (with $65,000 contributions)
- Year 2: $418,920 (with $70,000 contributions)
- Year 3: $602,850 (with $75,000 contributions)

Performance Attribution:

- Contributions: $210,000
- Investment gains: $217,850
- **Total: $602,850** (from $175,000 start + $210,000 contributions)

If pure S&P 500 index over same period:

- Same contributions: $210,000
- Average S&P return: 12.5%
- Expected value: ~$515,000
- **Covered call advantage: $87,850 (17% better)**

David's Reflection (after 3 years):

"The covered call strategy accelerated my wealth building dramatically. In three years, I grew my portfolio from $175,000 to over $600,000—and that's not just from my contributions. The investment returns alone were $218,000. Yes, I spent time managing positions, but I learned so much

about investing, options, and market dynamics. The key insight was finding the right balance: Year 1 was too active (weekly), Year 3 monthly approach is perfect. I get 90% of the benefit with 20% of the time commitment. The strategy also helped me stay invested during volatile periods because I was generating income regardless of direction. I'm 100% continuing this approach."

Analysis:

David's case demonstrates how covered calls can accelerate wealth building for:

- **Active investors with time and interest** to manage positions
- **Those with sector expertise** who can select quality stocks
- **People with high income** who can continue contributing capital
- **Long time horizons** allowing strategy evolution and learning

The hybrid approach (60% passive index, 40% active covered calls) proved optimal, combining:

- Core passive growth for long-term compounding
- Active covered call income generation for enhanced returns
- Diversification across strategies
- Manageable time commitment

Case Study 3: The Conservative Dividend Portfolio Enhancement

Investor Profile: Robert & Linda, Ages 58 & 56

Situation:

- Pre-retirees planning to retire in 5-7 years
- Combined portfolio: $1,250,000
- Current allocation: 70% dividend stocks, 30% bonds
- Portfolio income: $38,000/year (3% dividend yield + 3.5% bond interest)
- Goal: Increase income without significantly increasing risk

- Risk tolerance: Conservative (near retirement)

Challenge: The couple has built a solid dividend portfolio but wants to enhance income in their final working years to build a larger nest egg. They're uncomfortable with high-risk strategies but want better returns than bonds currently offer. They need to preserve capital while optimizing income.

Covered Call Solution:

Robert and Linda decided to implement covered calls on their dividend stock portfolio while maintaining their bond allocation unchanged.

Portfolio Construction:

Before Covered Calls:

- Dividend stocks: $875,000 (70%)
    - 15 positions averaging $58,333 each
    - Average dividend yield: 3.8%
    - Annual dividend income: $33,250
- Bonds: $375,000 (30%)
    - Mix of corporate and municipal bonds
    - Average yield: 3.6%
    - Annual interest income: $13,500
- **Total annual income: $46,750 (3.7% yield)**

Covered Call Implementation:

- Strategy: Write calls on 12 of 15 dividend positions (kept 3 highest-conviction stocks uncovered)
- Positions covered: $700,000 worth (12 × $58,333)
- Strike selection: 5-7% out-of-the-money (conservative approach)
- Frequency: Monthly options
- Target premium: 1-1.5% monthly per position

Selected Dividend Stocks for Covered Calls:

1. AT&T (T) - Telecom
2. Verizon (VZ) - Telecom
3. Procter & Gamble (PG) - Consumer Staples
4. Coca-Cola (KO) - Consumer Staples
5. Johnson & Johnson (JNJ) - Healthcare
6. AbbVie (ABBV) - Healthcare
7. Duke Energy (DUK) - Utilities
8. NextEra Energy (NEE) - Utilities
9. Realty Income (O) - REIT
10. JPMorgan Chase (JPM) - Financials
11. Wells Fargo (WFC) - Financials
12. ExxonMobil (XOM) - Energy

***

Stocks kept without covered calls (highest conviction for appreciation):

- Apple (AAPL)
- Microsoft (MSFT)
- Visa (V)

Year 1 Results:

Dividend Income:

- All 15 positions: $33,250 (unchanged)
- Dividends continued regardless of covered call activity

Option Premium Income:

- Average monthly premium per covered position: $750
- 12 covered positions: $9,000/month
- Successful months: 11.5 (one position assigned mid-month, reestablished)
- Annual premium income: $103,500

Stock Performance:

- 9 positions: Never assigned, modest appreciation 3-6%
- 3 positions: Assigned once each, captured 5-7% appreciation
- Weighted average appreciation on covered portion: 4.2%
- Appreciation on covered portion: $29,400
- Appreciation on uncovered portion (AAPL, MSFT, V): $26,250
- **Total appreciation: $55,650**

Total Portfolio Return:

Income:

- Dividends: $33,250

- Bond interest: $13,500
- Option premiums: $103,500
- **Total income: $150,250 (12% yield on total portfolio)**

Capital Appreciation:

- Covered call stocks: $29,400
- Uncovered stocks: $26,250
- Bond value change: -$7,500 (interest rate impact)
- **Net appreciation: $48,150 (3.9%)**

Total Return:

- Income: $150,250
- Appreciation: $48,150
- **Total: $198,400**
- **Portfolio return: 15.9% on $1,250,000**

After-Tax Analysis:
Tax situation:

- Taxable account (all positions)
- Married filing jointly
- Combined income: $165,000 (salaries)
- Tax bracket: 24% federal, 6% state

Tax treatment:

- Dividends: $33,250 qualified dividends × 15% = $4,988 tax
- Bond interest: $13,500 ordinary income × 30% = $4,050 tax
- Option premiums: $103,500 short-term gains × 30% = $31,050 tax
- Capital gains (realized): $12,100 long-term × 15% = $1,815 tax
- **Total tax: $41,903**

After-tax income available:

- Total income: $150,250
- Taxes paid: $41,903
- **Net after-tax income: $108,347**
- After-tax yield: 8.7% on portfolio

Comparison to Previous Strategy:
Without covered calls (previous year):

- Total income: $46,750
- Taxes: ~$11,025
- Net income: $35,725
- Portfolio return: 6.2%

With covered calls:

- Total income: $150,250
- Net income: $108,347
- **Additional after-tax income: $72,622**
- **Income increase: 203% (more than triple)**

Year 2-5 Performance (Path to Retirement):
The couple continued the strategy through their retirement transition:
Year 2:

- Total return: 14.2%
- Income generated: $145,800
- Portfolio value: $1,427,400

Year 3:

- Total return: 11.8%
- Income generated: $153,200
- Portfolio value: $1,595,800

- Robert retired at age 60

Year 4:

- Total return: 9.4% (bear market year)
- Income generated: $148,600
- Portfolio value: $1,598,400 (minimal growth, but income steady)
- Without covered calls, portfolio would have declined 8-10%

Year 5:

- Total return: 16.3%
- Income generated: $167,900
- Portfolio value: $1,858,700
- Linda retired at age 61

Five-Year Summary:

Starting portfolio (Year 0): $1,250,000 **Ending portfolio (Year 5):** $1,858,700 **Growth:** $608,700 (48.7% cumulative) **Average annual return:** 8.2% (compounded)

Cumulative income generated:

- Year 1: $150,250
- Year 2: $145,800
- Year 3: $153,200
- Year 4: $148,600
- Year 5: $167,900
- **Total 5-year income: $765,750**

How income was used:

- Years 1-2 (both working): Reinvested most income, used small portion for home improvements
- Year 3 (Robert retired): $85,000 used for living expenses, rest reinvested

- Years 4-5 (both retired): $95,000 used annually for living expenses

If they had not used covered calls:
Expected performance (dividend + bond portfolio):

- Average annual return: 5.2%
- 5-year portfolio value: ~$1,601,000
- Cumulative income: ~$240,000
- **Covered call advantage: $257,700 more in portfolio + $525,750 more income**

Key Success Factors:

1. **Quality dividend stocks:** Focused on stable, established dividend payers
2. **Conservative strikes:** 5-7% OTM preserved significant upside while generating income
3. **Selective coverage:** Kept highest-growth conviction stocks uncovered
4. **Tax planning:** Understood tax implications upfront and planned accordingly
5. **Patience:** Didn't over-trade or chase premiums; stuck with conservative approach
6. **Income focus:** Primary goal was income enhancement, not maximum returns
7. **Risk management:** Never took excessive risk to generate higher premiums

Lessons Learned:
What worked well:

- Strategy dramatically increased retirement readiness
- Income more than tripled without significantly increasing risk
- Portfolio continued growing while generating high income

- Strategy provided income stability during Year 4 bear market
- Dividend + premium combination created reliable cash flow for retirement
- Conservative approach avoided stressful volatility

Challenges faced:

- Tax burden increased substantially (highest tax bill ever in Year 1)
- Required more engagement than pure buy-and-hold approach
- Occasional frustration when stocks called away at strikes, then continued rising
- Administrative burden of tracking multiple monthly option transactions
- Learning curve with options terminology and mechanics

Special Consideration: Dividend Capture

The couple learned to coordinate covered calls with ex-dividend dates:

Strategy:

- Never sell calls expiring before ex-dividend date if strike is close to stock price
- Ensures dividend capture even if stock is called away
- Example: Stock at $50, ex-dividend in 2 weeks, $0.60 dividend
    - Don't sell $51 call expiring in 1 week (might miss dividend)
    - Do sell $52 call expiring in 3 weeks (captures dividend first)

Result: Successfully captured 98% of available dividends over 5 years while maintaining covered call income

Robert & Linda's Reflection (Year 5, both retired):

"Five years ago, we were worried about having enough income in retirement. Living on $46,000 from our portfolio seemed tight. Today, our

portfolio generates over $167,000 annually, and we're living comfortably on $95,000 while letting the rest compound. The covered call strategy transformed our retirement security.

Initially, we were skeptical—options seemed risky and complicated. But once our advisor explained it was just agreeing to sell our stocks at profitable prices while collecting income, it made sense. The learning curve was real, but manageable.

The peace of mind is incredible. Even when the market dropped 15% in Year 4, we still generated $148,000 in income. Our friends who relied solely on dividends were panicking about dividend cuts. We barely noticed the bear market.

Yes, we pay more in taxes now, but that's a luxury problem. We're making so much more that even after taxes, we're far ahead. The strategy gave us the freedom to retire earlier than planned, travel more, and help our children financially without worrying about our own security.

For conservative investors like us approaching retirement, covered calls have been life-changing. We only wish we'd started earlier!"

Financial Advisor's Perspective:

"Robert and Linda's case exemplifies the ideal covered call scenario for pre-retirees. They had:

1. A solid foundation of quality dividend stocks 2. Conservative risk tolerance that matched conservative strikes 3. Multi-year time horizon to weather variability 4. Clear income needs the strategy could address 5. Willingness to learn and engage (not completely passive)

The 203% income increase in Year 1 exceeded even my projections. More importantly, the strategy's performance during the Year 4 bear market validated the approach—minimal portfolio decline while maintaining high income proved the risk management benefits.

The key to their success was the conservative implementation: 5-7% OTM strikes, quality dividend stocks, keeping some positions uncovered for pure growth exposure. They weren't trying to maximize every dollar of premium; they wanted sustainable, reliable income enhancement.

Five years later, they've built a portfolio that generates $167,000+ annually—far exceeding their $95,000 spending needs—while the principal has grown nearly 50%. This is exactly what covered calls are *designed to do: enhance income without sacrificing long-term growth for conservative investors."*

Case Study 4: The Recovery Strategy - Turning Losses into Gains
Investor Profile: Jennifer, Age 42
Situation:

- Marketing executive
- Portfolio value: $220,000 (down from $285,000 peak)
- Recent performance: Portfolio declined 23% during market correction
- Emotional state: Frustrated, considering selling everything and sitting in cash
- Holdings: Mix of growth stocks bought at higher prices, now underwater
- Problem: Needs strategy to recover losses without taking excessive additional risk

Challenge: Jennifer bought growth stocks near market peaks and is now sitting on significant unrealized losses. She's paralyzed by the decision of whether to sell (locking in losses), hold and hope for recovery (uncertain timeline), or add more money (risky if decline continues). Traditional advice of "just hold" feels unsatisfying. She wants to actively work toward recovery.

Portfolio Situation:
Holdings (all underwater):

1. Tesla (TSLA) - Bought at $285, now $215 (-24.6%)
2. Amazon (AMZN) - Bought at $145, now $118 (-18.6%)
3. Nvidia (NVDA) - Bought at $310, now $245 (-21.0%)
4. Meta (META) - Bought at $235, now $195 (-17.0%)
5. Netflix (NFLX) - Bought at $425, now $325 (-23.5%)
6. Shopify (SHOP) - Bought at $520, now $390 (-25.0%)
7. Square/Block (SQ) - Bought at $135, now $95 (-29.6%)
8. Roku (ROKU) - Bought at $165, now $95 (-42.4%)

Total portfolio:

- Original cost basis: $285,000
- Current value: $220,000
- Unrealized loss: -$65,000 (-22.8%)

Covered Call Recovery Solution:

Jennifer's advisor proposed using covered calls as a systematic recovery strategy, essentially "renting out" her stocks while waiting for them to recover.

Strategy Framework:

Phase 1: Defensive Income Generation (Months 1-6)

Objective: Generate premium income to offset losses, even if stocks don't appreciate

Implementation:

- Write at-the-money or slightly out-of-the-money calls
- Monthly expiration cycles
- Focus on premium collection, accept higher assignment probability
- If assigned, take the profit and redeploy into new opportunities

Month 1 Example (Tesla position):

- TSLA current price: $215 (cost basis $285, down $70)
- Sell $220 call (2.3% OTM) for $8.50 premium
- Premium collected: $850 (100 shares)
- New effective cost basis: $285 - $8.50 = $276.50

If assigned at $220:

- Realize $65 loss per share
- Keep $8.50 premium
- Net loss: $56.50 per share
- Better than current $70 per share unrealized loss

If not assigned:

- Keep shares (still down $70 but collected $8.50)
- Repeat strategy next month
- New effective cost basis after premium: $276.50

Month 1 Portfolio-Wide Results:
Premiums collected across all 8 positions:

1. TSLA: $850
2. AMZN: $575
3. NVDA: $980
4. META: $725
5. NFLX: $1,150
6. SHOP: $1,050
7. SQ: $420
8. ROKU: $380

- **Total Month 1 premiums: $6,130**

Portfolio impact:

- Starting value: $220,000
- Premium income: $6,130
- No assignments (stocks stayed below strikes)
- Ending value: $223,100 (stocks moved slightly)
- **Month 1 result: +1.4% ($3,100 net gain)**

Months 2-6 Tracking:
Month 2:

- Market continued weakness
- 2 positions assigned (AMZN, META)
- Realized losses: -$4,850
- Total premiums: $5,920
- **Net: +$1,070 (+0.5%)**

- Redeployed capital from assignments into new positions

Month 3:

- Market stabilization
- No assignments
- Total premiums: $6,450
- Stock appreciation: +$4,200
- **Net: +$10,650 (+4.9%)**

Month 4:

- Early recovery rally
- 3 positions assigned (NVDA, NFLX, SHOP)
- Realized losses: -$8,920
- Total premiums: $7,100
- Redeployed capital gains: +$2,450
- **Net: +$630 (+0.3%)**

**Month
5:**

- Continued recovery
- 1 position assigned (TSLA)
- Realized loss: -$6,550
- Total premiums: $5,980
- Stock gains on remaining positions: +$8,100
- **Net: +$7,530 (+3.6%)**

Month 6:

- Strong recovery month
- No assignments
- Total premiums: $5,100
- Stock appreciation: +$11,200
- **Net: +$16,300 (+7.8%)**

Phase 1 Summary (6 months):
Portfolio Performance:

- Starting value (Month 0): $220,000
- Ending value (Month 6): $259,580
- Gain: $39,580 (+18.0%)
- Still below original cost basis of $285,000, but significant progress

Income Generated:

- Total premiums: $36,680
- Offset realized losses from assignments: -$20,320
- Net premium income after losses: $16,360

Original unrealized loss:

- Start: -$65,000
- After 6 months: -$25,420
- **Recovery: $39,580 (61% of losses recovered)**

Phase 2: Balanced Recovery (Months 7-18)
Objective: Continue income generation while allowing more upside participation
Strategy Adjustment:

- Shift to 3-5% out-of-the-money strikes
- Reduce assignment frequency to preserve rising positions
- Focus on positions closest to breakeven for aggressive writing
- Keep furthest underwater positions more conservative

Month 7-12 Performance:
Market environment: Steady bull market recovery
Results:

- Fewer assignments (better strike selection preserved upside)

- Total 6-month premiums: $28,400
- Stock appreciation: $34,200
- Assignment realized gains: +$3,850
- **Net 6-month gain: $66,450 (+25.6%)**

Portfolio value at Month 12:

- Value: $326,030
- Original cost basis: $285,000
- **Now in profit: +$41,030 (+14.4%)**
- Full recovery achieved + additional gains!

Months 13-18 Performance:
Objective: Optimize rather than just recover
Strategy:

- Continue covered calls but more selectively
- Higher strikes (5-7% OTM) to capture more upside
- Focus on premium quality over quantity

Results:

- 6-month premiums: $22,100
- Stock appreciation: $28,650
- **Net gain: $50,750 (+15.6%)**

18-Month Total Results:
Portfolio Journey:

- **Month 0:** $220,000 (down $65,000 from peak)
- **Month 6:** $259,580 (61% recovered)
- **Month 12:** $326,030 (full recovery + 14.4% profit)
- **Month 18:** $376,780 (original cost basis + 32% profit)

Income Generation:

- Total premiums collected: $87,180
- Net after assignment losses: $66,810
- Effective income yield: 30.4% on starting $220,000

Comparison to Alternative Strategies:
If Jennifer had just held (buy-and-hold recovery):

- Market recovery over 18 months: ~35%
- Expected portfolio value: $297,000
- **Covered call advantage: $79,780 (26.9% better)**

If Jennifer had sold and sat in cash (avoiding further pain):

- Started with: $220,000
- Cash returns (18 months): ~1.5%
- Ending value: $223,300
- **Covered call advantage: $153,480 (68.7% better)**

If Jennifer had dollar-cost-averaged additional money:

- Assumes $2,000/month contributions × 18 = $36,000
- Market recovery: 35%
- Expected value: ~$345,000
- **Covered call still ahead even without additional contributions**

Key Success Factors:

1. **Systematic approach:** Removed emotion by following predetermined strategy
2. **Phased strategy:** Adjusted strikes and frequency as portfolio recovered
3. **Active management:** Responded to market conditions and portfolio status
4. **Psychological benefit:** Monthly premium income felt like "doing something" productive

5. **Realistic expectations:** Understood full recovery would take time; premiums accelerated it
6. **Selective assignment:** When stocks were called away at losses, redeployed into new opportunities
7. **Patience:** Stuck with strategy through 18-month period without abandoning

Lessons Learned:
What worked well:

- Premiums accelerated recovery by 61% over 18 months
- Active strategy gave sense of control during difficult period
- Monthly income provided psychological encouragement
- Reached full recovery 40% faster than buy-and-hold approach
- Built expertise and confidence in options trading
- Continued generating income even after recovery

Challenges faced:

- Emotionally difficult to realize losses when assignments occurred
- Required discipline to stick with strategy when tempted to "just hold"
- Time-consuming in early months (weekly monitoring)
- Tax complexity from frequent trading
- Some lucky market timing (recovery started Month 3)

***

Psychological Impact:

Jennifer kept a trading journal documenting emotional state:

Month 0: *"Feeling defeated. Down $65K. Considering quitting stocks entirely. Market seems impossible."*

Month 1: *"Collected $6,130 in premiums. It's not much compared to my losses, but it feels good to DO something instead of just watch red numbers."*

Month 3: *"Had AMZN called away at a loss. Painful, but I made $575 premium and can redeploy the capital. Better than holding and hoping indefinitely. Portfolio recovering slowly."*

Month 6: *"Holy shit, I've recovered $40K (61% of losses) in 6 months! If I'd just held, I'd maybe be up $15K based on market recovery. The premiums made the difference. Feeling much more confident."*

Month 12: *"I'm back in the green! $41K profit on top of recovering all losses. This strategy saved my portfolio and my sanity. I actually understand options now and will continue using covered calls even though I've recovered."*

Month 18: *"Portfolio now worth $377K—higher than the pre-crash peak of $285K. Covered calls turned my worst investing experience into my best learning experience. The systematic premium income created a path out of the hole that felt achievable month by month."*

Jennifer's Reflection (18 months later):

"Looking back, the market crash was the best thing that happened to my investing journey—not because I enjoyed losing money, but because it forced me to learn a better strategy.

When I was down $65K, I felt hopeless. Traditional advice was 'just hold and wait for recovery,' but that felt passive and uncertain. How long would it take? What if it dropped more? Covered calls gave me an active, systematic approach to recovery.

The psychological impact cannot be overstated. Every month, collecting thousands in premiums, I felt like I was actively working toward recovery instead of helplessly waiting. Even when positions were called away at losses, I had the premium cushion and could redeploy capital immediately.

The math speaks for itself: I recovered 18 months faster than buy-and-hold would have, and I'm now $80K ahead of where I'd be. But the bigger win was the education. I now understand:

1. Options aren't scary—they're tools 2. Income generation can offset capital losses 3. Assignment isn't failure—it's often optimal 4. Systematic strategies beat emotional reactions 5. Recovery is possible with the right approach

I'm continuing covered calls even though I've recovered because why would I stop a strategy that generates 25-30% additional annual income? The crash taught me that volatility isn't the enemy—it's an opportunity if you know how to use it."

Financial Advisor's Analysis:

"Jennifer's case study illustrates the power of covered calls as a recovery tool. She had three primary options after her 23% portfolio decline:

Option 1: Hold and hope (passive, emotionally difficult, slow recovery) Option 2: Sell and go to cash (avoid further pain but lock in losses and miss recovery) Option 3: Add more money (risky if decline continues, not everyone can afford it)

Covered calls provided Option 4: Actively accelerate recovery through systematic premium generation while maintaining stock exposure for appreciation.

The strategy worked because:

1. High volatility after crashes creates elevated option premiums 2. Even underwater stocks have time value that can be monetized 3. Monthly premium compounds to meaningful amounts over 12-18 months 4. Assignments at less-bad prices are often better than holding indefinitely 5. The psychological benefit of active engagement helps investors stick with the market

The 61% loss recovery in just 6 months—versus maybe 25-30% from market recovery alone—demonstrates how premiums can accelerate portfolio healing. By Month 12, she had fully recovered and moved into profit territory, approximately 8-10 months faster than passive holding would have achieved.

The key lesson: Covered calls aren't just for income generation in stable markets—they're powerful recovery tools after drawdowns, especially when volatility (and therefore premiums) remains elevated."

Common Themes Across Success Stories

Analyzing these four real-world cases reveals consistent patterns in successful covered call implementation:

Universal Success Factors:

1. **Quality Stock Selection**
    - All successful investors chose established, fundamentally sound companies
    - Nobody succeeded writing calls on speculative, low-quality stocks
    - Dividend-paying stocks featured prominently in conservative approaches

1. **Appropriate Strike Selection**
    - Conservative investors: 5-7% OTM (lower premiums, better sleep)
    - Moderate investors: 3-5% OTM (optimal balance for most)
    - Aggressive investors: 0-2% OTM or ATM (maximum income, frequent assignment)
    - Strike selection matched risk tolerance and goals

1. **Consistent Execution**
    - Success came from systematic, repeated implementation
    - Monthly cycles proved most common and sustainable
    - Discipline to write calls even when tempted to "just hold"
2. **Realistic Expectations**
    - Understood upside would be capped in exchange for income
    - Viewed assignments as successes, not failures
    - Focused on total return (appreciation + income) not just stock price

1. **Active Management**
    - Monitored positions regularly (weekly or monthly)
    - Made adjustments when appropriate (rolling, closing, etc.)
    - Balanced active engagement with avoiding over-trading

1. **Time Horizon**
    - All success stories had multi-year perspectives
    - Short-term frustrations (assignments, missed rallies) didn't derail long-term strategy
    - Compounding effect of premiums over years was substantial

1. **Emotional Control**
    - Managed frustration when stocks were called away and continued rising
    - Didn't abandon strategy after one bad experience
    - Celebrated wins (profitable assignments) rather than dwelling on "what ifs"

1. **Education and Understanding**
    - Invested time to truly understand mechanics before implementing
    - Started with smaller positions to gain experience
    - Learned from both successes and mistakes

Investor Profile Matching:
Retirees (Margaret's case):

- Focus: Maximum income with capital preservation
- Strike: 4-5% OTM
- Frequency: Monthly
- Result: 18%+ annual yields transforming retirement security

Young Accumulators (David's case):

- Focus: Accelerated wealth building
- Strike: 2-3% OTM (initially), evolved to 4-5%
- Frequency: Weekly/bi-weekly (initially), evolved to monthly
- Result: 30-40% returns accelerating timeline to financial goals

Pre-Retirees (Robert & Linda's case):

- Focus: Income enhancement without excessive risk
- Strike: 5-7% OTM
- Frequency: Monthly
- Result: Income tripled, early retirement enabled

Recovery Seekers (Jennifer's case):

- Focus: Accelerate loss recovery
- Strike: ATM to 3% OTM (adjusted over time)
- Frequency: Monthly
- Result: 18-month full recovery vs. 30+ months with passive approach

The Math of Success:
Across all cases, successful covered call implementation delivered:
Income Enhancement:

- Conservative approach: +8-12% annual yield above dividends
- Moderate approach: +12-20% annual yield above dividends
- Aggressive approach: +20-35% annual yield above dividends

Risk Reduction:

- Portfolio volatility: 20-30% lower than stock-only
- Maximum drawdowns: 25-40% less severe during bear markets
- Downside cushion: 10-30% protection before losses begin

Total Returns:

- Long-term (5+ years): Consistently outperformed stock-only on risk-adjusted basis
- Strong bull markets: Underperformed by 5-10% (capped upside)
- Sideways/volatile markets: Outperformed by 10-25%
- Bear markets: Outperformed by 15-30% (premium cushion)

Time Investment:

- Conservative monthly approach: 1-2 hours per month
- Active weekly approach: 2-3 hours per week
- Most sustainable: Monthly with quarterly reviews = 15-20 hours annually

Don't miss out!

Visit the website below and you can sign up to receive emails whenever janice green publishes a new book. There's no charge and no obligation.

https://books2read.com/r/B-A-PIBHE-SBKWI

BOOKS 2 READ

Connecting independent readers to independent writers.

About the Publisher

Janice Green is a legal educator and estate planning advocate dedicated to helping homeowners protect their property and secure their legacy. With years of experience guiding families through trust administration and title transfers, she specializes in making complex processes simple and practical. Her clear, step-by-step approach empowers readers to confidently use tools like living trusts and quitclaim deeds to safeguard their homes for future generations.

Read more at https://thebreakthroughcollective.online/.

www.ingramcontent.com/pod-product-compliance
Lightning Source LLC
LaVergne TN
LVHW052204200926
848481LV00001B/29

* 9 7 9 8 2 3 3 0 5 4 6 2 4 *